THE FREE PRESS

New York   London   Toronto   Sydney   Singapore

In Search of
SUGIHARA

*The Elusive Japanese Diplomat
Who Risked His Life to Rescue
10,000 Jews from the Holocaust*

by HILLEL LEVINE

THE FREE PRESS
A Division of Simon & Schuster Inc.
1230 Avenue of the Americas
New York, NY 10020

THE FREE PRESS and colophon are trademarks
of Simon & Schuster Inc.

Designed by Carla Bolte
*Grateful acknowledgment is made to Koho Yamamoto for her rendering of
the Japanese character meaning "life."*

Manufactured in the United States of America

10 9 8 7 6 5 4 3 2 1

Library of Congress Cataloging in Publication data is available.
ISBN 0–684–83251–8

To some good people in my life:

*To my parents, who inspired me to meld determination
with compassion; to Father Takeji Ohtsuki of Kyoto, who first
told me about Sugihara in Kovno and about the setting sun
in Manchuria; and to the unknown rescuers during the Holocaust,
about whom we know even less than we know about Sugihara.*

Contents

Not "Standing on Blood"

Sugihara, the "Japanese Schindler"?

The Act

Dawn, August 2, 1940. A long line of Jews—ragtag, homeless, desperate—waits outside the Japanese consulate in Kovno, Lithuania. Among them is a somber twenty-six-year-old lawyer from Warsaw named Leon Ilutovicz. His dark Sabbath suit, which he tried to smooth for this morning's meeting, is hopelessly crumpled; but everything, including the tailor shops, has been closed in the past days. Chaos rules the streets of Kovno.

Like others, Ilutovicz recently escaped from Poland. With his own eyes he saw German soldiers in their formidable trucks, screeching to a halt in Warsaw's Jewish neighborhoods, grabbing Jews off the street for "work details." From the countryside, he heard reports of Jews packed into their synagogues, which were then set aflame; German soldiers had stood at the doors and windows, nonchalantly shooting at those who dared try to escape. The wall posters announcing new Nazi decrees against the Jews were becoming more strident and frequent. He had spent half the previous fall wandering through the forest on a trip that, by train, would have taken a few hours. Under the cover of night, he had stolen across borders, heading for Lithuania, "independent" Lithuania, caught between the Nazis and the Soviets, at that moment still allies.

Though there were early signs that it would be another hot day, Ilutovicz trembled in the early morning dew. He thought about his mother and father, his aunts and uncles, his many cousins and friends left behind. Virtually all would end up murdered by the Nazis in the ghettoes, slave labor camps, or gas chambers.

He had barely caught his breath since escaping. Yet he now faced an unanticipated threat from a different direction. The Nazis were bad enough, but these days Soviet troops, followed by their dreaded security forces, were swarming the streets. Since June 15, when the Soviets conquered Lithuania, Ilutovicz had seen many arrested; he had heard frightening stories about the terrors that Jews in the Soviet Union experienced during the past twenty years of Communist rule. It was enough to make Ilutovicz, ever the optimist, surrender his very last fantasies about Lithuania as a "safe" place to wait out the war. He'd escaped to here, but now had to escape *from* here as well.

As the line grew longer, he thought of the gloomy letter his father had received from his first cousin, in Boston, shortly before Leon left Warsaw. The New England Ilutoviczs had been making efforts in Washington, all frustrating, all unsuccessful, to obtain visas to bring family members to America. As he approached the head of the line, Ilutovicz, not a bad math student, was having difficulty calculating the number of years he would have to be on the U.S. quota list before these Yankee cousins could help. His nerves were bad. He knew his life depended on a piece of paper that the man at the window could provide.

Nearly eighty-seven years to the date after Commodore Matthew Perry forced Japan open to the West, vice consul Chiune Sugihara (pronounced chee-YU-nay Su-gee-hara) opened the curtain of the front window. Early mornings, he would enjoy stretching into his knickerbockers and digging about in the herb garden to the side of the consulate, the sun on his broad face. These reunions with nature were not as satisfying as he remembered from his rural Japanese childhood. But Sugihara was enough of the cosmopolitan to give contemplation on alien soil a try. Besides, it was exercise; the affable diplomat was beginning to exhibit the results of eleven months of culinary adventures at the best tables in Lithuania. He was a handsome man, 5'5", of ample proportions. His eyes were large, his thick hair neatly combed back. Now, with an extra chin, Sugihara was beginning to look portly.

Fog concealed the sun's first rays. As the vice consul gazed out of the rectangular front window, he could not quite tell what sort of day it would be. But that was not the only blocked view. The three-story white stucco building on Vaizgantas Street faced an open lot; the street snaked down to the town below. A black wrought iron gate marked the entrance. Through its lattice, Sugihara could usually see smokestacks, gothic roofs, and the golden dome of the Russian Orthodox church in the distance. This morning, though, the forty-year-old diplomat, coming from the backwaters of Japan, saw what must have appeared to him as strange-looking people, pushing against that heavy gate, clamoring to get in.

It was a scene that hundreds of diplomats in countries threatened or occupied by the Nazis would witness. Jews' scavenger hunts for visas were frequent, at least from 1933 to 1941, during the first nine years of Hitler's twelve-year rule. For the time being, the Nazis were largely satisfied to re-alize their vision of *Judenrein*—a world cleansed of Jews—as much by emigration from Europe as they subsequently would realize that vision through the smokestacks of Auschwitz. The lives of many Jews could have been saved not only by countries with more lenient immigration policies but by a diplomat here, a border guard there, who understood the dangers facing a fellow human being and merely stretched a rule or two.

This book is about that meeting between Leon Ilutovicz, the victim becoming a survivor, and Chiune Sugihara, the observer becoming a res-cuer. It is the story of the impersonal historical forces and the personal human choices that brought Ilutovicz and thousands of other Jews to Sugihara's doorstep. It is a probe into the culture and personality of the man who opened that door, an analysis of the making of a "mass rescuer." It is the story of an act that can teach us the simplest lesson about respon-siveness and responsibility in a not-so-simple world. "Do not stand on your neighbor's blood," as the Bible (Leviticus 19:16) puts it.

Sugihara is certainly not the only official to have become a mass res-cuer during the Holocaust.[1] Some are more famous. Why ponder such an obscure example of this transformation then? Thousands of Jews are alive today because of the heroism of Raoul Wallenberg of Sweden, but un-like Sugihara, he was sent under diplomatic cover to Hungary, specifically to rescue Jews. Wallenberg had behind him the support of at least two countries and their intelligence agencies. In Kovno, some, including Leon Ilutovicz, initially were assisted by the honorary Dutch consul, Jan Zwartendijk. After his government was deposed by the Nazi occupation of Holland, Zwartendijk was all but stranded. Yet with the approval of an equally stranded Dutch ambassador in Riga, L.P.J. de Decker, he agreed to issue some 1,200–1,400 visas, of questionable validity, to the Dutch

West Indies.[2] In a very few towns in Nazi-occupied Europe, such as Le Chambon in France, individuals and groups worked valiantly to save Jews.

And, of course, there is Oskar Schindler, now famous, yes, but still poorly understood. Most of what we do know about Schindler comes from Thomas Keneally's 1982 *Schindler's List* and Steven Spielberg's justifiably acclaimed 1993 film. But neither provides any biographical depth and insight that more than hints at Schindler's transformation into a mass rescuer.[3] Schindler grew up fairly poor, an ethnic German in the Sudetenland, on the Czech-German border. He experienced discrimination and rejection. As a child, he lived next to the town rabbi and likely played stickball with the rabbi's children. Another from this background might have been inhibited from joining the Nazi party and taking wholly voluntary initiatives in persecuting the Jews. Not Schindler! Yet he did become an imaginative and successful mass rescuer when exploitative relations evoked some personal feelings toward "my Jews," as he liked to say. This chronic gambler took self-sacrificing risks to out-fox Nazi officials; he committed his wealth and risked his life to save the 1,200 Jews of his factory in Cracow.

The life-saving acts of these mass rescuers render the story of their Japanese counterpart all the more curious and compelling. Sugihara grew up middle class, in a most homogeneous society. There simply *were* no Jews with whom to empathize. Sugihara's earliest exposure to Jews—from high school readings of *The Merchant of Venice* to a military training that pointed to Jews as fomenters of communism—were altogether negative. We know of no reason for him to have had any positive identification with the people he saw outside his consulate.[4] There is not the slightest cause to believe that Sugihara accepted any bribes, took any pleasure in danger, or was sent by anyone to rescue anyone. Common sense and conventional theorizing provide us scarce insight into his motives.

There is evidence, however, that even before Leon Ilutovicz and others arrived at his door, Sugihara was concerned about the Jews, whose lives, he knew, were in danger. He analyzed the situation in terms of the little he might help and the risks that he and his family would face. Sugihara was not one to act on whims.

Yet he *did* act. He started issuing Japanese transit visas, many, many visas, visas with long strings of characters dancing down and around the page, crowned by several official-looking seals. Sugihara ultimately granted them to anyone who applied, with whatever documents, and with whatever explanation for not having whatever documents! The more visas he would issue, the more Jews there would be in line. And when his hand tired from all that writing and signing, he allowed his assistants to produce rubber stamps. He even invited Jewish representatives inside to process the documents, with conveyor-belt efficiency.

He kept the consulate open longer than he should and missed no opportunity—even from the moving train window as he and his family finally left Kovno—to issue still a few *more* life-saving documents.[5] Sugihara had also spent his foreign service in all sorts of clandestine activities. This came in handy. He knew how to operate outside the rules, yet he did not implement "standard operational procedures" to prevent "unauthorized use" of his stamps and seals. A good number of forgeries—not necessarily of the highest quality—circulated as well; along the escape route, Japanese border guards, actually able to read the Sugiharan visas, were more than a bit curious as to why so many Jews seemed to have the name "Rabinowitz"!

On August 3, the very day after Leon Ilutovicz was trembling in line, the newly installed Soviet regime not so gently ordered Sugihara to close the consulate—immediately. His own government was sending him urgent cables; Jews were crossing Manchuria, arriving in Japan with visas from the Kovno consulate. But why did so many have this authorization, against the repeatedly issued regulations? At the end of August, the Japanese Foreign Ministry ordered him to move with his wife and three small children, including one newborn, to the German capital, Berlin. There, he knew, generosity to Jews was not particularly appreciated. Yet he continued to issue visas months later, even from Nazi-occupied Prague.

Leon Ilutovicz, like other survivors, speaks in hushed tones of what would have happened to him without Sugihara's help. When the Nazis captured Kovno from the Soviets less than ten months after Sugihara left, the overwhelming majority of those Jews who were not immediately shot died in ghettos and concentration camps. Ilutovicz joined thousands of Jews with Sugihara's visas who not only entered the Soviet Union but were able to leave it, via Japan, to begin new lives. For the past fifty years he has lived in New York City with his wife, active in civic and Jewish communal affairs.

Leon Ilutovicz was No. 819 on Sugihara's list—a document that I recently discovered in the archives of the *Gaimusho,* the Japanese Foreign Ministry in Tokyo. The discovery of this list, just at the time that Oskar Schindler was making his international celluloid reputation, pleased many Japanese. It seemed they would have a Schindler of their own. The list, inconspicuously filed in an altogether ordinary black loose-leaf marked "consular activities," fills thirty-one pages. It is followed by shorter rosters of Jews to whom Sugihara gave visas in 1941, in Prague and Königsberg, where he was stationed after Berlin. Each page is accompanied by a carbon copy. Other folios preserve some of the secret cable traffic from and to Sugihara in this period. Such a neat bureaucratic bundle, right there, in the musty Foreign Ministry archives; it was not what I expected of a dissident diplomat who seemed to issue visas with wild abandon.

There are many surprises in the evidence and the memories of Sugihara's act. Alas, he is the source of few. He died in 1986, near Tokyo; thus much of what was known about him heretofore comes from his wife, Yukiko, and older son, Hiroki. The story, as it is told, is that he asked permission thrice to issue visas, each time was denied authorization with increasing vehemence, issued them anyhow, and was fired after the war when he returned to Japan.[6] This is the standard story. A somewhat different one unfolds in the following pages.

In Japan, his deeds are now attaining equivocal popularity. The Japanese press, largely positive about Sugihara, occasionally will react with derision: "Swindler's List" ran one headline. Obedient citizens still have difficulty seeing this rule-flaunting renegade as a hero. But some subway-strapping salarymen, who have captured with their diligent labor and superior products so much of the global market share, seem to have time during their four-hour commutes to ponder the meaning of life, if not to enjoy it. Their perception of Sugihara as a rule-breaker, who, most important, sacrificed himself and was punished, seems to hold real appeal. Even among old Manchurian warriors and administrators active in the 1930s, now pensioners, there is a branch of his fan club; though some envy his fame, many seek vindication for Japanese colonialism in this strange story of "one of us," now a virtual candidate for sainthood.

Sacrifice has become a theme in Jewish memories of Sugihara as well. Among those Jews he rescued, he is often remembered as a *malakh* (angel), but with little human detail. In Israel, Sugihara's act received warm and enthusiastic public recognition as early as 1969. He was honored in Jerusalem but was not elevated to the ranks of the "Righteous Gentile." In accordance with the Israeli Parliament's legislation of 1953 establishing Yad Vashem, the government authority for research and commemoration of the Holocaust, Sugihara's risk in rescuing Jews, altogether praiseworthy as it was, was not deemed sufficiently life threatening. In 1985, shortly before he died, Yad Vashem had their own bout of rule-bending and anointed him a "Righteous Gentile" without changing the principle of honoring sacrifice and risk. Recent Sugihara commemorations have contributed to his international name recognition. They are sponsored by American West Coast organizations celebrating Japanese-Jewish relations and *not* caught up in notions of sacrifice.

In search of Sugihara, I have crisscrossed Japan, from the rice fields of his native town to the board rooms of conglomerates where his younger schoolmates still hold power; I have taken global jaunts from the archives of foreign ministries and spy agencies to the livingrooms of Holocaust survivors whom he helped rescue. I have done computerized network analyses of his associates in different periods of his life, trying to identify collaborators. Again and again, I tried to understand: Who was Sugihara? Why did he rescue Jews? Who helped him? Why was he punished? This book is an attempt to answer these questions.

Little in his background—one he shares with the colonial administrators and military men who brought us the rape of Nanjing and other incidents of mass destructiveness—explains his extraordinary behavior. And there are few clues in Sugihara's assignment in Lithuania. Visa stamping rated quite low as a priority; his crucial job was to spy on the Soviets and Germans in the planning that led to Pearl Harbor!

What we know from Sugihara's list itself provides little insight into the scope and magnitude of his act, even less into his motives. The list I found has 2,139 names, largely of Poles—both Jews and non-Jews—who received visas between July 9 and August 31, 1940. (Please tell Steven Spielberg that Nos. 1007 and 1008, Mordko and Chaim Szpilberg, may be his long-lost cousins.) It is far from complete; many who received visas from Sugihara, including children, are not on it. By statistical extrapolation, we can estimate that he helped as many as ten thousand escape; those who actually survived are probably no more than half that number.[7]

Were his rescue activities limited to issuing visas that may or may not have enabled their recipients to escape? Many survivors themselves have difficulty understanding how they traversed the dangerous, obstacle-laden exit route, out of Lithuania, across the Soviet Union, and into Japan, more than halfway around the world. Did Sugihara have a string of allies? Also, why did the Japanese government recognize his visas? Another Sugihara survivor, Dr. Isaac Lewin (No. 17), recently recalled that "the Japanese immigration authorities were lenient in scrutinizing the transit visas."[8] Inexplicably, mysteriously, did Sugihara activate the collaboration of others in this mass rescue, stirring up a "conspiracy of goodness?" Were his actions, as it were, contagious?

"Collaboration," "conspiracy," "contagious"—the very language we use to tame the mysteries of evil seems to fit so well with inexplicable goodness! What do we know about mass rescuers? How is it that we learn about all sorts of Japanese war criminals—not to mention Nazi mass murderers—but we read so little about someone like Sugihara? This may be more of a general problem than it appears to be. A recent bibliography of books on mass murderers, I was shocked to discover, lists 167 case histories, 36 general encyclopedic works, and 16 more specialized psychological studies.[9] Articles and popular treatments would increase this number many-fold. We seem to be fascinated by the story of the ordinary person, waking up one fine morning, loading a gun, and shooting into a playground of frolicking children or a crowded commuter train. The gruesome, to be sure, has important educational implications. We teach our children street smarts and provide them with vivid descriptions of the dangers lurking all over. Gawking at accidents might truly inspire us to drive more carefully. But the diversion of attention from the road is itself a major cause of "secondary" accidents; frighteningly, popular fascination with mass murder might conjure more violence than it deters.

On the other hand, a preoccupation with the self-sacrificial dimension of goodness carries its own problems. In liberal Western democracies, the making of heroes is often a suspect affair. One gathers that by legitimating societal truths, we are being enlisted toward still greater sacrifice. This may contribute to the great attention we pay to rogues, even to celebrities of questionable accomplishment, rather than to rescuers, people appearing to be ordinary in every way who commit extraordinary, life-affirming acts. Safety officials and military personnel who perform feats get their ticker-tape parades. Yes, but we quickly begin to lose interest in them and their sacrifice. Their own return to everyday, anonymous lives often is painful. Of late, social commentators and therapists have been talking about "rescuer trauma." It will not be long before someone, on trial for one heinous crime or another, will claim extenuating circumstances on the grounds of being a survivor of rescuer trauma. Can the heroic be instructive? Can it inspire life affirmation without demanding what might be considered violence to ourselves in the form of sacrifice?

Also, in regard to understanding the Holocaust, the time may not yet be ripe for us to search for silver linings. There is so much more that we must know about the making of mass murderers; anecdotes of rescue provide fraudulent happy endings to large-scale processes of destructiveness. Six million killed versus a few thousand saved—in that light, a preoccupation with rescuers becomes an unearned and unwarranted comfort. But as we know more about the Holocaust yet understand less—to paraphrase Saul Friedländer's apt statement—the story of Sugihara and the making of a mass rescuer should be part of what so baffles us.[10]

Rescue from the "top," as in the state-sanctioned case of Raoul Wallenberg? Or rescue from the "bottom," as in the case of many independently acting individuals? Where does Sugihara fit in? This book hopes to find the answer. The compilation of Sugihara's list and its preservation right there, in the very archives of the ministry that allegedly forbade, even punished what Sugihara did, raises many historical questions. It forces us to broaden our conceptualizations of the rescuer. But new documents or models will not explain away our early discovery and deepest sense of wonder about Sugihara. Why did he not do what virtually all the other diplomats across Europe were doing—shut the door?

These *Gaimusho* files even preserve complaints to the Japanese government about Sugihara's visas. There is a dispiriting letter written by Sir Robert Craigie, the British ambassador to Tokyo, on December 27, 1940. He had heard about the thousands of Jews who were escaping the Nazis and heading to Japan. He is not oblivious to the dangers confronting these Jewish refugees. But he is more concerned that many would now be able to make use of their immigration papers to enter the British mandate of Palestine. He warns the Japanese foreign minister, Yasuke Matsuoka, about what he calls the "dangers of personification." Whether he was warning against excessively humane responses or impersonations in forged documents is not clear. What is certain is that His Majesty's government will by no means feel obliged to recognize these unwanted Jews' entrance visas to Palestine, proclaims Craigie. He even tries to jolt the minister into action "to avoid the risk of such persons being stranded in Japan."[11]

The British ambassador's warning about the "dangers of personification" seems to go thoroughly unheeded. Why? Was there a secret Japanese pro-Jewish policy, idealistic or pragmatic? Did Sugihara strategize any cover-up? We have no hard evidence. But Sugihara could have been another of those rescuers about whom we know even less. That flood of refugees borne by Sugihara's visas could have been stopped at any point, leaving no one to tell the tale! Could it be that Sugihara's *determination* more than his *defiance* created some sort of loose conspiracy—even including his "drinking buddies" and the many who recognized his name among Japanese and Soviet officials, statesmen and border guards, up and down the Trans-Siberian and Manchurian Railroads?

How counterintuitive; conspiracies are invariably seen to bring out the worst in people.[12] But perhaps there is a different type of conspiracy, a "conspiracy of goodness," initiated by a person with great inner strengths that brings out the best in others, that "disinhibits" their care, their concern, their empathy? Perhaps what is truly contagious in such conspiracies is their ordinariness, their "banality." Hannah Arendt's renowned thesis about mass murderers, turned inside out, might be no less controversial when applied to a mass rescuer. No elusive motives, no depressive obsessions, no manic enthusiasms, no special indoctrination of any kind, no passionate love for Jews, no special relationship to Jews. If we looked hard enough we might even find reasons to resent Jews.[13] Might this describe the "banality of goodness"? And might Sugihara have been a most stellar practitioner?

The Search

For years, the story of Sugihara was filed in my consciousness more under exotica than anything else. Then, in February 1993, I was invited to inaugurate the first university program in Judaic studies established in the former Soviet Union. Vilna, "the Jerusalem of Lithuania," as Jews call their beloved city, now called Vilnius by the Lithuanians, had supported centuries of Jewish scholarship in its pious and more secular varieties. The political vicissitudes of the twentieth century have taken their toll on Jewish culture and those who appreciated it, but at the University of Vilnius, a feeling of renewal fills the air, even if there are hardly any Jews left to teach, research, and study. In this city, shadows of the past are ever lengthening.

The crystal chandeliers sparkle; the ornate plaster ceiling is recently restored. I note the government and university officials sitting on chairs upholstered in royal red frayed velvet. Behind them are a few students, and still farther back several of the aged partisans of the Vilna ghetto; for them, fifty years ago is as immediate as yesterday, and the yesterday that others experience is of little interest. At the end of a lecture, one of these men introduces himself. He recently retired after sixty-five years as engineer of the Vilnius Water Works. His unrivaled knowledge of its sewer system had enabled the partisans of this ghetto to be particularly mobile during the dark days of Nazi siege, and to provide something of a communications network for resisters in other ghettos. As we talk, he sketches on my lecture notes a map of the sewer system with the main escape routes demarcated. I will treasure that map. The partisans busy themselves these days arguing with the mayor's office for the right to place markers and memorials around the restored Old Town, where much of the ghetto once stood. Other citizens of Vilnius complain about the efforts of these militant octogenarians to make a "graveyard" out of "our" city.

Notwithstanding the joyousness of the occasion and the warm hospitality of my hosts, I feel chilled to the core. The extra sweater with which my family lovingly sent me off, the insulated ski overalls that I wore under my tweed jacket during other lectures in the same season and at the same longitude do not seem to be doing their job. Boris Yeltsin's efforts to pressure former Soviet satellites by cutting back on Russian fuel deliveries could account only in part for this profound cold from which I cannot escape, not for a moment.

Following my official duties, my generous hosts are eager to take me sightseeing. We visit places such as Ponar and the Ninth Fort in Kaunas, the Lithuanian name for Kovno, two hours' drive northwest from Vilna.

At these pastoral sites, Nazis and their zealous Lithuanian collaborators shot Jews into open ditches in the days before they introduced the higher-tech murderousness of Auschwitz and Treblinka. As I stand there, I ponder the prohibition against standing on blood. And I understand why it is difficult to feel human warmth.

That is when I think of Sugihara; he had been somewhere near here, I seem to recall. As I tour the former capital, Kaunas, and see the remains of its great Jewish civilization, I ask my hosts about the half-remembered story of the Japanese consul and whether we might try to find the actual chancery he occupied in 1939–1940. I saw a photograph of it once. With the help of a local Jew, we find the building on a small street, a few blocks from the city center. The stucco facade is virtually unchanged. The wrought iron fence is missing. But I excitedly verify the location by the curved staircase leading to the entrance.

Standing in front of the old consulate, I imagine the elusive Sugihara. His indefatigable hand is scribbling his life-saving bureaucratic formulas on scraps of paper. As the image comes into focus, I conjure up another hand, that of the infamous Dr. Josef Mengele, soon to be moving with the same precision at Auschwitz, sorting out Jews between immediate and attenuated dying. And behind him I see the hands of the millions of Nazi desk murderers, mere cogs in that big and efficient wheel of mass destructiveness. A loose cog can bring the wheel to a grinding halt, but these bureaucrats are experts at fragmenting responsibility, scheduling and allocating, signing and sealing the fate of others. I stand there transfixed in the −20 degree weather—centigrade or Fahrenheit, at that temperature, it hardly seems to matter. "On the site where a miracle occurred to our ancestors," the rabbis in the Talmudic tractate of *Berakhot* urge, "one must make a blessing." What blessing does one make, I wonder, on a Japanese bureaucrat?

Defrosting back in Boston, the image of Sugihara resists being refiled in long-term memory. Some cursory searches turn up a footnote here, a paragraph there, his rescue activities told as a tale of adventure more than edification. But nothing provides me with insight into the man or his background and motives, the act, its context and implications.

I busy myself in routine but begin to realize what effort it takes *not* to think of Sugihara. Horrible reports of "ethnic cleansing" in former Yugoslavia and the painful debate about American intervention prompt me to make a visit to the Balkans. Walks through destroyed villages remind me about standing on blood, and my heart pounds. In interviews with Bosnian refugees, I hear an old theme rise up fresh: "In the morning we sipped coffee with our neighbors and in the afternoon they returned and hacked us to pieces." That ancient warning emphasizing neighbors' blood takes on a frighteningly contemporary twist in our era of postmodern barbarisms.

I send an urgent message to friends in Kyoto, asking them if they know anything about Sugihara. This yields an immediate response from a T. Shino of Tokyo, who indicates that he has written a book on Sugihara and would welcome me to Japan and assist me in making my own inquiry. I do not know what to make of Shino's flattering presumption that I could understand anything in particular in the life of a man so separated from me by temporal and cultural gaps. Moreover, how am I to take the aggressive friendliness of the expert on Sugihara, who seems to happily invite competition?

I begin to ask questions about Sugihara that may lead me to his motives. I wonder about little Sugihara and his parents, the school boy Sugihara on the playground, the young man Sugihara and his first romance. Can I understand what made this man tick? Having spent the better part of the last decade analyzing structures of the Polish vodka industry two hundred years ago and the social structures of Boston real estate twenty years ago, I begin to wonder whether I would recognize a motive even if I saw one.

Sugihara himself was of heartbreakingly little help. He seems to have left little behind in his own words. If not for a few days out of his eighty-six years, his obscurity might have been well justified, and yet what Sugihara did during those days is all the more difficult to understand outside the context of what came before and after. As I painfully discovered, we have hardly any reliable information about who Sugihara was.

My new Japanese correspondent does not seem to appreciate my quips about whether Sugihara collected butterflies as a child and, if so, whether he took them apart or put them back together. My queries about material on Sugihara's early years and personality, the basic information needed for any interpretation of motives, do not seem to evoke much of a response from the otherwise solicitous, so eager-to-please Shino. Then a few days and round-trip faxes later, an express package arrives from Japan with a copy of Shino's book, bound in red and yellow with the by now familiar reproduction of Sugihara's visa. The considerate Shino has prepared a wooden translation of his book into English. Attached to it is a business card, "T. Shino, technical advisor." So this most likable and energetic Shino is, after all, himself a salaryman writing books on the side. In fact, as the forty-three-year-old civil engineer subsequently explains to me, he is an international consultant on mud. He helps plan tunnels, subways, and sewer systems. I remember the Vilna ghetto fighter and his map of the underground.

A particular detail in Shino's book catches my attention; Sugihara studied and subsequently taught in Harbin, at the school for training Japan's experts on the Soviet Union. He lived in that northern Chinese city from 1919 to 1935. "So, here," I thought, "here is the motive! Of course, the young man from the rice fields of Yaotsu would save all of these Jews in Kaunas because he knew all of those Jews in Harbin." Having myself visited Harbin in 1991 for some lectures, I had heard about its large and colorful Jewish community that existed from the late nineteenth century through the Chinese Communist Revolution. But in comparing Harbin in the post–World War I years with other multi-ethnic enclaves I have known, I realize that Sugihara might have resided in Harbin for a good period of time without actually knowing any Jews. Moreover, contiguity does not necessarily lead to affection. I still cannot pinpoint a motive. Even if Sugihara did come in contact with Harbin Jews, this still does not explain why he risked his career—and, likely, his life—to save some Jews.

Then again, information about his schooling, I begin to realize, might provide a few salient clues. Why did he transfer from Waseda University in Tokyo to Harbin? What influence did cosmopolitan Harbin, at the intersection of the Chinese, Japanese, and Russian cultural and political spheres, have on him? Indeed, Shino's passing reference to Sugihara's Harbin years suggests another tack of pursuit. Alumni organizations are more important in Japan than in many other places, acting as critical old boy networks. If there is a Harbin Gakuin, or college, alumni association, it could be a good place to start trying to collect Sugiharan impressions.

A few weeks later, I arrive in Tokyo and am welcomed by Shino. We greet each other like long-lost friends. His personality combines the sagaciousness of Charlie Chan, the—by now, politically incorrect—Asiatic Sherlock Holmes, with the soulfulness of Nahman of Bratzlav, the East European Hasidic master who poured his angst into uncanny tales that likely influenced Kafka. Soon, I am traveling around Japan with Shino, often accompanied by Japanese friends and former students, eliciting the memories of alumni of the Harbin Gakuin as well as Sugihara's relatives, his wife, sons, sister, cousins, nieces and nephews, and his bosses from later years. Interviews, Japanese style, with their ceremonial bows, gift giving, and abundant green tea, stir my feelings as they strain my bladder. My Japanese colleagues, ever concerned to fish for the "facts," quickly come to appreciate the way in which I cast my net more widely. The pursuit of Sugihara and what made him do good seems to bring out the best in people; I am offered much generous help.

Though the discoveries about Sugihara and the "field" conditions under which I was making them were so intriguing, I came close to quitting many times. Without the letters, diaries, and personal documents with which historians perform their craft, I would never be able to intuit why he became a rescuer. Just as I was about to give up, I remembered that Sugihara had a son living somewhere in Europe. For the sense of completion, I thought, it would be worth trying to track him down.

When Sugihara was first recognized and honored in Israel in 1969, he was asked by his hosts whether he had any special wish that his Jewish admirers could fulfill. He indicated that his youngest son, Nobuki, was not finding himself in the Japanese educational system and was at risk of going astray. The son was offered a full scholarship to the Hebrew University. But after two unfruitful years, someone had the good sense to guide him along a vocational track. The son was apprenticed to some Hasidim in the ultra-Orthodox town of Bnai Brak, where he learned the technical and business side of dealing with diamonds.

Nobuki Sugihara is still fluent in Hebrew and, when necessary, he can kvetch in Yiddish to get more favorable terms from a Hasidic diamond merchant. He has his father's intense gaze and a bit of his humor, too. He now lives in Antwerp with a home in Salzburg and a factory in Bangkok. In his spacious offices at the heart of the Antwerp diamond exchange, his Japanese associates sit on straw mats in the corner slurping their noodle lunches. Born in 1949, he has no personal memories of the days that made his father famous—yet they radically shaped his life.

Before I have a chance to ask Nobuki what I have asked every other relative and friend whom I have interviewed—for the words of his father—he pulls out a seven-page memoir in Russian, with an English translation. I am astonished. I would subsequently discover a more complete Russian version, likely the original, a Polish and Hebrew translation. Chiune Sugihara wrote this autobiographical fragment in 1967, in response to an inquiry made by a scholar then doing research on the Polish underground during World War II. Among other things, he summarizes his connections with Poles, particularly members of the underground, in Kovno, Berlin, and Königsberg in 1939–41.

Now, for the first time, in his few but very own words, I begin to feel more keenly Sugihara's personality and presence. But this unmediated encounter that I so craved perplexes me. Nearly three decades after the act that I am trying to understand, Sugihara remembers himself back in 1940 as defiant more than determined, a rule-breaker more than a strategizer. As for motives, this is all he has to say: "I acted according to my sense of human justice, out of love for mankind." No "-isms," no evocation of great ideas. A moving and earnest statement about goodness. But—dare I say it—is it not somewhat banal?

And, indeed, Sugihara admits that "after the war I did my best to forget the past." Understandable, for Sugihara as for many Japanese, those were years of pain, confusion, disorder, and reverses. Aging, moreover, brought with it a process of reinterpreting himself and his act. But there may be a pattern to his twenty-seven years of forgetting and revising. How does that pattern relate to Sugihara's Japaneseness and what his culture affirms, as well as what his own psyche might "repress"? Correctly read, how might this forgetting and revising provide significant clues into what did take place and what prompted him to act? The chronicler in 1967 and the actor in 1940 do not speak in the same voice. Is there any way in which we can learn more about the young man Sugihara in his formative years that will enable us to better understand what prompted him to act?

"The soul of the child of three," runs the Japanese proverb, "lasts for the rest of his life." But we know little about the child of three, or thirteen, or twenty-three, little that expresses his inner conflicts or that illustrates his good adjustment, little that shows that he was a rare genius or that points to the way in which he was altogether normal, little that reflects his rootedness in his own culture or that exemplifies his alienation and rebelliousness—in brief, little that would illuminate what might have made that young man a mass rescuer. His act is so full of light, his motives are so full of shadows. In the archives of the Gestapo and the Nazi German Foreign Ministry, the Lithuanian Foreign Ministry, the Soviet intelligence (NKVD), even in Washington among the intelligence intercepts of cracked top-secret Japanese codes, Sugihara barely exists.

But there is another approach. Understanding the transnational forces that shaped the world of Sugihara's childhood, upbringing, and adulthood enables us to derive far more from the few reliable facts that we *do* have.[14] Modernization and antimodernization, colonialism and decolonialism, nationalism and ethnic struggle, socialism and capitalism, and perhaps most important in the case of Sugihara, individualism and cosmopolitanism—all these forces help us understand this elusive young man.

Indeed, from our vantage point now we can see how these forces were truly formative. For what is life if not "lived forward but understood backwards," as Kierkegaard reminds us.[15] Ultimately, we want to learn lessons from Sugihara, even perhaps, most particularly from the "banality" of his goodness, from his capacity to "hear the voice of the oppressed," and the extraordinary quality of his acts. The silence of the observer threatens our civilization as much as the brutality of the victimizer and the anguish of the victim. We are overwhelmed by the muted cry of the abused and the abandoned, the hungry and the "ethnically cleansed" people. We have no clear precepts for intervention. We turn away as much out of confusion as indifference.

To understand how the passive observer becomes the engaged rescuer, evaluating motives and character may be important. Still, Sugihara's list, pulsating as it does with life, teaches us not to look askance at Schindler's identification with Jews, however self-serving it might have been initially. If, for whatever reason, Franklin D. Roosevelt, like Schindler, had ranted about "my Jews," millions might not have died. Nor would it be so bad if we could walk through the streets thinking "my homeless," or watch the news and feel "my Rwandans."

Nor should we need to defend a preoccupation with the ever-so-few rescuers as a distraction from mourning the millions, condemning the perpetrators, and learning the lessons of the Holocaust. The rescuer, arriving from "beyond the town wall," to use Elie Wiesel's fine phrase, overcomes the confusion that we all share about the moral ambiguities of intervention and the politics of the post–Cold War world. The rescuer has so much to teach us.

I have spoken with many who survived the war because of Sugihara They recall his face, his kind eyes, his courtliness. Some he even invited to sit down and have a cup of tea! Consulates, in the calmest of days, are stern places, not unduly convivial. But what Ilutovicz remembers most about that August morning, when he had his life handed to him, was this: Sugihara stamped his passport, looked him straight in the eyes, and smiled.

Chapter 1

The Young Man Sugihara

*The Summer of 1905 in Yaotsu, Kovno,
and Portsmouth and the Making of a Mass Rescue*

Between

He was born, as throughout life he would proudly recall, on January 1,
1900. From what we can tell about Sugihara, he would not have been impressed by the pedants who debate whether 1900 was the last year of the
nineteenth or the first year of the twentieth century. But over the course
of his life he did discover opportunity in being caught *between,* bridging,
as he did, such very different experiences of geography, culture, and tem-
perament—just as he straddled the centuries. It was what marked him the
most.

Both his parents were Iwais, not an uncommon name around Sugihara's hometown of Yaotsu, in Japan's Gifu Prefecture. But his mother's
family was among the few Iwais who could trace their lineage back to the
feudal lord of the region. This lent them considerable pedigree. Yatsu
Iwai, Sugihara's mother, was also the town beauty—some would claim
unrivaled in the entire prefecture. She seemed to have married beneath

her station in choosing Mitsugoro Iwai, for he descended from the untitled and unscrubbed Iwais.

Family legend has it that during Mitsugoro's military service in Manchuria and Siberia, in 1895, he contracted tuberculosis. In his confinement, he received an extra measure of care from an officer named Kosui Sugihara and, in gratitude, offered to become this man's adopted son, not an atypical practice in those years.[1] But some family members attribute the name change to less noble reasons. Around this time, Yaotsu initiated a new postal delivery service; one Sugihara had a better chance of getting the right mail than dozens of Iwais.

Yaotsu lay at the "navel" and *between* the two lobes of that island-country of Japan. Gifuites, as I learned in my travels there, are very proud to point out how they compose the heartland of their country. This centralized location was prized by many feudal warriors: "Control Gifu and you control Japan!" they would proclaim, while devastating its countryside. The region was coveted for its rich agriculture and thick forests.

Sugihara was also born precisely *between* the Sino-Japanese War of 1894–95 and the Russo–Japanese War of 1904–05. In that first war, Japan, like the Western powers that it both admired and resented, became a colonial powerhouse of its own, attaining degrees of control over Chinese and Korean territory. The war's outcome set the stage for Sugihara's early career as a colonial administrator.

In the Russo-Japanese War, the Japanese were justifiably impressed by their military triumph over the "Western" power of Russia. But many believed they were unjustly deprived in the diplomatic war that followed, under American sponsorship, in Portsmouth, New Hampshire. The treaty signed there raised Japan's international status but deepened its distrust of the West. This twin result set the stage for the second half of Sugihara's career in Europe and Russia, as he struggled mightily to understand his country's position *between* East and West.

We twist the kaleidoscope of Sugihara's life and discover such fascinating shapes and configurations. Take his birth year, 1900, when his country was placing itself, once more, between a Western power and an Eastern neighbor. At the time, the Japanese joined the British in trying to suppress the Boxer Rebellion in China, but not without experiencing profound confusion in choosing allies. That confusion continued into the 1930s, when Japan again had to opt between alliances with the United States and Great Britain or Nazi Germany and Fascist Italy. In each case, much of Japan's decision depended on who would best protect it from its dreaded neighbor, Soviet Russia.

Sugihara would become one of Japan's top experts on the Russian language and the Soviet Union, someone who thrived at the geographic and cultural stress points, at the intersection of East and West. Hence his assignment in Kaunas, some thirty-nine years after he was born in Yaotsu, where his skills came to their utmost fruition. He was ideally equipped for his roles—the official job, that is, and the unofficial one of rescuer that he assumed. For the former, he was to monitor developments that would determine on which side of the erupting conflict—soon a world war—Japan should place itself. For the latter, he created strange and wonderful alliances with remarkable agility.

In short, there came a moment when Chiune Sugihara stopped investigating what was good for his country and ended up plain *doing* good. We want to comprehend that golden moment, but we must approach it from yet another vantage. To understand the makings of a mass rescuer, we must try to understand the circumstances of the mass rescue. This includes most specifically the background and active involvement of those rescued. For Sugihara, in becoming a rescuer, entered into a relationship. A rescuer, in other words, needs "rescuees."

For instance, what historical forces brought Jewish rescuees to Kovno? What forces shaped East European Jews? What were the psychological and cultural sources of their unrelenting initiative? As chaos prevailed, where did they find courage to leave the warm, the loving, the familiar behind? What fortified them against the comforts of denial or fatalism? What "facts" and "forces" brought Sugihara together with those whom he tried to rescue, and what was the nature of their interaction? In short, why did thousands line up outside his door?

We will try to understand the lives of rescuer and rescuees *backwards,* as Kierkegaard helpfully suggests. To understand that mass rescue, we must understand another point in time and several points in space. It is 1905, and we are visiting Yaotsu, Japan, Kovno, Russia, and Portsmouth, New Hampshire. This itinerary will help us understand the relationships among Japan, Russia, and the United States, as well as to chart the path that leads to that fateful meeting between Sugihara and the Jews who converged with him in Kovno in the summer of 1940. Along the way, there are many ironies for us to savor, and mysteries to contemplate.

Yaotsu: Provincial Origins of a Japanese Cosmopolitan

It is the end of the late spring rainy season and I moistly wonder how the young man Sugihara endured the humid heat. The mayor of Yaotsu, having heard of my interest in this favorite son, has planned a reception and tour in my honor. The festivities begin with the ceremonial exchange of business cards; all the mayor's assistants bear cards with laminated photos of the Sugihara monument, with its chimes and reflecting pool. It's all quite genial, but soon I perceive some nervous stirrings. In misdirected faxes over the past weeks, the mayor's office has been trying to ascertain whether the honored guest would prefer bread or rice with his lunch. This now had to be resolved. "Ours" and "theirs," Japanese and foreign are still laden with explosive meaning, hard to comprehend for those of us accustomed to walking out our doors on any day and finding within a sphere of five blocks a global variety of foreign eateries. That the young man Sugihara chose such a cosmopolitan existence more than three quarters of a century ago suddenly takes on new implications. At lunch, I demonstrably savor both bread and rice.

I am taken to the site of the Sugihara home, close to the Kiso River in town, and then to Grandma Iwai's home up in the mountains, not far from the monument constructed in the early 1990s. Joe Iwai, a second cousin on Sugihara's maternal side, accompanies me. As we drive through Yaotsu, I try to picture scenes from Sugihara's childhood.

Of course there's no record. But if our knowledge of Chiune's early years is so scant, still there is much we can infer. In truth, for a child growing up in a provincial town such as Yaotsu, the summer of 1905 may not have been particularly memorable. The days were stiflingly hot; the evenings provided little reprieve. It was cooler, though, four miles up the hill at their maternal grandmother's house, amid the pine and bamboo, one of the boys' favorite haunts. The five-and-a-half-year-old Chiune Sugihara, with his brother Toyoaki, eight, had more time on his hands than most of the village children, who might have had to help dust their parents' stall in the market or pluck weeds in the family rice paddy. For the Sugihara boys, the oldest of five brothers and a sister, the summer of 1905 was carefree.

On long, hot summer days, Chiune hung around the swimming hole in a convenient bend of the Kiso River, a few meters down the road from their small wooden house at the town center. Wearing a cotton kimono, perhaps with cloth shoes rather than thongs so they could run faster, Chiune and Toyoaki would carefully finger the ten-sen coin their mother would give them for a snack, at the cake store, or the rice cracker shop, or the baked sweet potato stall. For a change of scenery, the Sugihara boys could head over to the Arakawa River, a full kilometer from home. Among the urchins who did not have to work in the field or the marketplace, there was a sixth sense as to where the gang was hanging out on any given day.

At five, he already had broad shoulders and large, piercing eyes that would evoke much comment in later years. Even at that age, he could swim all the way across the river.[2] Chiune was a good athlete, big and strong, able to compete with his older brother's friends. After a cool dip,

Chiune, Toyoaki, and their friends would uncover the bamboo poles they had stashed in the brush. With saintly innocence, they might pass by an unsuspecting horse and rider, and stealthily pluck a few tail hairs to use for fishing line. A dig in the muddy riverbanks for earthworms and the youngsters would be all set. The day would be truly perfect when the older children on the way back from work would stop off for a swim and then build a fire to broil the day's catch. Seventy years later, Chiune would remember those late afternoons in Yaotsu with great nostalgia.[3]

On other occasions, Chiune and Toyoaki would sit on the riverbank for hours on end watching fishermen catch trout with the help of tethered cormorants. The locals still pride themselves on the sweetness of Gifu Prefecture's *ayu*. As my tour continues, I read a tourist brochure, which cites no less a personage than the emperor of 1200 years ago who enjoyed the local trout, and Charlie Chaplin, who "was especially delighted with cormorant fishing." No wonder. I watch as one sleek bird soars gracefully over the water, patiently waiting to spot a shimmering school. It quickly swoops down and nabs the fish in its large beak. Just as the cormorant is about to enjoy the fruit of its labor, the fisherman pulls the leash with its loop around the bird's neck. The excited bird surrenders his anticipated dinner only to be allowed another opportunity to soar. I can't help but muse how Chiune would pay careful attention to this technique. He would become so adroit at pulling strings, after all.

Daily life in Yaotsu provided the Sugihara boys with many other lessons about the pecking order, as it were. It was no longer the village it once was, even a generation earlier when their parents were growing up. Then, the town consisted of a few extended families and everyone knew each other, for better or worse. The shameful threat of "losing face" was as effective as any police force in maintaining order. Yaotsu, like other provincial towns across Japan, was becoming a magnet for rural folk drawn to city life but not quite resourceful enough to make it to Tokyo or Osaka, or even one of the prefectural capitals such as Nagoya or Gifu City. Between 1890 and 1920, Yaotsu's population grew to 3,528, double what it had been. Today, the town has a population of 15,000. Suddenly, aspects of city life were trickling down to the towns. Moreover, the "new faces" in Yaotsu, unattached to regional dynasties, or local families of standing and reputation, were less concerned with losing face.

As such, Mrs. Sugihara was becoming a bit more uneasy about her sons wandering through the marketplace during the lazy summer days of 1905. There had always been teahouses in town. But now some newly opened teahouses raised suspicion as to what exactly was going on behind the wooden lattices.[4] Still, there was much to keep the boys occupied without getting into trouble. Carts and wagons were beginning to make an appearance on the streets, the technological spinoff of the war in Manchuria. Lanes were consequently laid down to accommodate more horses and riders. With the new vehicular traffic, the boys often would have to duck into doorways and alleys. There they would pass mothers and daughters, sitting on stools at the entry to their houses and weaving cloth for a new kimono, or cooking dinner on an outdoor stove. They might peek into the paper maker shops until someone chased them away.

Many farmers kept their horses on the Kiso River side of town, near the rice paddies. Sometimes Chiune and his brother would cut across these paddies on the way home, occasionally getting scolded by a farmer for weakening the walls of the irrigation channels. As dusk fell, they would pass the bathhouse, where men, women, and children would be coming and going, dressed in their *yukatas,* cotton kimonos. Yaotsu night life was still fairly subdued; it would be six or seven years before the town got electricity and telephones, more than a decade before it opened its first library.

Class and Déclassé in Yaotsu

The Sugihara sons fell somewhere in what we might call the middle of the Yaotsu hierarchy. They were neither akin to the wealthy few young-sters who left town for their parents' summer homes in the mountains or at the seashore, nor the children worked to the bone in family enterprises in the fields or marketplace. The Sugiharas had samurai connections, though, inauspiciously, they lay on the mother's side of the family. This placed Chiune, once more, in between, part respectable, part déclassé.

I wonder whether this borderline position, this marginality, made him all the more receptive to the strange, even the stranger? The West was making itself felt even in little Yaotsu in 1905. Yaotsu's kimono-clad parents celebrated *Bon,* Japan's August Buddhist festival, swaying to the beat of drums and shuffling their feet in circle dances paying homage to an-cestors' spirits. On the next morning, on the same field, cotton kimono–clad children, swinging their baseball bats and clonking around the bases in their wooden clogs, were paying their homage, now, to the spirit of the West. Indeed, *yakyu,* as baseball is known, had become the rage in Japan, since its introduction by an American professor in 1873. Chiune would become an avid player.

Not all the townspeople were pleased with this youthful preoccupa-tion. American imports still evoked complicated reactions, even a half-century after Commodore Perry forced the end of Japanese isolation. Inazo Nitobe, one of Japan's greatest educators, statesmen, and harmonizers of East and West, could not contain his scorn for baseball: "A pickpocket's sport," he called it, concerned that a game that relied on "stealing" bases was morally deleterious.[5] Nitobe was a Johns Hopkins–educated Quaker who in the summer of 1905 was busy readying his book *Bushido: The Soul of Japan*. It celebrated the Japanese martial spirit of chivalry, dismissed various corrupting Western influences, and became vastly popular.[6]

That summer offered the Sugihara boys still another form of entertainment besides swimming, fishing, and baseball: what you might call propagandistic roadshows. The Ministries of Home, Education, Army, Agriculture, and Commerce would send out their provincial officials to press one issue or another on townspeople around the country. At one meeting, the good citizens of Yaotsu would be chastised for, say, succumbing to the latest Western fad of owning watches, a useless trinket in the eyes of the authorities. At another, they would be adjured to the attribute of punctuality! The Ministry of Agriculture asked rural citizens to stay put and work the land, while the Ministry of Commerce tried to recruit workers for new urban factories. Tokyo's ministerial rivalries were being played out in the field. No wonder these messages conflicted. Local pundits claimed that if Yaotsu's farmers attended all the meetings sponsored by the Ministry of Agriculture alone, there would be no time left for the crops.

Still, the meetings were fairly popular, though more for the food, drink, and magic lantern shows, of course, than the buffet of ideas. The Sugihara boys could make a few fast passes on the refreshment table if done discreetly, while their parents listened to the orators. Indeed, the Yaotsu branch of the Meat Eaters Association, which urged citizens to improve their physique by eating more beef—the better to compete with Westerners—may have been a particular draw for the brothers. In his later years, Chiune, the bon vivant and gourmand, used what he learned in restaurants all over Europe. The lads were probably less engaged by the "haircut club," however, a group advocating that young women abandon traditional Japanese hairstyles in favor of Western coiffeurs. Other representatives of the "Local improvement movement" focused on the need for Japanese to surrender such cherished habits as soup slurping and the public display of toothpicks.[7] Sugihara's family was at least partly amenable to modernization, but many others weren't. Some such meetings were infiltrated with ardent champions of the old ways. A patriotic veteran, perhaps, or the scion of a samurai family, might hurry to the front of the crowd, the sleeves of his kimono ballooning in his haste. He would begin a predictable harangue about the evils of the West.

There would be a moment of uncertainty as those within hearing range would have to decide, was this part of the carnival atmosphere or something else?

Some of these speakers would lovingly recall the recent Sino-Japanese War years, how the people were more patriotic then, practicing *shobu shobu,* the local variety of extreme patriotism, the war songs, the mock drills, the open and violent expression of hostility toward the enemy. In those days, teachers and local officials, too old to go off to war, tried to create an all-consuming martial atmosphere on the home front. Now, though, Tokyo officials refrained from stimulating excessive degrees of patriotism, remembering, perhaps, how difficult such things were to control at the end of the last war.[8]

What was being argued vociferously during Chiune's childhood—by everyone from ministers to locals to humorless missionaries of anti-reform—was no less than the essence and future of "Japaneseness." How is such Japaneseness best expressed and by whom is it best represented? Are citizens, primarily committed to the collective good, who are patriotic, loyal, traditionally inclined, and skeptical about the West, the best Japanese? Or can you exert Japaneseness by striving for social harmony while expressing your unique qualities, which may include an appreciation of modernity?

These issues had been hotly argued in Japan for some time.[9] In the summer of 1905, however, the debate took place in a different key. For suddenly, Japan was winning its first major confrontation with a Western power. This created a new set of ambivalences, influencing how Japanese identified with both East and West, shading how they searched for security in the old and tolerated the frustrating and unfulfilled promises of the new. National integration was supported largely by patriotism. But the big question—the one that would fiercely confront Sugihara's generation in their youth and early adulthood—was whether Japan could achieve solidarity in peacetime and *without* the threat of an enemy, whether distant, close-by, or within.[10]

By the beginning of the summer of 1905, the direction of the war was clear, and in towns like Yaotsu anxiety was decreasing. The townspeople sighed with some relief. Russia would *not* be invading Japan, as feared. Japan's stunning victories, rather, had secured it a considerable foothold on that same stretch of land on which Moscow, Berlin, and Paris were situated. But the enormous cost of financing the war was beginning to strain the people of Yaotsu. And the first sons of Yaotsu were returning, many injured and broken, and some only as ashes in urns. A steep price was paid for Japan's new prominence.

Kovno, Kowne, Kaunas:
Declining Empire, Rising Nationalisms

We are eager to learn more about Sugihara, the rescuer, without delay. The nationalist and socialist revolutions brewing in a Russian city such as Kovno in the summer of 1905, even the peace treaties negotiated in Portsmouth, were far away from the swimming holes and rice fields of Yaotsu. They would seem to have little effect on the young Sugihara and his family except insofar as they contributed to the ending of the war. Yet to understand the culture of "Post Russo-Japanese War" Japan in which Sugihara grew up, we must make some side trips. Moreover, in the Kovno of 1905, we can observe the germination of forces that shaped rescuees just as we find in Yaotsu formative influences upon the rescuer, as we anticipate that fateful meeting thirty-five years later.

This one place has three names. Some call it Kaunas, recalling a Lithuanian gentry that prevailed until the end of the fifteenth century. Sentimental Poles, harping back to the nearly three centuries of Polish domination that followed, call it Kowne. The Russians, who annexed much of Poland and Lithuania in the eighteenth century, call it Kovno, as do the Jews. Sugihara arrives in Kaunas—under Lithuanian sovereignty since World War I—and leaves Kovno at the end of summer 1940, after the Soviets annex Lithuania and he helps thousands escape.

In the summer of 1905, children are swimming in the two channels of the Neeman that wind through town and separate it from suburban Slobodka. Though the Russians are now fighting Japan, most residents of the city are not unhappy about Russian losses. The tyranny and corruption of the tsar's administrators made Kovno a simmering cauldron of Polish, Lithuanian, and Jewish nationalisms, as well as socialism, and various combinations thereof.

If Russia was the enemy then Japan, perhaps, was a friend, because it shared that same enemy. Support for this "enemy's enemy" had lately grown quite brazen. Indeed, a personification of this stance is Joseph Pilsudski, the most important leader of interwar Poland, who was born not far from Kovno in 1867. In 1904, as the leader of Poland's underground labor party, he made his way to Japan to seek support for a well-timed Polish rebellion that might strengthen the Japanese position against Russia. "Citizens of Yaotsu and Kovno, unite," might have been Pilsudski's call.

Roman Dmowski, the leader of the centrist nationalist party and Pilsudski's arch rival, also made the pilgrimage to Tokyo. He begged the Japanese not to incite such rebellion. Not only would the rebels be squelched, with a horrible cost of life, he argued, but the ensuing chaos would inadvertently strengthen the Russians. Dmowski seemed to convince the Japanese government to err on the side of caution, much to Pilsudski's dismay.[11] But, apparently, Dmowski did not convince members of his own party. At the very moment he was making his plea in Tokyo, two young members were receiving a secret course in sabotage in a Paris hotel room from Japan's military attaché to France.[12]

And then there was the mysterious Colonel R. He grew up not far from Kovno when Sugihara was growing up in Yaotsu. And he would be lurking in the background as Sugihara distributed visas.

Whatever came of those aborted alliances, the foundations were established for empathy between Poland and Japan for several decades, and through many different sets of leaders. The bonds were strong. Indeed, even though Poland and Japan ended up on opposite sides after Pearl Harbor, they still worked together clandestinely, cooperating in code breaking and spy rings. As we shall see, the Polish-Japanese connection plays a role in Sugihara's act in the Kaunas of 1940.

But what was going on in Kovno in 1905—but one of the vibrant Jewish communities of Eastern Europe—and what are the political and cultural forces that shaped those who would line up outside Sugihara's door? Many, many developments. Zionism and cultural rennaissance, for instance, were thriving, as an eighteen-year-old Kovno woman named Devora Baron shows us. Baron expressed the tragic choices of her generation in rich allegories, as one of the first writers in the renewed ancient Hebrew language. That summer, she left Kovno for her parents' small village nearby, to write. In her story "Mountain of Shade," *har zel,* she played with a pun on the name of Theodore Herzl, the leader of political Zionism, whose death the previous year many Kovno Jews were mourning. She tells of a hot Sunday afternoon when a few young Jewish women take a boat ride on the Neeman and seek the protective *har zel.* But they are not sure whether this meaningfully named mountain—and the promised land to which it points—will ease their way. Can peace be attained through worldly activities, such as actually going to the mountain? Or can real peace be secured only by faith, here symbolized by the old Jew of their parents' generation who is studying a sacred text about enchanted mountains?[13] In other words, emigrate to Palestine, or stay where one is and participate in a rich and varied Jewish life? Is one's homeland in the mind, or can one actually see and touch it?

While floating down the river, the Kovno group passes some simple peasant women at work in the lush fields. They hear them singing, "Soil, our mother, you have given birth to us." Intuitively, Baron's women can identify with these women, with their joy in the land. But drawn as they are to the beauties of nature, as Jews they feel the gap between the home of their birth and the imagined homeland of their history. It is all so wrenching. They don't even have the Hebrew words to translate the peasants' passions, that language for centuries having been relegated to prayer and study.

It would take several more years before Devora Baron would make for Palestine. Many like Baron, lovers of Hebrew, lovers of Zion, would still be in Kovno when Sugihara arrived. For some Kovno Jews in 1905, leaving for Palestine was less of a dilemma. In the months since the beginning of the war, of the more than forty murderous pogroms that had raged across Russia, Kovno alone was the site of two. It was a good place to leave.

What choices did Jews have? Gone were the days when the *khappers* (grabbers) prowled the streets of Jewish towns, kidnapping children for twenty-five years of military service. But during the Russo–Japanese War, it was still difficult for Jews to avoid conscription. The folklore of the period is replete with tales of men mutilating their rifle finger or sneaking out of the ranks, some to escape to America. In the end, some thirty thousand Russian Jews soldiered for the tsar. Relative to the Jewish population as a whole, this figure represents a much higher proportion in the army than native Russians.[14]

One of those unlucky recruits was a Russian Jew named Josef Trumpeldor. Like Baron, this young man would also became a Zionist, eventually emigrating to Palestine. Trumpeldor was the son of a victim of the *khappers* and himself the victim of tsarist bureaucrats and their quotas who rejected the talented Trumpeldor from dentistry school. With little reason to be patriotic, he nevertheless volunteered for a unit involved in particularly dangerous missions. Jewish heroism, he believed, would advance Jewish rights in Russia.

Trumpeldor fought on, even after losing an arm to a Japanese mortar shell at Port Arthur. Here he writes to his parents on February 2, 1905: "People with two arms will envy me. . . . The Japanese are treating us as well as could possibly be." A generation of Russian-conscripted Jews had the same experience. They were treated better as prisoners of war than as civilians back home! Not only that, Japan turned out to be the spawning ground for an intense form of Zionism. During his enforced period of contemplation as a POW on the island of Nippo, Trumpeldor founded the first *moshava,* a Zionist agricultural collective. The former Tolstoyan pacifist became a hero of the Revisionist Zionists, who turned him into a symbol of militant nationalism. In fact Trumpeldor died in 1920 while defending one of the northernmost settlements in the land of Israel. These were his last words: "It is good to die for one's homeland."[15]

Men and women like Baron and Trumpeldor would one day line up in front of Sugihara's consulate. The initiative they took—so integral to Sugihara's act—drew from venerable sources.

Of course, to borrow Baron's image, there were plenty of Jews, in Kovno and throughout Eastern Europe, who would rather study the mountain than move to it. Like the soup-slurping samurais with whom Sugihara grew up, for these Jews any concessions to the West were anathema. For many Jews, revitalization movements such as socialism or Zionism, religious reform, Hebrew or Yiddish renaissance—movements with Western roots—were more problems than solutions. The Yeshivot, renowned Tora academies located in Kovno and its environs, were part of a network of renewed traditional institutions stretching from Lithuanian towns such as Mir to the Polish city of Lublin.

Kovno had a special reputation for its *mussar shtibels,* special rooms designated for ethical contemplation. One of the all-time favorite inspirational books among these spiritual types was *Heshbon Hanefesh (Calculus of the Soul),* a disguised Hebrew rendition of Benjamin Franklin's moral accounting system, fostering, perhaps, as did Franklin's *Poor Richard's Almanack,* a touch of entrepreneurialism. These academies were vital places, crowded with students. They rejected the new but were not above innovation within certain parameters. Like the venerable Ninth Fort, constructed to protect against attacks from the West, the revitalized Yeshivot provided such defense against assaults of the modern.

In the summer of 1905 when military incursions, pogroms, and revolutionary movements were threatening Kovno from all sides, the Yeshiva compound certainly was more substantial than the poorly designed defense apparatus of the tsarist military architects. And thirty-five years later, those otherworldly Yeshiva *bukhurs* (students) and *mussarniks* (meditators on ethics) would help facilitate Sugihara's actions. Some even demonstrated advanced managerial skills in coordinating apprehensive Jews to take advantage of the Japanese *malakh* (angel), Sugihara's escape routes.

Portsmouth: The End of a War, the Beginning of a War

Tuesday, August 8, 1905, a hot, windy day. Anything that floated lined Portsmouth harbor in anticipation. The steamers *Dolphin* and *Mayflower* were chugging to the New Hampshire seacoast from Oyster Bay, New York, where President Theodore Roosevelt had first welcomed and introduced the Russian and Japanese delegations. The three countries hoped to end the war here in this New England navy town, so very far from where it began. As the gleaming steamships entered the harbor, police had to use force to calm the crowd, now standing several abreast along the water's edge. Even the local urchins, diving for pennies off Pickering Wharf or playing baseball in South Park on any other summer day, were dressed in their Sunday best, waving tiny flags. The towns-people did not know much about the war's particulars, but they were proud of their role in trying to end it.

Portsmouth, New Hampshire, had its share of summer celebrities in those days. True, it could never quite compete as a wealthy vacation spot with Newport, Rhode Island, one steamship day closer to the financial centers of New York and Philadelphia, or Bar Harbor, Maine, for those rich enough to spend a whole season away from such hubs. Usually, any visiting dignitaries came to break champagne bottles against new hulls; many a famous frigate had been built in the Portsmouth Naval Yard—and many a sailor cherished rum-soaked memories of carousing on Water Street. As one local historian, full of civic pride, put it: "Portsmouth would have to take a back seat to none of them for the pure viciousness and depravity of its night life."[16]

Not the most sedate place for pinning down a treaty, perhaps. But some in the President's inner circle expressed concern that Newport or Bar Harbor socialites might upset the talks by shunning the non-Christian, nonwhite guests. Portsmouth clinched the deal, in the end, because of its naval base. Superior telegraph facilities would enable the diplomats to communicate with their governments. Superior guards and gates would keep at a distance nosy journalists who wanted to communicate with their readers.

A year before, Roosevelt began the trek that led to Portsmouth, dur-ing the early salvos of the war, at a point when nobody seemed very ea-ger to end the fighting in Manchuria. Indeed, Britain and Germany were not unpleased to see both Russia and Japan tied up in such devastating fu-tility. Roosevelt himself was facing elections in November 1904—his first presidential run since inheriting the office from his assassinated predeces-sor, William McKinley. Mediating this conflict would truly be a high-risk proposition, he knew. But as an avid reader of Darwin and champion of manifest destiny, the old Rough Rider was firmly convinced America would soon be a world power. The time was ripe. Still, he had little rea-son to believe that he could roughride himself back into the White House and then onto the Nobel Peace Prize in 1906, for playing the in-ternational power broker.

Initially, it was not simple for the President to decide which combatant the United States should support. Roosevelt was not without sympathy for tsarist Russia. "Russia, and Russia alone of European powers has been uniformly friendly to us in the past," he said.[17] But whatever tolerance the bully pulpit user had for an autocratic regime, he did not appreciate actual bullies. TR was outspoken in condemning the Kishinev pogrom of 1903, for instance. In those days, the brutal state-sponsored murder of forty-nine Jews in the southern Ukrainian city of Kishinev still aroused indignation. What he once pointed to as a "uniformly friendly" regime he now tagged as a "menace to higher life of the world." Loyalties had shifted. "Our people have become suspicious of Russia," he said. "And I personally share that view."[18]

As Roosevelt grew more sour on Russia, Japan seemed the sweeter potential ally. Ever the enthusiast, the President had recently taken a shine to Japan; the charger up San Juan Hill appreciated the samurai spirit and even began to take wrestling lessons from a certain Professor Yamashita.[19] "Dealing with a government with whom mendacity is a science is an extremely difficult and a delicate matter," he said disparagingly, speaking of Russia. In contrast, Japan seemed upstanding. Its interests in the Yellow Sea were, after all, not unlike those claimed by America in the Caribbean, under the Monroe Doctrine. The Japanese and Americans had more in common, thought Roosevelt and Secretary of State John Hay, than was first supposed. As Hay put it, there's no reason to "lose sleep over the 'Yellow Peril.'"[20]

Japan might have enjoyed a measure of support among the Western powers. The war did begin with Japan's efforts to force Russia to uphold the Open Door policy regarding trade in the areas of northern China that it controlled. Europe supported Japan's stance. But then things went too far, too fast. Japan's recurring victories made many worry about its future influence; it was possible Japan would win *too big* against a European power, throwing the East–West balance out of whack. So by the spring of 1905, those European powers, usually not too eager to allow America the prestige of a diplomatic victory, had changed their tack. They began nudging the warring parties toward Portsmouth.

The Russians had been prepared for war in every other way but militarily, and the Japanese quickly exposed their bluster. Only a few days before the Japanese attacked them at Port Arthur, in southern Manchuria, on February 8, 1904, Minister of Interior Vyacheslav Plehve told Minister of War Aleksey Kuropatkin this: "What we need to hold Russia back from revolution is a small victorious war."[21] Tsarist officials' responses to social and economic ills were no more reality oriented than their attempts at military preparedness. That same minister of the interior who had spurred the battle against internal "enemies" also suggested: "There is no revolutionary movement in Russia, there are only the Jews who are the true enemies of the government."

But pogroms against "true enemies" did not seem to add to Russian fierceness in confronting the Japanese. The Russians were defeated repeatedly on the battlefields of southern Manchuria. By the spring of 1905, Russia had virtually lost its navy in battles in the Strait of Tsushima. The tsar's admirals had organized this task force with spectacular incompetence.

It was now clear to everyone, besides tsar Nicholas II and his advisers, how difficult it would be to stanch the flow of unrest and revolutionary fervor.[22] Bringing the Russians to Portsmouth was no simple matter. On the Japanese side, conversely, there seemed to be some calculation of realistic military goals. In April 1905, when photographs of a hunting-trophy-laced reunion of President Roosevelt and his Rough Riders ran in the press, the Japanese ambassador to the United States, Jutaro Komura, was quoted as saying, "I notice that the President has got two bears. We would be satisfied with one." But still many Japanese were unenthusiastic about negotiating. In the government and on the streets of Japan, many felt that in both the Sino-Japanese War of 1895 and the Boxer Rebellion of 1900, Japan had fared better in combat than in diplomacy. Nevertheless, by June 1905, after consolidating its hold on Port Arthur and Mukden, destroying the Russian fleet in the Strait of Tsushima, and, following its final grab for Russian territory on the island of Sakhalin, Japan was ready to negotiate.

At this point, the bankers—on both sides—were happy to give Roosevelt more than a hand in getting their clients to Portsmouth. Jacob Schiff, a prominent American Jewish leader, no fan of the tsar and his pogrom-makers, had already backed three bond issues for Japan totaling $260 million on most favorable terms.[23] A fortuitous meeting in London with Korekiyo Takahashi, the vice governor of the Bank of Japan and financial commissioner of the government of Japan to New York and London, later minister of finance and premier, marked the beginning of Schiff's heavy funding of the Japanese side, as well as a lifelong friendship between the two men.[24] Schiff's assistance would long be remembered and appreciated in Japan. It would also foster some residual pro-Jewish sentiments there, as well as some exaggerated beliefs in Jewish power. Schiff helped Roosevelt steer Japan to the negotiating table by quietly letting his Japanese clients know that he was becoming uneasy about the additional bond issues they would surely need if the war were to continue.

The Japanese, likely, did not realize in 1905, nor in subsequent years of lauding Schiff and that bright moment in Japanese-Jewish relations that, astonishingly, a rogue French-Russian Jew was raising considerable sums for the other side. Wheeler-dealer Artur Raffalovitch paid generous bribes to the French press to paint a rosy picture of Russia, so he could exaggerate the security and profitability of Russian bonds to French pensioneers and their agents. For a time, Russia was a hot investment. But by the summer of 1905, Russia's military performance had grown so poor and its domestic situation so volatile that Raffalovitch was no longer convincing, and bond prices began to dive. Like Schiff with Japan, Raffalovitch and the Jewish bankers he represented were not eager to extend the Russian credit line.[25]

To the last moment, no one had confidence that the Russians and Japanese would actually agree to meet. Yet, on a billowing August day in 1905, in unlikely Portsmouth, the Japanese disembarked from the *Dolphin* and the Russians streamed off the *Mayflower*.[26] Following the dignitaries' words of welcome, a marine honor guard struck up a rousing march and fired a deafening gun salute. A parade proceeded down Congress Street, appropriately considered for the occasion the Nevski Prospekt of Portsmouth. The crowds were huge and varied; as the *New York Times* reported, "farmers rubbed elbows with spruce Bostonians."[27] The delegates would soon settle down in the opposite wings of the grand Wentworth Hotel in nearby Newcastle. The head of the Russian delegation, Sergei Witte, was dissatisfied with the accommodations, complaining that the bathtubs were too small for his 6-foot, 6-inch portly frame and the American food was overly spiced. The Wentworth's otherwise uninspiring variations on boiled potatoes and fish, however, may well have convinced the flamboyant minister to get down to business and not linger in Portsmouth.

During the twenty-eight days of talks, the press delighted in keeping track of the various sideshows: who was going to church, who was buying what where, and, of course, who was hanging around with the "summer girls . . . dying to know celebrities."[28] Other visitors to the Wentworth (receiving less press attention) included a delegation of Jewish leaders, headed by Jacob Schiff, to meet with Witte. The count's old-world charm had served him well in the past, in talks with other Jewish leaders such as the founder of political Zionism, Theodore Herzl.

But it did not seem to work with these particular bankers. In response to an appeal for their brethren in his country, for example, Witte claimed that reports of Russian Jewish suffering were exaggerated. The removal of their legal disabilities, he said, would do them more harm than good. Schiff, in accordance with reports from all sides, responded with less of his usual calmness, tact, and diplomacy to Witte and to his fatuous claims.[29] Notwithstanding the tone of their exchange, Schiff sent a check for $10,000 to the Russian ambassador in Washington to provide for the "needy and stricken of Russia." To ensure that there be no misunderstanding, he sent a comparable sum for the same purpose to the Japanese consul in New York.

Reporters never tired of contrasting the two main players, the "envoy of the Tsar" and the "plenipotentiary of the Mikado," "as unlike each other as any cultured human beings could be." The very difference of those representatives seemed to bode badly. How could they possibly agree on any resolution?

Nevertheless, the delegates did leave Portsmouth with a treaty in hand. A historic marker in the Portsmouth Naval Yard still attests to the moment:

> In this building at the invitation of Theodore Roosevelt, President of the United States, was held the peace conference between the envoys of Russia and Japan, and September 5, 1905, at 3:47 P.M., was signed the Treaty of Portsmouth, which ended the war between the two empires.

The war was ended, borders and spheres of influence redrawn. True, the Russians and Japanese overcame hopeless complications by coming together on foreign shores. But in timeworn fashion, the treaty that resulted was seen as preparing the way for future disasters. Most glaringly, the Russo-Japanese War exposed Russia's weakness to its own people; the treaty did little to revitalize that country, for war led to revolution.

For the Japanese, the treaty provided more than a badly needed respite. It enabled Japan to gain its primary war aims, including tacit international recognition of its stake in Korea, control over a segment of southern Manchuria, and important railroad concessions beyond the so-called "leased territories" of China. Japan emerged as a major power.[30] On the other hand, the Portsmouth legitimation of Japanese colonialism set the stage for four decades of problems, zigzagging across Sugihara's life and reaching right up to the door of his consulate in Kaunas. In Portsmouth, Japan became a more "modern" country, relative to the isolated society it had once been. It also became a more "Western" nation in emulating Great Britain and the United States, the powers it most admired in the West. Now Japan, too, possessed colonies.

Except that, by the turn of the century, colonialism was falling out of fashion. It would take two world wars before real decolonization would begin, but the ideology's heyday was fading. Japan was late to enter the imperialist club and would resent how its own versions of "manifest destiny," the idealism with which it saw itself assuming "burdens" in China and Korea, would be debunked as aggressiveness. Why was its self-interest exposed while the West's was concealed, simply because the West had begun earlier? The Japanese felt humiliated. This Occidental double standard hopelessly confused pro-American sentiments in Japan.

Moreover, Japan did not receive indemnifications at Portsmouth. The payment it demanded directly from Russia was more than money; it was a palpable admission of fault. Japan's perceived failure in this aspect of the negotiations seemed to strengthen the belief, in years to follow, that another round of war with Russia was absolutely "inevitable."[31] That America in Portsmouth "deprived" Japan of its full victory provided another source of resentment that would influence Sugihara's generation.

The signing ceremony on September 5 lasted for seventeen minutes. A special Te Deum was offered at Christ Church by the Russian Orthodox archpriest from New York City. The Japanese, it was noted, did not attend. They arranged their own local events, including judo demonstrations, accompanied by "a dragon and small parasols, and a temple complete with idol." They made donations of $10,000 to the governor for the needs of the state, $1,000 to the Old York Historical Society and York Hospital. They left tips for the hotel staff. Komura quickly returned to Japan by way of Cambridge and his alma mater. A brisk trade began in treaty conference momentos, including the chairs, table, and pens with which the agreement was concluded. Various Portsmouth brewing companies heralded their beer as the "most potable beverage that [the Russians and Japanese] had tasted in the US." President Roosevelt said that peace was good for the Russians, good for the Japanese, and "mighty good for me too!"[32]

The new status achieved by Japan may have encouraged arrogance within its borders and envy outside. Belief in the Yellow Peril became more prevalent as Japanese colonialism intensified, providing the climate for a measure of hatred between the allies and Japan experienced nowhere else. The life and career of Sugihara unfolded against the background of those Portsmouth provisions and the "inevitable" second round of Russo-Japanese conflicts that it instigated. It pointed Sugihara down the path to Kaunas.

"Post–Russo-Japanese War" Japanese Culture: A Tax Collector in His Own City

What was Sugihara doing while those lumbering steamships sailed into Portsmouth harbor, we wonder? And what was he thinking as the tsar's recruits, on their way to fight Yaotsuans in Manchuria, were whipping up a pogrom in Kovno?

His father, Kosui, certainly had reason to think of those events. Sugihara Sr. was not lacking patriotism, though he did not serve in the war. Perhaps he was older than the call-up age at the beginning of the troubles, or was exempt because of old battle wounds. Had the peace negotiations in Portsmouth not begun, Kosui Sugihara might soon have been drafted to serve along with the younger men in town. But the good news from Manchuria made that seem unlikely. And besides, wasn't he the Emperor's own tax collector-in-residence, serving his country by pen if not by sword? Chiune may have wished for a more romantic, heroic figure, but at least his father had some standing in town.

But if the young Sugihara was looking for heroes, all he had to do was glance at the photograph of one plastered all over town. The picture showed General Maresuke Nogi accepting the surrender of his Russian counterpart, General Anatolii Mikhailovich Stoessel, in Port Arthur. The defeated commander is standing tall, in full uniform and with full armaments. Everyone in town had heard the story of how, even before the surrender became official, General Nogi sent to his vanquished enemy fifty chickens and one hundred fresh eggs. All young Japanese, like Sugihara, were to learn from General Nogi's example that even when confronting one's enemy, one must respond with compassion, never humiliation.[33] It was a matter of national honor. The hunted bird flying near the Emperor's portrait, as the Japanese aphorism goes, must be protected. I wonder, did Sugihara remember that aphorism and example years later when hunted Jews came to his door?

At any rate, the Japanese could afford to be generous in victory. But that victory would leave them richer in spirit, if little else; it was an open secret that the government's coffers were depleted. And Chiune's father, trying to cover the cost of feeding bested Russian generals and the interest on foreign loans for the war effort, now became one of the new "soldiers," serving at the fiscal front. It was an important job, though not an easy one. To be the tax collector in the same small town in which one lives is a thankless burden, and surely not the best way to win friends, particularly during those days of war against a modern, Western power, when expensive new props in the theater of an ever-more-mechanized warfare were as necessary as the right cast of soldiers.

In short, Japan's military planning was sharper than its financial planning. Men like Chiune's father had to cover the gap. Other citizens could contribute by planting trees or by building up their savings accounts. In fact, patriotic Japanese citizens did increase their deposits during the war—as much as twentyfold the national average—making those sums available for government spending. But who was more responsible for providing for the costs of men and matériel than His Majesty's local tax collector? Even so, one doubts the erstwhile Iwai was looked upon as a great patriot such as the soldiers returning to town. Fear—respect, maybe—but not admiration for Kosui Sugihara.

Even though Japan appeared to have the advantage and the war was about to end, it probably was not a smooth period for Sugihara's father. The pressure on him and his colleagues to build up the country's fiscal reserves was mounting. The majority of levies were collected as a land tax, but most farmers and peasants kept scant written records of their income.

Their plots were distributed in different areas, making collection difficult. Some of their secondary businesses, such as the sale of mats woven from rice stalks, were especially thorny to track. Whatever taxes supplemented the land tax—head, income, property, irrigation use, and enterprise taxes—were inadequate. The tax rate approached the confiscatory and many simply didn't pay up.[34]

How did Sugihara Sr. feel about the "rough stuff" that now had to be used, sometimes against the poorest of peasants, to keep up with the quotas imposed by his bosses in Tokyo, and what did his son think about that? We have no information about the response of either. But clearly it must have been a factor in their relationship. Indirectly, Kosui's position created the circumstances for his son's colonialist career. It was the tax collectors, after all, who fueled the growth and power of the modern state by developing paper-and-pen strategies for taxing citizens at a rate far beyond what could be brought in through old-fashioned arm twisting. Here is one telling detail: whatever their specific tax collection techniques, Kosui Sugihara and his colleagues made pawnshops the fastest-growing business in town.[35]

Sometimes patriotic fervor, in the wake of military victories, would make Kosui's work a bit easier. Then the locals would show more positive feelings toward their absent but demanding landlord, the state. The country was starting to believe in itself. For some Japanese, proud memories of military triumphs unleashed a greater sense of patriotism, which could be channeled into an eagerness to compete with the West. But the West, they felt, was not playing fair. The Japanese had only to look at Portsmouth to see how the politicians were mishandling things. The negotiated treaty left something unresolved, and Japan was thus robbed of its victory. Yes, the Japanese identified with General Nogi's grand chivalrous gestures to the enemy, but that didn't mean they desired anything less than a full victory. The riots in the Hibiya district of Tokyo and elsewhere, soon after the treaty signing in Portsmouth, expressed these frustrated hopes for monetary and territorial compensation.

Soon thereafter, in early 1906, a new series of urban riots, motivated by the decline in living standards, erupted. Crowds burned streetcars in Tokyo, seemingly in response to the full-blown postwar recession. Japanese patriots had great difficulty understanding why the war should be as ravaging for them, the winners, as it was for the Russian losers. If Japan was so victorious in battle, why not in diplomacy? In a small town like Yaotsu, there was little comprehension of the new international economics of warfare. By now, in fact, Japan's interests were as dependent on New York and London as Tokyo and outbacks like Yaotsu. How could most Japanese grasp that Jacob Schiff, the New York banker, and Kosui

Sugihara, the Yaotsu tax collector, were actually partners, if unacquainted, in funding Japan's war efforts? It made one's head spin.

"Ah! It's a money world!" ran the words of one of the favorite songs of Chiune's childhood, and whether this was an "ah" of condemnation or celebration, it's hard to say.[36] The period 1905–12 is not exactly heralded for its idealism. "Everyone today is talking and writing about the struggle for survival, even the proverbial four-year-olds, all know about it," Japanese were saying. The fiercest battle in this struggle for survival was played out during a deep recession brought on by the costly Russo-Japanese War. Japanese were now forced to work harder simply to stay in place, let alone get ahead. Some reacted by taking risks, being innovative, and producing new goods and services. As in Kovno, the spirit of Benjamin Franklin was alive and well among Japanese in their own Poor Richard–like aphorisms. "One day spent in idleness is a day behind," as they said back then.[37] Of course, some of these entrepreneurs benefited mightily, but far more failed miserably.

Indeed, the entrepreneurialism that so colored this new "money world" of Chiune's later childhood corresponded with profound ambivalence for the urban and urbane.[38] In these years, the West and the modern (closely associated in the minds of most Japanese) were often vilified. They were seen as contaminations, yet certain current ideological movements, like socialism, for instance, cut both ways in Japan. Some decried it as a product of enemy Russia, but others, especially intellectuals, felt it spoke to their culture of collectivity. Still, the influence of Marx and Tolstoy, or, for that matter, George Washington and de Tocqueville, was felt by many to be alien to Japaneseness. These ways of thinking might be seductive, but they were misleading and must be resisted.

This ambivalence intensified through Sugihara's growing years. *Bushido,* the feudal ethos, may have been extolled more than wicked *besoboru* ("baseball"), another name for the American game, but not all Western imports were condemned. It was not unusual for the Japanese to appropriate Western ideas to express their fear of Western encroachment and envy of Western success. While opposing occidental colonialism in Asia, for example, many Japanese could simultaneously support Japan's growing empire. Pan-Asianism was homegrown manifest destiny, was it not? Competitiveness with the West became an abiding concern for Chiune Sugihara's generation, in what they both approved of and deprecated. "The world says that America is civilized," as Sugihara would tell one Jewish refugee in Kaunas some thirty years hence. "I will show the world that Japan is more civilized . . ."

This was an endless problem for Sugihara and his peers, then; they were unable to sort out or evaluate the effect of the West on their lives.

Both to express their fears and simply to orient themselves, many thus embraced extreme ideologies of the right and left—rustic sentimentalism, chauvinism, and nativism on one side, with strange admixtures of nationalism and socialism on the other. Here we find the source of some of the potent and destructive ideas that became real political forces in the 1930s, each arising at critical moments in Sugihara's career. But at the same time, the taproots of cosmopolitanism and compassion, courage and defiance were also taking hold on his personality. They would one day create a remarkable man and a remarkable action.

And Kosui Sugihara? What was his relationship to the modernizers and antimodernizers? Practical, but also eclectic, for he had long local ties, was married to a family with property and status, and was close to the city fathers—conservative sorts, we might suppose. Yet he went about in Western attire in a period when trousers and jackets, in a small town like Yaotsu, would come under scorn. In his off hours, the Emperor's servant was even known to go out Western dancing. He was also one of the most frequent patrons of the new local movie houses, not places where he'd likely bump into his philistine friends.

All these conflicts—modernism versus tradition, East versus West, state government versus local—coalesced in the arena of education. Here is where father and son had to stake their ground. Chiune began school shortly after the war, just when Kosui, as an imperial tax collector, became deeply involved in debates over financing education. The importance of education was constantly emphasized throughout the Meiji period, from 1869 to 1912, and scholastic reforms were initiated with great fanfare. Indeed, reformist edicts became catechisms that young people would have to recite along with their other lessons. The crux of the problem was that the imperial government tried to centralize control of education, but the school budgets were provided locally. This dual control inflamed a debate.

How to pay for teaching, therefore, became as complicated as what to teach. Until now, both educators and politicians had been divided among themselves on "traditional" and "modern" approaches to education. Some believed the purpose of education was to convey filial respect and the values of Japanese society in the service of the state, transmitting native Shinto and Confucian tenets. Others sought "knowledge throughout the world" to produce learning that was "useful to the nation," pedagogy that stressed enlightenment and utility, universal dimensions of education. Still others, particularly those concerned with the weakening of rural life and its wholesome ways, called into question the very usefulness of education. They dismissed the debates, calling them the problems of the "educated idle."[39]

Tokyo itself sent out contradictory signals, as postwar economic realities began to exert their full impact. At about the same time, the Ministry of Education added two years to the amount of mandatory education required for Japan's sons. Kosui Sugihara's bosses in the Ministry of the Interior began criticizing municipal governments for spending too much on school construction. Budget cuts ensued. The salary of teachers, never opulent but at least reasonable in the earlier Meiji period, now fell beneath the level of artisans, below the poverty level.

The squabble for tax yen in a tight economy placed Sugihara's father in a keenly difficult situation. Between 1906 and 1911, when Chiune was in the local village school, education consumed the largest portion of town and village budgets, averaging 43 percent on a national basis.[40] A campaign, now initiated by the state and prompted by competition for tax money and fear of the insidiousness of foreign ideas, questioned the value of so many Japanese receiving so much instruction. Even Ministry of Education officials spoke of "the evil of too many people harboring hopes of higher education." Doctors "were increasing like bamboo after the rain."[41] These sentiments were captured in a popular song of the day: "I will be a doctor of laws, you a doctor of letters. So let's go to the pleasure quarter, our parents in the country are digging yams."[42]

With Toyoaki already in school and Chiune soon to start, Sugihara Sr.'s professional and personal interests could not help but clash in the summer of 1905. For it was the municipal tax collector, after all, whose efforts would fund public spending for his own boys' education. Naturally he would want them to have the best opportunities. Yet as an imperial bureaucrat, Kosui was forced to be an advocate of the state's antieducation campaign, and was thus obliged to join in the attacks on the "educated idlers." In other words, he had to act one way, even though he thought another. Here was no simple yam digger; Kosui was cosmopolitan enough to know that education led to getting ahead. And Chiune, who showed an inclination to "spare no effort when doing anything," by his father's plan, showed great promise.[43] Kosui wanted him to be a doctor. It did not matter one bit that physicians and other professionals were "springing up like bamboo." National aims were one thing, personal ones something else entirely.

The Making of a Masterless Man in Modernizing Japan

Sugihara Sr. moved around a good deal in the years immediately following the war, perhaps because of his own idiosyncrasies or the awkwardness of being a tax collector. With increasing bureaucratization of the Emperor's tax system, assignments were shifted to maximize utility rather than to maintain personal relations. In 1907, the Sugiharas lived in Kuwana City in Mie Prefecture. In the same year they moved to Gifu City, where Chiune attended the Nakatsu Elementary School. In April 1909, at the beginning of the Japanese school year, the Sugiharas relocated to nearby Nagoya, where Chiune attended the Huruwatari School. In 1912, he completes sixth grade; his report card from that year indicates he is a straight-A student and he misses only two days of classes. In 1917, he graduates from the Higi Fifth Junior High School in Aichi Prefecture.

The record is tiresomely sparse, of course. We see that Sugihara moved around a lot and got good grades. But we still know so little as to what went on in his mind. Some facts, some forces—it's not enough. If we are to understand anything about his subsequent actions in Kaunas, we must know something about his personality or as some, including Chiune himself, might have called it, his soul.

Perhaps in our pursuit of Sugihara, then, we must consider other methods by which to give chase.[44] We have touched on the alleys and rice paddies of Yaotsu, the conflicts within a modernizing Japan, the play of international relations. What influential legends, even movies, may have shaped his early thinking and aspirations?

It is an afternoon in 1907, at a first showing of *The Forty-Seven* Ronin, filmed on the new movie back lots in Kyoto. This is an epic tale of Japan, first published in the early eighteenth century and since studied by young people for edification and inspiration. It is also based on a true story. Even for the children of the "money world," this story was among the "most popular entertainment of the time."[45] Kosui, a cinema devotee, we recall, may well have taken his older sons with him on that particular day. From one source or another, however, it is reasonable to assume that this tale was a part of Chiune's education. How does this so very popular tale inform us of the world in which Sugihara grew up, and how might it have contributed to the making of this mass rescuer?

The legend concerns a good and mighty provincial leader, Lord Asano, who is loyal to the Shogun. Lord Asano is much beloved by his hundreds of retainers but is essentially a country bumpkin; in spite of Lord Asano's unpolished ways, the Shogun honors him by making him, on a particular occasion, one of the masters of ceremonies. One Lord Kira, a sophisticate more familiar with the ways of the court and a jealous rival of Lord Asano, has long made himself available to such provincial lords as an adviser on these occasions. But Lord Asano is so pure, naive, and unconversant with courtly procedure that he bungles his transaction with Lord Kira by not offering him the right gifts for his services.

The urbane Lord Kira decides to take revenge. He wrongly advises Lord Asano how to dress and act for the occasion. Asano's resulting humiliation is profound. When he realizes what has happened, he responds as any man of honor must: he pulls a sword against the humiliator. This only makes things worse, for Lord Asano, in that singular and restorative gesture, thereby violates a most sacred rule of the court. Kira receives only a minor wound, but the fate of the good Lord Asano is sealed, as is the fate of his many loyal retainers, too. Because of the corporate responsibility implied by the feudal contract, his retainers must surrender their property and, in good form, submit to *seppuka,* ritualized suicide. Asano's wisest and most loyal retainer, Oishi, who if he had been present at Kira's misdeeds would surely have corrected the advice he received, returns just in time to bid farewell to his master and take charge of the collective suicide of some three hundred other retainers.

But then the loyal and grieving Oishi decides that even these three hundred acts of devotion will not restore Lord Asano's *giri,* his good name and honor. Only vengeance against Lord Kira will do that. The plotting will require much delicacy. Kira himself is close enough to the Shogun to be somewhat protected, so first, then, Oishi must ascertain who is indeed loyal. Like the biblical Gideon, he separates the men from the boys, then he instructs those who have proven to be the most loyal—in actuality, only forty-six—to divorce their wives, sell their daughters, wallow in drunkenness, and do everything to appear other than a well-organized, goal-oriented conspiracy.

This ruse is perpetrated with great deliberateness during a period of twenty-one months. The "masterless men" indulge in lives of "debauchery" to make their "enemy relax in watchfulness," to throw Kira off their trail. This will make the surprise attack more dramatic, Kira's murder more painful, and the revenge for the *ronin* all the sweeter. On the snowy night of December 14, 1703, they slay Kira and then commit suicide.[46] Their graves in Takanawa, near Tokyo, are visited by many pilgrims to this day.

Many Japanese, I was astonished to find out in my travels, staunchly associate this story with uncompromising loyalty. It deeply moves them. It symbolizes a central tenet of their culture. But those sharing the Western Enlightenment tradition, not raised in a system that sentimentalizes certain courtly traditions, are likely to respond to the tale with a troubled sense, even a measure of indignation. "All that bloodshed and misery," we might ask, "because a practical joke went awry, because someone had to restore honor?" Ruth Benedict emphasizes the zealous concern with *giri,* with honor, name, "face," the "initiative and ruthless determination" with which, in this "non-Western" society, a hero "finally settles incompatible debts to the world and to his name by choosing death as a solution." The American anthropologist's book, *The Chrysanthemum and the*

Sword, with whatever flaws, continues to be influential in Japan and abroad to this very day.[47] But an older contemporary of Sugihara's comments on *The Forty-Seven* Ronin might provide more insight into the meaning of this story for Sugihara himself and the *mentalité* with which he becomes a mass rescuer. Inazo Nitobe spent the post Russo-Japanese War years as Tokyo University's first professor of colonialism, training administrators who would become Sugihara's colleagues and providing legitimacy for Japan's rising empire. He sees this saga as "representative" of the tendency of the Japanese to be "spontaneous and guileless" in their responses. "In times when cunning artifice was liable to pass for military tact . . . this manly virtue, frank and honest, was a jewel that shone the brightest and was most highly praised."[48]

Nitobe, we puzzle, is the man who dismisses baseball because it promotes "stealing bases." Yet he lauds Oishi and his co-conspirators, who even sell their sisters into prostitution to "catch off base" their enemy Lord Kira! *They* are "spontaneous and guileless"? What's going on here? Is this really a tale about impulsiveness, immediacy, and pure action? In fact, every move in this story appears carefully planned. Why should spontaneity be considered more of a "manly virtue, frank and honest"? What inhibitions are there for Japanese to strategize action? Or, as is more likely the case, why is it so important to conceal from others and even oneself that a reaction is carefully planned?

Each scholar finds a conflicting subliminal message, particularly as to whether guile is good or bad. But neither pays attention to the "aesthetics" of the cover-up. The loyal disciple Oishi's dissembling may be exquisitely choreographed, but his disloyalty to his family (especially the female members) is far less enchanting.

Sugihara is so often seen as a rule-breaker operating with *defiance* and *directness,* so uncharacteristic of most Japanese. Yet perhaps his behavior was actually *extremely* Japanese. In understanding his mass rescue effort, we must try to answer not only *why* he did it but also *how* he did it. For like Oishi, Sugihara not only enlisted others to his cause—but also *concealed his strategy.* He acted very much like a *ronin.*

End of Childhood, End of an Era

Chiune's later childhood was bound by two events accompanied by loss. In 1910 Japan annexed Korea, and his father, soon thereafter, joined the colonial civil service there. For Kosui this may have been a good resolution of personal and professional problems, a fresh start, but his departure left the family divided. From then on, Kosui was little more than an intermittent presence in Chiune's adolescence.

On July 30, 1912, another event took place, the death of the Emperor. The month of funeral rituals and public mourning created a solidarity in the "money world" unknown since the threatening days of 1904–05. But just as the Meiji Emperor, whose reign had become synonymous with Western-oriented reforms, was about to be buried, Japan's foremost hero of the Russo-Japanese War stole the show, as it were. General Maresuke Nogi, whose picture Chiune had seen in the Yaotsu alleyways, kneeled before a photograph of the Emperor and, with his wife beside him, committed suicide in the traditional samurai manner outlawed some 250 years before.

To this day, the Japanese periodize their lives in accordance with certain years of imperial reign. The death of an Emperor is deeply experienced as the end of an era, and his passing might have entailed a solemn celebration of Japan's modernity.[49] But the general's suicide cast too long a shadow, and mourning quickly turned into questioning. Which direction would Japan follow? Backward or forward?

In the late summer of 1912, uncertainty and anxiety prevailed in Kovno and Portsmouth as well as Yaotsu. In Kovno, revolt against Russian domination, in the name of one "-ism" or another, was in the air. At the Portsmouth Naval Yard, fitters were working extra shifts to build the new battleships that would enable Teddy Roosevelt's America to cement its leadership under Woodrow Wilson, and through the world war that was a few years off.

In Yaotsu, the young Chiune felt distinctly unmoored. Not only had he lost his own father to the Emperor's colonial administration but also two more father figures in the Emperor and the general. Here was impending manhood and he had no guides. But a new father figure, himself a *ronin* of sorts, would provide for Kosui Sugihara's precocious second son. Chiune would learn to be a "masterless man," in his own unique ways, full of "ruthless determination."

Chapter 2

Sergei Pavelovich

The Making of a Colonial Official, 1919–31

We live during breathtaking times
Be brave, Japanese students!
Let us make Russia and Japan brothers
Long live the friendship
Between East and West!
We are pioneers of the new sunrise;
East is asking West for help;
We are dreaming of Moscow walls
And Volga, and Dnieper, and Ukraine
And the Caucasus magical secret
Neighbor Eastern countries
Are half-asleep in the darkness
They are suffering deeply!
Lead us, "Aurora"

—from the Hymn of Japanese Students of the Harbin Gakuin National University

The tricolor is rent
The star of glory is falling,
Wings of the wild eagles are losing their strength,
Evening casts its dark shadow at the Kremlin.
Who can be a brave one
Among 100,000 iron cavalrymen?
The tower of the synagogue is tall,
And we enjoy the friendship of the people,
After clearing away the dead branches and leaves.
The synagogue shows no shadow of opulent spring.
There is no moon on the Ural Mountains,
When everybody seems lost like sheep,

Oh, now it is the time of confusion,
I will stand up for justice.

—from the Harbin Gakuin National University Dormitory Song by Kunio Nakajima,
   Class of 1923

The water from the Sungari River runs for thousands of miles.
Soon my grave will be built in the fields of India, Persia, or Turkey.
Manchuria is not my final goal. I will go much further beyond the Ural and Altai
   mountains.
I rest my head on the lap of a beautiful maiden.
I am a patriot and my life is for the cause. I will die a hero's death.
Marry your daughter to a man from the Harbin School.
Because unlike all those dandies, we have guts, we are determined.

—from the Harbin Gakuin National University School Chorus[1]

"Military Preparedness in Civil Garb . . ."

His name was Shimpei Goto, and his countrymen called him *oo-buroshiki,*
the man with the large wrapping cloth, a Japanese euphemism for a man
with many ideas. Indeed, Goto was a German-trained medical doctor
whose hectic public life included stints as foreign minister, minister of the
interior, mayor of Tokyo, and colonial official in Taiwan and then
Manchuria. His prominence was such that he was even dubbed "Japan's
Teddy Roosevelt."[2] The preceding song lyrics give a good sense of this
oo-buroshiki's robust spirit; Goto founded the Harbin Gakuin as a national
academy in 1919. Sugihara enrolled that same year. Both lived "during
breathtaking times" to be sure.

As with Chiune and Kosui Sugihara, we know little about the interaction between Chiune Sugihara and this other father figure.[3] But we can
infer and speculate on that relationship by examining those situations they
did share. From this perspective, the evidence for Goto's influence on
Sugihara's life is as abundant as it is clear. Let us begin, then, by learning
a bit about Shimpei Goto's way of thinking. Here he is, speaking shortly
after the Russo-Japanese War:

> The Russo-Japanese War will probably not conclude this situation in
> Manchuria in a single war. Will a second war actually come some time in
> the future? . . . We must occupy a position in Manchuria wherein we are far
> in the lead and, full of vigor and vitality, confront our rival with fatigue. . . .
> In short, colonial policy is *bunso teki bubi,* military preparedness in civil garb.[4]

Goto's civil garb had several layers: He wanted to organize the *civil*
realm with military efficiency. The colony thus set up would demonstrate

to other nations how *civilized* Japan truly was. Japan's moral superiority, manifest in this talent for *civilizing*, would bestow the justification for its colonialism. For Goto, Japan and its colonies were all of a single cloth, inextricably meshed. Each colony provided a disguise, a motive, and springboard for military control. In this simple but somewhat paradoxical phrase, *bunso teki bubi*, Shimpei Goto, Japan's foremost theoretician and enactor of colonialism, described the environment in which the young Chiune was trained. Might he also have been suggesting the pretense with which Sugihara, the very representative of Japanese "military preparedness" sent to that volatile Nazi-Soviet divide on the eve of World War II, saved thousands of Jewish lives?

A half-century after Japan's territorial empire collapsed in World War II, its colonial heritage still arouses strong feelings, both polemics and apologetics. Men like Goto and Sugihara helped create that ambivalent legacy. Indeed, a significant part of Chiune's professional life was spent in the Imperial Japanese Army, the Foreign Ministry, the Manchurian Foreign Ministry, and other related intelligence agencies. We must take glimpses behind the doors of these now-vanished institutions; knowing more about Sugihara's early professional experiences, we hope, will provide us with some understanding of what he brought with him to Kovno.

From 1919 to 1935, Sugihara, in ways that we will never fully know, was an active participant in Goto's world of *bunso teki bubi*. Goto orchestrated the "civil garb," the hospitals and schools, the buildings and factories, the mines and harbors, the thriving economy of interwar Manchuria. The Japanese colonial strategy was to inspire awe; when the colonized saw how much Japan could do for them, they would gratefully comply.

"My grandfather was a real liberal," Goto's granddaughter, Kazuko Tsurum, told me one summer afternoon in 1994. She is now a retired professor of sociology at Waseda University, another of Sugihara's brief academic stomping grounds. But is it the little girl, overwhelmed by Grandfather's genuine accomplishments, that remembers Goto, or the critical sociologist, analyzing tragedies of good intentions?[5]

This is just one of many rosy reminiscences I encounter. One July morning in 1994, I call on Masami Okitsu, the chairman of FM-Nakayushu Broadcasting Company and a member of Harbin Gakuin class of 1938. Summer rain pours down, giving even this modern side of his venerable city, Kumomoto, the feeling of a Kurosawa film. Okitsu is flanked by male assistants and a retinue of uniformed office women, who bow upon entering and leaving. It is a distinctly unsentimental scene. Yet tears come to the chairman's eyes when he recalls his lost Harbin days—and foremost in his memory is Shimpei Goto.

Okitsu proudly details how the old-style Meiji bureaucrat, while studying in Germany, picked up on ideas that animated so many student princes in the late nineteenth century, particularly the idealism and mysticism of Tolstoy, which Goto reformulated into the language of the civil service code, and expertly spiced with Japanese nationalism. The mix produced, in essence, a Japanese version of manifest destiny, an ideology for colonialism sounding much like the Boy Scout Code of Honor. At the same time, Goto imported some distinctly unscoutly concepts; in the 1890s, he translated into Japanese some of the same German texts on biological racism that would excite the first generation of Nazis.

Talking with Okitsu this sodden day, I find myself seeing Goto as a man divided; as a bureaucrat, he could not realistically implement those high ideals taught at the Harbin Gakuin. Okitsu becomes particularly maudlin when he remembers the school code: 1. Do not be a burden to others; 2. Take care of others; 3. Do not expect rewards for your goodness. I ask him for memories of Sugihara, and he quickly warms to a story, as if it were a tale of the Master Goto's teachings. It runs thus: during a flood in which Chinese residents of Japanese-controlled Manchuria suffered particularly heavy losses, Sugihara pulled on his boots and went out to survey the situation in the countryside. There, he gave the flood victims some encouragement rather than, in timeless bureaucratic form, remaining deskbound and filing his report, sight unseen.[6] This was typical of Sugihara, says Okitsu. He took Goto's code most seriously when events demanded in Kovno years later.

But Goto, as liberal and humane as he might have been, must also be remembered as the theoretician of the clearly illiberal "military preparedness." The colonial regime of Manchukuo came to brutalize the colonizers and estrange the colonized. The West condemned the "puppet regime." Most Japanese preferred to focus on the civil garb: without their best intentions and altruism, they maintained, primitive northern China would never have been developed. Weren't they also protecting their unruly neighbor from its "Western" neighbor, the Soviet Union? Didn't the USSR, after all, want to spread the malignant ideology of communism to Manchuria, then to China, Korea, and the other "backward" countries of Southeast Asia? Where would Manchukuo be without benevolent Japan?

This disparity between civil garb and military preparedness—plus the West's sour disapproval—prompted many Japanese to become indignant, self-righteous, and xenophobic. It was especially galling when Great Britain and the United States, themselves colonists, criticized Japan's policy in Manchuria. The hypocrisy was too much. Years later when Sugihara, the disciple of Goto in Kovno, observed how Jews were treated by other nations, he found the West sorely wanting: "Who is more civilized?" he asked. The East, was his answer, clearly the East; he would prove it. "Oh, now is the time of confusion," says the Harbin Gakuin song. "I will stand up for justice."

"Pioneers of the New Sunrise, Friendship between East and West . . ."

At Portsmouth, Japan, the island-nation, had indeed surrendered its isolation, whatever else it might have gained. The ink on the treaty was hardly dry when Edward Harriman, the American railroad tycoon, arrived in Tokyo, lobbying the government for the railroad development rights to southern Manchuria. Long-isolated Japan could suddenly be connected with a world transportation venture. Doing business with the prominent American would improve Japan's standing in the international community by evidencing Japan's support for the "open door policy" and international cooperation in China. Rioters in the streets of Tokyo, disappointed that the Japanese politicians in Portsmouth had not exacted indemnities from the Russians, wanted to give clearer expression to Japan's "special interests" in Manchuria. But leaders who realized that the war had depleted Japanese coffers made the strongest argument; they emphasized that Harriman would help fill them back up.[7] Harriman's plan was close to being pushed through.

But Goto ultimately prevailed. The point of Japan's stake in the railroad was not to shore up revenues, Goto argued, but to colonize Manchuria. The railroad would provide the opportunity for 500,000 Japanese to settle there over a ten-year period. If we cede railway rights, Sugihara's mentor pleaded, we end up weakening our control. Indeed, in less than a year after the conclusion of the treaty, the government established the South Manchurian Railway Company (SMR), which would manage Japan's economic interests in Manchuria. Only Japanese and Chinese would be allowed to invest in what came to be called the "chopstick alliance." When offered in Tokyo, the stocks were oversubscribed by a factor of a thousand. The official had gotten his way.

By November 1906, Goto was appointed president of the SMR. He wielded immediate influence. With speed and decisiveness, he deployed work crews to lay new single and double tracks. He built warehouses, docks, administrative buildings, and housing as well as a new hotel in Darien, and launched negotiations with the Russians to connect the SMR line with the Chinese Eastern Railway in the north, not far from Harbin. Orders were placed to the United States for 180 new locomotives and 2,060 railway cars; Goto demanded rapid delivery.

But a railroad, in Goto's hands, was far more than a mode of conveyance. The railroad's right-of-way—233 square miles—was sufficiently ample that by 1931, even before Japan changed its Manchurian colonizing style from control to formal annexation, it included 105 cities with managers trained to promote de facto annexation.

Known as the "proposal madman," he seemed able to roll the poses of man of the Enlightenment, patriarch, and micromanager all into one. He established research institutes to study the region's rich resources, plot economic enterprises, and plan the social environment that would encourage Japanese to settle in Manchuria, strengthening Japan's stake in the region.[8] The resulting stream of intelligence covered a broad range of Manchurian, Chinese, and Russian endeavor; reports were published on everything from their folklore and natural resources to their economy and potential level of rebelliousness. He urged members of his growing staff to trust him and, as he said, "be a member of a great family."

This family, though, had its share of problems; in the areas of Manchuria over which the Japanese were given control at Portsmouth and beyond, the Japanese inherited serious conflicts between the Chinese and Russians. Goto had two concerns: that the conflict not disrupt Japanese plans and that those plans in no way foster Chinese-Russian solidarity against Japan!

China's centralized governance was becoming weaker. But Goto knew that nothing would better unite and stir latent Chinese nationalism than the arrogance of foreigners, particularly Japanese. At the same time, he might have considered Japanese-Russian relations a matter of secondary importance. After all, at Portsmouth, the Russians had ceded their rights in those areas of southern Manchuria where Japan was now active. Reports were arriving that the tsar was losing his grip on power, not to mention reality; the number of Russian strikes and demonstrations was growing ominously. Nevertheless, while still advocating personal politeness to the Chinese, Goto chose to bet on the political future of the quasi-European Russians rather than the declining Sino state. He repeated Japanese adherence to the open door policy.[9] Goto began to post "railway guards," most often thinly concealed Japanese soldiers and intelligence operatives, every fifteen kilometers of track, in accordance with the Portsmouth Treaty.[10]

After little more than two years of working on the railroad, Goto was recruited into cabinet and ministerial slots back in Tokyo. But he came to be known as the SMR's "eternal President," and these later, higher positions enabled him to influence the colonization of Manchuria even more.

A tour of duty with the SMR—management of its related enterprises and agencies, work in its research institutes—became an important experience for young careerists like Sugihara in Japan's military and far-flung bureaucracy. Others included two of the better-known officials later brought before the World War II Tokyo War Tribunal: Yosuke Matsuoka, known as the "talking machine," who defended Japan's Manchurian policy before the League of Nations and led his country's brazen walkout. Matsuoka subsequently became a foreign minister. He was the man to whom Sugihara reported, trading telegrams about the thousands of Jewish refugees milling around in front of the Kovno consulate.

Then there was Shigenori Togo, another Japanese minister of foreign affairs at the beginning of World War II, who also logged time on the SMR. One of Japan's experts on Germany, his hatred for the Nazis was prompted by his experiences while ambassador to Berlin in 1937–38. But Togo's attitude, particularly as ambassador to Moscow in 1940, may have had consequences far beyond the personal for some desperate Jewish refugees. Precisely what his relationship was with Sugihara remains a mystery.

Matsuoka, Togo, and Sugihara learned statecraft in Goto's colonial administration and they also learned about each other. It was just one more unanticipated consequence of Goto's military preparedness behind civil garb; these SMR research institutes trained several generations of Japan's experts in fields as diverse as construction and sanitation to using arguments from world religions to influence public opinion. The latter was practiced by one such expert, Setsuzo Kotsuji, who completed a doctorate in Semitic studies in the United States and wrote a grammar on Hebrew in Japanese. In 1940, Kotsuji intervened at the highest levels on behalf of Sugihara's refugees. In 1959, he even converted to Judaism.[11]

But these apparent seats of Enlightenment, these famed research institutes, had their dark side. Dr. Goto, with his interest in the same Darwinian pseudoscientific racist tracts that drew Hitler, would have been shocked at "studies" coming out of the establishments he founded. During World War II, biological warfare tests were conducted in a secret laboratory near Harbin; the Japanese army's "military preparedness," run by the infamous Unit 731, led to the brutal torture and murder of several thousand in horrible "medical" experiments. Harbin's biological bombs were responsible for thousands more civilian deaths—and might have been used against millions more.[12]

Apart from Goto's research institutes was his school. The Harbin Gakuin lasted from 1919 through 1945 and graduated approximately 1,585 students. It seems to have been founded as Goto finished his term as foreign minister, during which he orchestrated various Siberian excursions, sometimes teaming up with the United States and Japan against the fledgling Bolshevik state. True to the linkage he perceived between military and cultural efforts, a training institution was altogether appropriate.

Exactly why and when the Gakuin was transformed from a mere language school of some Japanese-Russian Association to a fullblown academy is not at all clear.[13] Several generations of Japanese colonial
administrators and "Russia hands" would be trained at that institute, including the young man from Yaotsu, the son of another colonial bureaucrat posted in Korea.[14]

From the Provincial to the Colonial

In about 1910, when Japan's gradual annexation of Korea was formalized,
a small but tough bunch of soldiers, police, and bureaucrats was selected
to run that country—among them Kosui Sugihara. It seems to have been
more of a lateral transfer than a promotion, from one imperial bureau to
another. Whether Chiune, his mother, and his brothers actually spent any
time in Korea when Kosui was first getting established there is unclear. As
far as we can tell, the older sons were in school in Japan, boarding perhaps
with distant relatives, and the mother seems to have remained in Yaotsu.
The family was decidedly scattered. Sugihara's father, it appears, was not
much of a father in those years.

The Japanese colonial administrators in Korea acted considerably dif-
ferently from their counterparts in Formosa, Taiwan, and the "leased
territories" of Manchuria, where Goto was in charge. In fact, Goto's concern for the sensibilities, if not the rights, of "his" natives was nowhere
matched by his Korea-based colleagues. Here, the Japanese seemed to
want to reenact the coerciveness that they themselves had felt under
Commodore Perry in 1854. Thus, a "state within a state" was set up, gov-
erned by officials with little accountability to the Diet in Tokyo—not
much "civil garb" in these parts.[15] The colonization of Korea was brutish;
in 1895, diplomat/military officer Goto Miura unilaterally ordered the
Korean empress assassinated and placed the emperor and crown prince
under house arrest. After 1905, the Japanese exacted concessions from the
Koreans, as authorized in the Portsmouth treaty, in lieu of indemnities
from the Russians. Defenders of Japanese colonial policy provide evidence for rapid economic development during this period.[16] The human
costs of these policies are patently clear; production may have been up
but Korean autonomy was all but destroyed.

Back in Yaotsu, tax collectors were not known for their gentle techniques; neither were colonial administrators in Korea. Was Kosui Sugihara involved in harsh methods of governance? We do know that he soon
developed other interests. In Korea as in the American Wild West, speculative opportunities were available to an administrator of his background. Whether he found himself a pensioner with discretionary time

and capital or simply seized a moment ripe for entrepreneurial "cashing-in," Kosui soon retired from the government and turned to real estate. He was aided by the decade-long Japanese land survey of Korea; it was justified as an instrument of good governance but in the hands of these officials soon became an excuse for expropriations. Deals were there for the making.

Kosui Sugihara bought some land in the Korean countryside and established a Japanese-style inn in Seoul. He also took a concubine, as Chiune's older brother, Toyoaki, visiting his father in 1915, discovered and immediately reported back home. Yatsu, his wife, quickly joined him in Seoul, we hear. We do not know what happened to the other woman. We do know that after their reunion, in October 1916, the Sugiharas had their sixth child, Ryuko, a daughter. Yatsu helped Kosui run the inn until her untimely death several years later.[17]

We have no information as to Chiune's whereabouts in the two years that followed his graduation from the Number 5 Prefectural High School of Aichi on March 16, 1917. We do not know about his relationship with his father during these years of separation. Perhaps they were now living together in Seoul; perhaps Chiune was there for an extended visit. But father and son were now very much in conflict. Kosui wanted his son, following an ancestor's example, to become a physician. Never mind the doctors reportedly were "sprouting like bamboo," that frugal bureaucrats were supposed to oppose excessive and expensive education. Chiune seems to have wanted to study English, possibly with the goal of becoming a teacher. We know what kind of salaries, in virtually all societies, the members of that profession make. Father and son argued bitterly.

Moreover, conflict at home was accompanied by conflict in the streets. The situation for Japanese in Korea was altogether tense. On March 1, 1919, Korean nationalists rioted through the streets of Seoul and even in the countryside. The Japanese suppression of this movement was bloody and successful. It was not the kind of street scene that Chiune liked; he left for Tokyo and entered the English division of the normal school at Waseda University on April 1, 1919. The father's anger and disappointment were intense: Kosui disowned his son.[18]

With great difficulty, Chiune tried to support himself through his first year of college. But it soon became apparent this tactic was untenable. Japanese universities were elitist institutions with few provisions for work/study or scholarship students. By November 1 of that year, his name, the record indicates, was struck off the enrollment list at Waseda University.[19] For another man this might have been the end of his chosen career of being a teacher. For Chiune, who even half a century later was called by his Moscow colleagues "the teacher," it was, in fact, the beginning.

While struggling to support himself, he was directed by a newspaper announcement to an exam to be given on July 16, 1919. It was drawn up by the Foreign Ministry, and it entitled fourteen students to study abroad with subsidies. He passed (no easy task—it was highly competitive) and selected Spain as his first choice. But the one Spanish fellowship went to someone else. He next opted for one of the three positions available in Russian.[20]

What insight do his language choices give us into the soul of Sugihara? Spanish and Russian; this was a man attracted, perhaps, to passionate cultures, to warmth, whether from the climate or the bottle (Sugihara would become a connoisseur of vodka). For a young Japanese to try and master any European tongue denotes an extra measure of venturesomeness, we might also assume, in contrast with Chinese or Korean, which, as different from Japanese as they are, could still be perceived as somewhat familiar. Moreover, to study a colonial language would surely prove a more practical undertaking. If Sugihara was bent on one of the European cultures, though, one might at least have expected him to begin at the top; in Japan, German was prized over English, trailed by French; other than issues connected with the Philippines and Japan's growing diaspora in Latin America, the Spanish-speaking orbit was not at the crux of Japanese foreign affairs. And Russian? What was the status of this language of the enemy?

Japanese reactions to anything foreign were always complicated; Russia was viewed as Western but not clearly so. The historical moment when Sugihara chose Russian as his special language was precisely when the image of Russia was in flux. In the past, Japanese who delved into Russian culture did so because they were curious about the Russian intelligentsia. They wanted to read Pushkin and Tolstoy, study the Russian politics of nihilism and anarchism. True, Russia had been an interloper on Japan's borders, but it also intrigued as a culture.

But now an increasing number of Japanese, including politicians, military men, and government officials, were deeply concerned by the "contagiousness" of Bolshevism.[21] In contrast with 1905, when the Polish Pilsudski's anti-Russian scheme failed to enlist enthusiastic support in Tokyo, Japanese intelligence officers now shared Russian secret codes with Polish nationals. Indeed, they helped the Poles break the Soviet blockade of Warsaw—which seeded the relationship that would blossom, two decades later, in Vice Consul Sugihara's consulate in Kaunas. In fact, just as Sugihara tackled Russian, a dramatic preoccupation with Soviet culture was getting underway. In 1919, hardly anything was translated from Russian into Japanese; a decade later nearly three hundred works of literature, literary criticism, art, and the social sciences were published in translation.[22] Whoever this young Yaotsuan was and for whatever reason he first opted for Spanish, ultimately, he picked a "growth industry."

Harbin Gakuin: The Training of a Secondary Elite

On September 2, 1919, Chiune Sugihara was ordered to Harbin and given an annual scholarship of 1,600 yen. He arrived on October 6, in time for the second semester, which began November 1.[23] Still a teenager, he had sufficient time to settle into his dormitory as he was is-sued the "prescribed school uniform and school cap."[24] While, in general, students could start only at the opening of the academic year, the charter indicates that exceptions could be made.[25] Perhaps Chiune had some pre-liminary knowledge of Russian, allowing him to join the students who had begun six months before. Monthly tuition came to 35 yen covering "textbooks, commodities, clothes, food, pocket-money, medicine, and the school field trip."

Even after paying his transportation costs from Tokyo, Chiune seems to have been left with a comfortable sum, thanks to the Foreign Ministry.[26] Unlike his colleagues at Waseda, the sons of wealthy merchants and high-level government officials, many of the students in Harbin seemed to hail from humbler backgrounds. Various employers sent would-be employees to the Gakuin for training, in return for their expertise upon graduation. The main sponsors were apparently railroad companies and governments of different prefectures.

Harbin had once been little more than a small Chinese village on the Sungari River. In Goto's time, the "metropolis" was emerging not only as the administrative center of the railroad but as the very control point of Russia's colonization of Manchuria. Goto was fond of Harbin; the *Mittel-europe* atmosphere of the town reminded him of his student years in Ger-many. It was a cosmopolitan city, "Paris of the Orient," as some said.[27]

Even after secondary-school years in Nagoya, living in Seoul with his family, and spending time in Tokyo, cosmopolitan Harbin must have overwhelmed a young man from Yaotsu. Like most of the students at the Gakuin, Chiune was beginning his career as a colonial administrator. But Chiune was taking his first steps in becoming something more than that, also. One day, he would be considered perhaps Japan's foremost Rus-sophile and, despite his father's discouragement, a great teacher.

But life was not all work and no play. Chiune became an ardent partic-ipant in what Nitobe derisively called the "pickpocket's sport." The Harbin Gakuin's baseball team was named Aurora, for the Japanese em-blem of the rising sun. It was the strongest squad in Manchuria, and the players wore white. The baseball season in chilly Harbin was fairly short, and Chiune clearly missed it in 1919. By the time he arrived in late fall, the Sungari was sufficiently frozen over for hockey, though, another sport that the athletic Chiune relished. But conditions were less than ideal; the Chinese in Harbin had created huge craters on the hardened river by carting away blocks for their intricate ice sculptures. Chiune would have to make it through a long, dark winter before he could stretch for line drives at first base.

During that bleak season, when not carousing with his classmates, Chiune would work on his game of GO. This quintessential Japanese game falls somewhere between chess and checkers. But the goal of GO is not so much to get to the other side, to neutralize or capture the opponent's pieces, as in those games better known in the West; it is to encircle the opponent's men in ever-expanding and more tightly enclosed clusters, wonderful training for a colonial administrator. Baseball, GO, Russian, his fellow students, and friends in Harbin—these were the beginnings of long and significant involvements for Sugihara.

When Sugihara began at the Harbin Gakuin, there were fourteen faculty members, mostly Japanese, with academic degrees. Russian language and culture courses were taught by native speakers with Russian diplomas, including one woman. One of the Russian language instructors seems to have gone to Yale. Some faculty members also taught at other local schools. A certain Professor Gogvaze, for example, gave classes at the First Harbin Public Commercial School, where the students were Jewish and White Russian. When, as was often the case during his lectures on accounting, Gogvaze had discipline problems, he would try to shame his charges into obedience, castigating them as to how attentive and courteous were his Japanese students over at the Gakuin.[28]

The school could accommodate 190 of such well-behaved students, if the inventory of classroom desks is a reliable indicator. The first graduating class in March 1923 had forty-six students; a year later, the total was up to sixty-three.

The program demanded thirty-six hours per week of class attendance. Half of that was devoted to Russian reading, writing, grammar, conversation, and translation, particularly from Japanese. But students were encouraged likewise to study a second language. They could choose among Chinese, English, German, and French when enough of them were interested. Additionally, there were requirements in ethics, physical education, Chinese classics, and an array of more practical courses in such areas as economics, finance, trade, merchandising, business math, calculations on the abacus, bookkeeping, business writing, business, and geography, primarily of China and the Soviet Union.

Much learning took place outside the classroom as well. It was actually part of Goto's educational mandate: "Try to see, hear, meet, study as much as you can." This certainly explains why Goto did not choose a more secluded environment for his Gakuin. Harbin was a fine place for budding Russia hands to wander in; for reasons long forgotten, the city preserved the siesta tradition, more logical in areas where weather induced drowsiness. The town work ethic included long breaks—and Chiune took advantage of them.

On a typical afternoon, he might leave the Gakuin complex and amble down Uchastkovaya Street, the densely settled but relatively small Japanese district. Seasoned Harbinites liked to joke about the number of barber shops with Japanese proprietors in this neck of the city. They were apparently established with the encouragement of one Japanese intelligence agency or another as neighborhood sounding posts. There is something about hot lather on the face and cold steel on the throat that makes even circumspect men less cautious in conversation. Most Harbinites could also predict when clandestine Japanese military forces were going to provoke trouble: sandbags would suddenly appear and disappear along Uchastkovaya Street, around the barber shops and beyond.

Picture Chiune passing through many different sections of town, each with its own feel. Novogrod seemed to be a mixed Russian and Chinese area, the slums of Nachalovska largely poor Chinese. Pristam, leading to the river harbor, was where many of the middle-class Jews and Russians resided. As he walked along Kitayskaya (Chinese) Street into the Commilo center of Harbin, he would pass the synagogue, then the Churin Department store, redolent of brewing coffee. Perhaps he might stop off for a treat in the nearby Matsuura department store, owned by Japanese. And, of course, in the windows of Eskin Brothers, a textile and haberdashery shop owned by Jews, there was always something new to glance at.

Harbin is probably where Sugihara saw Jews for the first time. In Japan and Korea where he had lived, there were virtually none. What was often a carefully guarded secret in towns and cities of Europe was no secret in Harbin—Jews were among the earliest settlers. Indeed, the man who initially selected the site on which to build Harbin was a Jew from western Russia named A.I. Shidlovsky, who in 1895 was planning the Trans-Siberian railroad.[29] Other Jews settled in Harbin upon being demilitarized after the Russo-Japanese War. It seemed a decent alternative. Here they would not face the same restrictions and lack of economic opportunities that plagued the Jews back in the Pale, the areas of Russia to which Jews were legally confined.

By the time of the revolution, Jewish professionals as well as destitute Jewish refugees started to arrive in droves. Some did not intend to stop in

Harbin and, in fact, chose the eastern route to avoid war-torn and pogrom-plagued western Russia, the Ukraine, and the quickly disintegrating Austro-Hungarian Empire. These refugees did not have money for transit or became separated from other family members, or lost contact with relatives in America who could send them visas and steamship cards. This caused a great deal of confusion around Harbin—just around the time that Chiune arrived.

The chaotic situation prompted a visit from "Captain" Samuel Mason of Providence, Rhode Island, in 1919, representing the New York–based Hebrew Immigrant Aid Society (HIAS). The Russian-born accountant had distinguished himself during the Spanish-American War by trying to organize a Jewish branch of Teddy Roosevelt's Rough Riders. They were called the Touro Cadets, named for America's first synagogue, in Newport, Rhode Island. While it is not certain that the Cadets got much beyond demonstrations at fund-raisers in New York City, no less a personage than the famed Zionist Theodore Herzl expressed "the keenest interest" in the captain's efforts to improve "the physical fitness of our people."[30]

As the Great War was coming to its end, Theodore Roosevelt's vision of the United States as a global power was being realized. With America's star rising, the power and prestige of its Jewish community also ascended. Such organizations as the American Jewish Committee, the Joint Distribution Committee (JDC), and the HIAS had been peripheral to the major centers of Jewish life, their leaders not particularly influential beyond the U.S. borders. But after World War I, when the Jewish communities of Europe were divided, they saw a unique opportunity to step into the breach.

When Mason arrived in Harbin, he was returning to America from Irkutsk, where he organized and convened the Jewish National Council representing some sixty Jewish communities of the Urals and Siberia. They constituted a sort of "underground railroad" that would act in concert with the JDC and HIAS in America to help Jewish refugees escape. The terminal point was Japan. Its port of Yokohama was the most significant for Pacific crossings, and its government was sufficiently sympathetic to issue transit visas for these Jewish refugees. In the past year, Mason had successfully moved 1,706 refugees (including 106 non-Jews) from Europe, across Japan, and to the United States. The Harbin branch of this operation remained intact up to World War II.

Colonial official-in-training Chiune Sugihara probably knew nothing about Samuel Mason's mission in 1919. During the many years of his residence in Harbin, he may have seen these refugees walking down the street, sitting in cafés, waiting forlornly with overstuffed suitcases at the railroad station. Years later, during his career as an official in Harbin, he may well have been privy to information about organized efforts on behalf of foreigners. We have no idea. And Sugihara unobligingly presents us with no hints as to how he remembered anything of this in Kaunas, 1940. Still, irony of ironies, could Samuel Mason ever have imagined that one of those unassuming, green Japanese cadets would perpetrate an act of rescue far larger—and more critical—than his own?[31]

When Chiune first arrived in Harbin, there were approximately 10,000 Jews in residence. By the 1920s, as he scaled up the bureaucratic ladder, the city's population counted 13,000 Jews, 13,000 Japanese, 120,000 Russians, and 339,000 Chinese.[32] When he moved from Harbin in 1935, the Jewish population had dwindled to about 5,000. Mostly, they had left because of a rising sense of lawlessness. An unholy alliance had been forged between the increasingly powerful Japanese military and the increasingly dependent White Russian fascists—which resulted in predatory behavior against the Jews.

"The White Russians were our enemies," Evsey Domar remembers. "They would wait for us after school and beat us up." A retired MIT professor of economics, Domar grew up in Harbin, a city his family considered a haven—at first. In 1914, his father in Lodz, Poland, decided—enough! There was no end to antisemitism in the lands of the tsar. Domas Sr. accepted a brother-in-law's invitation to migrate to the "Wild East" city of Harbin. He was excited about the new beginnings.

Some years before, this relative had gone into business with a Chinese partner and was now doing well enough to help the *mishpuha* (extended family). Evsey was only a few months old when his family left Lodz for Harbin, just ahead of the bloodshed erupting across Europe with the onset of the Great War. They rented an apartment from an entrepreneurial Chinese landlord who utilized the newly improved railroad connections to rotate his wives and concubines between Harbin and his *"shtetl"*—the professor, to his and my amusement, uses the sentimental Yiddish phrase for village—"back home." It was a safe life for awhile. But there was always an undercurrent of unease; even young Evsey wondered why so many of Harbin's barbers were Japanese. But as Japanese nationalism climaxed, particularly after the "independent state" of Manchukuo was proclaimed, many Japanese took to, as Domar says, "acting badly." The professor still shudders as he remembers the change.

For the White Russians, Harbin was deemed a "Little St. Petersburg," for its broad avenues, late-nineteenth-century imperial-style buildings with their stucco facades and domes and playful imitations of the Moorish, plus, in later years, a few Stalin-style eyesores.[33] Traces of the original sleepy Chinese village were still visible. But as one Russian historian put it, Harbin was "a particle of the fatherland transplanted to a foreign country . . . with the Chinese Eastern Railway . . . the first and unique Russian colony."[34] As the terminus of the connector line that Goto had constructed between the South Manchurian Railroad and the Russians' Chinese Eastern Railway, Harbin provided an ideal nexus for the rising clout of the "unique Japanese colony" in northern Manchuria. If civic activities were to conceal military efforts, as Goto hoped, railroads would be the vehicle for their twin advancement.

Notwithstanding Russia's rivalry with Japan, it was extremely eager to cement an alliance; both countries wished to weaken China's stake in Manchuria. In 1914, Japanese Foreign Minister Kikujiro Ishii proposed that "if Russia could yield to Japan the railway between Changchun and Harbin at the highest price," Japan "might comply with the Russian wishes."[35]

And then the Russian Revolution thundered forth. Not surprisingly, it greatly complicated any diplomatic relationships developing in Harbin; when it came to Manchuria, suddenly China and Japan would have to answer to two sets of Russians competing for the day-to-day management of the Chinese Eastern Railway.[36] The city became a refuge for various train-taking White Russians, monarchists, Mensheviks, and others rendered misfits by the Bolsheviks; it became thoroughly unwieldy.

The White Russian railroad managers organized a Far Eastern Volunteer Corps to combat Bolsheviks in Siberia. Adding to the confusion around Harbin were streets full of troops from the isolationist United States. They had barely recovered from World War I's end and were now joining old friends and old enemies in trying to figure out who were the *new* friends and enemies. From mid-July 1918, under the guise of rescuing some stranded Czechoslovak troops who had deserted the Austrian Army, U.S. troops, with a very limited mandate for engagement, joined the anti-Bolshevik Siberian expedition, even helping to run the railroad for a period of time. Fear of the Bolsheviks and their sway in chaotic China became the abiding trump card of the White Russians.[37]

Shimpei Goto was foreign minister at this time; in subsequent years he would be proud to be remembered as the "architect of the Siberian intervention." Whatever *bunso teki bubi* really meant to this "real liberal," the "civil garb" that cloaked the "military preparedness" throughout Manchuria was all but threadbare. In the prevailing disorder, Japan saw opportunity, and it compelled China to agree to the stationing of sixty thousand Japanese soldiers in the Chinese East Railway zone. By July, the Japanese General Staff of the military was urging the cabinet in Tokyo to overrun the whole of Manchuria. On August 12, 1918, the Japanese

Army conquered significant areas of Siberia and Manchuria, which they occupied for the next four years.

In view of Japan's growing imperialism and military power over the next few years, the fact that support for this proposal was tepid in large segments of Japanese public opinion, even with Japan's colonial successes, is of vital note. Where Goto stood on the issue of direct annexation is not clear. But the growing strength of the military and its support for annexation provides the backdrop for Sugihara's whole professional life in Manchuria. The skills that he acquired in navigating between pro- and anti-annexation factions in Manchuria helped him also steer between pro-German and pro-Allied factions at a later time.

In this "time of confusion," to quote the Gakuin song, in and around Harbin, it must have been quite difficult for the "pioneers of the new sunrise," the Gakuin's students, to busy themselves conjugating irregular Russian verbs. Nevertheless, Chiune's scholastic performance seems to have been more than adequate. On September 29, 1920, he was given his annual tuition scholarship, even presented with a two-hundred-yen raise. But he had little opportunity to spend his bonus in Harbin at baseball games or parties; these were not normal times.

Sugihara, the Soldier

In October 1920, Sugihara was ordered to take a leave from his second year of studies and return to Japan for military training. He left Harbin on November 15 and stopped off in Seoul on November 20, presumably to visit his parents. On December 1, he became a one-year "volunteer" soldier in the 79th unit, 9th company of the Ryuhzan Infantry, stationed not far from Seoul. As his sister, Ryuko Nakamura, tells me, Sugihara's strongest memory of almost sixteen months in military training is based on an incident quite independent of soldiering. One day in August 1921, he was taking aim on the rifle range when suddenly an officer approached him with the message that his mother had died, in Seoul. Though the organizational culture of the Japanese Army certainly supported a stiff-upper-lip response, Chiune could not hold back the tears.[38]

In September 1921, he passed the examination to be promoted to corporal; by December 1 he became a sergeant of the first reserve and his active service was completed. On March 31, 1922, he received an honorable discharge from active service but continued in his position as a reserve officer. In 1924, he passed the examination for promotion to second lieutenant of the first reserve; by 1928, he was promoted to the second reserve.[39] It is altogether likely that in the squabbles between factions and ministries that so characterized the Japanese administrative presence

in Manchuria, particularly in the 1930s, Sugihara's double commission—
military and Foreign Ministry—made his situation all the more complicated. Webs of group affiliation are not as cherished among Japanese as
loyalty to one group. On the other hand, his army affiliation and service
did make him well known in certain circles. This, as we shall see, proved
at times to be useful.

Sugihara, the Teacher and Official

Masami Tsuji, 85 years old, still spry and lucid, studied with Sugihara
during the short period when Sugihara was himself a student and before
he became a bureaucrat. We spoke one wet spring morning at his home
outside of Kumamoto, the capital city of Kyushu, Japan's southern island.
Where Tsuji came from there was a belief that young men should discover their fortune abroad, a useful message for a Japan assembling its empire. In truth, though, much of Tsuji's prosperity came from his postwar
work reviving the Nagasaki bus company, after the bomb dropped.

We sit in a Western-style living room but there are hints of its Eastern
double behind a sliding partition. Outside, I can see a lily pond and rock
garden, surrounded by a few dwarfed trees in the inner courtyard. Only a
few years younger than Sugihara, Tsuji recalls how his young teacher in
the early 1920s was already a legend. After his military training, Sugihara
returned to the Harbin Gakuin as a language instructor. For one thing,
Sugihara was absolutely fluent in Russian, a daunting accomplishment to
his students, who were struggling with the strange sounds and irregular
forms of that language. For another, Sugihara seemed to be able to dispense with that unique combination of shyness and arrogance that inhibited other young Japanese men. Sugihara was open, expansive. He traveled
in the Harbin Russian community with ease.

While he taught Russian language at the Gakuin, Sugihara seems also
to have had some involvement with the Japanese Consulate in Harbin. I
imagine these were good days for him. It was spring, and though there
were not enough people to play baseball at the consulate, he managed
to cobble together a team by inviting some employees of the South
Manchurian Railroad to play with the consulate members. He called the
team *Ryoman: Ryo* meaning consulate and *man* for the Manchurian Railway. Plus, at the tender age of twenty-two, Sugihara had already achieved
his childhood fantasy of becoming a teacher—and on a higher level than
his status-conscious father could ever have imagined.

"I first became acquainted with Sugihara in 1922," says Giichi
Shimura. "I was catcher. Sugihara played first base. He really loved baseball! That's how we met first time. We did good things together and we

did bad things together. We were buddies." Giichi Shimura has done a lot in his close to a century of living and is eager to tell about his adventures to anyone who will listen. He is particularly proud of his association with his younger and, now, more famous friend from Gakuin days. We spoke at his home in Tokyo on a pleasant early summer morning. All around the long sitting room are American flags crossed with Japanese flags, extending to the front alley way, all to make American guests feel welcome. With long white beard and robe, he sits in the lotus position on his divan, looking like a saint, but speaking like a rogue.[40]

In those years, Harbin, as Shimura tells me, was a hotbed of ethnic, religious, and political diversity. Indeed, with the consolidation of Communist rule across the Soviet Union, the Russian enclave of Harbin was becoming a Noah's ark of émigrés. Many were making clandestine preparations for returning to spark one revolution or another or were Bolshevik agents, in Harbin to keep tabs, provoke, and subvert. Some were plotting underground countermoves of their own, hoping to spread communism to the vast lands of China and throughout the Far East. And, of course, there were Russian Jews; some of them, at one time or another, may have been Mensheviks, if not Bolsheviks. But most of them simply wanted to live far away from Russian antisemitism, in its tsarist or newer forms. The battles that had been raging across the Soviet Union would soon, many feared, be enacted here in Harbin. There was plenty to keep the few Japanese spies/officials in town, even young trainees such as Shimura and Sugihara, very, very busy.

Exactly when teaching and studying at the Gakuin ended and his position as an official became full-time is not clear. We do know that the year 1924 is a fateful one for Sugihara, professionally and personally. On February 8, his attachment to the Ministry of Foreign Affairs was made official, and he became a clerk, pay scale 7th class. He was assigned to Manchuria but sent back to Tokyo, perhaps for training. It is with no small measure of pride that Goto, on February 13, 1924, writes the vice minister of foreign affairs, Tsuneo Matsudaira: "The Japanese Russian Association School at Harbin which we are running is steadily developing, thanks to the help of your ministry. We had forty-six first graduates last spring and three of them were recruited by your Ministry for Foreign Affairs as interpreters. It was a tremendous honor for us." Though Sugihara is not listed as a graduate—perhaps because the Gakuin still did not have its charter when he left—it is likely that he is among those for whom Goto sees "a tremendous honor."

This time, Tokyo was almost unrecognizable to Chiune, for an earthquake had devastated much of the city. Mayor Goto was embroiled in controversy about its reconstruction. To him, the natural catastrophe was nearly a blessing in disguise. Tokyo, he argued, could improve its infrastructure at a reduced cost. Mindful of new types of water, sanitary, and subway systems, the mark of great cities, Goto energetically promoted heavy capital investments, albeit without success.

Whether Goto had time to see some of his star students who were in from Harbin is not clear. Sugihara's baseball cohort, Shimura, did have personal contact with the elderly Goto. But he is not at all certain whether Sugihara met their school's founder. In any event, while in Tokyo, Sugihara received another appointment, which in recent years has raised some suspicion. On March 31, he became a *shosa,* a second lieutenant in the army. In this capacity he seems to have had connections with the cabinet. We can well imagine how all sorts of agencies were after a piece of Sugihara because of his superior abilities in general and his Russian language skills in particular. Rumor now has it that his career shifts point to mischief of a very suspicious sort. A recent article in the *Japan Times* presses the point that Sugihara was likely working not only for the *Gaimusho,* the Foreign Ministry, as is well known, but that he had a special connection with the *Naimusho,* the Ministry of the Interior—and some of the dreaded agencies of counterintelligence!

For the *Japan Times,* it seems, proof positive for Sugihara's untrustworthiness is the manner in which he conducted his personal life. As the *Times* (and other reports) would have it, Sugihara was, among other objectionable things, a drinker and a womanizer![41] Multiple assignments and lateral moves, in the Japanese civil service and corporate world, however justified administratively, always leave questions about personal loyalties.[42] It was hard to pin Sugihara down, harder to know which titles were fronts, and for which activities. For a man with many masters, Sugihara was increasingly acting masterless and independent-minded. He would pay for this dearly.

Another seminal event took place in 1924. Though it occurred far away from Sugihara in Tokyo, it exerted a fateful influence on his careers as a Manchurian official and as a mass rescuer years later in Kaunas. A San Francisco school board passed regulations to exclude Japanese children, an injustice that provoked heated comment back in Tokyo. The public debate in the United States not only ended up justifying discrimination but also provided a supportive environment for the most restrictive immigration policies affecting Jews and Japanese, in particular, for decades to come.

Would-be Jewish émigrés, in fact, were now forced to stay and cope with the crescendo of antisemitism in Central and Eastern Europe, since this Immigration Act put an end to America as a safe haven. Fifteen years hence, America's closed doors would make it all the more difficult for one

Japanese official to open his doors. And even though thousands of Jews received Sugihara's visas, many could not take things a step further. Without a U.S. visa, they paused a moment too long, some ending up in the ditches of the Ninth Fort and other renowned places in the geography of horror.

At the same time, some Japanese with limited opportunities in their island economy, who might have joined their families in San Francisco or the Mississippi valley, now became prime candidates for immigration to Manchuria. This provided greater resolve and reality to the "proposal madman's" plan for Japan to capture Manchuria demographically. With the doors to the United States closed, the Japanese would turn to Goto's land of the flowing Sungari. Once welcome at Portsmouth, the Japanese now felt shamefully snubbed.

To be sure, Japan's rivalry with the United States and Great Britain over trade rights and parity in naval tonnage, and, in later years, Western responses to Japan's policies in China, contributed to anti-Western sentiments within Japan. But the discriminatory sentiments expressed in these exclusionary acts fueled Japan's righteous indignation; this was a serious blot on the reputation of a country that many Japanese wanted to admire. The nation that forced Japan open, that so staunchly tried to maintain Japan's commitment to the open door policy elsewhere in the Far East, was now closing its own doors to Japanese. "Which country is more civilized?" Japanese asked. It was a question that Sugihara would grapple with, again and again.[43]

Sugihara, the Lover

Giichi Shimura blithely begins to tell: "Sugihara and his friends liked going to the 'wetties.'" My informant dangles a foot unlocked from the lotus position over the edge of the couch, as he gets more caught up in his story. Who knows his motive, whether it's self-aggrandizement, even envy and malice. I think about my responsibility to Sugihara and his reputation, my readers and the historical record, my feelings about the man and purpose in studying his life, and, ultimately, what in the world I am doing in this strange place with this strange man, listening to steamy stories on this steamy summer day! But what Shimura remembers yields rich insight into Sugihara's character.

Tokyo of the 1920s: Yoshiwara, the world-famous and much-imitated pleasure zone of the old city, full of music, dancing, food, and, of course, the famous geisha ladies.[44] The three Manchurian Musketeers are Sugihara, Shimura, and their boss, Chu'ichi Ohashi, then the Japanese consul of Harbin. Shimura tells how they first stopped at the Turkish bath. But he promptly corrects himself; the old colonial official from Manchuria, abundantly experienced in the vagaries of ethnic sensibilities, is quick to remember the diplomatic implications of what can give offense, even, as it turns out, in the name of a bathhouse. Concern for the feelings of Tokyo's Turkish legation had, at some point, led a government official to ask that the name of the baths be changed. Now, he proudly indicates, it was called "Soapland." They soak for a bit, then indulge in much liquid refreshment in the teahouse, and next move on to the geishas. As Shimura continues, I can almost smell the street's wood-and-charcoal fires, and see various "showrooms" that display women ranging from the adolescent to the matronly, dressed in red and purple, smiling at the passersby. Through their painted faces, they feign shyness, some rhythmically sucking on their long bamboo pipes.[45]

There were only about one hundred authorized houses in Yoshiwara then, far fewer than in its heyday during the seventeenth century. The trio picks a small establishment called the Tamanoi, where there are precisely three women. It is a most congenial setting for the three guests as long as they were celebrating the evening together. But insofar as the gentlemen would go off for more dyadic experiences including possibly, but not necessarily, intimate entertainment in the private rooms upstairs, some decisions about "distributive justice" had to be made. This was not a simple matter, for one of the geishas particularly caught the eye of all three.

Even now, seven decades later, Shimura vividly remembers her. "She was a very dignified lady, respectable, and quite graceful," he says. She had almost no cosmetics but was wearing a type of kimono called an "oshima" of "extraordinary beauty."[46] He pauses whimsically. "I wanted to buy her!" But for Japanese, even when involved in leisure activities, rank and status prevail. The Honorable Consul General would have the companionship of the woman who caught all of their attention.

Shimura ends up spending a restless night back at his own residence, craving the first geisha, and resolves to return to Yoshiwara the following morning. But when he reaches the Tamanoi, he discovers that Sugihara had already been there earlier that morning with the same purpose in mind! "Sugihara," his old classmate sighs painfully as if all this occurred yesterday, "Sugihara was always a step ahead." He pauses and adds, "And often he was going a step too far." But neither Sugihara nor Shimura won this round. Rank rather than determination prevailed. Consul Ohashi bought the geisha from the Tamanoi proprietors and took her back with him to Manchuria, an arrangement that was apparently not that unusual for the time.

This took place in 1924, I presume. On one of his résumés, I later read:

"December 22—Report of his marriage." Sugihara's wife, Yukiko, in her memoirs reports being born in 1913. In none of the recent scurrilous reports on Sugihara had I heard about his child bride. Quickly, I realize there must have been a *first* Mrs. Sugihara! Shimura and others corroborate: I further discover that her name was Klaudia, she was Russian, and she might even be alive today!

Klaudia: The White Russian Connection

Suddenly the kaleidoscope with which I have been viewing this story takes a turn; that's why he did it, I think. Our provincial young man from the backwaters of Japan was not so provincial. He married a Russian Jew, he ended up liking Jews, and, ergo, rescued them when he had the opportunity. A hidden Queen Esther. But could this be? Lots of influential people, married to Jews, did not end up saving or even being particularly friendly to them. I further realize that my assumption of his marriage providing the motive is even more tenuous. When Sugihara was rescuing Jews in Kaunas, he was married to Yukiko; there is no doubt about that. What happened, then, to his first marriage to this would-be Queen Esther? Obviously, it had gone bad. How can we assume that he was predisposed to do anything on behalf of Jews? But was I not overlooking an even more fundamental point? The Russian wife—how do I know that she was Jewish Russian? Perhaps she was White Russian or even Red Russian?

"Beautiful, clever, and tough," concede some of Sugihara's aged friends from the Manchurian civil service, when speaking about this wife. In their old age, they have taken on the affectations of samurai and are not enamored of memories of the younger Sugihara as a free spirit. Reluctantly, they fill in details with airs of disapproval unmitigated by the passing of time. Last they knew, she was living in Australia. Through various friends and relatives with some Down Under connection, I sent out the word that I was desperately in search of the erstwhile wife of the great Sugihara. I mobilized everyone I could, from a well-placed Washington friend with Australian roots to my dear aunt who knows lots of Hadassah members in Australia's largest cities. For some time, the results, I had to acknowledge, were disappointing. Then one day, staring at the fragments of names I had gathered, I realized that a few r's and l's could be exchanged with some benefit. I forwarded the new information to my contacts.

Aunt Helen's team triumphed. Late one night I received an excited call from one of her Australian volunteers. In examining old telephone books in the Sydney Public Library, "Apollonov," one of the names I had for Klaudia, appears. I quickly place a call to Michael Apollonov, who turns out to be Klaudia's grandnephew. Yes, he says, she is alive but frail at ninety-three and in an old age home. It is October and I am less than inclined to make long trips. Winter vacation is two months away, reduced rates on flights booked in advance—it seems best to postpone. A week later, another late night call from Sydney about Klaudia's failing health reminds me that, for ninety-three-year-old interviewees, one does not wait for frequent-flyer bonuses.

Within thirty-six hours I am walking down the corridor of the St. Sergius Home for the Aged, in Cabramatta, a Sydney suburb. The nurses receive me with an iciness bordering on hostility. I cannot figure out why. The walls are lined with pictures of the last tsar and his family; the pastoral scenes are straight out of Pushkin. Russian Orthodox crosses hang everywhere. Since the days of Gorbachev, this enclave of White Russian culture begins to feel somewhat futuristic rather than hopelessly archaic. I have a different set of associations with White Russian culture from stories that my great-grandmother told me a long time ago. The air is close, thick with ersatz sanitary odors. What a place to pursue Sugihara! I try to control my primordial fears.

I introduce myself to the head nurse and even present a business card with academic credentials. No one here has heard of Chiune Sugihara. Suspiciousness is not diluted (nor does anyone seem to be impressed) by the fact that I have traveled ten thousand miles to visit one of their feeble patients. Still, I am grudgingly led to Klaudia Semionovna Apollonova Sugihara Dorf. She sits in a chair, but one can tell she is now less used to being perpendicular to the horizontal. I have no difficulty identifying her with the beautiful woman in the photographs on the wall, dressed in kimonos and gay 1920s fashions, with gloves and parasol, then as now, deceptively frail.

No need for any introduction, it turns out, nor any attempts on my part to make her remember her "late first husband," as she calls him. She gets right down to work. "There were two dogs on the second-floor balcony, such beautiful little pups," she says, in the passionate accented English so typical of Russian émigrés. "One of them fell down. Sergei Pavelovich went up to the dog and tried to help him. He wrapped the injured dog in his coat jacket and quickly took him to the doctor. Sergei was always kind, always wanted to help somebody. He was kind to people and also to animals. He was friends with everyone."

The nurses stand nearby in the hallway to overhear our conversation. Other than a few distant family members who visit her with decreasing frequency, no one has paid much attention to this patient of two decades. Why is this Klaudia Semionovna enjoying celebrity status, they wonder? The uncollected lunch tray with slightly nibbled boiled chicken and kasha wobbles on the night table. "How many years I was married to him I do not remember," says Klaudia. Her eyes never leave mine. They met in Harbin some time in the early 1920s, I find out. Her parents came from the nobility, and had an estate in central Russia. Chiune was attached to her family. "He was sorry for people who lived in poverty," says Klaudia. "He was sorry for people who were something before and then had nothing."

I ask how they met. Klaudia, the older daughter raised with anticipation of a pampered life, now had to resort to waitressing to support her family. One day a handsome young Japanese official came into her café and sat alone in the corner. "Why are you sitting alone?" she asked. Neither remained that way for long. "Why did he prefer a Russian woman to Japanese women?" I ask. She reads my thoughts. "He loves Russian people, he understands them." Her shift into the present tense is jarring. Suddenly, he is present to me as well, in a way that he had never been before. By standing with him in the streets of Harbin coddling an injured dog or surveying the flood-damaged homes of Chinese coolies, I can better stand with him in the streets of Kovno looking at the "people who were something before and then had nothing." I feel the past rise up to touch me.

The nurses listening in from the other side of the door are stirring. Every few moments, it seems, someone enters with one pretext or another. A vacuum knocks about noisily. "What did he call you?" I ask Klaudia as she lifts a cup of tea to her lips with a hand that is amazingly steady. "Yukiko," she answers. "Isn't that a beautiful name?" I nod. "And what did you call him?" I ask. "Sergei, Sergei Pavelovich. I was very young, sixteen. He brought me candies. He was not selfish. He so much loved to dance. He would take me dancing at the Fantasia. I saw his kindness to people and animals. I was young and not very experienced. So I took him to my place and I loved him."

Suddenly the door bursts open. The buxom head nurse runs in, wildly gesticulating, flailing her clipboard. "Pogrom," I think. "Mrs. Dorf!" she screams without the slightest bit of modulation in her voice. "Mrs. Dorf!" Now she sounds like a schoolmarm about to give one of her charges a scolding. "Do you really want this man to ask you these questions?" Klaudia looks at me. Then she looks at the nurse. I realize that I must carefully prepare my response. The moments pass. She looks at me again and then she looks at the nurse. I am buying precious time in preparing my defense against elderly abuse. Suddenly Klaudia's leathery cheeks begin to stretch into a smile. Now she is looking at neither and both of us at the same time. "Yes, I want this man to ask me these questions," she says. "I want to remember my late first husband."

The senior nurse now walks backward in retreat, grabbing the luncheon tray as if this were the only reason for her entry to begin with. Other than a few more incidents with the vacuum cleaner, I am left in quiet with Klaudia. "Why Sergei Pavelovich?" I continue, my pulse returning to normal. "This was the name that was given to him by the old priest. Sergei was close to Sugihara and the priest's name was Pavel, so Chiune made him like his father." Yet another father figure, I wonder? Klaudia goes on: "The old priest gave us his blessings. I didn't want him to change his religion, I didn't press. But he became Russian Orthodox."

The young Japanese official, who was raised in an environment in which religion was but one more set of loyalties to the state and who was himself not particularly prone to theological musings, actually had himself baptized. And for love, it seems. Or maybe it was the music, the incense, the candles, even the teachings that carried sensual appeal to this warmhearted Japanese man. Whatever the case, the Emperor's civil servant was now vowing loyalty to the saints of Smolensk.

Decades later, as I glean from many interviews, Sugihara's samurai friends find this behavior strange. They remember the White Russian women of Harbin with fondness, but also apprehension. Those women played piano, they were educated, they were assertive, and, with a blush and distant look, Sugihara's buddies will admit, those women were sexually demanding. Shimura and others recall that for many of the students, it was "a common custom to have relationships with the ladies." What more convenient way was there for an ambitious young Japanese official to improve his Russian than to have a "native speaker" mistress? But to marry one, to take on her religion? This was unseemly.

But in taking on a new wife, a different religion, and a fresh name, our twenty-four-year-old Sugihara may have found what he craved: a new family structure, complete with a replacement father. In traditional Japanese culture, a wife joins her husband's family, but Chiune/Sergei was throwing in with Klaudia/Yukiko's. Indeed, the Apollonov family, as Klaudia tells me, moved into the Harbin Japanese consulate with Chiune or, more likely, into the consular compound, which included lodging for the staff. It was not unusual for Japanese officials in Harbin to cultivate relations with the White Russians. They shared the same concern for the spread of communism, after all, particularly in regions of the Far East, like China, where Japan had its own imperial ambitions. Perhaps the Emperor's loyalists especially identified with the tsar's loyalists. Yet to bring into the consulate not only a White Russian wife but her family as well? This may have been a good example of Sugihara's taking things "a step too far," as his friend Shimura so aptly noted.

Klaudia also explains that her father, during his difficult period of adjusting to exile, became a "policeman," likely a guard on the Russian-controlled Chinese East Railway. "Sergei Pavelovich went as a friend of my father to the railroad to see where he worked," she says. "He went to see him, probably to help him. He showed kindness not only to the government but to ordinary people. He was very good to my father and invited him to come to our house. My father came, my girlfriend who came from my town and was working for the government—she came too. He loved Russian people because he loved me and I am Russian."[47]

Sugihara helped his father-in-law—and also may have been given help in return. Semion Apollonov was nicely useful in terms of the information he could provide. During the Russian civil war, he and his sons had fought with Ataman Semyonov, the viciously antisemitic leader, who in the years following the revolution was supported by different combinations of foreigners, including the Americans, who wanted to somehow get a foothold in the country. Legend has it that Semyonov returned to Manchuria from the Siberian Intervention via railroad cars full of booty, while leaving behind secretly buried barrels of gold.

His most serious and sustained patrons were the Japanese, who saw in him a puppet leader of the "liberated Russia." Semion Apollonov had achieved the rank of colonel in Semyonov's forces and, according to a family tradition, worked for the rogue White Russian leader in Darien after the civil war. Sugihara was active in the Manchurian White Russian community, recruiting spies who would return then to the Soviet Union or who would be held in reserve for that time when Russia would be "liberated" by Semyonov's forces.[48]

Sugihara's contacts within the White Russian émigré community could have proved quite fruitful. For a Japanese intelligence officer, it would be smart to buy an occasional drink for one of those Russians who held insider information on activities up and down 950 miles of the CER's line, not to mention the thousands more miles of Russian concession surrounding the tracks. But Sugihara's installing of the Apollonovs in the middle of the Japanese compound raised some questions about who was spying on whom. Shimura, who spoke with consistent kindness about his former friend, conceded, "I often wondered about this." Others are far more blunt in questioning his loyalty.

As our talk proceeds, I ask Klaudia if her husband had any Jewish friends. She registers no special awareness. I mention specifically a Yako, seemingly a Jew whom other friends from the Harbin period seem to remember. "He was very kind to people, animals, Jews and not Jews. He was very kind to people," she says. "Whoever came was his friend. He knew Russian so well. He was well educated. He had gone to Moscow University before I met him. He was friends with everyone." I am not sure what to make of this. Neither his Japanese family, friends and former colleagues nor the Japanese Foreign Ministry personnel records report this early visit to Moscow. But it makes sense; his Moscow stint may account for his excellent Russian and might be the source of some Russian contacts as well.

Another story that Klaudia repeated several times throughout our meetings was meant to illustrate Sergei Pavelovich's kindness to people and love for Russians, yes, but it also hinted at the dynamics in their marriage. Clearly, she had much control. The story concerns the arrangements she made to take care of Sergei during her summer vacations to Japan. Klaudia would go off to Kamamura, then a resort, now a bedroom community, on Tokyo Bay, hiring a Russian woman for sexual liaisons with her husband in her absence. Upon returning to Harbin, the chauffeur would drive her to the woman's house, where Klaudia would offer a ten-dollar bill for her services. But money was not the issue, it seems. The woman, as Klaudia tells it, was so disappointed that Klaudia was now back and her visits from Sergei would end that she pouted with envy and would hardly look at Klaudia.

Sitting with this impressive woman, I have one more question to pose, however gingerly. I am emboldened by the fact that on this second and likely last meeting with her, other than recurrent vacuum cleaner sounds coming from the tiled halls, the nurses have left me alone. Klaudia is repeating herself and seems somewhat confused. The letters from Sugihara that her relatives assured me she had, she claims not to possess. But she assures me that they loved each other to the very end (Sugihara died in 1986) and indicates that there had been intermittent communication between them, however indirectly. "He thanked me for my love for him, always long loving letters." She still possessed the box in which Sergei had sent her his last gift: a kimono. I look at the postmark. It is 1981.

Sugihara's résumé for January 20, 1936, states, "Report on divorce." More officiously, it adds, "December 30, 1935, divorced by mutual consultation." His friends rival each other in the insistency of their claims that Chiune dumped Klaudia. "He loved her," Shimura states unequivocally. "But he also wanted to be consul. I warned him that if he really wanted to get the promotion he should not have such good relations with Russian people." By the end of 1935, the White Russians in Harbin had outlived their utility to the Japanese; it was clear they would never regain power in the USSR. Could it be that Sergei Pavelovich, "kind to people and animals," succumbed to the spirit of the times and divorced Klaudia, who had become by then a liability? Klaudia is dozing. It would soon be time for me to head back to the airport. Would I now have to come to terms with a singular fact? Did Sugihara divorce the woman that he loved for no better reason than to advance his career?

"Mrs. Dorf," I blurt out. There is alarm and pleading in my voice. "Could you please tell me . . . Do you remember why Mr. Sugihara divorced you?" She opens her eyes and straightens herself in the armchair. "Sergei Pavelovich . . ." She speaks with firmness. "Sergei Pavelovich did not divorce me. I divorced Sergei Pavelovich." She says it as if there would be little to add to set the record straight. I feel sheepish. I had not even considered such a possibility. "I was a cold woman but somehow men loved me," she says. "He thought that I couldn't have children. But I went to the doctor to have an abortion. He never knew. I never told him. He was very sad. He wanted a child. I had more than one abortion. The doctor was my friend and told him nothing. I was just selfish. He was never cruel. Sergei Pavelovich was never cruel. He said, 'I understand. I know you want your own countryman.' He thought I had a lover but said that he was not angry. I didn't want children. I regret it. I told him to marry someone and have children because I didn't want children and he wanted children."

Klaudia knew more than she wished about bearing and raising children. During those chaotic days that the Apollonov family was fleeing from the Bolsheviks, they spent long nights on freight trains and in sheds with other refugee families. The adolescent Klaudia had too many opportunities to see the effects of child labor, and to see its sometimes fatal results. Her own carefree years were cut short by the responsibilities that she had to assume in raising her extant younger brothers and sister, in lieu of her mother; the Bolshevik ouster of her family was a trauma that rendered Mrs. Apollonov unable to cope. "It was my regret," Klaudia repeats now, in a trembling voice. "I didn't want to have babies."

It is time to take my leave. I ask her once again about letters from Sergei Pavelovich. She does not have any. But she reaches up to the wall behind her and pulls down the photographs that I had been staring at all through our meetings. "Please, take," she says, giving me also a frayed envelope of photographs that her "late first husband" had sent her over the years. In the taxi, I glance at Klaudia in kimono, Klaudia in gay 1920s garb, and photographs of Sugihara in the 1970s standing outside the Kremlin. Shattered loves, shattered worlds.

Hardly had I recovered from chronic jet lag when I received a message from her family: Klaudia died soon after my visit. The nurses spoke of her last days, in which she appeared to be happier than they had ever seen her. The head nurse who had given me such a hard time now spoke of the extraordinary calmness with which she died and the "beatitude" on her face as she lay in her casket. A few old friends paid their last respects, remembering her as the pious widow of a Jewish doctor; no one knew her as the passionate wife of "Sergei Pavelovich" Sugihara. "Yes," I could hear

Klaudia saying in that firm, accented voice of hers. "I want to remember my late first husband."

Later I would be able fill in some details about the life Sergei and Klaudia led together. My primary source was Sugihara's sister, Ryuko Nakamura, who was orphaned at four in Seoul and died in late 1995. She had run a karaoke club in Gifu City for many years. Ryuko and Klaudia had been close. "In better days, they drove in an elegant carriage," she said of the Apollonov family. When the Bolsheviks came to their town in central Russia, Klaudia's oldest brother was arrested. Klaudia used her female charms to convince his jail keepers to release him. But some time later, a less friendly bunch of revolutionaries stabbed this same brother to death in front of his mother's eyes. She never recovered from the shock. The family fled, wandering pennilessly, arriving in Harbin just after the revolution.

The Sugihara/Apollonov residence seemed to be a favorite gathering spot. Ryuko spent the early 1930s with her brother and his Russian family in Harbin. "There were two drawing rooms and an additional parlor just for women," Ryuko marveled to me. "Even the cold storage was two times the size of an eight tatami-mat room." As I found in my travels, these were impressive dimensions, even to contemporary urban Japanese. Ryuko described the grand parties thrown at her brother's wildly spacious Harbin quarters. "Chiune would connect the two rooms with ten mahjongg tables. Fifty or sixty military personnel, including the special mission commander and intelligence officers," she proudly recalls, would come to these soirees, hosted by the young Japanese official and his beautiful White Russian wife.

Ryuko emphasizes that Chiune always provided well for Klaudia and her family, even after their marriage ended. After the divorce, he bought her a house in which to live, another property to rent out for income, and even a cabin near the Sungari River to spend the short Harbin summers. He paid all school expenses for the three youngest Apollonov children and found jobs for the others. Klaudia soon married a Mr. Dorf, according to some reports a Jew. They spent the war years in Shanghai and then emigrated to Australia. The Apollonov siblings scattered, some even returning to the Soviet Union.

At this juncture, we seem to be more privy to Sergei Pavelovich, the lover, then Chiune Sugihara, the colonial official. But what was he doing when he was not giving grand parties, or helping the Apollonovs, or being kind to "people, animals, Jews and not Jews?" Whatever suspicion his marital ties from 1924–35 had aroused, his career was not exactly frozen. He advanced steadily in rank and in salary, and received some recognition for his good work. His résumé notes: "June 30, 1927—Pay scale became

6th class. June 30, 1927—Pay scale became 5th class. November 16, 1928—Rewarded Memorial Award by the Award Bureau." Of course, it is possible that his advance would have gone higher and faster without Klaudia. But the fact that he was not a graduate of Tokyo University seems to have been the deciding factor. It pretty much relegated him to secondary positions within the two-tier civil service, notwithstanding his ability and his achievements.

Sugihara, the Writer

Though Sugihara responded personally and vigorously to crises rather than doing what bureaucrats do—observing from a distance and scribbling a report—he was not above using the written word to further his government's aims. During the Klaudia years, *General Survey of the National Economy of the Soviet Union* was published by the Europe and America Bureau of the Japanese Foreign Ministry. The text opens with a dedication from the publisher: "We recognize that this book owes much to the compilation by Secretary Sugihara, consulate of Harbin, in service on December, 1926."

This bulky *General Survey,* in all of its 608 pages, provides not even an opaque window into Sugihara's soul. As controversial as any writing on the Soviet Union had to be at that time, it rarely moves beyond the descriptive, and avoids the overtly political. There is no rousing endorsement of capitalism and counterrevolution, but no backing of the Soviet's various economic policies and plans either. One colorful phrase does show Sugihara's hand, though. He disparages the efficacy of building Soviet industry while restoring agriculture, if these efforts are not also linked to the growth of markets. The tactic makes as much sense, he says, as "climbing a tree to go fishing."

Sugihara's tome must be compared with two larger series—a six-volume Research Series on Workers' and Peasants' Russia and an eight-volume Series on the Russian Economy—that were published by the South Manchurian Railway research institute in Harbin, shortly before Sugihara finished his own book. This institute had assembled a great deal of material on the Soviet Union. Its researchers through the twenties (and even to a surprising degree in the thirties) seemed to be able to state their positions without kowtowing to any ideological line.[49] Much like medieval monasteries, these institutes appeared to be the safest place for unconventional thinkers, in the best tradition of their "great liberal" founder, Shimpei Goto.

But the atmosphere at the Foreign Ministry, where Sugihara was posted at this time, was quite different from the SMR institutes. It's hard to know how much this fact accounted for the bland neutrality of Sugihara's *Survey*. Self-censorship might explain his reticence; he was probably mindful of what his bosses really wanted to hear about the Soviet Union. Whatever the reasons for this arid treatment, it would appear to indicate Sugihara's success as a diplomat. He kept his poker face.

What sort of work was Sugihara performing, apart from his book? "Information," says Giichi Shimura, cryptically. "Sugihara and I did a lot of bad things together." When pressed he concedes, "preventing rebellion." Against whom? For what? He is playfully silent, protective of his secrets of seventy years ago. What we cannot learn about Sugihara's professional life in his Harbin period from coaxing Shimura for his reminiscences, we might interpolate from Goto's proposals. In 1925 in Tokyo, the retiring Mayor Goto would attempt one last round of negotiations with the Soviets on behalf of his beloved project, first outlined shortly after the Russo-Japanese War: to solve Japan's security and overpopulation problems by colonizing Manchuria and Siberia with Japanese residents.

> If within ten years, by managing the present railroad we are able to induce 500,000 Japanese to emigrate to Manchuria, we will not have to commence hostilities recklessly despite Russian strength. Control over the tempo toward war or peace will fall firmly in our hands. Even if Russia were to defeat us in battle, we would still not lose the foundation to recover our successes.[50]

In southern and northern Manchuria and Siberia, through the twenties, there were large areas in which China and the Soviet Union crossed conflicting claims of sovereignty and varying degrees of control; Sugihara and Shimura, among Goto's many disciples, were strengthening Japanese outposts, to be followed perhaps by outright annexation. Shimura tells of the intrigues instigated by nations many miles away, the violence of local warlords asserting control, and the venomous ethnic battles that these Japanese colonies confronted: In Nikolaevsk, Russia, near Vladivostok, some time before Shimura and Sugihara were posted there, the new Soviet forces had tried to assert their sovereignty; they massacred seven hundred Japanese diplomats and residents. Nikolaevsk became the Japanese Alamo. From now on, levels of mistrust scaled dizzily upward; it would be the job of men like Sugihara and Shimura to work within this context.

Even such dangerous volatility would not deter the determined Goto. But the arrival of Soviet Foreign Minister Adolf Ioffe for negotiations precipitated riots in the streets of Tokyo and assassination threats. Goto had his own misgivings in regard to the commissar, claiming that "his Jewish character was bad." Stalin seems to have agreed. Just as Goto was reciprocating the visit to Moscow to continue negotiations, Stalin purged his Jewish foreign minister, Ioffe, along with his Jewish arch rival, Trotsky. At this point, even Goto had to recognize that little could be accomplished with the Soviets through negotiations and settlements. Goto disappointedly returned to Tokyo. In the last years before his death in 1929, Goto gave up on his Manchurian dream and poured his efforts into another vintage colonial institution: the founding of the Japanese Boy Scouts!

Neither the Master Goto nor the disciple Sugihara found it easy to be a Japanese Russophile in these turbulent years. Still, Chiune's talents did not go unnoticed among his colleagues—as an official, as a spy, and, yes, even as a lover. Sergei Pavelovich Sugihara may have been both doing good work and getting into a lot of trouble because of his ease with Russians and his good contacts in the Soviet Union. What deterred his professional advancement—his personality, his marriage, his movement in and out of agencies—might have been precisely what enabled him to accomplish extraordinary feats at a later time. The colonial official Sugihara may not have been on the roster of elite universities. But the jovial Sugihara, with his dashing Russian wife, was certainly in the memory of quite a few army officers and government officials; human connections can matter more than official ones.

Perhaps we can try to fill in the gaps of broken and lost memories. It is winter 1940, perhaps, on an unspeakably cold, star-filled night. A Japanese official stands at a remote border crossing in Siberia. To take his mind off the cold, he thinks back on his youthful days at the Harbin Gakuin. He stamps his feet, wraps his scarf tighter, and sings songs to pass the time.

Lead us, "Aurora"
Sun is rising soon.
You are showing the right way
For Peoples of the East! . . .
The source of life moves East

A train arrives, steam billowing whitely against the black sky. A motley bunch of Jewish refugees tumble onto the platform, a sweep of trampled dignity, frayed elegance, frightened faces. They present scraps of paper of dubious validity but bearing a signature "Vice Consul Sugihara." Sugihara! So this is what he does now! What fine parties he and his Russian wife gave back in Harbin, full of food and drink and light and warmth. The official is transported for a moment, remembering. What seemed so far away now blossoms in his mind, all the more vivid against the tense bleakness of Siberia.

Nevertheless, the official tells himself, he must go by the book. A transit visa is a transit visa. Are these documents really valid? Look at these people! Could Sugihara really have issued transit visas to people who do not appear to have any means and anywhere to which to transit? Doesn't this contradict the orders coming down from superiors in Tokyo?

In a few moments, there will be pleading men and women, crying children, piles of luggage to move, forms to fill out in triplicate, accommodations to be made, perhaps for several days as they wait for the next train in the opposite direction to take them back to Europe and oblivion. The official is wrenched from his happy reminiscences, torn by turmoil and conflict; he yawns from anticipated exhaustion as he trembles for an endless moment in the cold. But then, at the sight of Sugihara's signature, his spirits again soar. "I will stand up for justice," he thinks, the lyrics rising up.

Sugihara is not a fool. Sugihara is not a villain. Surely he knows what he is doing in issuing these visas. In honor of those fine days, the official decides. He waves the travelers through, as that old school tune keeps playing in his head. "The source of life moves East," he sings softly. For these Jews, the words are truer than he knows.

Chapter 3

The Honorable Chiune Sugihara

*The "Gorgeous Life" and the Making of the
Diplomat/Spy, 1931–39*

When he arrived in Kaunas in September 1939, Sugihara discovered chaos and fear, but he'd been in many such situations before. Eight years ago, he'd found himself caught in the crossfire between rival masters, as an officer in the Imperial Japanese Army and as a Manchukuo official, during the Manchurian Incident and with the establishment of the Manchukuo state in which his career bloomed. This dual position demanded great navigational skills; Sugihara had to be diplomat, spy, and bureaucrat, each demanding he do certain "bad things." It was a precarious existence.

Let's go back to Harbin, then, the scene of Sugihara's first and deepest lessons. It is mid-September 1931, and Uchastkovaya Street is solidly lined with sandbags. The Japanese barbers had been particularly gregarious with their clients lately, teasing out bits of information here and there. One of the more colorful and better known of these Japanese barbers is Konstantin Ivanovich Nakamura, who, like Sergei Pavelovich Sugihara, has mastered the Russian language and, for that matter, the Russian ethos.

Like Sugihara, Nakamura also had a Russian wife and converted to Russian Orthodoxy. But unlike Sugihara, by then a well-established diplomat and Russia hand in the Japanese consulate, no one seemed to know exactly who this Nakamura was. In addition to his haircutting establishment, he held a varied reputation as a drug pusher, child molester, and pimp specializing in prepubescent prostitutes. But his success at living above the law with impunity, joined to the unwillingness of Japanese representatives in Manchuria to enforce any charges brought against him by Chinese officials, signaled that he had some special connections.

On September 19, those connections became patently clear. Rumors were circulating about an incident—a train blown up, Chinese soldiers apprehended—that occurred the day before in Mukden, 350 miles to the southwest of Harbin. Nakamura immediately convened a group of White Russians, whom he had cultivated for many years. As they gathered at his barber shop, he distributed revolvers, rifles, and hand grenades and instructed them to protect Japanese and White Russian property. The Chinese could be on their way, but worse, the Soviets were close on their heels.

He said that the Kwantung Army, the army based in Japan's "leased"-in-Portsmouth colony of Kwantung, in South Manchuria, would now have to "free the people of Manchuria from the Communistic Chinese Army" and help "patriotic" Russians like themselves "liberate" their motherland from the Soviets. Cheers rose up all around.

The barber soon identified himself as the "secretary-interpreter" of the *Kempei,* the Japanese intelligence agency nominally responsible for investigating and suppressing military and civilian dissidence. Its reputation for the efficient dispatch of "special offenders" was exceeded only by its successes in the profiteering of its own staff—bribes, extortion, even drugs—justified, of course, in the name of Japan's "past sacrifices" for Manchuria. The other major intelligence arm, spying mostly on the Soviet Union, was called the *Tokomukikan.* Colonel Kenji Dohihara, known as "Lawrence of Manchuria" for his wild schemes, represented that agency.[1] Though his precise relationships are not known, Sugihara moved in these circles.[2]

The Mukden railroad bombing was blamed on the Chinese, though it was actually the handiwork of Japanese intelligence. Those officials, with dramatic flair, left Chinese corpses, dressed in military uniforms, near the damaged tracks, aligned carefully in the mud facing in the direction of a close-by Chinese military camp. This arrangement made it seem as if the now-corpses were the perpetrators; one only had to note the "evidence" of their own bloody footprints.

Japanese technicians planted the blast with such skill that the damaged rails would not impede the next express train carrying Japanese shipments. What was equally well planned was the massive Japanese military response to this "Chinese" provocation. Japanese soldiers would no longer have to pose as "railway guards," as dictated by the compromise made between the haggling Japanese and Russians at Portsmouth in the summer of 1905. Now they could be real soldiers. Undercover agents such as Nakamura, living, as did Sugihara, in Russian-controlled Harbin, could now "come in from the cold."

The Manchurian Incident of September 1931 was by no means unique in its violence. It was preceded and followed by actual and attempted assassinations of Japanese ministers, storming of the Imperial Diet, and other conspiracies done for the sake of, if not in the name of, the Emperor. The perpetrators were most often young military officers, acting at times with the tacit approval of their superiors. Funding often came from large Japanese corporations, or from the highly ultranationalist clubs stocked with representatives from the military. Between 1927 and 1937, 634 right-wing clubs were established with 122,000 members.[3] Throughout the government and even in the military itself, there was awareness of the dangers of the military making, not merely executing, policy. But little was done to punish this "rule from below."[4]

Where was Sugihara when all this was happening? His two résumés and other reports indicate that he was very much present.[5] On March 1, 1934, he is honored for "contributions to the foundations of the country," presumably the Japanese puppet state of Manchukuo. Fewer than two months later, on April 29, he is given an award for "contributions during the incident, 1931–1934." His prize includes 150 yen. Sugihara was "involved" in still another way. The Manchurian Incident was nurtured by the pan-Asianism, "scientific colonialism," and *"bunso teki bubi"* of his mentor, Shimpei Goto. As that notion of "civil garb" was becoming all but unraveled, Sugihara could now observe how the cumulative effect of years of Japanese "military preparedness" was beginning to burst at the seam.

Yet it is no simple matter to intuit what his reaction to these events might have been. A man like Sugihara may have endured relations with the typical Japanese "militarists" and their allies in the Foreign Ministry that were often, even at best, strained. The frequency with which he changes jobs is some evidence for this. Nevertheless, liberalism and reformism among many Japanese were not wholly dissociated from support for Japanese imperialism.[6]

Wherever Sugihara was on the pivotal night of September 18, he seems to have been back in Harbin during the following months. The Kwantung Army was in no rush; annexing Chinese territory was not considered a problem. Already, it seemed to be falling easily. But the territory that the Soviet Union claimed as a corridor to the Chinese East Railway, the railroad line shared with the Chinese, with rights ratified in the Portsmouth Treaty—that was another story. Harbin, the stronghold of Soviet interests in Manchuria, became a test case for the Soviet stake in Manchuria. Harbin's prominent Japanese Russia hand, Sugihara, must have been busy in those days.

Even as audacious a military commander as Colonel Dohihara spent a lot of yen hiring agents provocateurs, plus fomenting imaginative and dramatic incidents within Harbin to keep the Soviets guessing. Japanese soldiers at stations along the CER jostled and provoked Soviet railroad officials by demanding transportation to Harbin to assist their endangered countrymen. Telegrams flew back and forth from Moscow seeking to interpret the finer points of the Portsmouth Treaty.[7] Japanese expansion was presented as Japanese self-defense, as Dohihara's soldiers would launch an occasional mortar shell into the center of Harbin. And his colleagues elsewhere, as far away as Shanghai, planned a few imaginative incidents in their own military theaters of operation to deflect world attention away from Harbin.[8]

Within Harbin, the sizable White Russian population lived with a heightened level of anxiety. Might Stalin "come to the rescue" and take over their slipping haven? The Chinese did little to disabuse them of such fears, while the Japanese commissioned assaults upon them to force these White Russians to welcome entering Japanese troops.[9] They did welcome them, with fairly open arms. At first, the Japanese were far preferable to the hated Soviets. They seemed the least onerous of rulers, though Harbin's Jews flourished more under the old cross-alignment of forces, with no strong identification with the Chinese, Japanese, White Russians, or Soviets. But as their security and influence in Harbin's economy was challenged by the influx of Japanese, many Jews began to pack their bags for seemingly calmer places in China.

Evsey Domar, the future MIT economics professor, had seen upheaval before, in Poland. Still, those days in the fall and winter of 1931–32 left an impression on him. He remembers how the Japanese became ever more brazen behind their sandbags, and being surprised by this transformation. He was long led to believe—even by his beloved teacher, Professor Gogvaze, moonlighting at Sugihara's old school—that the Japanese were paragons of decorum. Years later, Domar registers as much surprise as indignation at how the Japanese, expanding their territory and hardening their rule, as he says, began "acting badly."[10]

Ryuko Nakamura, Sugihara's sister, remembers the night of February 5, 1932, when "Lawrence of Manchuria" finally did conquer Harbin. As the gunfire became louder and less distant, Chiune got ready to leave for the Japanese consular offices. Klaudia, her mother, and two younger brothers were anxiously watching developments from the living room. This Japanese diplomatic compound might have become a tempting target for Chinese soldiers and militia about to abandon the city. Chiune, Ryuko says, warned them, "It is dangerous. Do not stick your heads out of the window," but Ryuko was overwhelmed by curiosity. The servant said to her, "Young lady, if you want to see what is going on outside, I will take you upstairs." Ignoring her brother's admonition, Ryuko "stood at the window for a long time watching the gunfire flashing like fireworks."[11]

But exploding projectiles and shattering glass, as Chiune warned Ryuko, were not the greatest dangers on his mind. The imminent entry of Japan's military into Harbin was precisely the kind of event that could get out of hand. The "Manchurian crisis" was, in fact, a double crisis; it was as much the expression of the Japanese domestic crisis—a breakdown in authority—as it was a crisis in the international order. And Sugihara stood at the juncture of the two.

Chiune ran through a night streaked with the comets of exploding artillery shells. He sped around courtyards and ducked into doorways as he made his way from his home to the administrative building of the Japanese Consulate. Under different circumstances, he might have brought a bottle of the strongest vodka, perhaps some home-brewed Russian beer from the "eight tatami"–sized cold storage beneath the apartment where he lived with Klaudia and family, and food from a White Russian or Jewish shop on Kitayskaya Street, to share at the meeting in the consulate that evening. Military and intelligence personnel in the Kwantung command would be there, many of them colleagues and former schoolmates.

They viewed Tokyo's hesitation over massive incursion and annexation as still more evidence of the moral decay into which all Japan, but particularly its leaders, were now slipping. Opposition to their efforts to expand Japanese control over Manchuria could be nothing more than further evidence that their beloved country was being taken over by the hated Communists. Soon Stalin, not the Emperor, would be in control; class struggle would replace *kokutai,* their cherished belief that the Japanese people made up one large family headed by the Emperor.[12] If for no other reason, they had to move now, forcefully, against the Communist infiltrators. Amileto Vespa, an Italian spy, reports the soliloquy of his Japanese "handler": "We must show no mercy, no weakness. We must work on the principle that it is better to punish 1000 innocent than to allow one single propagandist to remain at large."[13]

The young Kwantung officers experienced still another threat to their vision of the New Order and the future of Manchuria: America and other Western countries. If Sugihara's jingoistic colleagues felt fear and disrespect for the Soviets, they felt actual hatred for Westerners who appeared to disrespect them. Undoubtedly, America would interfere with such a noble effort to "civilize" Manchuria. The Americans, English, French, and other Europeans could not allow the Yellow Peril to thrive, but American threats of economic sanctions against Japan were mere talk, the Kwantung partisans believed. They reassured each other that, militarily, America was in no position to impose its threatened blockade. Here is how one such officer put it:

> They believe that their countries have special rights in the Far East. Every time that Japan tries to move a step they try to find some foolish reason for interfering. We Japanese do not recognize such rights. America has its Monroe Doctrine; we, too, have ours. The whole orient is our sphere of influence and must fall under our control. Korea, Manchuria, Mongolia and, before long, China and Siberia as far as Irkutsk will all form one single Empire, the Empire of Japan, governed by our great Emperor; the only Emperor who can truly be called heavenly, since he is a descendant of the Sun Goddess and all the Japanese are sons of Gods.[14]

These young officers would not accept the possibility that Headquarters had a different but, nevertheless, legitimate estimate of the international situation, or that field operators might raise questions of tactics even though, ultimately, it was their duty to accept orders.[15] Sugihara knew how some of his friends described what was wrong in Tokyo, how they would voice the purity of their motives, and evoke the beauty of their vision for the future of Manchuria. "Let the world not be deceived by our internal strife, our political assassinations, our economic problems," as one of his colleagues might have allayed his fears on that evening. "These things are not signs of corruption; on the contrary, these are signs of patriotism."[16]

In spite of their fevered idealism, however, these Kwantung officers were not yet ready to commit *seppuku* (suicide). They would risk their lives, maybe, but not ritually sacrifice them. The officers could certainly take the heat for occasional clashes with poorly organized Chinese troops and the suspicion that their deeper penetration into Manchuria was arousing at the League of Nations in Geneva and major capitals. But a full-fledged confrontation with the Soviets, with tepid backing from Tokyo, might be the end of a few military careers. They could proceed, under the rubric of a divided homeland, only so far.

The Russia hand arrived at the consulate meeting on that critical evening rather empty-handed. For years Sugihara had been monitoring the goings-on in the Soviet Union. By now, he usually could anticipate what Russians were thinking and respond in kind with near overwhelming self-confidence. It appeared to be instinctual, but now he was forced to move beyond instinct. In the past months, in particular, he had been brutally busy trying to make sense of the posturing of Soviet government officials on the "Manchurian crisis." His fieldwork entailed spying on the spies, as it were. There were drinking buddies among the White Russians who had spy networks reaching deep into Siberia on the one side, through Outer Mongolia to the Trans-Baikal on the other.

Sugihara also had close ties with the Soviet Russian residents back in Harbin. The night he ducked mortar shells to enter the Japanese Consulate for his planning session with the Japanese military and Foreign Ministry officials was his last opportunity to assess the full array of Soviet intentions. Surely his colleagues ultimately would turn to him: Will the Japanese decision to take full control of Harbin and environs incite massive Soviet responses? He was not sure whether he felt safer inside or out.

Whatever sounds were coming from Moscow, this Soviet hand might have anticipated that Stalin was not going to be provoked into a war over Manchuria by some Japanese military thugs.[17] The Soviets were drawing the line against Japanese incursion farther to the west, on the borders of Outer Mongolia, and to the east in defense of their maritime provinces and the valuable port of Vladivostok. They did not need armed combat to draw those lines, even to increase their influence in the region. Stalin's Comintern had more effective means to spread communism and Soviet influence in China throughout the Far East and even in Japan itself without risking a war that would be perceived as distant and unpopular in the heartland.

What Chiune and the Kwantung officers could not anticipate was that Stalin had far better information on Japanese intentions and the capacity to act on those intentions: his spy ring, headed by the German journalist Richard Sorge, had become well positioned and productive by that time.[18] From Sorge, Stalin knew that Japanese territorial ambitions exceeded their control over a provincial capital here and a railroad corridor there. And if the "Japanese fascists" were to become the "Napoleons of the East," using Manchuria as a launching pad for attacks of Soviet territory, Stalin might have mused, the same fate would await them as the "Napoleon of the West."

More recent history provided another precedent for Sugihara and other Harbin Gakuinites among the Russia hands around town who had special memories of "Goto's folly," the Siberian multinational intervention during the Russian Revolution. The sense of futility and disappointment that was the legacy of that effort might have encouraged

Sugihara to advise caution at the very same moment he was humming to himself old school songs about the "pioneers of the new sunrise . . . dreaming of Moscow walls." In the end, it must be said, we do not know what Sugihara advised.

In the days that followed the Japanese conquest of Harbin and other areas of Manchuria, the Japanese military heard Soviet pronouncements against intervention, an admission of what they suspected—that the Soviets, in fact, could not defend their interests in Manchuria against Japan, at least not at this point As the truth came out, the Japanese responded to the Soviets with scorn and even greater aggressiveness. But Sugihara was relieved at the plain words. For an official who had spent much of his career trying to secure the rights of his government in Manchuria, the approach of Japanese soldiers into Harbin, with no countervailing threats from the Soviets, must have made him happy.

Amileto Vespa, the Italian spy in the service of the Japanese, describes the excited anticipation of some Harbinites, particularly the White Russians, over the Japanese conquest. They thought this was the beginning of a White Russian state in Manchuria, if not the harbinger of liberation from the Bolsheviks for their entire homeland. "Poor, foolish, deluded people! Their *'Banzai!'* shouting was to be of short duration," as Vespa said. Chinese and Jewish Harbinites, according to his description, were too jaded for such illusions.[19]

"Short duration," indeed. A few days after the Japanese asserted control over Harbin, some Chinese officials, collaborating with the Japanese, announced the secession of Manchuria from the Republic of China, or what was essentially Chiang Kai-shek's Nationalist government in Nanjing. In early March, the independence of Manchukuo was proclaimed.

To make the new state appear legitimate beyond question, Lawrence of Manchuria virtually abducted the last emperor of China, Hsuan-t'ung, whose reign had not been very happy or successful. In 1912 (at age seven) he had taken early retirement. Lawrence's men now groomed him for a comeback as the emperor of Manchukuo.

As part of this same effort to legitimate their conquest, the Japanese accepted the League of Nations commission to investigate the circumstances of the Mukden Incident. The Lytton Commission, headed by the British Victor Alexander Lytton—baron and earl, not exactly the most convincing symbol of opposition to colonialism—surveyed the situation in Manchuria for six weeks, starting on April 20, 1932. Early in the fall, it issued its report. The Kwantung Army's action of the previous September, the commissioners unhesitatingly declared, could not "be regarded as measures of legitimate self-defense."[20] Japanese claiming otherwise were met with undisguised scorn: "The Independence Movement which had never been heard of in Manchuria before September, 1931, was only made possible by the presence of Japanese troops," read the report.

Japan's assurances, made in Portsmouth and after, that it would effectively preserve an open door in China did not impress members of the Lytton Commission. They reported back to the League of Nations that what in fact took place in Manchuria was a Japanese conquest and annexation. Again, what Tokyo perceived to be a military victory turned into a diplomatic debacle. Japan would continue to have difficulty convincing anyone it was engaged in a "moral crusade, the fulfillment of her mission in Asia" rather than "an imperialist war of greed and aggression," as the common phraseology of the day had it.

Japan made one more effort to win over public opinion for "Greater Asia Prosperity." The University of Oregon–educated former Goto disciple, future president of the South Manchurian Railway, foreign minister, and Sugihara's boss, Yosuke Matsuoka, represented Japan at the League of Nations in November and December 1932. The "Talking Machine," as he was called, made a clever effort to reverse the erosion of support for Japan's position by using compelling, Western-resonant images to foster identification with his beleaguered country. Here, Matsuoka goes so far as to compare Japan to the crucified Jesus:

> Humanity crucified Jesus of Nazareth two thousand years ago. And today? Can any of you assure me that the so-called world opinion can make no mistake? We Japanese feel that we are now put on trial. Some of the people in Europe and America may wish even to crucify Japan in the twentieth century. Gentlemen, Japan stands ready to be crucified! But we do believe, and firmly believe, that in a very few years, world opinion will be changed and that we shall be understood by the world as Jesus of Nazareth was.[21]

The man who said of himself "While I am a Christian, I am a Matsuoka-Christian" undoubtedly had heard about Jews and antisemitism. Perhaps he knew some Jews during his years in Portland and learned how some still blamed them for the crucifixion. Jews had a reputation for subversiveness too, judging by how overrepresented they were among Communists. For Matsuoka to link the opposition to Japan's Manchurian policy with a little antisemitic imagery was probably more of an effort to create a coalition of his "enemies' enemies" rather than a conscious or unconscious expression of antagonism toward Jews.

But whatever his motive, the tactic struck a chord with only a few countries. Indeed, all of El Salvador, the Vatican, and possibly the Dominican Republic initially recognized Manchukuo. In a few years, though, the potential ally Germany, the spy partner Poland, and an increasingly fascist Hungary established diplomatic relations.[22]

New Careers

March 9, 1932, the day on which the independence of Manchuria was declared, seems to have passed in Sugihara's life without repercussions. But shortly thereafter, his career begins to accelerate. On March 31, he is ordered to make an official trip to Korea, followed by a circuit around Tokyo and Harbin. At least according to one source, by April 5 he is doing some sort of work for the Foreign Affairs Department of the fledgling Manchukuo government. On May 18, he is promoted to second interpreter of the embassy. On the same day or so, he is placed in a different civil service category, that of high ranking officials, but now in the Ministry of the Interior, rather than his customary Foreign Affairs Department. He is ordered by the Imperial Cabinet to work in the Soviet Union. All these seemingly dazzling career successes are undercut by a strange report soon thereafter: "He left his position for personal reasons. He received a temporary pension of 930 yen."

What personal reasons could make him abandon his new assignment and keep this avid Russophile from going to the Soviet Union? True, it was no place to take his wife, Klaudia, with her prominent anti-Bolshevik background. But it certainly was not unusual for a Japanese diplomat to travel without his wife. Perhaps he was fearful that his own connections with White Russian expatriates in Manchuria would endanger him in the Soviet Union.

But most likely what these strange inscriptions on his résumé indicate is that he undertook some intelligence mission in the Soviet Union. "Personal reasons" may have been the phrase that covered his tracks. It states he did not go, when it seems likely he did. Both résumés are unusually vague. No city is mentioned and we find no record of his visit in Soviet sources. Perhaps what is indicated is a pro forma resignation from one agency before he takes up his post under the auspices of another agency in the Soviet Union. Indeed, as some former associates still whisper to derogate him, he had something to do with the Ministry of the Interior, which was then associated with some of the harshest counterintelligence agencies.

Was he caught in intra-agency squabbles and intrigues between the Ministries of the Interior and Foreign Affairs, between civilian agencies and whatever claims the military had on him?[23] Could it be that he was being detailed to the South Manchurian Railroad to assess how Japan should prepare its negotiating stance for the purchase of the railroad? Indeed, about a year later, as his résumé lets on, he was deeply involved in those negotiations.

With the Manchukuo economy booming as it was, perhaps Sugihara did take a "leave." And he used that leave to assist the Japanese *zaibatsus,* the large trade and manufacturing companies, who then (and now) held special relationships with the bureaucrats. Comparing Sugihara's career to those of other government officials at this time, we find such examples. Matsuoka himself takes a few spins through the "revolving door" between the South Manchurian Railway and the Foreign Ministry. Sugihara's occasional boss, Chu'ichi Ohashi, who accompanied him and Shimura to the "wetties" in Yoshimura, at one point took a leave from government to go into the lumber business, as Shimura tells us. Whatever else is going on in the background, it is clear that the Manchukuo administration is getting organized, that the Japanese hold on the polity and economy is firm, and that Sugihara is part of all this.

In pre-Manchukuo days, Ohashi had been Japanese consul general in Harbin; in the spring of 1932, he was named Manchukuo's vice minister of foreign affairs, and a member of the Supreme Council. He needed someone proven to be reliable to help him with his new duties; the fact that his former subordinate, Chiune Sugihara, also hailed from the same Gifu Prefecture was not irrelevant. The sense of *han,* the particularly intense and exclusive Japanese version of the old-boy network, the personal attachment that Japanese feel in relation to small groups and shared experience rather than more rationalized and impersonal forms of discipline, was strong then among Japanese, as it still is today.[24]

Ohashi could trust, as Shimura tells us, that Sugihara would be loyal to him. In 1940, as parliamentary vice minister of the Japanese government, an ally if not a friend of Matsuoka, Ohashi initialed cables arriving from Sugihara in Kaunas. Did Ohashi reciprocate that loyalty at a critical moment to his visa-issuing fellow Gifuite and protégé? But that part of the story will have to wait.

In the meantime, with the consolidation of Japanese rule in parts of Manchuria after 1932, many members of the civil service were transferred to the administration of the "puppet government" of Manchukuo, including Sugihara and Shimura. The good side was that the new administration probably provided more opportunities for nonelite men who, typically, came from the provinces, were without family connections, and did not attend Tokyo University. The bad side was that Manchukuo had fallen more under the control of the Japanese military than the Foreign Ministry, though the latter had trained and employed most of these colonial administrators.

Suddenly, Sugihara's peers felt the brunt of the militarism then growing at home. Considering the increased frequency of political assassinations and other "dirty tricks," working in these bureaucracies was probably not altogether pleasant for Sugihara. By that spring, the second-tier official Chiune Sugihara was in an upper-echelon position. He was the director of the Manchukuo Foreign Ministry, working for Ohashi. These days, the Chinese peddlers and rickshaw drivers on Kitayskaya kowtowed to Chiune as well.

In Harbin now there were nods toward establishing a semblance of democracy, but mostly there was chaos checked by military might. Some nine competing military, police, intelligence, and counterintelligence agencies, with overlapping mandates and domains of authority, contributed to the tangle. Corruption flourished. Indeed, it was not unusual for individuals extorted by one agency to be released, only to be extorted by another agency. These agencies spent much of their time locked into murderous battles against one another to control lucrative concessions, rather than the political and security work for which they were sent to Manchuria.

Notwithstanding their reformist agenda for their own country and people, Japanese officials eagerly took lucrative bribes to look the other way on drugs. More opium dens opened in Harbin and elsewhere in Manchukuo, primarily serving the Chinese. The morphine trade involved what was now, quite literally, over-the-counter transactions; customers, wrist-up, inserted their cash-clutching fists into bank-teller-style windows. A tug on the cash, a prick in the veins, and they were happily on their way. "Junior doses" were available near schools, ensuring the long-term profitability of the trade. Futuristic innovation such as "home delivery" and sophisticated advertising schemes—leaflets dropped from airplanes and billboard use of banknotes displaying beautiful engravings of poppy blooms—helped increase sales.

Under these circumstances, it did not take much bullying of small farmers to convince them to grow poppy seeds rather than soybeans. The old strategy of keeping Chinese coolies happy on drugs, Japanese officials would argue, is better for all concerned. Better that, they said, than tamping down their political rebellions. Sometimes Japanese officials achieved even greater economic stakes for their organizations and themselves by rationalizing markets, founding the Manchukuo Opium Monopoly Board, and by offering licenses and concessions for specific territories.

Similar incentives and modes of organization could be used to get White Russians to transform more and more available supplies of grain and potatoes into vodka. White Russian families, preoccupied with remembering their ancestral estates, townhouses, and all else that they lost to the accursed Bolsheviks, often were crippled by nostalgia and anger, and unable to adjust to the new realities. Japanese "entrepreneurs" and officials, often working in partnerships, induced and tricked White Russian women into prostitution, also providing the customary rake-offs for the different police, military, and intelligence agencies.[25] For clients with other preferences, there was no shortage of Japanese women arriving regularly from Osaka, Kyoto, and other cities, dressed in bright kimonos and quickly driven through the streets of Harbin in open cars to promote their establishments.

Harbin's Jews were particularly vulnerable to extortion. Our Italian spy/memoirist, Amileto Vespa, in his book *Secret Agent of Japan* under the apt chapter heading "The chief goes berserk," reports on a conversation he had with his Japanese handler in regard to future policy:

"These Russian toughs will help us in putting the screws on certain rich Jews and Russians whom we do not like," said the handler. "I want to take their fortunes away from them and kick them out of Manchuria. When they leave, it will be with empty pockets." Vespa protested, "'All Jews are not bad,' I dared say; 'I know many Jews in Manchuria who are perfect gentlemen, who conduct their business honestly, who are glad to see the Japanese in Manchuria.' The Chief jumped up and rushed at me as though he wished to grab me by the throat. 'How dare you talk that way to me? How dare you defend the Jews? One more word like this and I choke you! The Jews are all swine! All Europeans are dogs. That's why we shall throw them out of China and the Pacific. But the Jews are still worse. . . . The Russians whose names I have given you are the ones who are going to do the dirty work for us. We Japanese do not want to soil our hands.'"[26]

Only ten days after the establishment of the Manchukuo state, Sugihara's fellow Russia hand and well-known pimp, Kostya Nakamura, ordered some White Russian thugs to kidnap a wealthy Jewish pharmacist named Kofman, in Harbin. Though his wife posted an $18,000 ransom, Kofman's cut-up remains were left on a Harbin street. On August 24, 1933, Nakamura was involved in another Japanese–White Russian joint venture, this time whisking Semeon Kaspé off the street. Kaspé was the son of Josef Kaspé, one of Harbin's fabulously wealthy citizens. Semeon was a talented Jewish violinist who had trained in Paris. Though the French consul's active intervention threatened to make it an international scandal, Kaspé's tortured body was found the following December after long ransom negotiations failed. At the large funeral Harbinites from every background, including Japanese, expressed indignation. The head of the Jewish community, Dr. Abraham Kaufman, denounced the murderers and those behind them. The insinuation was clear to all and Kaufman received an unfriendly visit and threat-filled warning from the *Kempei*.[27] The exodus of Jews from Harbin quickened.

Sugihara knew well the foundations of such racism and xenophobia. Likely, he too had heard pronouncements similar to those conveyed by Amileto Vespa in the name of his Japanese handler:

The Japanese are the only divine people on earth; that is the only reason why they never mix with other people. Our culture is sacred and likewise sacred is everything Japanese. We have no intention of imparting our civilization to the people whom we have conquered or shall conquer. They will disappear. The Korean will be eaten by vices; the Chinese will be victims of opium and other narcotics; the Russians will be ruined by vodka. They will be annihilated. Alone the descendants of Ameterasu-O-Mi-Kami, the Sun Goddess, will people our Empire. And this is but the first part of the programme of the tasks which the Gods have given to our people. The second phase calls for the conquest of India and of all the islands in the Pacific; also Siberia as far as the Ural region. Do not smile at these declarations. The Gods do not lie. The destiny of Japan has been outlined by the Gods. Nothing can stop Japan from becoming the greatest Empire on earth![28]

The Emperor cult was now imposed on the very population whose heterogeneity was to be cherished in accordance with the ideological pronouncements of Manchukuo. Manchurian citizens were to bow in the direction of Tokyo and when not doing that, to bow deferentially to the Japanese official at hand. This *Wang tao,* or the Kingly Way, a quasi-secularized Buddhist notion, was used in Manchukuo to evoke a general terror, which was supposed to lead to love and respect. Much as he may have disapproved of such obeisance, Sugihara probably garnered his share of enforced bows and even may have had to enforce these rules upon others.

Meanwhile, the work of a Russia hand was changing rapidly. In the twenties, when Sugihara and Shimura had left the Harbin Gakuin and were getting their first jobs, the Russia desk of the Imperial Japanese Amy, the police, or any of the intelligence agencies in Manchuria were not high energy centers. These were the easiest of subsections where Japanese officers and officials could while away their time—as we know Sugihara did—playing baseball or GO. The new Bolshevik state, through the end of the decade, was seen as a threat, but more philosophically than militarily. How much could one fear of strategists who, as Sugihara put it, "climb a tree to go fishing"?

But not long after the Manchurian Incident, base running and opponent encircling, as in a GO game, spawned new applications. The "pioneers of the new sunrise" needed to wake up from their somewhat sleepy existence. Notwithstanding Soviet purges and famines that lulled Japanese military planners into complacency (this is an enemy?!), the Soviet economy was shifting into high gear. Suddenly, the quantity and quality of Soviet armaments, tanks, and even aircraft began to rise, and before long Manchuria was being surrounded on three sides.

Until the Manchurian Incident, military attachés were assigned to only three of the USSR's neighbors: Poland, Latvia, and Turkey. These countries were selected as points from which to organize intelligence efforts against the neighboring Soviet Union. Such efforts were coordinated by the Harbin branch of the Tokumukikan intelligence agency, and Sugihara was likely involved. As he indicated in his 1967 memoirs, his connections with Polish intelligence were particularly close, even warm. Japan, as we recall, had hosted General Pilsudski as well as his rival Dmowski during the Russo-Japanese War, even coaching a few Polish patriots in urban terrorism.

Also, during the Bolshevik encirclement of Warsaw in 1920, the Japanese had provided the defenders of the city with Russian codes enabling them to break the blockade. In the thirties, as Japanese military planners began to take the Soviet threat more seriously, Poland in turn helped Japan with Moscow's codes. The symbolic logic faculty of the Jagiellonian University Department of Philosophy, in Cracow, probably the best in the world, produced an interesting array of code makers and breakers alumni. On one of his forays to Europe, Sugihara brought back some of their codes. Washington- and London-based code breakers, some with Polish backgrounds, cracked the crucial Japanese Purple codes in mid-1940, just in time to provide Allied intelligence information on Sugihara's activities in Kovno.

In the thirties, military attachés were added to other Japanese embassies to keep tabs on the Soviets. Their ranks were bolstered by diplomats who also had military commissions, like Sugihara; unbeknown to their host countries, they were deployed abroad not only to organize trade fairs and cultural events and to issue visas but also to collect military intelligence. Scantily disguised Japanese army couriers would take the Trans-Siberian Railroad monthly to deliver new codes to embassies in the USSR and different parts of Europe. Along the way they would observe all they could, including military and air bases, troop movements, arsenals, new weapons, and fortifications. Sugihara was likely one of these observers, from time to time.

Working on the Railroad

Even if Sugihara never made the history books for his activities in Kaunas, he might have won a minor citation for his role in averting a second Russo-Japanese War. His smaller story unfolds: on June 2, 1933, Sugihara, now in charge of the Manchukuo Foreign Ministry office in Harbin, receives an angry protest from the Soviet consul general concerning Japanese violation of the provisions of the Portsmouth Treaty. Nothing new about that. The two powers were often at loggerheads. But the situation surrounding the Chinese Eastern Railway has become so dangerously explosive, and the solution, at least to some, is so patently clear, that Soviet and Manchukuo delegates decide to meet in Tokyo.

A U.S. intelligence report of the time sums up the conflict: "the weakest point strategically in Japan's control of north Manchuria now lies in the Russian ownership of the Chinese Eastern Railway. . . . the Japanese War Office has undoubtedly decided that a war with Russia is inevitable." The railroad, it concludes, plus other valuable Soviet assets such as the too-close-for-comfort Soviet airbase in Vladivostok "must be taken before the Russian Soviet becomes too powerful militarily."[29]

There was a long history to all this. Even back in Sugihara's student days in Harbin, the Chinese Eastern Railway had been a serious flashpoint. Ownership and management agreements, made years earlier between the tsarist and Chinese governments, never really worked. But with the establishment of Manchukuo, the Japanese knew their moment had arrived. The Nationalist Chinese government was out of the picture, factionalized and weakened as it was. But the official presence of Soviets in Manchuria was a thorn in Japan's side, a constant threat of spreading communism in Manchuria, China, and even Japan. As for the Soviets, the once profitable CER had become a losing proposition. Banditry—some of it sponsored by the Soviets or Japanese against each other, some self-inflicted to justify more damaging attacks against each other—resulted in delayed shipments and spoilage.[30]

To protect their stake in the railroad, the Soviets began transferring locomotives and rolling stock onto other lines in their territory. In retaliation, the Manchukuo authorities ordered a halt to freight traffic between the CER and the Trans-Baikal Railway. Acts of sabotage with unidentifiable sponsorship were perpetrated against targets even reaching at times beyond the boundaries of Manchuria on the Trans-Siberian Railroad. These attacks raised the profits of the bandits as well as levels of indignation on all sides.

While the Japanese leadership agreed that the Soviets must be eliminated from Manchukuo, none agreed on how, precisely, this was to occur. The Japanese Army was not particularly supportive of the plan to negotiate for what would become prize booty in a second Russo-Japanese War. The Foreign Ministry was more sanguine about arriving at a deal. Sugihara, both soldier and diplomat, Japanese civil servant and Russia hand, was caught in a serious conflict. But he soon elected to join those seeking a negotiated settlement, including those Japanese most committed to rapid, intense, large-scale development of Manchukuo and its natural resources. He became an international deal maker.

A prominent ally of Sugihara in these negotiations was the young, handsome, suave, and most promising diplomat, Shigenori Togo. Togo would one day write about the negotiations, from his Tokyo jail cell in 1946. He was an accused war criminal at the time, recently Japan's foreign minister during World War II. Among the claims he made for having been on the side of peace, he cited his active role during the early thirties in the transfer of the Chinese Eastern Railway. The Soviets, he explained, had, "intended to liquidate the imperialistic inheritance from the Czarist days, thereby gaining as much income as possible." They also wanted to "eliminate sources of dispute with Manchukuo, and even with Japan."

But the Soviets, Togo emphasized, had still one other major incentive on that morning in June 1933 when they complained to the director of the Manchukuo Foreign Ministry in Harbin, Chiune Sugihara. The rise of Nazi power on its Western border made it quite necessary for the Soviet Union "to prepare for the new situation," as Togo commented years later. Nevertheless, internal divisions between the Japanese and Manchukuo representatives on the one side, and the Russians on the other, made the negotiations precarious and protracted. The sides were far apart on selling price and on terms.

What was Sugihara's role in the negotiations? As Vice Foreign Minister Ohashi's assistant, he was out in the field contending with dangerous bandits, an assortment of unreliable Russians of different political and military stripes, and Chinese who had little reason to be friendly to a Japanese official about to sell off their stake in the railroad. His job was to count and evaluate the railroad's assets. At the same time, he was collecting intelligence reports from his many contacts inside and outside the USSR about the actual passenger and freight traffic on the former CER, now called the North Manchurian Railway by the Japanese. He was comparing this volume to the volume on alternate lines going around Siberia and factoring in time saved to project future profits generated by the railroad, when it would supposedly be managed better under the Japanese. And he was collecting intelligence on the precise number and locations of locomotives and rolling stock that the Soviets were stashing away on their side of the border, information his colleagues at the negotiating table in Tokyo could use against their Soviet counterparts.

Armed with Sugihara's reports, Togo and Ohashi were able to cite actual figures, thus exposing how inflated the Soviet asking price (one billion gold rubles) was. Togo seemed to be conciliatory and resourceful in moving the negotiations out of dead-end positions. But Ohashi, we hear from Soviet reports at least, was antagonistic. He disputed the Soviet's CER investment figures, challenged their claims to exclusive ownership, and bickered over the rate of exchange. The Soviet delegates reported that the quarrel between the Japanese Foreign Office on the one hand and the Military and Manchukuo Foreign Ministry on the other "was being revealed with absolute clarity." Moreover, Ohashi, it would seem, wanted to prolong the negotiations, if not promote their breakdown.[31]

"While the negotiations were thus stumbling," Togo tells us, "the Foreign Office of Manchukuo conspired with a few Japanese Army officers and caused the seizure of a large number of the Russian employees (of the railroad), whereupon the Russian representatives insisted that they could not continue the negotiations unless these employees were released." Whoever these high-level conspirators were, Togo adds, they got virtually what they wanted: "The negotiations were thus on the verge of collapse." Sugihara, now secretary of the Manchukuo delegation, must not have been pleased with the rising power of the militarists and other antinegotiations factions on his side. And they were not very pleased when Sugihara and his colleagues managed to keep the Soviets in for another round.

For the better part of twenty-one months the negotiations continued. Though the Japanese were interested in the Soviets bargaining directly with the representatives of the Manchukuo government, thereby providing it recognition, if only de facto, Togo realized that he himself must take matters in hand. "From then on the negotiations proceeded with the USSR on one side and Japan on the other, and I naturally became responsible for them."

Ultimately, it was the Soviets who most likely broke the stalemate. They realized that their recalcitrance would only strengthen the Japanese "Attack Russia" faction. A war would probably end with Soviet territorial concessions plus the loss of the railroad, for which, if they stayed at the table, they might still receive payment, even if less than expected. Moreover, the Nazis were causing the Soviets real worries. Better to lay low. A war on two fronts had to be avoided at any cost.

Japan and the Soviet Union: "Peace" and the "Inevitable Second Russo-Japanese War"

On March 23, 1935—within days of Hitler's announcement that he was rearming Germany in defiance of the Versailles Treaty—Japan and the Soviet Union concluded their negotiations. The Union of Soviet Socialist Republics signed an agreement with Manchukuo to cede "all rights concerning the CER, its subsidiary enterprises and properties." In turn, the Manchukuo government paid 140 million yen, considerably less than the Soviets' initial asking price of 300 million yen, but 50 million yen

more than the Japanese had offered at the outset. Sugihara's careful estimates may have helped both sides move closer to a realistic price.

In Tokyo, a ceremonial signing of the protocols took place that morning with expressions of optimism made by Soviet, Japanese, and
Manchurian officials. Ohashi represented the latter, though the list of at-
tendees makes no mention of his assistant. In Harbin as well there were
speeches and toasts. Nor is there a record of Sugihara attending that
event. Wherever he was that day, one assumes Sugihara felt joyful. After
all, he had successfully completed a difficult assignment and must have
been pleased to have helped forestall the "inevitable war."

Yet for many Japanese, including his friends in the Manchukuo administration, feelings ran to the bittersweet. For the hawks who believed that
a second round of a full-scale war with the Soviets was "inevitable," the
peaceful settlement of the conflicts surrounding the railroad meant a lost
opportunity for launching a preventative war against the USSR; Japan
had blown the initiative. They well might have blamed Sugihara for his
hand in this. Indeed, no agreement was reached on a nonaggression pact,
long sought at least by the Soviets.[32] But Togo reports that his government "did not consider the time opportune for such a pact."[33]

No, both countries were far from any permanent vision of "peace."
For the Soviets, their agreement to retreat from Manchuria seemed
merely tactical. A Japanese intelligence officer in Harbin remembers asking Soviet railway workers whether they were not sorry about leaving
Manchuria after so many years of effort and was it not painful for them
to observe the "utter defeat" represented by their sale of the CER to
Japan? "No! No!," they replied, "We will get the railroad back sooner or
later—and free of charge too!"[34] The time-out would actually enable
them to strengthen their defenses on three sides of Manchukuo.

In fact, without the distractions of Japanese skirmishes over the railroad, they could better complete their Five-Year Plan, augment troop positions, and increase armaments. Newly assembled bombers, placed on
their airstrips near Vladivostok, would one day threaten Japan's "paper
and matchwood cities," in the words of one Yurenev, the Soviet ambassador to Tokyo. Indeed, he rather undiplomatically boasted that he
thought the Japanese industrial centers could be destroyed, perhaps in one
night's raid.

The time-out could also lend the Soviet Union a chance to improve its
standing in world opinion—while Japan continued to pay the price for its
annexation of Manchuria. Clearly, the Bolsheviks were winning the image game. The Soviet Union was entering the League of Nations just as
Japan was resigning in protest and increasing its isolation. The Soviet
Union was bettering its relations with the United States and China, just

as Japan's relations with those countries were becoming more and more strained.

Jewish Conspiracies, Jewish Colonies

In 1935, as the last Soviet railroad official and commissar departed, the Japanese won true control over Manchuria and began seizing opportunities to develop and colonize it without interference. There should have been much to celebrate. But the Japanese government was riven by factions. Intrigues substituted for politics, while policy decisions were difficult to forge, more difficult to enforce.

Among the many proposals for the development of Manchuria, one hinged on providing a haven for Jewish refugees, at least those who were well connected and endowed. As Hitler became more aggressive, highly trained scientists, engineers, and musicians were now leaving Germany in growing waves, desperately seeking work and home. This was an extraordinary opportunity for Japanese, so committed to accelerated development of Manchukuo. Yet antisemitism was also cresting in Japan and Manchuria, as elsewhere. The Japanese had their translation of the *Protocols of the Elders of Zion* and their own special fascination with conspiracy theories. Ironically, just as Japan was discussing the creation of a Manchukuo Jewish "haven," the Jews in Harbin, frightened by kidnappings and other violence, were trying to leave.

But the Japanese government had another reason to consider the usefulness of Jews in Manchurian schemes. In 1935, just as they were withdrawing from Manchuria, the Soviets began to publicize plans for establishing an autonomous Jewish region of Birobidzhan near the Amur River, on the Manchukuo border. The Soviets, in planning Birobidzhan, had three expectations. First, Jewish settlers could provide a first line of defense against Japanese troops pouring over the borders. Second, Birobidzhan was a convenient dumping ground for pushing purged Jews (Mensheviks, etc.) out of the mainstream. Third, and most important, Birobidzhan would help rectify the Soviet image just as reports of Stalinist brutality were seeping out.

Unlike their Teutonic and Anglo-Saxon counterparts, the Soviets were helping their Jews, they boasted. This was the era of the antisemitic Nuremberg Laws and British mandate anti-Zionism over Palestine. In bright contrast, the Soviets were creating the first Jewish "homeland" in two thousand years! Soon the Birobidzhan railroad station would sport a sign—in Yiddish—designating this landmark. The settlement of a few thousand Jews enjoying their "Jewish form, Soviet content" culture was played up through Soviet propaganda organs, at least until the next purge.

That the Soviets, in developing Birobidzhan at this particular moment, might have been prompted by military considerations as well as propaganda goals was not lost on the Japanese. Its site on the Amur River lay just a bit upstream from where the Red Army had clashed terribly with the Kwantung Army. If the Japanese Army should ever invade Soviet territory, argued Mamoru Shigemitsu, later one of Japan's foreign ministers during World War II, this new Jewish state of Birobidzhan would threaten Japan. "It was founded near to the military center of Habarovsk," as he wrote, "in order to take advantage of Jewish influence over world opinion."[35]

In 1934, while Manchukuo Foreign Ministry Vice Director Chiune Sugihara was anxiously trying to keep diplomats and locomotives on the right track, Colonel Norihiro Yasue was enjoying the fruits of professional success. This military expert had just published a book entitled *Yudaya no hitobito (The Jewish People)* under the auspices of something called the Military Club, with an introduction by a former minister of the army. It was a strange melange of backhanded compliments, praise, traditional stereotypes, and antisemitic allegations. This equivocal attitude is rather typical of Japanese antisemitism; such literature emphasized Jews' political and economic activity, as well as the harm they cause through their efforts to control and dominate.[36]

Yasue had begun his career during the Siberian Intervention after World War I, as a lieutenant in the Japanese combat forces. There he encountered Jews escaping from the Russian Revolution, as well as fleeing White Russians who blamed the disaster that had befallen "Mother Russia" on the Jews, those enemies of "Christ and the Tsar." The Imperial Japanese Army, always eager to have well-trained experts in any field where the need might arise, sent this budding Jew hand, in 1927, on an educational grand tour of the major Jewish communities of Europe and Palestine.

During the thirties, Yasue was posted in different parts of Manchukuo where he seemingly spied on Jewish communities locally and abroad, and acted as a liaison when the Japanese government wanted to convey messages or implement policies. In the late thirties, he encouraged several Jewish leaders in Harbin to organize three conferences of Far East Jews. It was more than coincidence that speaker after speaker at these well-publicized meetings praised Japan for its kindness to Jews; they knew Manchuria could become a welcoming destination. The Japanese wanted to populate Manchuria, if not with Japanese then at least in a manner where Chinese influence would be reduced. Jews could act as ballast. Might there have been some Japanese thinking about a Birobidzhan for the Manchukuo side of the border, to enlist "Jewish capital and ence" for the benefit of Japan while containing the dangers of "Je communism" in remote colonies?[37] It would seem so.

Yasue was dismissed from the Japanese military in 1940. "The Nazis asked that my father be fired because he was so pro-Jewish. Yasue was taken prisoner by the Soviets at the end of the War and disappeared into the Soviet Gulag," says his son Hiroo Yasue, a retired businessman, who has made it his life mission to rehabilitate and make known the father who vanished in his childhood.

"My father was not an antisemite," Hiroo told me one steamy day in August 1994 while sitting in the Tokyo American Club, overlooking the sprawl and smog. It is an appropriate setting in which to discuss Japanese colonialism. "I will do everything that I can to prove this. Why, the Jews themselves honored him!"[38] Yasue Jr. spoke as if he'd been challenged on this point many times before:

> They have two most important books, the "Golden Book" and the "Silver Book." Both are believed by the Jews to be divine. The Golden Book has the name of world-famous Jews and the Silver Book, the names of foreigners who have contributed to the Jewish people. But my father's name was inscribed in the Golden, not the Silver Book. The Jews wanted to express special thanks to my father for what he did for them. Also, they put his name in the Golden Book in 1941 because they wanted to appeal that the punishment of the Japanese Army was unreasonable.

In this bizarre theory, he seems to refer to a fund-raising device of some Jewish organization; names are inscribed in lieu of a donation. As far as we know, this book has no metaphysical powers!

The Japanese stance toward Jews, as Yasue so distilled, was full of contradictions. The *Gaimusho* archives contain an impressive collection of antisemitic literature, much of it American vintage: Posters declare, "Onward Christian Soldiers" and point to the dangers of "International Jew Baruch," "Fellow-Traveller" Ickes, Dorothy Thompson "Levy," and how "Kosher La Guardia" and the whole "Jew-Deal" crowd are "Baiting" friendly nations!" Threats of war in America come from nowhere other than the Jews, they insist: "The American people have no quarrel with Germany or Japan. They do not want to fight either nation. And neither do the Germans nor the Japanese want to fight us."[39] In poring over these vile and well-preserved folders full of antisemitica in the Foreign Ministry archives, one senses a naïveté, even earnestness among Sugihara's generation. Some of these officials seem genuinely to have wanted to know who the Jews are, and why they are so disliked.

Better to co-opt Jews, perhaps bring some where the Japanese can keep a close eye on those Jews. Indeed, a dateless but probably early policy paper, "How to Manage Jews (in Japan)," stamped "Top Secret," adumbrated such themes:

(1) Japanese trade relies on Jews. It was developed and is managed in the hands of Jews. If Jews oppose Japan, it will severely damage our trade. (2) We have to win Jews over to our side to lead foreign investments. We need much capital to develop the power of the product in Manchuria. If we make enemies of the Jews it will be impossible to draw capital from overseas because Jewish influence on the global financial world is extremely large. (3) When America and Britain put economic pressure on Japan, we have to utilize Jews. Jews have strong racial connections so that it will be disadvantageous if we mistreat them. (4) Rejection of the Jews will hasten the invoking of the Law of Neutrality of America. Since the occurrence of the Manchurian Incident, the Law of Neutrality of America is about to be invoked. But it is still being held back because of the economic relations between America and Japan. If Jewish feelings are hurt, if they abandon the profits of trade, and if 4,500,000 Jews agree to the Law, it will be surely invoked. (5) 2,000 Jews now live in Japan. Most of them, in Tokyo and Yokohama, are teachers and musicians. Most of them, in Kobe and Osaka, are involved in trade. About 20,000 Jews live in Manchuria and Northern China. We believe that they will not have any bad effects on Japan. This situation is very different from America or the European countries. In these countries, Jews are spreading inside the national institutions and governments cannot control them. But in Japan such a situation will never happen. If some dangerous social elements come into Japan, then we can regulate them by usual orders like prohibiting communists from entering Japan. We actually do not need to exclude Jews just because they are Jews. We should try to utilize them and not to provoke Jewish antipathy. Jews in the world are watching our attitude now. We have to show them that there is no possibility of Japanese discrimination against Jews.

Exactly how pervasive this attitude was cannot be ascertained. From the number of like proposals lingering in the *Gaimusho,* it would seem to be more than the work of a few Jew hands such as Colonel Yasue. And from the manner in which such proposals link the situation of Jews under Japanese control to concern with American policy, it seems most likely that they stem from an emerging pro-U.S. faction. Could it be, I began to wonder, that Sugihara was so motivated to rescue Jews because he represented a pro-U.S. faction? And these cohorts thus helped him to succeed?

"Manchurian Development," the "Quasi War," and Sugihara Suspected

While the Jewish question was debated, the Japanese now poured themselves into the construction of Manchuria. New cities sprang up in barren spaces, and the number of factories increased from 430 in 1931 to 1,853 in 1940. Around 5,300 kilometers of new railroads crisscrossed the country, some propelling along the Asia Express, an elegant high-speed train that ran from Darien to Hsinking at speeds comparable to the fastest in Europe and America. The worldwide Depression had hit rural Japan hard, yet now agricultural workers could find jobs in fast-growing Manchuria. Indeed, such development "was inspired by a host of utopianist visions which looked to empire as the panacea for Japan's socioeconomic crisis."[40]

Notwithstanding Japanese dominance and chauvinism, the notion of a Greater Asia assumed that different people would live side by side. The need for skilled people was so great that even Jews were welcome and were coming.

However much Manchukuo became a boomtown that could beat the West with faster trains and larger sanitary systems, it was still just a wilderness with armed garrisons. Tensions hadn't declined as much as the Japanese had hoped. In 1935 alone, there were 152 border skirmishes with the Soviets. Each country continued to infiltrate the other with spies and agents provocateurs, retaining a state of "quasi war." Whoever instigated these incidents, the Soviets were becoming more of a formidable opponent, while the Japanese, with increasing frequency, were getting beaten.

Only a few months after Japan's purchase of the railroad, the Seventh Congress of the Comintern met in Moscow in July 1935 and passed a resolution to carry on the fight against Japan, Germany, and Poland's "imperialistic ambition of world redivision."[41] The Japanese made their own counterthreats: "If the Soviet does not cease to annoy us," as War Minister Sadao Araki said, "I shall have to purge Siberia as one cleans a room of flies."[42] Strong talk, but out in the field, Araki's men watched as the Soviet military presence grew in numbers, skills, and armaments. The "Strike South" military faction had been arguing that the Imperial Japanese Army should do a "clean-up" job, once and for all, on its southern neighbor, China. That faction included Colonel Dohihara (nicknamed "Lawrence of Manchuria") and Lieutenant Colonel Kanji Ishihara, with whom Sugihara had some association going back to pre-Manchukuo days.[43]

These plans to strike China were now thwarted. Only yesterday, it seemed, the Japanese had signed treaties so the Soviet Union would cease to be their enemy. Yet now the Bear was up to its old tricks—and once again Sugihara was caught in the middle. On July 1, 1935, just three months after Manchukuo concludes the purchase agreement of the North Manchurian Railway, Sugihara's résumé notes the following: "He left his position at his own request." How much that "request" was forced must surely have been at least somewhat.

"It is generally believed that Sugihara quit his job in Manchuria and then returned to the Japanese Foreign Ministry because he did not like the way in which the Japanese army was controlling the Manchurian government," says Tadakazu Kasai, a friend of Sugihara's. "But I know that the Japanese army and military police suspected that Sugihara was working for Russia since he had very intimate relations with Russians in purchasing the North Manchurian Railroad and he had access to much information. He was sent back to Japan." Though Kasai has had no access to much "information" for years, he is evasive and censors himself in a demonstrative manner. Sugihara, Shimura, and Kasai all served in Manchuria together, alternating between civil servant, diplomat, and spy. Kasai was sent directly to Berlin in 1938, where he represented the Manchukuo government all through the war years. He and Sugihara met up there in 1940. Now Kasai is eighty-six; we spoke at his home in a suburb of Nagoya.

Kasai remembers Sugihara with fondness, as a generous person, eager to help and take care of others, loyal to his students, and loving his work. In Harbin, Sugihara hired Kasai for summer work. Like Sugihara, he came from Gifu Prefecture and graduated from the Harbin Gakuin. Sugihara even introduced him to his younger sister, the memory of which makes Kasai blush more than half a century later. But what most impressed Kasai was Sugihara's Russian fluency, his comfort with Russians, his intuitive sense of how to get along with them, his superb negotiating abilities, and the abundant warmth that he evoked in Russian circles. "I overheard two Russians arguing with such vehemence, but when I got closer I realized that it was actually no one other than Sugihara speaking animatedly with them," he recalls.

Kasai depicts Sugihara much as the colonialist who has "gone native," a man somewhat alienated from his fellow countrymen, and more devoted to his relations with White Russians and Jews around Harbin. "Sugihara had relations with Jews," Kasai confirms, though he does not remember the specifics. These connections probably enabled Sugihara to facilitate Manchukuo's purchase, with Japanese guarantees, of the North Manchurian Railroad from the Soviets. But in the end, his superiors were anything but grateful. Sugihara's excellent command of Russian and his coziness with the Russian side caused the Japanese military police to suspect Sugihara was double-dealing. The Russian wife didn't help; it was easy to imagine he was passing on even more valuable information to the Soviet side than he was receiving.

"Mr. Ohashi had a close relationship to the military in Manchuria," says Kasai, referring to Sugihara's boss. "When the military wanted to force out Sugihara, Ohashi did not stop it. I was once questioned by the police after attending a party at Sugihara's home. They wanted to know what was being discussed and who was there. I told them that we had conversations on ordinary topics."

In short, some of Sugihara's colleagues betrayed him; others lent him support. Even though he seems to have assessed the railroad's value in a very businesslike manner and concluded the deal at an advantageous cost to his government, none of this lifted him above suspicion. Perhaps his very *competence* was ground for resentment. Kasai makes it clear that Sugihara's independent-mindedness and trouble with superiors did not begin on a 1940 summer morning in Lithuania.

Japan and Germany: The Hollow Alliance

Gifu Prefecture already had a beachhead in Berlin when Tadakazu Kasai arrived there in 1938 as secretary in the Manchukuo Consulate. Colonel Hiroshi Oshima, born to one of the prefecture's most prominent families, was on his own fast track in the German capital since his arrival as military attaché in 1934. Indeed, he quickly developed close personal relationships with high-level Nazi officials—including Adolf Hitler. Having the "fraternal government of Japan" represented by such a prominent fellow Gifuite certainly helped the young, unworldly Kasai get settled in the German metropolis and promote the interests of the supposedly "independent state of Manchukuo." Whether it was primordial *han* sentiments that influenced the "Extraordinary Envoy" Oshima later to choose the no-longer-so-young man Sugihara from Gifu Prefecture for his most sensitive mission is not clear. But as we observe the complex relationships that develop between Japan and Germany and the bravado with which Oshima operated from his arrival in 1934 as military attaché, we begin to anticipate Sugihara's dispatch to Kaunas in 1939. At a critical point, the high-flying, daredevil Oshima, the most ardent promoter of Japan's alliance with Nazi Germany, while trying to remain credible to his new buddies in Nazi Berlin and influential in Tokyo, slipped. He needed help. He needed someone he could trust, as Sugihara would put it a few years later. He needed "new eyes."

Oshima, only six years older than Sugihara, was to German culture what

Sugihara was to Russian: expert and aficionado. The two hands were good at what they did and full of self-confidence in the presence of foreigners. But unlike Sugihara, Kasai, and Shimura, Oshima was born to a prominent wealthy family. The German and military connection went back at least a generation in the Oshima clan. His father, a contemporary of Shimpei Goto, was one of the first young Japanese students to attend the great universities of Prussia. Lieutenant General Ken-ichi Oshima traveled Europe extensively during his public career, which spanned the 1890s to World War II, and served in the highest military, civil, and imperial circles.

Hiroshi Oshima studied German in the military academies and Army Staff College and, like Sugihara, made an impression with his fluency.[44] In his first overseas assignment, Oshima was sent to the fledgling Weimar Republic, accompanied by Hideki Tojo and Tomoyuki Yamashita, later famous for the important roles they played in World War II. Oshima's personal relationship with these powerful military officers would prove highly useful when he arrived in Berlin in the thirties. Their support helped him successfully negotiate with the Nazis. He was the right man in the right place.

Oshima's instructions from Tokyo were clear; he was to determine Germany's likely stance should a second Russo-Japanese war break out. He also was ordered to establish cooperative intelligence efforts against the Soviet Union. Oshima was seeking a new partner to fight more effectively against the Soviet Union, as Sugihara, on the other border, was making efforts to remove an obstacle to peace. The great fear was fighting a two-front war, and the great trick was to catch others—particularly your enemies—in such a two-front war. This took considerable finesse.

Oshima seems to have made his debut in German society with the help of a German businessman named Friedrich Wilhelm Hack, who had served as an adviser to the South Manchurian Railway. At the time he met Oshima, Hack was using his Japan connections to peddle planes and weapons to the Japanese military. He was eager to introduce the new military attaché to his old friend Joachim von Ribbentrop, another rising star with particularly close ties to Hitler. After several meetings in Ribbentrop's drawing room, Oshima was brought to meet the Führer himself, who similarly took a quick liking to this exemplar of Oriental military virtue. I imagine the two discussing the values of *bushido* while listening to Wagner! Perhaps his admiration for Oshima, though, led Hitler to create the category of "honorary Aryan" with which to dignify Oshima and his people. However else Hitler would rationalize his deviations from Nazi racial theory, he seemed to like being photographed with his Japanese friend; perhaps he especially enjoyed how he towered over Oshima, by at least half a head!

Oshima cut quite a figure in Berlin. As one hostess said of him, "Colonel Hiroshi Oshima is as slick and smooth as an eel. . . , extremely intelligent, shrewd, and versatile. He repeatedly emphasizes the similarity of Japan's national ideology with that of Nazi Germany."[45] Soon he was making statements and writing enthusiastic articles on National Socialism and its New Order worthy of a Goebbels. German faith in Hitler, he wrote, "has brought afresh the great and phenomenal achievement; today over 80 million Germans—From the Meuse to the Memel, from the North and Baltic Seas to the Alps frontier—are really 'ein Volk und ein Reich,' great, strong, and invincible!"[46] Some years later, in April 1942, Goebbels himself would comment that "Oshima spoke extremely eloquently in favor of the Axis policies. He behaved very cleverly and tactfully. . . . A monument ought later to be erected in his honor in Germany."[47]

Oshima's diplomatic accomplishments paled beside his propagandistic feats, however. The more impressed he became by what he observed in Berlin, the less he seemed to understand the complex reactions that all this evoked in Tokyo. This becomes most apparent in 1936, with his efforts on behalf of the Anti-Comintern Pact, the German-Japanese Agreement against the Communist International. The pact had few teeth. It was very limited by secret protocols attached back in Tokyo, since some of Oshima's colleagues did not went to antagonize the United States and Great Britain. Indeed, the pact was a double failure. Ultimately, it did little to strengthen any Japanese-German alliance, plus it did not provide Japan a freer hand for completing its war in China by neutralizing Stalin with the fear of encirclement.

Besides, Stalin's spywork was too good. Once again, the German journalist Richard Sorge was able to penetrate high levels of Japanese circles and inform Stalin of Japan's limited backing for this pact. But FDR and the U.S. State Department took the Japanese-German alliance unduly seriously, and their resultant antagonism and threats weakened the position of the Japanese pro-U.S. faction. Oshima could thank America for indirectly strengthening his pro-German position.

Tokyo was not the only place where the Nazis roused ambivalence. The Japanese Embassy in Berlin itself was divided over alliances with the Nazis. Even Oshima's boss, Ambassador Shigenori Togo, was more pro–United States and Great Britain. By the fall of 1938, Oshima won the bureaucratic battle, though; he was made ambassador to Germany and Togo was given Moscow as a consolation prize. Togo and his German wife, Emily Gizaka, whom he married in 1922, left just before *Kristallnacht*. Her son Guido from a first marriage, a brilliant but emotionally unstable young architect, was institutionalized during their Berlin posting. The Nazi takeover of her beloved country and her son's condition threw her into an uncharacteristically deep depression.

The following year, in Moscow, the Togos received word from the German authorities that Guido was dead. His demise, the Germans said, was due to a "heart condition"; his cremated remains would be forwarded. Was Guido's death part of German experiments in killing off the handicapped at the end of the thirties? Such techniques would subsequently be used to murder Jews. Guido's death continues to be a family mystery nearly six decades later. Whether or not Togo himself had information or intuition that Guido might have been a victim of Nazi euthanasia is not known.[48] What is clearly remembered is Togo's hatred of the Nazis.

Remembering Guido, did Togo and his wife harbor any special sympathy for Jews as their "enemy's enemies"? Did this prompt them to be helpful when thousands of Jews with Sugihara's visa began to pass through Moscow in 1940 and months later, when Togo was back at the Tokyo *Gaimusho?* In his postwar memoirs, Togo claims to have expressed such sympathies. In 1936, a German-Jewish musician, Josef Rosenstock, was appointed the conductor of the Tokyo Philharmonic Orchestra. The German Embassy mounted an ongoing campaign to have the Japanese government dismiss him. Indeed, no less than Togo defends the Jewish musician's appointment.

And Sugihara? How is he conducting his own career? The files reveal the minimum, but one can read between the lines. On August 29, 1934, in the heat of the negotiations for the sale of the railroad, he receives a significant promotion to director of the Foreign Affairs Department of the Manchurian government. But whatever the basis of his success at that time, it is short-lived, as we have already learned. Sugihara "left his position at his own request," on the following first of July.

That same day he is registered as having returned to the Foreign Ministry, presumably that of Japan, where he is assigned to the Personnel section of the Minister's Secretariat. On July 7 he packs his bags and returns to Tokyo, arriving on July 15. On July 23, he receives still another assignment, "ordered to work for the section of Information Department," a department of the Foreign Ministry having more to do with intelligence, we suspect, than with public relations. This new assignment takes place just when the Comintern issues a statement condemning Japan for its aggression in China. He seems to be in Tokyo for the better part of 1935. On December 30, he and Klaudia are divorced, "by mutual agreement," as his résumé blandly puts it.

The Tokyo that Sugihara roamed, suddenly wifeless, was much different from the Tokyo of his Waseda University days, almost two decades before. It had been largely reconstructed after the devastating earthquake of 1923, and the political terrain had changed considerably, too. Shortly after Sugihara arrived, a group of young officers tried to take over the government. There had been political assassinations and attempted coups earlier in the decade, but this pointed to a new level of insubordination. The conflict between ministries and the military that Sugihara had to grapple with in Manchukuo was now plaguing the center.

As ever, the Japanese were wrestling with the question of Western influence, both inside and outside the country's borders. Out of Japan's total population of 65 million, the number of Westerners never exceeded 10,000 and of those not more than 900 were Jews of various nationalities. Most of those were Sefardim from places such as Baghdad, Bombay, and Shanghai. Some had arrived in Japan via Harbin and Manchukuo. Even among the newly arrived German Jews, some continued to represent the largest and most powerful German companies such as Krupp A.G., the infamous armament manufacturer that several years later worked to death thousands of Jewish slave laborers. As the relationship between Nazi Germany and Japan grew closer, the Japanese government became more attuned to Nazi antisemitism and, in some ways, more puzzled by it. Perhaps Jews were disagreeable, but why would a country turn them away, only to lose their talents, skills, wealth?

Coming Back from the Cold: New Discoveries in Tokyo

Sugihara's career unfolded between alliances and "nonaggression pacts" made and broken, between moments of cooperation and more frequent moments of deep distrust—between Germany and Japan, Germany and the USSR, and, as we shall see, bearing most on his Kaunas rescue of Jews, Japan and the Soviet Union. As I have stressed, most Japanese had little knowledge of Jews and received their basic information from the research of "Jew hands" such as Colonel Yasue, who conveyed all sorts of conflicting impressions. If the Jews are so disliked, the argument went, there must be something truly wrong with them.

At the same time, the Japanese were drawn to some of the gifted and resourceful Jews who were losing important positions in Germany and were leaving the country (like the new conductor of the Tokyo Philharmonic). At a time when Japan was rapidly industrializing, the availability of Jewish scientists, engineers, and entrepreneurs was a temptation. That the Germans were prepared to dispatch these Jews, for whatever reasons, was deemed by some Japanese as wasteful; it did not enhance the image of Germany among them.

Out of politeness to an ally rather than out of principle, the Japanese would sometimes gingerly comply with German efforts to boycott Jews and their products. Foreign record distributors, for example, would be asked to drop the recordings of Jews from Japanese distribution—until it was realized that the European musicians best known and honored in Japan were Jews. It is important to reiterate, however, that the Nazis usually encouraged Jewish emigration, even after the beginning of the war in 1939. There were profits to be made in transporting Jews, and Hitler was primarily concerned to be rid of them by whatever means. It was only at a later date that the Nazis would pressure their Japanese allies against sheltering Jewish refugees in Shanghai.

What might best reflect the curious attitude of the Japanese government comes to us allegedly from the pen of Yosuke Matsuoka, the most pro-Nazi of Japanese foreign ministers, in the fall of 1940. Significantly, this is precisely when Jews with Sugihara's visas were beginning to arrive in Japan en masse. At the end of 1940, Matsuoka reportedly wrote to a Jewish businessman, "True, I concluded a treaty with Hitler but I never promised him to be an antisemite. And this is not only my personal opinion but it is a principle of the entire Japanese Empire."[49]

A truly delightful memoir, written in 1971 for his grandchildren by a German Jew named Hans Straus, evokes the realities of Tokyo in the period preceding Pearl Harbor:

> "Excuse me, are you connected with the Jewish Consulate?" Hans Straus thought only for a split second and said, "Yes." I knew the Japanese could not imagine any group of people without proper and orderly representation. They knew that German Jews were no more covered by the German Consulate and therefore a Jewish Consulate was not so far-fetched. The caller on that day was a Mr. Suzuki of the Ministry of Interior.
>
> "We have a rather difficult case. There is a gentleman in Tokyo who is very sick. He is in the hospital but has no family to take care of him. Would you please make the necessary steps?" I asked, "Is he Jewish?" "Well, not exactly, he is a negro, if that interests you, and he plays the trumpet at the Florida Dance Hall. I am afraid he has tuberculosis. He says that Jamaica is his country. We contacted the British Consulate and they told us that they know the man who claims that he lost his passport, but they are not at all sure that he is a British subject. They rather rudely—I have to tell you—declined to take care of him and that is the reason why I am coming to you." I told Mr. Suzuki that the Jewish Consulate would be highly pleased to fulfill the wish of the Japanese Government whose charitable attitude towards wayward aliens we so greatly admire.[50]

Hans Straus was born in Würzburg, Germany, around the turn of the century, like Sugihara. As an employee of a German record company, he was sent to Japan in 1932 to deal with some trademark issues. The negotiations, to his good fortune, took longer than expected. Hitler came to power in January 1933. Rather than return to the threatening situation in his homeland, Straus decided to bring his wife and two sons to Japan. He became the adviser on Western classical music and export manager to a Japanese record company.

Two other German Jews in Tokyo, Ernst Baerwald and Henry Steinfeld, "decided to meet (with Straus) when the occasion demanded it and organized help." Baerwald, a native of Frankfurt, while fighting in the German Army in World War I, had fallen prisoner to the Japanese in China. Four years later he was freed, having developed a fascination with Japanese culture and Buddhism, and decided to stay. He represented I.G. Farben and continued to be a director long after the Nazis made the employment of Jews by German corporations strictly illegal. Unbelievably, the company, later convicted by the Nuremberg War Tribunal for its brutal exploitation of Jewish slave labor, was willing to retain a useful Jewish employee and director, at least at the beginning of the war.

Henry Steinfeld I know about only through a letter of his that I found in the *Gaimusho* archives from August 13, 1940, requesting visas for his brother Gideon and his wife, Reha, "both of Christian faith but Jewish parentage, [who] have found life in Germany under the present circumstances and for reasons well known to your Goodselves hard to bear." There he writes that he has been living in Japan for thirty-two years, assisted the Japanese army as an interpreter, has owned a house in Tokyo and a summer home in Chuzenji, and has represented for thirty-four years the same German trade company from which he "had to retire" recently. More tales from Straus:

By the year 1938 I had become quite well known among Japanese industrialists as a supplier of experienced—and inexpensive—man power. One day I got a call: Mr. Yamaguchi, the President of the Tottori Iron Works, requested my visit. Mr. Yamaguchi received me in his spacious office, surrounded by at least a dozen of his aides. I was duly impressed. Yamaguchi motioned me to be seated: "Mr. Straus, I have heard many good things about you—do you have an expert on armor-plating?" I looked straight at him: "Mr. Yamaguchi, I have the complete list of Jewish experts available in Germany and also in Shanghai, and if somebody would, indeed, have such an odd profession as an armor-plating expert, I would know it. I can assure you that we don't have such a man." Mr. Yamaguchi smiled: "I think we can help you. We have found in the library of the Imperial University in Tokyo a book on armor-plating written in the German language and published in Vienna in 1914. It was written by a man named Friedrich Ratsky. He is just the man we want to have." "Mr. Yamaguchi," I said, "I do not know whether Mr. Ratsky is alive or Jewish but I will try to find out."

Straus sent a telegram to the Jewish community of Vienna, now under German occupation, searching for Ratsky. "Four days later I had a reply from Vienna: 'Thanks for your utmost kindness, Friedrich Ratsky left Vienna for Trieste boarding steamer Hie Maru stop will arrive Yokohama hopefully on schedule.'" Straus describes how he returned to Yamaguchi's office. "You are a lucky man indeed. Not only is Mr. Ratsky alive and Jewish, but I have been authorized by him to negotiate an employment agreement with you." The Japanese industrialist offered a salary far more than what Straus could have imagined.

Straus next describes his surprise when receiving Ratsky with his "Tyrolean hat with a kind of huge shaving brush on top." As it turned out, the expert on armor plating was little more than an expert on padlocks. Before Straus could regain his composure and figure out how to salvage the situation, he noticed that Mr. Yamaguchi and at least twenty of his employees were waiting, all deeply bowing! The obliging Japanese employer had prepared comfortable housing including a "very pretty housekeeper for him," as Straus writes, as well as a Japanese language tutor.

Straus called a meeting of his colleagues in the "Jewish Consulate" to consult on how to handle the situation. Should they reveal to the steel company that the Jew it sought to hire was not really competent, or let the Japanese industrialists discover for themselves? Before they could decide what to do, Mr. Yamaguchi again called Straus. The Japanese Navy refused to allow the steel mill to employ a foreigner for the shipbuilding task at hand. Mr. Yamaguchi, shamefacedly, paid off Ratsky for his entire two-year contract before dismissing him.

The Viennese Jew hardly had enough time to celebrate his good fortune when a competing steel mill, with better connections in the navy, received approval to employ this foreigner and offered Ratsky a job. Straus pointed out to the company that Ratsky was not exactly competent. But they did not believe him. Again, before Ratsky could be put to the test in any way, the president of the second steel company approached him and paid him an enormous sum on his unfulfilled contract as severance fee. Mr. Fujimura informed Ratsky that while his company initially had received approval for his employment from the navy, when the first employer heard, it complained about the discrimination. And so he, too, was now forced by the navy to break his contract and would pay it up in advance. Ratsky made a generous contribution to the Jewish community and used the rest of the money to bring his extended family from Vienna.

In time, Straus would have a wide range of experiences in seeking em-

ployment, dealing with cultural misunderstandings, and mediating between government officials and newly arrived Jewish emigrants. Once, an
elegant but faded beauty of Central European origins came to introduce
herself to Straus. In her prime she had been a ballerina of some prominence, and Straus was duly impressed. Several weeks later, a police official
appeared at his doorstep. He asked Straus whether he knew Miss Goldberg:

"Yes I do. She had once been at our house." The police official continued:
"Mr. Straus, I do not want you to misunderstand me. I believe that we
Japanese are not—allow me to say—as narrow minded as you Westerners
sometimes are. We have much more understanding for human nature and
are less harsh than Christians of the West are." After additional hesitation,
the police official blurted out, "She is selling her charms as far as we can
make out." Straus said, "That's impossible! She is a homely old woman."
"Mr. Straus, tastes are different in this world and the honorable aged profes-
sors of the university don't share your opinion. And if Miss Goldberg, as I
said before, would restrict her business to the honorable elderly gentlemen—no objection. But recently, she has thrown her considerable charms
at the students and that is something about which we are concerned. Not
about the sexual aspects of the situation—in that we are not interested—but
we have to protect our young people from the dangerous ideas of undisci-
plined Western Democracy."

Again, Straus was able to settle the disagreement by convincing this
refugee to confine her attention to the senior faculty. Shortly after, Miss
Goldberg asked the Jewish Consulate for assistance in bringing over her
sister: "Does she—eh—practice the same profession?" the Jewish Consulate was eager to know. "Oh no, my sister is a dressmaker." The Jewish
leaders were delighted, there being a considerable demand for those skills
utilizing Western styles. As soon as she arrived, word about the new European dressmaker spread quickly. The most aristocratic women of Tokyo
came to be measured and commissioned new gowns for the New Year's
ball. The night before Christmas, the dressmaker's workshop burned
down with all the new gowns. The ladies of the diplomatic corps were
faced with the unbearable: to appear with last year's dresses at the Imperial Reception.

Sometimes, the experiences were not so amusing, as when the Jewish
leaders had reason to believe that a Jewish emigrant was being compelled
to spy for the Soviets. Through housing arrangements that the Jewish
leaders had made, this charge of the Jewish consulate became socially
close with the brother of Prince Fumimaro Konoe, the prime minister. "I
was flabbergasted," writes Straus.

The Jewish community lived a very precarious life. The Nazis tried their best to convince the Japanese that we were just a bunch of Communists and should be turned over to the military police for questioning. . . . And now, the Jewish committee had put a Soviet spy into the home of a Japanese family closely connected with the Prime Minister's family!

In desperation I rushed home to get together with Steinfeld and Baerwald, but they were both at a summer resort four hours away. I took the next train at nine o'clock in the evening. I met my friends. Baerwald just listened and then just said that he was taking the next train to Tokyo. Only later did we learn that that very night at three thirty in the morning he had the Prime Minister woken up, dragged out of bed, and told him the whole story—thus saving our group from disaster. The Jewish Consulate, as we can see, had good connections but was appropriately cautious.

The "Jewish Consulate" indeed did have good connections. While Ernst Baerwald was pulling Japanese prime ministers out of bed in the middle of the night to rescue them from Soviet spies, his brother, Paul Baerwald of New York, was involved in a different sort of rescue activity. As president of the American Joint Distribution Committee, the organization established by American Jews to coordinate refugee relief efforts, he received a letter from President Franklin D. Roosevelt, dated April 18, 1938:

The White House, Washington

My dear Mr. Baerwald:

The Government of the United States has invited a number of other governments to cooperate with it in the constitution of an International Committee charged with the responsibility of facilitating the emigration of political refugees from Germany and Austria. It has been my hope that this committee might be enabled to relieve in large measure the suffering and the distress of many thousands of persons emigrating from Germany and Austria and desirous of obtaining refuge in some other part of the world but who, if they were not assisted, would find themselves in most instances without funds and without documents of identity.

As stated in this Government's invitation, we do not propose any change in our existing immigration law. Furthermore, the cost of the work of relief must be borne through contributions obtained from nongovernmental sources.

In order that the people of the United States may be enabled most effectively to further the work to be undertaken by this International Committee, I am appointing an American committee to act as an intermediary between the International Committee and the many organizations within the United States which are dealing with this problem of political refugees.

Three months after Roosevelt's letter, Paul Baerwald was one of six American representatives at the Evian Conference, on the French side of Lake Geneva. Representatives of thirty-one countries met to discuss the resettlement of refugees persecuted because of their race, religion, or political convictions. But the conference was doomed to failure before it even started. The primary reason for this failure is suggested in FDR's letter; FDR and the State Department, by resisting any efforts "to propose any change in our existing immigration law," rendered those Jews trying to escape the Nazis as surplus population with nowhere to go. The pride that Baerwald felt in participating, as he wrote years later to his grandchildren, was not matched by significant rescue of endangered Jews; as such, he did little more than to lend tacit legitimization to the State Department's "do nothing" policies.

But Ernst Baerwald, at the "Jewish Consulate" in Tokyo, and other Jews in Tokyo, Yokohama, and Kobe were able to relieve the "suffering and distress," as FDR phrased it, of a measure of emigrating Jews. How their acts dovetail with Sugihara's it's hard to know. Certainly, though, Straus & Company evoked a helpful attitude on the part of the Japanese government. Admittedly, Sugihara was probably not acquainted with any German Jews of Tokyo in the brief period in which he resided there, but traveling as he did in government circles, he must have developed a sense that Nazi antisemitism was not an integral part of the German-Japanese alliance.

Sugihara may have observed that high officials, prepared to do all sorts of business with Hitler and harboring anti-Western sentiments of their own, still took Hitler's racial rantings with a grain of salt. Perhaps at that point, our "Information Department" official concluded that Japan was going to pursue an independent policy in regard to Jews. It would combine expressions of lofty ideals and practical considerations, emphasize Japan's publicly stated rejection of racial discrimination, and enlist Jewish influence and wealth in Japan's interest. Such a policy was not voiced consistently, and by all Japanese officials. The threat of "Jewish Communism" and general xenophobia prevented that, but, as Straus found out, the Japanese dealt with Jews in their own singular fashion.

On April 7, 1936, as his résumé matter-of-factly states, Sugihara remarried. Her name was Yukiko Kikuchi, and they met through her brother. At the time, this brother was a Tokyo insurance salesman who frequented the Foreign Ministry as part of his sales territory. One night he invited Sugihara, perhaps one of the livelier bureaucrats upon whom he was trying to impress the limits of mortality, home for dinner. There, he introduced his twenty-one-year-old sister, fourteen years Sugihara's junior. The Kikuchis were a well-educated family, modern in their ways.

Yukiko's parents, as she proudly tells me later, met playing tennis, quite unconventional for the time.

In 1990, she wrote her memoirs. Here she recalls her first impressions of her future husband: "In spite of it being the first meeting, he smiled. . . . Every time I asked some questions, unexpectedly, Chiune gave a joyful smile, looked at me directly, and answered with sincerity. . . . It seemed strange that he tries to talk to me in a sincere fashion, strange because in those days there weren't any men who listened to women nor did they take them seriously." Not very much time passed before Sugihara was expressing serious intentions, as well. When she asked him, "Why do you want to marry me?" Sugihara promptly responded, "Because you are a person whom I can take to foreign countries."

Keenly aware that "at that time, a love marriage was not easily allowed," she reflected more pragmatically that "marriage with an older man might provide more security for my future rather than a marriage with a young man." What, in fact, Yukiko felt for Chiune she does not say, and whether this was intensely a "love match" is not clear. She seems to have liked the idea of going abroad as a diplomat's wife, living, as she puts it, the "gorgeous life."

But Siberia hardly qualified as gorgeous. Chiune left the day after their wedding, on April 8, for the bleak cities of Petropavlovsk and Uska, as clerk of ministry affairs. Yukiko did not join him even if she was "the kind he could take to foreign countries." By mid-September, he left his post in Uska, returning to Tokyo for four days to attend the birth of his first son, Hiroki. Sugihara was now the father that Klaudia had never allowed him to be.

Instead of returning to Uska, he was sent to Hokkaido, the Japanese island closest to the maritime provinces of the Soviet Union. On December 26 he received another promotion, "second interpreter for embassies, seventh rank for high officials, Cabinet, fourth grade," with a salary of 1,300 yen. In the wake of Oshima's success in forging an Anti-Comintern agreement, if not the more comprehensive alliance that the Nazis wanted, Sugihara was ordered to work in the Soviet Union.

New Wanderings

It is difficult to reconcile the different reports of what Chiune was doing from the last days of 1936 through August 1937 and precisely where he stopped on the road to Kaunas. His two résumés state the situation quite clearly: December 26—Ordered to work in the Soviet Union." Three published and seemingly independent sources confirm the order; one seems to describe the fact. Yet for reasons that are decidedly cloudy, both

Yukiko and the Sugiharas' son, Hiroki, insist that he got nowhere near the Soviet Union.

Mrs. Sugihara remembers that, in 1937, her husband was to be posted in Moscow. That was only logical, for everyone was struck by his eloquence in Russian. "When he spoke Russian, his eyes would grow large and his face would change," she says. Intriguing use of image, this, for it seems Yukiko is proud to claim "not looking Japanese" even without the transformative powers of language. Her hair was wavy and almost brown, her eyes larger and lighter than those of most of her countrymen.

But somehow Sugihara did not go to the USSR. Perhaps *because* he could get around so well in a Russian ambiance, Yukiko suggests, the Soviet government stalled. It's hard to know quite what she means. And indeed, her memoirs conflict with *The Ministry of Foreign Affairs Report,* the internal yearbook of the *Gaimusho.* It contains two entries, describing in detail his appointments, promotions, and salary scales for the army and Ministry of Foreign Affairs. The first entry elusively states that he is "appointed as seventh rank, second lieutenant of the Army Infantry and the seventh degree high commissioner of the second degree interpreter at the embassy where he is presently on duty." The second entry indicates that he is "appointed to be second degree interpreter, receiving fourth grade salary, to hold office in the Soviet Union."[51]

But a listing that I discovered in the archives of the Soviet Ministry of Foreign Affairs curiously points to the presence of both Sugiharas in Moscow. In *Le Corps diplomatique au Moscou* for the end of 1936 and the beginning of 1937, Sugihara is listed, accompanied by his wife.[52] Strangely enough and in contrast with other listings for the diplomatic corps at this time in Moscow, the address of the Sugiharas is not included. The listing for July 1937 mentions Chiune, not Yukiko, and again, no address. By January 1938, there is no Sugihara. And still another source places him as the chancellor of the Japanese consulate in Petropavlovsk in 1936 and second interpreter in the embassy in Moscow, 1937–39.[53] These listings are sufficiently official and divergent in detail for us to assume that a simple mistake is not being transmitted to us in different versions.

During the years he was a colonial official—for the Japanese or for the Manchukuo government—there are indications that he visited the Soviet Union, as we have seen. The record shows he traveled around Soviet-controlled areas of Manchuria and Siberia, and Klaudia was quite specific about this. Sugihara's successful negotiations with the Soviets in the first half of the thirties aroused suspicions about him in his own country. Now Japanese-Soviet relations had become even more complicated and strained. Sugihara found himself caught—no surprise by now—between different factions.

Another man who found great power in slipping between diverse factions now enters our story. He was known as little more than Colonel R., or that "pesky Pole," as Walter Schellenberg, the head of Germany's Foreign Intelligence Services, called him, with the deference paid to a worthy opponent.[54] Sugihara seemingly never met him though Rybikowski certainly became a most important collaborator. My own association with Colonel R. began, colorfully, one morning in October 1994.

The phone rang. "I am Rybikowska," my caller exclaimed with a familiarity that I, scanning my memory embarrassed, simply could not reciprocate. Upon her insistence that I should intuit the significance of her call, embarrassment turned into annoyance. Suddenly I recalled that I had placed an author's inquiry in Polish newspapers around the world in the hope of finding non-Jewish Poles saved by Sugihara. I'd had more luck finding the Jews he'd rescued up until now. "Did you get a visa from Sugihara," I asked with renewed interest in my caller. "No, I did not." Terse, this woman.

Three days later a package arrived from Dr. Sophie Rybikowska of Montreal. In it were photos, high school graduation diplomas, military records, and personal letters of her late husband, Michal Rybikowski, better known as Colonel R.! But at the time this still did not mean much to me. Then I saw mention of a Polish battalion banner. It had been returned to Colonel R. by some of his agents via "a Japanese diplomat in Kovno." Now it was beginning to dawn on me. Sugihara had several personal assistants in Kovno who were Polish. I never understood why he had foreign nationals working for him but figured qualified Poles were easier to come by in Lithuania than Japanese.

In a few days I was off to Warsaw, armed with a letter from Dr. Rybikowska authorizing me to examine her husband's papers at the archives of Polish Military Intelligence. Judging from previous experiences in Eastern Europe, even after 1989, I had little confidence I would be let in. Quite the contrary, though. The director, his helpful archivists, and an efficient Xerox machine opened new vistas on the story of Sugihara. It seemed Schellenberg's "pesky Pole" had grown up near Kovno, at the juncture of Polish, Russian, Lithuanian, and Jewish cultures. Rybikowski became an ardent Polish nationalist. "I studied at University of Wilno (Stefan Batory University) history and civilization. This last [subject] is my main interest and this knowledge of civilization that helped me to understand and work closely with Japanese," as he wrote to a British professor in 1978.[55]

After World War I, Rybikowski joined the army of the reborn Polish state and studied at its military academy. He specialized in understanding "German behavior" and for a time was the head of that branch of Polish military intelligence specializing in spying on Germany. "This position gave me possibility to contact many Japanese which were those days in Poland," he writes.

In the late thirties, many Poles, including some high in government and military circles, were pro-Nazi. As Hitler made demands for territory, they sought the path to accommodation to preserve their own position and wealth. Rybikowski was among those military officers who were convinced that war with the Nazis was inevitable. But he was anything but pro-Nazi. He assiduously prepared for the impending occupation by organizing underground cells of resistance and even recruited informers in Germany itself.

To that end, he devised a cover as a somewhat jovial Latvian business-man, name of Peter Ivanov, who shuttled between Berlin, Scandinavia, and the Baltics. In about 1938, he set up a secret course for future leaders of the Polish underground, whose curriculum included basic elements of subversive action, clandestine radio communications, establishing net-works, the use of explosives, and whatever else promising young spies should know.

Among Rybikowski's star students was a Captain Alfons Jakubianiec, better known among his friends as "Kuba," who was militarily trained and, as Rybikowski proudly emphasizes, from a solid "patriotic upbring-ing." The disaster that had befallen Poland, for someone of Kuba's back-ground, merely illustrated the wisdom of the aphorism of Poland's *"Ronin,"* its unruly gentry: "For lack of order Poland stands." Even if Poland had not effectively resisted conquest, perhaps *because* it was not bound in the conventional order of other nations and states, it would ul-timately demonstrate some mysterious order and strength.

Colonel Rybikowski regarded his student Kuba as "a man meant to be working at a higher level of network building."[56] Apparently, Sugihara thought the same thing. In 1940, Jakubianiec and his friend Jan Stanisław Daszkiewicz received jobs in Sugihara's consulate in Kaunas, later follow-ing him to Berlin. Their association with Sugihara would contribute to the success of his rescue activities, but to understand how, we must ex-plore a bit more.

From Harbin to Helsinki

At the very same time that Kuba and Daszkiewicz are somewhere in Poland, in training for unknown contingencies, Sugihara was being groomed for something more than a consular secretary and interpreter. In 1938, a Japanese embassy official in Paris requests Sugihara for a special assignment, surrounded by secrecy.[57] Shortly after, he is dispatched to

Finland, although it's hard to pinpoint why. Finland was certainly an important listening post for goings-on in the Soviet Union, and there Sugihara could take advantage of "nordic neutrality" to spy on the Soviet Union and Nazi Germany.

After twelve years of marriage into a prominent White Russian family, Sugihara was surely the Japanese Foreign Ministry's expert on Slavic spy networks, now made more accessible in a neutral country. Outside Finland's borders, all sorts of liaisons could be made—the Poles and Japanese had a long history of working together against the Russian Bear. As we now know from Colonel Rybikowski, Polish intelligence was considerably better prepared for a German attack than the Polish Army. While that intelligence service's main base of Baltic operations at this time was in Sweden, Sugihara may have been establishing Finnish-based connections that would service him well in Kaunas.

My principle informant for Sugihara's posting in Finland is Yukiko. The Sugiharas had to take the long route from Japan to Finland, across oceans and, by rail, traversing the United States and then through Europe rather than passing through the Soviet Union. Remember, he had not been allowed to work in the USSR, albeit for murky reasons. For Yukiko, who brought her sister along to help with their baby, the journey was quite an eye-opener. Her memoir conveys the pain and pride of Japanese modernization and her own heightened self-consciousness.

On the German ocean liner *Bremen,* by then prominently flying a Nazi flag, Yukiko observes how plump, middle-aged European wives sunbathed on the deck during the day and in the evening dressed up lavishly, brandishing sparkling jewelry. The jewelry, Yukiko realizes, are heirlooms that European but not Japanese women receive. Still, she tries to make the best of this difficult situation, spending "most of the time in my kimono which I had brought from Japan." She was conspicuous because "I wore an especially gorgeous kimono. People came up to me and touched the sleeves all the time." It was not easy to dance in a kimono, nor chat with the others with her scant German, nor remain polite in the face of blithely racist questions. Why, some Europeans asked, was she not yellow?

Equally complicated were relations within the Helsinki embassy, as she discovered on her arrival. Minister Hideichi Sako had left his wife back in Japan and was all too eager to have Yukiko act as a substitute hostess at events. The young couple was on duty, as it were, every evening in the minister's residence, where they lived. In late 1938, though, Mr. Sako was transferred to Warsaw, a pivotal position for Japanese intelligence in Eastern Europe and fortuitously for Sugihara, perhaps a placement helpful to his own later activities in Kaunas. Upon Sako's departure, Sugihara became acting minister. "The post [as] the wife of the Acting Minister was too much for me," Yukiko admits. In addition to the taxing entertainment schedule, during that period she gave birth to their second son, Chiaki.

Yukiko also remembers something about Chiune that bears mentioning, if only for what it says about his character. In Helsinki, at age thirty-eight, he learned to drive. "Our driver used to be a principal of a driving school, so my husband decided to learn from him," Yukiko recalls. "Several days after he received his driver's license, the driver came to me and said, 'Our car was stolen.' My husband wasn't there. A few hours later we could hear the car coming into the Legation. As we hurried to the car, we saw my husband getting out of the car with satisfaction. Though he had gotten a driver's license, he usually had to sit quietly in the car while the driver drove. My husband, who really wanted to drive by himself, tried to drive at night secretly. It was his personality to always do what he wanted to do."

Most likely, Sugihara did what he wanted to do with spywork, too, though it was less the cloak-and-dagger variety and more through direct observation. The Japanese Legation had its share of spies. Yukiko suspected the White Russian wife of the second secretary, Mr. Izumi, who, she mentions in passing, was later "a friend of my husband." The woman was making suspiciously frequent trips to Switzerland, and later she was revealed to be a spy, though Izumi himself was eventually exposed to be a "great spy, probably greater than Sorge," as Yukiko says. This was the environment in which Japan's proficient Russophile spent 1938 and the first eight months of 1939.

Helsinki must have seemed familiar somehow to Sugihara. The Japanese had an affinity for Finns, who also had good reason to feel threatened by the neighboring Soviet Union. During the summer of 1939, Japan was fighting an undeclared war against the Soviets in Manchukuo. Sugihara paid careful attention to occasional statements, as from Leningrad party chief Andrei Zhdanov, that if the Germans were to attain any influence in Finland, the Soviet Union would deliver to Finland "such a crushing blow that the enemy will never again turn his eyes on Leningrad." Both the Japanese and the Finns, then, knew what the cost could be for not balancing alliances between the Germans and the Soviets.[58] The negotiations for territorial concessions that Stalin forced on the Finns and that led to Soviet attacks the following winter, shortly after the Sugiharas departed, showed the Japanese what could happen in Manchukuo.

Meanwhile, not far from frozen Helsinki, Ambassador Hiroshi Oshima in Berlin, usually "slick and smooth as an eel," was distinctly paralyzed. The Hollow Alliance grew even hollower as the Nazis grew more dissatisfied with the weaknesses in their 1936 agreement with Japan. They wanted the Japanese to keep the Soviets tied up while they conquered

Poland. But Oshima, squirming within the myriad of ambivalent forces back home, could not deliver the military alliance the Germans so desired.

By spring of 1939, Hitler knew he had to try another approach if the Reich were to stay on schedule. Oshima's friend and partner in designing the Anti-Comintern Pact, Ribbentrop, secretly began shuttling between Berlin and Moscow. Stalin, he discovered, wanted to take back parts of Poland that the tsarist government had lost, and he demanded the Baltics as a sweetener as well. Hitler agreed but countered by setting aside Lithuania as a geographic buffer between Nazi Germany and the Soviet Union. It was to be an independent state, a bargaining chip.

The Japanese were stunned by the August 23 Russo-German Pact. Did Hitler try to convey to Oshima, soon to return to Tokyo, that the pact was a tactical and temporary move and that he had other plans for the Communist regime? That we do not know. But what we do know is that Lithuania began to look more and more like the "Switzerland of the East" albeit one with many Jews and borders that were easier to cross. We also know that these developments finally pointed Sugihara on his way to Kovno.

Chapter 4

Roads to Kovno

"A City Full of Memories"

The Move

Sugihara speaks of his transfer from Helsinki to Kaunas in his 1967 letter to Dr. Roman Korab-Zabryk, an historian of the Polish underground:

> As future consul in Kovno, where there were no army detachments at all, I soon realized that my major task would be to provide the General Staff [of the Imperial Japanese Army], and not the Ministry, all information based on events and rumours regarding the Lithuanian-German occupied border regions, and any indications regarding the end of the [Nazi-Soviet Nonaggression] treaty and preparations by the German armies to attack the USSR. We needed new eyes in Lithuania.

In the last days of summer and the first days of autumn 1939, when the Sugiharas were moving to Kaunas, there was much other movement throughout the world. Leaders were shifting their nations out of old pacts and into new alliances, and refugees were resurfacing wherever they could. In Eastern Europe, some Poles were fleeing the Nazis, some the Soviets, while the Jews among them knew they had to escape both. At first, Lithuania seemed like a safe haven, or so many on Sugihara's list must have hoped. There are the Zells and the Warhaftigs, Irene Dynenson and her family and Irene Malowist and hers, Victor Erlich, the secular socialist, and Ben Fishoff, the pious Yeshiva student. And Moe Beckelman, however he got there from the Bronx. Michal Rybikowski, a.k.a. Colonel R., a.k.a. Peter Ivanov, was also in Lithuania in those days, a long curved feather in his green felt hat, a warm, carefree smile on his face, a forged Latvian passport stashed in his breast pocket.

Japan and the Baltic states had established good relations in the interwar period, given their common enemy, the Soviet Union. At Versailles, the Baltics had been ceded their independence from the crumbling tsarist empire, but these small states, caught between empires, had not emerged as centers of significant political or economic activity in the years between World War I and World War II. Now, with international tensions reaching higher levels, it was hard to know whether they could ultimately retain their independence. Though their political viability was questionable, their strategic location was not. The United States, though it had maintained a low-level office in Kaunas since the early days of Lithuanian independence, was represented through Riga, Latvia. It was only about two years earlier that this changed with the appointment of Owen J. C. Norem, who presented his credentials as Envoy Extraordinary and Minister Plenipotentiary.[1]

Sugihara's transfer had been in the works for at least two months, probably longer. Shojiro Ohtaka, the Japanese consul general in Riga, handled the initial negotiations. On July 12, 1940, Ohtaka was reporting to Foreign Minister Arita in Tokyo on his discussions with the Lithuanian government to create a consulate in Kaunas, the capital. In the *Gaimusho* there seems to have been concern over whether this new post required a full professional diplomat or merely an honorary representative. Several other countries employed the latter in Kaunas; a Japanese citizen who happened to live in Lithuania, for example, or perhaps even a Lithuanian citizen who had ties to Japan could perform an ambassadorial role. Whatever reason there might have been for keeping things low-key without insulting the Lithuanians, Chiune Sugihara was a good compromise—not a full diplomat, yet not a regular civilian either. Except for the short transitional period in Helsinki when he was acting consul, his appointments had been in the secretary and interpreter categories.

But even if Sugihara were being sent to do more than sign a few visas and organize Japanese-Lithuanian cultural exchanges, assigning him the title "vice consul" would provide just the right cover, plus the Personnel

Office at the *Gaimusho* could be placated as well. No matter how dire the circumstances for posting Sugihara, it would look disapprovingly upon this nonelite Foreign Ministry employee, with no Tokyo University degrees, making an unacceptable professional leap to ambassador.

On August 2, 1939, the Lithuanian government gave its approval to the *Gaimusho*'s candidate, and on that day, the Japanese consul general in Riga notified Foreign Minister Arita that "The Lithuanian government permits us to send Sugihara as consul."[2] Sugihara was still busy at work in Helsinki gathering intelligence and filing his frequent reports. As late as July 21, he sent off two reports on "Western Politics." On August 9, Ohtaka could reassure his boss in Tokyo that he would have the appointment ratified by the Lithuanians in writing.[3] By September 2, Sugihara had taken up his new post. On September 14, he sent a progress report to Ohtaka in Riga and Arita in Tokyo. The new vice consul to Lithuania was becoming not only visible but, through the literary genre of the diplomatic cable, vocal: "It is very difficult to find houses here," he writes. "I was working in the hotel for a while, but it is very inconvenient, and also the Foreign Ministry of Lithuania want us to open the consulate formally."

With refugees streaming into Kaunas, Sugihara was not exaggerating his housing problems. The cable continues:

> I searched hard for a house and finally found one. It is at the Eastern part of the city near the houses of many ambassadors. It is three stories and we can rent the first and second floors. . . . This is the only house we can find here. . . . The owner said that there is another person who wants to rent this house so he wants our answer before the 19th of August [September, more likely]. Please respond as soon as possible as to whether or not we should rent this house.

Sugihara enclosed the architectural plans for the proposed chancellory.[4] Three days later, Ohtaka sent a letter to the *Gaimusho* following up on Sugihara's request.

> Consul Sugihara wants to open the consulate on 20th September if there is no problem with you. Expenditures will be 20,000 lit, Lithuanian currency (about 870 English pounds). This does not include the payment for the safe, Japanese and Western tableware, and decorations. To open the consulate, we need a telegram code and a safe for telegrams. So I would like to send Sugihara to Berlin to receive some codes from the Embassy in Berlin and to buy a safe for telegrams which costs about 50 pounds. Please permit his official trip.[5]

In subsequent cables, Sugihara preserves the record of his move and the establishment of this new consulate, down to the last detail. But all this minutiae sheds little light on why, in the war's early days, this was taking place. Why a new Japanese diplomatic post in the backwaters of Lithuania and why Chiune Sugihara? What did the Japanese hope these "new eyes" would see?

The Polish Connection

To answer these questions, I plowed through hundreds of diplomatic cables, plus Sugihara's letter to Dr. Korab-Zabryk. I also visited Dr. Korab-Zabryk, now an octogenarian, in his tiny Soviet-style apartment in Warsaw. It is a chilly day in November 1994. The markings of austerity indicate, if nothing else, that this survivor of nearly forty-five years of communism, a regime that rewarded those intellectuals upon whom it could rely, was not to be bought.

In the 1960s, Korab-Zabryk searched for and identified Japan's first and only consul to Kaunas. It was no easy task. The Communist rulers at the time were inconsistent in their attitudes toward the World War II Polish underground, at times heating up old rivalries, making out of some heroes, others criminals. Though it was not his primary intention to seek out Sugihara, raising the Jewish issue was doubly risky. The extent to which the Polish underground and government-in-exile assisted Polish Jews was a matter of controversy when Korab-Zabryk searched for Sugihara, as it continues to be to this day.[6] Furthermore, in the Warsaw of 1967 and 1968, when Korab-Zabryk was trying to document what went on in the Kaunas of 1939 and 1940, another "old fighter" of the Polish underground, Mieczyslaw Moczar, was leading an antisemitic campaign to eliminate the very few Jews still remaining in Poland.

As it turned out, Korab-Zabryk did not have far to search for Sugihara. "I first met him in the lobby of the Hotel Ukraine in Moscow some time in the sixties," he told me. "He was part of a Japanese trade delegation living in Moscow at the time. He had changed his name to Sempo Sugiwara." The Polish savant explains that this is another possible reading of the Japanese characters representing his names. "For the future, please use these names when writing to me," Sugihara/Sugiwara writes to Korab-Zabryk, on July 21, 1967. He actually seems to have worried that his rescue of Jews in Kovno would be discovered in the Soviet Union and that the negative responses to his past would jeopardize the only job, after World War II, that provided him with a modicum of dignity.[7] "I always had a feeling that he was an unhappy man," Korab-Zabryk recalls.

The historian asked the former diplomat seven questions about his interaction during the war with Polish intelligence officers. He wanted to know how they maintained an intricate international network of spies, how they kept themselves and others informed of what was going on in their occupied country, and how they paid their way with the Allies by plying them with reliable and valuable war secrets. Sugihara responded in Russian, question by question. Because of Korab-Zabryk's perseverance, we have part of Sugihara's story in his own words:

In the autumn of 1939, I opened the first Japanese consulate in Kovno, at that time the temporary capital of the bourgeois Lithuanian republic, following the orders of the Japanese Foreign Ministry. Although there was a Japanese embassy in Riga, this consulate came under the direct authority of the Foreign Ministry and there were no relations whatsoever with the embassy in Riga. As you already wrote, the ambassador of the Riga embassy was Mr. Ohtaka but in Kovno there was only me. It is well known that during these few years prior to the Second World War, one could observe an extremely active and fanatic movement among young officers belonging to the Japanese General Staff who desired to establish more intimate relations with the German fascist army. One of the active leaders of this movement was the Japanese ambassador in Berlin, H. Oshima, who was a lieutenant-general in the Japanese army.

To some extent, General Oshima had influenced the conclusion of the Triple Military Pact between Japan, Nazi Germany, and fascist Italy and apparently he had been warned beforehand by Hitler regarding Germany's intention to attack the USSR in the near future. Since General Oshima was not completely sure about the correctness of Hitler's information he wanted to check it himself and as he was jointly responsible for said pact, he was also concerned about: "Did the German army really want to attack the USSR?" The matter was such, in view of the apparent attack by the Germans on the USSR from the west, the Japanese General Staff was extremely interested to transfer as quickly as possible the best part of the Japanese army in Manchuria, near the USSR-Manchu border, to the southern islands in the Pacific Ocean.

My consulate's main task was to rapidly and accurately determine the time of the German attack. It became clear to me that this was the reason why the Japanese General Staff had urged the Japanese Foreign Ministry to open a consulate in Kovno. . . . The circumstances made it clear to me . . . that Hitler did not want to inform General Oshima regarding the detailed military plans. . . .

One year later, on 31st August 1940, I was ordered to close the consulate upon a suggestion made by the new Lithuanian authorities. On 31st August, I left Kovno, a city full of memories, as my late third son was born there, taking with me the consular properties, documents and my family and I travelled to Berlin.

The tone of the letter is more melancholic than nostalgic. "Kovno has been a city full of memories," Sugihara writes, not because of the "gorgeous life," as his wife called their diplomatic lifestyle, or the lives he saved with his visas, but his son, Haruki, who would die nine years later. The Sugiharas seem to think it was the chaotic times of his birth that weakened the boy and made him susceptible to the leukemia that eventually killed him. "After the war I did my best to forget the past," writes Sugihara.

What is so immediately striking about this letter is the complex sponsorship of Sugihara's mission and the intricate lines of reporting. He tells about the involvement of Ohtaka in Riga but makes clear that he reported directly to Tokyo. He speaks of the Japanese Foreign Ministry, for which he works, but emphatically claims that other agencies had the actual stake in his placement at this seemingly insignificant outpost. What appeared a routine posting soon revealed itself to be something quite iconoclastic.

Sugihara's selection as these "new eyes" should not be surprising. We have seen how he and his colleagues were trained for the dual roles of diplomat and spy. What seems to have upset Sugihara as he became settled in Kaunas was the realization of whom he was working for: the "extremely active and fanatic movement among young officers belonging to the Japanese General Staff who desired to establish more intimate relations with the German fascist army," he writes. In other words, Japan's pro-Nazi faction and its leader, Sugihara's fellow Gifuite, General/Ambassador Hiroshi Oshima. Is Oshima the force behind the creation of the new Kaunas post? If so, the irony is almost too exquisite. For Sugihara actually claims that he, mass rescuer of Jews during World War II, was in fact supposed to be assisting the most rabid pro-Nazi faction of his country.

I set to puzzling this out. First of all, the archives are silent about Oshima's involvement in establishing the consulate in Lithuania. And other than the September 1939 trip that Sugihara allegedly took to Berlin to purchase a safe deposit box and to pick up codes at the Japanese Embassy, we know of no contact between Sugihara and Oshima during this *initial* period of his assignment. In fact, Oshima was in Tokyo and *not* in Berlin for most of the time that Sugihara was in Kaunas. Even if Sugihara's memories are reliable, even if out of historical sequence, what his writing does convey is the emotional background for Japanese-German relations. It is certainly a "hollow alliance" at this moment, full of desperation and distrust.

It seems Sugihara had to provide information to members of certain elite coteries who were sharply in conflict with other elite coteries. Those whom he was servicing were in the army but also in the Foreign Ministry; the members of each branch were staking their careers and the security of their country on the intentions and assurances of an inscrutable foreign leader, Adolf Hitler. They were speculating on the opportunities that his plans would provide for Japan, and most were advocating a stronger alliance with Nazi Germany. They must have been mercurial masters for the new vice consul.

Indeed, by late summer 1939, as the Sugiharas were packing their bags in Helsinki, the Japanese Army, which had become so powerful in its country's politics, was sinking into deeper and more serious trouble. Its most visible officer, Oshima, who had charmed his way into the highest Nazi circles, could no longer slide out of multiple troubles. More than a million Japanese troops were tied up in what seemed a never-ending war in China, a war that was also severely complicating Japan's relations with other countries. The United States was threatening sanctions that could jeopardize Japan's vital supplies. The Soviet Union, China's most important ally, was less favorably disposed to resolve its conflicts with Japan. Border skirmishes in the Nomonhan area of Manchuria also threatened to escalate into the much-fretted-over second Russo-Japanese war. Everywhere it looked, Japan was beset.

Meanwhile, German Foreign Minister Ribbentrop, Hitler's favorite, was trying to strengthen the 1936 Anti-Comintern Pact. The Nazi leaders so much wanted to conclude an expanded agreement with Japan before they began their push for *Lebensraum,* territorial quest in Poland and points east. This agreement, if it could be passed, would encircle the Soviet Union. It would provide the basis for a Berlin-Tokyo and a Berlin-Rome axis. In exchange, Oshima wanted his Nazi friends to support his country's policy in China, stressing Japan's and Germany's mutual animosity toward communism.

Neither side gave, though. Hitler was quickly losing patience with Japan, with its intrigues behind the scenes, its coups in the street, and its endless political dickering in the cabinet and Diet. He disdained Emperor Hirohito's perceived lack of authority, and the fact that Japanese generals could not enforce their decisions. Besides, with Chinese and Soviet border skirmishes, Japan was too tied up to behave like a valuable ally. Hitler had shared his vision of New Orders with Oshima, supporting Japan in its efforts to legitimate Manchukuo and defy the League of Nations, much as Germany had done. But could Hitler rely on Japan as a partner when he controlled Central and Western Europe? Would Japan be able to run Europe's Far Eastern colonies? Having just devoured juicy morsels of Czechoslovakia, Hitler wanted to stay on schedule. But Japan was a military as well as a political disappointment. It was demonstrating scant ability to pin down Soviet forces in Manchuria, which thus failed to leave Germany a free hand in Central Europe. Hitler had to find some other arrangement.

There is evidence that Ambassador Oshima had an inkling that an "unthinkable" Nazi-Soviet rapprochement was being discussed; other diplomats seemed to pick up such intimations.[8] When Ribbentrop actually raised the suggestion in May, Oshima sulked and refused to listen. He is reported to have said that such talk, even in jest, would end their friendship. Such a threat evidently did not nettle Ribbentrop. The German foreign minister preserved the friendship but simply stopped informing Oshima of his negotiations with the Soviet Union.

Then again, perhaps Oshima really *did* know about Hitler's short-term plans. Japan, in fact, with its special relationship to Poland, was trying to negotiate a German-Polish agreement to the last minute to stave off Hitler's invasion.[9] Could it be that Hitler was already discussing with Oshima his plans to eliminate the "Bolshevik-Jewish Empire," thus trying to convince his Japanese friend that the pending agreement with Stalin was nothing more than a temporary tactical move?[10] Was Oshima trying to pressure the Japanese who wanted their country to improve relations with the United States and Western Europe with these threats of Nazi-Soviet détente? Was Oshima trying to convince factions of the army, the navy, ministers and Diet members that the real stake in tightening alliances with the Nazis was preventing the Soviet Union from moving its best troops, heretofore pinned down on the Western front, into Manchuria exactly when border skirmishes between the Soviet Union and Japan were intensifying?[11]

Sugihara's indication that "the Japanese General Staff was extremely interested to transfer as quickly as possible the best part of the Japanese army in Manchuria, near the USSR-Manchu border, to the southern islands in the Pacific Ocean" suggests another selling point of Oshima's. With the weakening of Western Europe's hold on oil-rich colonies in the south, such as the Dutch East Indies, Japan would be far less vulnerable to U.S. pressures. Was Sugihara, in his letter, a bit confused in his geography? Was he imagining the oil fields of the Dutch East Indies a bit to the east of where they are located, or was he accurately conveying contingency plans for a more "determined," a more bold confrontation against the United States in "southern islands of the Pacific Ocean" should the United States interfere with Japan's supply lines? Was Sugihara in Kaunas to provide intelligence for an early feasibility study of Pearl Harbor?

Sugihara may be providing us with a report, more accurate and insightful than we might have guessed, on Oshima's thoughts and activities at the time. Whatever was going on between Oshima and Hitler, it is clear that Hitler proceeded with his plans. The Führer also urged his military commanders to maintain "secrecy . . . even from Italy and Japan." Such subterfuge made Sugihara's posting to Lithuania even more vital. Oshima wanted him to observe whether Nazi military planning against its new Soviet "ally" was proceeding as Hitler promised Oshima it would. Having staked his career and the security of his country on Hitler's actions, Oshima needed Sugihara badly.

In ways no one could anticipate, Japan did help Germany prepare for its attack on Poland. On August 20, the Soviets, having lost patience with Japan and its border skirmishes, launched an offensive against the Japanese in Manchuria. At the same time, fearing a two-front war, the Soviets signaled to Ribbentrop that they were now ready to seriously negotiate an agreement. Hitler, altogether delighted, is alleged to have said, "Now I have the world in my pocket!" Not one to be too disturbed about his breach of the 1936 Anti-Comitern Pact with Japan, Hitler expressed an extra measure of satisfaction in outmaneuvering that country: "I have found that Japan does not go with us without conditions. . . . Let us think of ourselves as masters and consider these people at best as lacquered half-monkeys who need to feel the knout." So much for "Honorary Aryans."[12]

Whether Oshima was truly shocked by the announcement of the Soviet-Nazi nonaggression pact or knew it was coming, he obligingly offered Foreign Minister Arita his resignation. Arita did not have the time to consider whether or not he should take too literally Oshima's gesture of ritualized contrition, for he would shortly resign too. The cabinet, with its close ties to the military, fell on August 28 as Japanese citizens angrily reacted to Germany's betrayal. On August 30, Nobuyuki Abe, who had more moderate army ties, became prime minister and acted as foreign minister for a month until he could find a replacement for Arita.

By the end of September 1939, Oshima was on his way back to Tokyo, joined by the sacked Japanese ambassador to Italy. Notwithstanding the unhappy circumstances that led to his resignation, Oshima was warmly sent off from Berlin with Ribbentrop himself asking the Japanese government to place his friend in some position where he could contribute to the improvement of Japanese-German relations. From the winter of 1939 to the winter of 1940, when he was reappointed ambassador to Berlin, Oshima addressed many Japanese audiences about the importance of the Japanese-German alliance. And when he wanted to communicate with his Nazi buddies back in Berlin, it was alleged, he would simply go over to the German Embassy in Tokyo, where he was afforded German ciphering services. Having left his man behind in Kaunas, Oshima was better able to operate in Tokyo. Nevertheless, through much of the period that Sugihara worked in Kaunas, German-Japanese relations palpably cooled. For a while, Japan cast about for other alliances—even rapprochement with the United States was not out of the question.

The Japanese felt yet another loss from their now hollower alliance with the Germans. Part of the deal that Oshima tried to strike with the Nazis was to share intelligence on the Soviets. Now that source had pretty much dried up, and at the crucial moment. Japan needed another outlet. The logical substitute was Poland, with whom the Japanese had a long-standing, fruitful relationship, as we have touched upon.

Shocked as they were by the Nazi-Soviet pact, the Japanese did benefit from one of the pact's "secret protocols." They were losing miserably to the Soviets in the "undeclared war" on the Manchurian border, in part because of poor intelligence. On September 15, the Soviets inexplicably called for a cease-fire. Two days later, Foreign Minister Molotov announced: "Events arising out of the Polish-German war have revealed the internal insolvency and obvious impotence of the Polish State. . . . The population of Poland have been abandoned by their ill-starred leaders to their fate. The Polish State and its Government have virtually ceased to exist. In view of this state of affairs, treaties concluded between the Soviet Union and Poland have ceased to operate."[13] The Soviets had averted a two-front war, and Poland would suffer accordingly. The Japanese, although sorry for their Polish friends, were relieved that those Soviet tanks, now moving through eastern Poland, were not plowing through western Manchuria. Poland was again divided and annexed, and Poland's Jews, as ever, were being assaulted from *all* sides.

The View from Vaizgantas Street

On October 17, 1939, Vice Consul Chiune Sugihara was settling in at his quarters on 30 Vaizgantas Street. Within just a few weeks, he completed the move from Helsinki to Kaunas, relocated his family, procured codes and a safe from Berlin, and presented his credentials to the Lithuanian government. And now he had succeeded in finding such an ideal location—good garden, nice views—and was ready to open the doors of Japan's first consulate in Kaunas.

These were no small accomplishments, considering the tumble of recent events. It was only a month and a half since the Nazi blitzkrieg against Poland had begun. The world—and Japan's relationship within that world—had been transformed. France was connected by treaties to Poland and, with England, decided that appeasement would not work with Hitler. America continued to assert its neutrality. The Nazis halted their conquest in Eastern Europe at the Bug River for the time being, just a few miles west from where Sugihara now lived. A few miles east, the

Soviets were completing their mop-up operations, the Nazis having given them free reign under the Nazi-Soviet pact. "Independent Lithuania" was encircled.

Remarkably, Sugihara's Lithuanian neighbors seemed less worried about recent events than he would have expected. While surrounded by two predatory countries, now actively carving up and devouring a third, rumors circulated around Kaunas that Poland's tragedy would gleam a silver lining for Lithuania. Little love was lost between Lithuanians and Poles. They did not even have full diplomatic relations, though the two countries shared a union going back to the fifteenth century. Vilnius, which had been the capital of Lithuania centuries ago, was captured by Poland shortly after World War I when both countries gained their independence from the Russian Empire. Now, talk on the street was that the Soviet Union was going to return now-Polish Vilna to the Lithuanians, making it Vilnius once again. A minor favor was asked of the Lithuanians for this grand gesture of historical rectification: it must allow in twenty-five thousand Red Army troops.

For years, it was Sugihara's special responsibility to interpret Soviet activities to his government. As of late, especially in Helsinki, he had developed a "subspecialty," reading between the lines of these manifold "nonaggression" agreements and reporting the implications for Japan. Inevitably, there would be various "secret protocols," yet through his special connections, he tried to pin them down. But back in Tokyo, governments were falling, politicians were making and breaking their careers, ministries and the military were divided, all because of the pacts.

Should Japan finally seek an agreement with the Soviets? Should Hitler's friend and Sugihara's compatriot, Ambassador General Oshima, slip back into Berlin and conclude the pact that Hitler had been seeking for three years, even if it might lead to open conflict with England, France, Holland—even the United States? Perhaps Japan's estrangement from the Nazis could be turned to advantage. As Sugihara observed, so much had changed since September 1 and the Nazi-Soviet attacks on Poland. Under the new circumstances, could public opinion in FDR's isolationist America, so negative to Japan at least since the Manchurian Incident, be made more favorable? Sugihara was the "new eyes," sitting at the explosive point where "nonaggressors" were meeting. What should Sugihara's advice be?

In the course of trying to discern the pacts and spy for his country, Sugihara tapped into the Polish underground, inheritors of the legacy of Josef Pilsudski from a quarter-century ago. It started at a party at the "neutral" Swedish consulate, down Vaizgantas Street. Sugihara needed to better staff his own consulate and made some inquiries about the help problem in town. He was looking for a valet, in particular. A referral was made—a young Pole named Boleslav Rozyki.[14] Thereafter, Sugihara seemed to hire Poles, ending up with a staff peculiarly overtrained to be butlers, drivers, and secretaries. They became highly skilled at bringing him information. though as we shall see, they grew just as adept at spying on their employer, too.

One of Sugihara's staffers who strengthened this "Polish connection" was Lieutenant Stanisław Daszkiewicz, from Colonel Rybikowski's circles in the Polish underground. Daszkiewicz's 1948 memoirs, recently discovered in the archives of the Polish military intelligence in Warsaw, detail his espionage activities, first behind Lithuanian, then behind Soviet lines, and the beginning of his work for Sugihara in Kaunas. After Poland fell, Daszkiewicz escaped the Nazis by crossing the Lithuanian-Polish border. But soon he had to hide from Soviet troops who were rounding up Polish military officers, most of whom were never heard from again. With the help of Poles who were Lithuanian citizens, he obtained fake papers for the name Jan Stanisław Perz. Here is a telling passage:

> After a few days in Kovno, I went to Vilnius illegally. I went to the town hall and asked the local official to destroy the papers of persons who held high positions before the war. Two ladies at the office were assigned the task of manipulating the registration cards of the refugees. I carried on the increase of the contact network and set about penetrating the Soviet agent network.

Daszkiewicz soon returned to Kaunas, where he made contact with the British Consulate. He quickly began to practice the espionage skills he had learned in Rybikowski's spy school before the German conquest of his country.

> I established contact with Captain Alfons Jakubianiec (pseudonym Kuba). He helped me obtain a job in the Polish Affairs Department since I knew the region and the people coming in and out. We gathered intelligence, issued certificates, forged documents. Field work was getting more intensive due to rumors that either Germany or Russia was going to take over Lithuania. I received much information from the secretary of the Finnish consulate. The Finnish consul himself was well-disposed toward the Poles and offered much information about German movements.

This was precisely the type of information that Sugihara needed for Tokyo. One wonders, therefore, whether his Polish connections begin with the hiring of a valet, or earlier? In view of Sugihara's Finnish connections, was he, too, receiving information from the Finnish consulate? In that murky world of espionage, all sorts of connections might have been possible. In his own memoirs, Rybikowski writes about his visits to

Kaunas and his efforts to make connections with his star protégés. Even within this small Polish underground, they feigned not knowing each other for fear of counterspies; indeed, he and Jakubianiec made sure to walk on opposite sides of the street. It was vital for someone they trusted to get romantically involved with a chambermaid, so that she might provide an empty hotel room for a quick meeting and exchange of information. If it was not safe to talk, they could at least leave an encoded message scratched on the bottom of a desk drawer.

After passing through Kaunas in October with a side trip to the newly annexed Vilnius, Rybikowski moved on to Paris. This was the first base of operation of the Polish government-in-exile, until France also fell to the Germans, in May 1940. Then the base moved to London. Around February 1940, under whatever guise, Colonel Rybikowski made another trip to Kaunas. His contacts with Kuba "revealed leaks and the necessity of further descent into secrecy," he writes. On the other hand, he was delighted to observe that "Kuba's cooperation with the local Japanese consul, Sugihara, was proceeding very well." He adds, "Sugihara had great respect for him, and valued his courage, inventiveness, and initiative. This made me very glad because I know that the Japanese are very stern and demanding in relation to their surroundings."

By the spring of 1940, Col. R. was back in Riga establishing his "permanent headquarters" there "with the local Japanese military attaché." This "permanency" lasted only three months, until the Soviets took over Latvia on June 15. Rybikowski then inserted himself in the Stockholm office of the Japanese ambassador to Sweden, General Makoto Onodera. Onodera was Japan's spymaster for Europe and part of a pro-American faction back home. Before Pearl Harbor—even after!—he tried to promote an alliance between Japan and the West. Some of the most valuable secrets of the war were exchanged here in Stockholm, thanks to Rybikowski and Onodera.

With the arrival of Sugihara, Rybikowski claims, Kaunas became a well-established point, even a hub, for Rybikowski's greater espionage and resistance plans. The network stretched from Rome and Lisbon through London, Paris, Berlin, Stockholm, Warsaw, Białystok, and Kaunas to Moscow, and then to Tokyo using Japanese diplomatic couriers. "The plan involved a slow progressive penetration of Germany while maintaining contact with Warsaw," explains Col. R.

We are more than a bit startled and confused: Could it be that an indiscretion at a cocktail party in Kaunas led the "small Japanese consul" to an embroilment with big Polish spies? Or did Sugihara intend to hire Polish spies, only saying he needed consular "help" to draw them in? In that case, did he betray his original backers, the pro-Nazi faction, by serving the pro–West faction instead? As a rescuer of Poles, including Polish Jews, can we still believe Sugihara that he alone made this virtuous decision, or should we follow Rybikowski's lead and examine Sugihara's role in some higher level of Polish-Japanese cooperation?

Let's identify "higher level," first of all. Rybikowski mentions several top Japanese military officers such as General Kiichiro Higuchi, Army General Staff second bureau chief in Manchukuo, and Lieutenant General Masataka Yamawaki, vice minister of war. Higuchi and Yamawaki may have been anti-Nazi.[15] They may also have harbored warm feelings toward their old ally Poland, perhaps even for Polish Jews, with nostalgic memories from visits to Poland in their cadet years. Higuchi even rescued a trainload of nearly frozen Jewish refugees who had been stranded on the Manchukuo border in late 1938.[16] The two may have maintained relations with military and intelligence officers such as Rybikowski or at least remembered them well enough to initiate or respond to proposals for collaboration. Sugihara may have been selected as the perfect go-between. He probably knew and was known by these Japanese officers from his long stint in Manchuria/Manchukuo. The ultimate questions, then, are these: could he have anticipated support for his rescue activities, and did he receive support or not? Was there a "conspiracy of goodness," and who initiated whom?

While we cannot answer these questions at this moment, we do have considerable evidence that Sugihara was mindful of what was happening to Jews and, for the first time that we can ascertain, acquainted with some Jews. As Lithuania filled with Jewish refugees, "Sugihara asked about the discrimination against the Jews marking them with the David stars on their clothes and on the doors of their houses," says his old Harbin buddy and protégé, Tadakazu Kasai, who visited with Sugihara in Berlin and Kaunas in this period. "Mr. Sugihara was fully aware of the Jewish people," he adds. Before long, Sugihara satisfied his curiosity about the Jewish experience from more than secondhand reports.

On October 11, not far from the Metropole Hotel, where the Sugiharas were still lodging, the Te Deum in the cathedral and the church bells accompanied pogroms in the street. The Soviets announced that Vilna and its environs would be returned to the Lithuanians; the Lithuanian residents of Kaunas had their ways of "celebrating."[17] Undoubtedly, Sugihara saw or heard these attacks.

But Sugihara at this time became privy to more than Jewish suffering. There was a sizable, well-established indigenous Jewish community of all classes, even the opulent. Most local Jews responded to the Nazi threat through a generous outpouring of assistance to refugee Jews. Few thought of packing their own bags. Some gaiety began to return to the people of Vilnius, following the frightening month or so under Soviet occupation. The new Lithuanian masters had their own scores to settle with the Poles and the "Communist Jews," but their inefficiency proved to be a humanizing force. Some local Jews began to think that they were vindicated in resisting panic.

Sugihara would occasionally drive in his black Buick southeast rather than to the northern border regions, in order to visit the more cosmopolitan and less formal city of Vilnius. At a party during the days when the Soviets were making their retreat in the second part of October, Sugihara seems to have met a dashing young Jew in his early twenties. That summer, Boris Minkowitz had returned home from Grenoble, where he attended the École de Commerce, to visit his family. When the war broke out on September 1, he could not return to France. The son of an international flax dealer, one of Lithuania's wealthiest Jews, Minkowitz and the Japanese diplomat seemed to make a good impression on each other. He invited Sugihara to meet his family at the large mansion on Chopin Street, where Mrs. Minkowitz had the servants polish the special silver used on Sabbath and holidays. The Sugiharas would become frequent visitors.

Boris's youngest brother, Moshe, sixteen at the time, remembers the visits of the "kindly and dignified diplomat" to their home. What influence did *these* new friends ultimately have on the making of that mass rescuer? Moshe Minkowitz, Americanized into Michael Menkin, is virtually the only member of his large family to survive the Holocaust. The grandfather and New York diamond merchant remembers the last time he saw Sugihara, the man who he claims simply acted, with no "high levels" behind him, as Sugihara's Polish friends claim. Sugihara was standing at the Kovno train station, with his family, perhaps ten and a half months after the young Moshe first met him, his consulate now closed by the Soviets. Even as he was about to board a train for Berlin, Sugihara "was still stamping visas," Michael Menkin, with tears rolling down his cheeks, remembers.

But let us go back to the opening of the consulate. In mid-October, Sugihara, his family, and staff finally moved in from the Metropole. He set to fixing more household matters, of which there was still much to be done. Sugihara's instructions now apparently were to report not to Riga or to Berlin but to the Foreign Ministry directly. A change of government in Tokyo prompted him to again explain the provisions of the lease:

> There are many consulates nearby, but transportation is inconvenient. The next house is not too close and the opposite side of the road is open land. So it is suitable for our special circumstances. We rented the first and second

floors. There is a resident of the third floor. Although we did not need the whole house, I asked the owner to rent it to us to keep matters secret. But the resident did not agree to transfer residential rights.[18]

Incredibly, more than a half-century and four political regimes later, the same resident still lives on the third floor. Her name is Jadvyga Ulvydaite, and she continues to be "unwilling to transfer residential rights," though unlike Sugihara, she cares little about "keeping matters secret." Her memories of the ambiance if not of the details of the activities provide us with a fuller sense of our subject.[19]

"He was quite beautiful, his face. I had never seen anyone Japanese before," says the now matronly Mrs. Ulvydaite. When she first met him, she was nineteen years old, newly arrived in Kaunas with several of her brothers and their families. "He never visited us upstairs, at least I did not ever see him here," she continues. "But perhaps he was here to take his son home. Mr. Sugihara's son would play in our apartment. We were neighbors, not friends," she is careful to emphasize. "Sometimes they would treat us to some ice cream which they would send upstairs with their servants. But my brother, he was sometimes invited to consulate parties and to drink tea. Sugihara even offered him a job, but my brother refused."

But if Sugihara maintained a proper distance from the young woman upstairs, it was not out of indifference or callousness. She remembers, as if it were yesterday, the exchange that they had one day when she was looking sad. "He stopped me, telling me that he knows that I am very sad. 'There must be a balance between good and evil in the world,' he said. 'Therefore, it is absolutely necessary, sooner or later, that everything in your life will improve. Evil,' he said so reassuringly to me, 'the evil in your life will be outweighed by good! There is no reason that you should surrender to despair.'"

But even with the time that he would take to give words of encouragement to a neighbor, Mrs. Ulvydaite remembers how hardworking Sugihara was. "Early in the morning he used to work in a small garden just in front of his windows. People would sometimes gaze at him but that was only because of his fine face, not because of the way he acted. His character was not different from others. He was a person of high culture." Mrs. Sugihara had her own schedule of activities, the neighbor on the third floor remembers. "She would often go out to do shopping, but never alone, always with a car. She never worked with her husband in the garden. I never saw her in the office."

"There were two maids, a driver by the name of Boleslav, and two consulate workers. The consulate workers were not Lithuanians, but they spoke Lithuanian. People said that one of them was German. We would exchange friendly greetings when meeting in town. They drove me home on several occasions. Mr. Sugihara spoke to other neighbors also. They loved him too. The Sugiharas were very kind and friendly, very kind and friendly, indeed. They were so polite and we lived in a wonderful relationship of a truly loving neighborhood." And when the Jews started coming, I ask? "When the Jews began coming to the Consulate, everybody approved of what was going on here," she answers.

Then she amends this last statement a bit. "The neighbors were not so interested in was going on here with the Jews. When passing by they sometimes spoke to the Jews for a while. But they were not interested at all, I have no doubt whatever." She reports how the Jews began to visit the Consulate in the spring of 1940, their numbers increasing with the summer. "The line was long, perhaps 200 meters long. People were standing there with their children. They were in panic that they would not get visas. We tried to calm them down. 'Sugihara is a wonderful man,' we would tell them. 'He would not refuse you help.' While all this was happening, she insists, there were no policemen or soldiers to be seen in the area.

"We never talked about saving Jews," she adds, speaking of people of the neighborhood. "On the contrary, I would say, we were trying not to speak about all that. I felt sorry for the Jews waiting for visas on the street around our house. There were many of them and they even pitched a tent. And they slept in their tents just in front of the house. I was used to entertaining them to dinner in my own flat, I gave them sandwiches, tea. I would allow them to use the bathroom. We allowed the weaker ones to lie down on the sofa. You know, they should give me an award for helping Jews!"

But with all Jadvyga Ulvydaite's good will toward Jews, the painful decades of Soviet occupation have chipped away at Sugihara's reputation, even though "everybody approved" his rescue effort here. "People thought that maybe he collaborated a bit with the Russians, do you understand me?" she says. In the end she does feel privileged to have lived all these years in no ordinary home. "This house is sacred. Right now they want to privatize the apartments. I think there must be a museum." She sighs. "But nobody cares."

In that "sacred" house, consular work was supposed to be rudimentary, a cover for high-level spying. The precise nature of that spying we may never know, for even if any of those records were preserved, they have yet to be discovered in the archives of the different states that had an interest in Sugihara's activities.[20] We have but scant information about Sugihara's drives in his big black Buick to observe troop movements on either side of the border, of his discussions with various informants. We do not know who in Tokyo read his reports, and who else may have received his precious information. But we do know about this consular work— because no one cared as much about covering it up.

Other Roads to Kaunas

What could not be kept secret, of course, were the lines on Vaizgantas Street. Just who was standing out there, and why? Shortly before Bernard Zell died in 1985, he and his wife, Rochelle, née Berek, and Ruchel Zielonka, numbers 789 and 790 on the Sugihara list, had written a joint memoir. It is powerful in its unpretentiousness, a remarkable tale of how they escaped the fate that befell their families, communities, and a third of their people. Mrs. Zell, an active octogenarian and matriarch of her large and prominent family, provides me cogent commentary on their rescue. We spoke over the phone from her home in Chicago.

On October 15, 1939, the Zielonkas arrived in Vilnius from Poland. They were in search of a place where they would be "safe from both the Germans and the Russians," as their memoir states. And from there they imagined a better place, safe from the Poles and Lithuanians as well, an "open window," as they put it, far away from a Europe that was quickly becoming the graveyard of their dreams.

Wealthy, young, full of energy and initiative, they had just spent three nights in a cold and drafty cattle car. "To add insult to injury, the floor was covered with leaflets, in Polish, of a highly antisemitic nature, the type used in Poland against the Jews before the war broke out," Bernard recalls. They had been on the road for more than a month and a half since leaving Sosnowiec, a small town in western Poland. A successful grain broker, he had also been dabbling in real estate. Thinking that Hitler's audaciousness in making claims on Poland could never exceed the areas of Silesia (once part of Prussia) where he and Ruchel lived, he decided that geographic diversification to his real estate holdings would be the safest hedge. He recalls:

I made contact with some real estate people in Warsaw. On August 24th, I got on a very modern train called the "Torpedo Train." While we were in the station at Piotrkow, I heard newsboys on the platform yelling, "Extra, extra, extra!" I got off and bought a paper. The paper carried a report that the German foreign minister, Joachim von Ribbentrop, and the Russian foreign minister, Vyacheslav Molotov, had signed an agreement the day before, the "Nazi-Soviet Nonaggression Pact." I had an instant feeling that this was the beginning of the end. I crossed the tracks and got on the westbound train to return home to Sosnowiec. The train arrived in Sosnowiec at 2:00

P.M., and it took ten minutes for me to walk home. I told Ruchel, "We're leaving on the next train, at four o'clock."

Ruchel protested, but she quickly packed their baby, Julie, and whatever clothes they could carry. They left behind their household, businesses, and substantial bank accounts. From the train station awaiting the 4:00 P.M. eastbound train, they called their closest relatives and warned them to join. But Berek's parents wanted to stay with his brothers and sisters. "They were unhappy to see us go—they literally refused to believe what was to happen," the Zells remember. At one point Berek even left his wife and daughter in a town along their escape route and returned to his hometown to convince friends and relatives to escape before it was too late. Everyone around them was staying. That had the fatal lulling effect.

During the first days of September, Ruchel and Berek experienced Nazi bombing on the Polish towns in which they sought shelter at night, and ducked strafing of the long lines of refugees by day. By September 4, they were receiving reports that the Nazis had shot thirteen Jews in their hometown of Sosnowiec. They moved east, from town to town, staying with the owners of the local wheat mills. These were people with whom Berek had done business but often had never met. The Jewish homes along the way were crammed with refugees. He writes:

> We were finally able to rest in Luck. We had no choice; there was no place else to go. Luck was close to what was then the Russian border, and we didn't want to cross into Russia. We were afraid of the Russians, afraid they would take our money and leave us to starve, or worse, they might send us to a camp in Siberia. And even if these things did not happen to us, we could forget about an open window to the world in Russia—you could not leave that country whenever you wanted. But as it turned out, the Russians came to us. Everything was still moving with great speed. . . . On September 18th, we watched Russian troops, with their tanks, marching into Luck. The whole city came out to watch the death of Poland.

Suddenly they heard that the Soviets were returning Vilna to the Lithuanians. Having just been annexed by the Red Army in Poland, they could make a visaless passage to Vilna because now both these places fell under Soviet jurisdiction. And if they could be in Vilna when the handover took place, the borders would cross them rather than they would cross the borders, they thought; it could be as good as leaving the Soviet Union, visalessly! "We arrived in Vilna on October 15th, a beautiful afternoon," Bernard recalls in his memoirs. "We stood there in the middle of Polanka Street and wondered what to do next."

The two Irenes—both are numbers on Sugihara's list. But what different fates that ledger conceals! Childhood friends, they still are close, one living in upstate New York and one in Miami, both having married, raised families, and arrived at comfortable retirements. In 1941, Irene Rothenberg, née Malowist, number 2016, escaped with her parents via Kaunas, the Soviet Union, Japan, and, ultimately, San Francisco. Irene Steinman, née Dynenson, number 566, was separated from her family. For her, the road to Kaunas was just the beginning of her tribulation.

The Dynenson and Malowist families had been close friends in their hometown of Lodz, in western Poland. As war clouds began to gather in August 1939, the families often met to discuss the situation. "At the end of August 1939, my parents and the Dynenson family, on the basis of their knowledge of international affairs, recognized that Germany would invade Poland," Irene Malowist Rothenberg tells me.[21] (From now on I will use maiden names to keep the stories straight.) "I remember the crucial conference at which our families made the decision." In view of the fact that Lodz was the major textile center of Poland, they thought, the city would be most vulnerable to air attacks. It would be a good idea, they thought, to send wives and children eastward to escape possible bombing.

The Dynensons left Lodz for Sarny, a small Polish town near the Soviet border, on August 29, 1939. "It was the last day that civilians were permitted to travel on trains," says Irene Dynenson.[22] "On the 30th mobilization was declared effective on August 31st. I do remember friends seeing us off at the station laughing at what they called our 'war hysteria,' and predicting that we'd be back in a week to be laughed out of town."

Irene Malowist's family had a more difficult time: "The Germans invaded Poland on September 1, 1939. My father, as a physician, was an officer in the reserves, was mobilized and ordered to leave Lodz instantly on Sept. 6. He walked out of our home with literally nothing but the uniform on his back. The army retreated, luckily eastward. On September 17, 1939, the Russians invaded from the East, as part of the Hitler-Stalin pact, the Polish army was disbanded and Dad tried to find Mother and me."

Malowist continues:

Polish officers were ordered by the Russians to report for internment. Dad reported and had the extraordinary luck to be received by a young officer who gave him a pass for travel on Russian military transports in order to find his family. Furthermore, when Dad saluted and offered to report back as soon as possible, the young Russian told him to get out, burn his uniform, and never come back. The officer was Jewish. Dad had no other clothes, so Mom had his uniform dyed black. It still looked like a uniform, though, with the high leather boots.

"There was a combination of fortitude and luck, and good people helping along the way," Irene Malowist reflects, as she remembers the family of her childhood friend. "Some weeks later we received a telegram stating that 'Lidochka is marrying a Lithuanian. Come to the wedding. Sara.' We didn't know anyone named Lidochka!" It seems the Dynensons had gone to the Central Post Office in Vilnius on October 15, 1939, and sent as many such telegrams as they could to their friends back in Poland. Irene Dynenson, twelve years old, was particularly concerned that her best friend from home receive the message. Years later, Dynenson remembers, "we got there at the beginning of October 1939 and within a short time we found out that Vilnius was to become part of Lithuania. My mother's name was Sara. The border was through a town called Lido. We sent telegrams to friends and relatives who had escaped to Eastern Poland. Quite a few people who received our telegram came to Vilnius and eventually also received Sugihara's visas and were saved."

"We didn't know anyone by the name of Lidochka," Irene Malowist says, "but soon understood the message with gratitude when we heard rumors that Wilno was being given to the Lithuanians by the Russians in exchange for military bases." "Lidochka" was code for "Lido," adds the grateful friend, Irene Rothenberg. "The telegram was from my friend's parents. They saved us." The Malowists next got on the train to Vilnius. "We were absorbed by Lithuania, escaping the Soviets for a vital year in which to try to arrange further flight. We accomplished that with the help of 110 miracles and several kind persons, including Sugihara. The Dynenson family was to follow us within a week."

Some arrived at Sugihara's door as individuals, or as groups of friends. But some also arrived as leaders and members of well-organized movements. Such was the case with Zorach Warhaftig, number 455. I spoke to him at his son and daughter-in-law's apartment in the heart of Jerusalem, where he sat at a table surrounded by adoring grandchildren and stacks of folios on Jewish law. Warhaftig is the former minister of religion of Israel. He signed Israel's Declaration of Independence and served in every government from its founding until his retirement a few years ago. Short and compact, the ninety-year-old is deliberate in every gesture. His rhetorical skills are as sharp as they must have been years ago when arguing a case in a Polish court, or calling for action among the *haverim,* the members of several religious Zionist factions he led, or addressing the Israeli parliament. But when he talks of his late wife, Naomi, passionate grief overwhelms him. I ask him about how he wound up in Kaunas.

In 1939, Zorach and Naomi had been married for almost a year and a half, but they had never had a honeymoon. He was a lawyer and his Warsaw practice was flourishing; his leadership in local, national, and international Jewish and Zionist organizations would have consumed a man of normal levels of energy and ability. But Warhaftig was formidable; vacation was not a word in his lexicon. Still, in August 1939, he was asked to attend the Twenty-first International Zionist Congress in Geneva. Naomi would join him and perhaps this could count as their delayed honeymoon. A few days on the lake and in the mountains would be an unanticipated blessing.

They arrived in Geneva in the flush of August. But soon the delegates abandoned their discussions to huddle around the radio, listening with intense despair to announcements of the nonaggression pact that had just been signed on August 24 by Ribbentrop and Molotov. "The Twenty-first Zionist Congress was brought to an unexpectedly abrupt close and those attending it dispersed in a somber mood," Warhaftig remembers. Dr. Chaim Weizmann, president of the World Zionist Organization, parted from the participants with these words:

> I need hardly tell you about the present world situation. Darkness besets us and it is hard to see through the black clouds. . . . I have no prayer but this: that we may all meet again alive. If, as I trust, we survive, our work will continue. Who knows—perhaps out of the very darkness a new light will shine upon us. . . . Together with you, I pray that this may come about. The Glory of Israel will not fail!

Though altogether mindful of the dangers they faced, the delegates from Poland were eager to return home. "We knew we simply had to get back to our families in Warsaw and do our duty as loyal Polish citizens," says Warhaftig. "At no time in the past had our Jewish and civil responsibilities coincided so harmoniously as they did now." After several days of difficult negotiations, Warhaftig and his Zionist friends arranged for a "sealed" train to take them back to Poland via Yugoslavia and Hungary, rather than Germany. On September 2, the second day of World War II, they looked out the train's windows and saw their first Polish refugees escaping Poznan. The Polish patriotism of these Zionist delegates was not diminished by the heckling from the train of defectors on the next track. "Jews, go back to Palestine!" they shouted. Warhaftig and his wife arrived in Warsaw in time to volunteer to dig antitank trenches on its outskirts, though doubting their effectiveness in halting the Germans.

By September 7, with the defense of Poland in a shambles and members of the government in flight, the Warhaftigs joined several of their Zionist friends in escaping eastward. No sooner had they left Warsaw than the Germans closed their pincers around the city. In the next days they walked by night, trying to avoid German bombardment and strafers, as well as equally dangerous Polish soldiers, drunk, defecting, and now wholly out of control.

Sometimes they'd come upon a village with Jewish residents who would offer them food and shelter. Naomi was pregnant and having a particularly difficult time. They tried as best they could to celebrate Rosh Hashana, the solemn New Year, in barns and in the fields.

"Our original plan had been to make for Brest-Litovsk and report there to the army," Warhaftig tells me.

As a result of the prevailing chaos, however, and since news had reached us that there was no one there in charge of mobilization, we decided to change direction and head southeast toward Lutsk (Luck) on the way to the Romanian border. Our journey from Warsaw, mostly on foot, had taken eleven days. We were completely exhausted, but our mental anguish was far greater than any of the privations we had experienced. The dead bodies of refugees had made our route an unending scene of horror.

Refreshing themselves at Luck among Zionist colleagues, they, too, spotted the same opportunity for a visaless transfer to Lithuania if they hurried. Overnight, that country was becoming a vast asylum for Polish Jews. Warhaftig thought of the many borders that he would have to cross if ever he was to see the Holy Land. Those crossings, he knew, would require visas. Borders were closing but the word was getting out.

"I shall never forget," a frightened Polish Jew wrote anonymously:

During the first few weeks of this mass exodus, the Red Army guards permitted everyone to cross the border and frequently showed a sympathetic attitude. About the fifteenth of October, however, the borders were suddenly shut tight. The sentries were no longer friendly, and frequently towns and villages near the border were searched for refugees who had somehow got across. Those caught were shipped back to Nazi Poland. Soviet border guards shot at anyone trying to cross the border. Nazi guards, in turn, fired at anyone trying to get back. The unfortunate refugees, caught between two lines of fire, had no choice but to remain in a no-man's land along the border.

Meanwhile, the weather had grown bitterly cold and many froze to death. Only after great difficulties could Jews living in the border towns receive permission from Soviet authorities to bury the dead and the murdered. I myself witnessed the tragic burial of a seventy-year-old man, a young mother and her three-month-old baby, all of whom died of exposure.

Thousands eventually gathered in these no-man's lands. Nazi guards would have "fun" with them, and their cries would be heard on both sides of the boundary. Local Jews did their utmost to help them, frequently sharing their crowded quarters and last pieces of bread. On the other side, the Red soldiers stood grimly and silently holding their guns ready. When finally the refugees had reached a point of desperation, they stampeded past the Soviet guards. Several were shot, but most of them got across after overpowering the sentries by sheer weight of numbers. Sometimes Red soldiers who sympathized with these unfortunates disregarded the orders of their superiors.

Another way to cross was devised by a Jewish waiter from Warsaw. After eight days of hunger and cold in no-man's-land together with thousands of others, he made a red flag out of a piece of cloth, and led a march of refugees toward the border, all singing the "International" at the top of their lungs. The Soviet guards, confused by this unusual scene, lowered their guns and allowed most of the people to enter the country.[23]

While the Warhaftigs contended with Soviet troops and drunken Polish deserters, young Ben Fishoff, number 2070, was studying at a Yeshiva near Lodz.[24] He was all of fifteen in the summer of 1939. If Warhaftig's tale demonstrates the resourcefulness of a Zionist, a community leader, a brilliant and powerful professional, Fishoff's exemplifies the otherworldliness and social insularity but determined respect for life of the Yeshiva world. The Yeshivot in Eastern Europe were in the midst of a mysterious renaissance. By all expectations, they should have succumbed to the more benign forces of acculturation in the modern world rather than the Ninth Fort and concentration camps, where most of the *bukhurs* (students), not saved by Sugihara, ended up. In those perilous days, Fishoff's fellow students and teachers were sorely divided; how, they wondered, should one understand evil? For many, recent events appeared to constitute a pogrom, if bigger than usual. Such a classification actually had a taming effect, under the circumstances, giving frightened Jews a sense of the familiar! "We have overcome such violent enemies in the past and we shall again in the future," seemed the consensus. In the fall of 1939, who could know that there was something altogether new in Nazi totalitarianism and its war, not mere pogrom, against the Jews? The most pious had long believed that suffering has meaning, that Jewish history is the record of God's love for the Jewish people, and that, most important, most contrary to everything happening in the fall of 1935—*Gut vet helfen,* God surely will come to our rescue. For such believers, it was all the more difficult to take one's life in hand, leave a loving family, a warm and caring community, and actively escape.

Today, Ben Fishoff is a leader of the Aguda Movement, the moderate wing of Ultra-Orthodox World Jewry, and makes his living as a representative of Sony, a job that in part sprang from his years in Japan. I met with him in his spacious midtown New York City office, where pictures of his children and grandchildren line the desk and walls. With the Manhattan skyline looming behind him, Ben Fishoff began to tell me his story.

The Fishoffs had prospered in their little town outside Lodz, even though the Polish economy was backward and Jews suffered discrimination. They imported dried fruit from Romania, which provided a secure existence without interfering with their piety. In the summer of 1939, young Ben was living away from home at a Yeshiva called *Darkai Noam* (Paths of Pleasantness). "The war broke out on Friday," Fishoff remembers. "I took the train home, a short distance but did not arrive until 10 P.M. after the Sabbath had begun." The Fishoff family deliberated and decided to stay put. They had their summer home away from the industrial city of Lodz, where they would be safe from German bombing. Matters went from bad to worse through the fall, though. By late fall, after the border was already sealed, Fishoff decided to try for Lithuania. "The situation was increasingly dangerous, but with the horrible things that the Nazis were doing, there was little possibility to learn in the Yeshiva in Poland anyhow," he reasoned.

On the way, he stopped off in Warsaw, a risky move. But as a young devotee of the Gerer Rebbe, a Warsaw-area Hasidic master who regularly received tens of thousands of Jewish pietists, Fishoff had to bid farewell to his master no matter how dangerous travel had become. By now, the German-Lithuanian border was heavily guarded on both sides. Fishoff joined other groups of desperate Jews trying to find the right place to cross or the right smuggler who could bribe the right guards.

Another person might enjoy recounting his clever moves and close brushes with death, but Fishoff is uninterested in elaborating on that part of his escapade. Instead he reminisces about how good it was to get to "beautiful Lithuania" and how delighted he felt to join its great Yeshivas. Arriving in Vilnius in December, he enlisted in *Yeshivat Hakhmai Lublin,* recently transferred from the Polish city of Lublin. After several months, he transferred to one of the great Lithuanian Yeshivot, the Telse Yeshiva, named for that Lithuanian town.

Ben Fishoff, the Yeshiva *bukhur,* the other young men, the rabbis of the Telse Yeshiva redoubled their efforts in study, in prayer, in fulfilling the commandments, in moral self-reflection. Less time was spent on the issues of the day and even less on theological agonizing. *"Ad ki yaavor zaamo,"* until God's wrath would pass, some thought. The more the world spun out of control, the more news arrived about German and Soviet brutality in Poland, the greater delight *bukhurs* and rabbis took in strengthening their studies. True, some Yeshiva officials had to deal with the day-to-day problems of constant food shortages, of police and government officials making one outrageous demand after another. But the world outside was still kept at bay.

Meanwhile, across the Atlantic in New York City, rabbis were setting up the *Vaad Hahatsule* (Rescue Committee) to help the Yeshivot. Letters went back and forth, but no one was quite sure how to act. Fishoff was one of those eagerly checking the mail each day, along with his friend Nathan Gutwirth, from Holland. The two hoped to hear from their families. But Gutwirth also had a more local correspondent; he had become friendly with the Dutch representative of Philips Electronics in Kovno, a man named Jan Zwartendijk. Zwartendijk would send Gutwirth an occasional Dutch newspaper so he could keep up with soccer scores back home. That correspondence, for Gutwirth, for Fishoff, for many, many people proved to be life-saving.

Fishoff has retained a spiritual outlook on his own rescue in Kaunas. He believes, in the words of the Hasidic Master of Belz that he is so fond of quoting, that Jews who survived the Holocaust were able to "see how hundreds of angels actually accompanied and watched over them during the course of those bloody years." For him, Sugihara was one of those angels. "I owe him more than my life," says Fishoff, nodding to the photos of his extended family. "I am thirty-seven people!"

Among those on the road to Kaunas were upholders of many different traditions. Polish Jewry between the two world wars was rich in political and intellectual ferment, and even relatively small towns would support several Hebrew and Yiddish periodicals representing various factions of socialism, Zionism, and other religious and cultural stances. Victor Erlich, number 1684, was a product of such diversity.[25] He harmoniously combines the graciousness of the Polish aristocrat, the broad intellect of the Renaissance savant, and the *heimishness,* the warm folksiness, of the East European Jewish intellectual, all garnished by his contagious laugh. Even at Yale, where he taught Russian literature, people would whisper of the energetic man in his eighties what had been said through his growing-up years: *"Dubnovs an einekil"* (Dubnov's grandson). Victor Erlich was the grandson of the great leader and historian of East European Jewry, Simeon Dubnov.

Erlich and I met in the Branford College common room, where he seemed to naturally belong, amid heavy walnut paneling, the well-worn sofa, the intricately carved stone fireplace, the leaded-glass windows, and the inevitable bottle of well-aged and very dry sherry. With his parents, Sophie and Henryk Erlich, brother Alexander, and sister-in-law Rachel, he left Warsaw on September 7, 1939. "We proceeded eastward as far as

Pinsk," Dubnov tells me. "Our arrival there roughly coincided with the entry of occupying Soviet forces. On October 1st, Father, a leader of the Jewish Labor Bund, was arrested by the NKVD. The rest of us promptly left for Vilna. We assumed, wrongly, that he was being held in the Vilna prison." Victor never saw his father again.

It seems the NKVD had inherited the political Most Wanted list of twenty years ago. They wanted to settle scores with Henryk for his Menshevik leanings. This was not the first time Victor and his family were political refugees. His parents had lived and worked dangerously for years trying to replace the tyrannies of tsardom with a more humane government and society in which Jews would be full participants. In 1918, as the Bolsheviks consolidated their rule in his parents' beloved St. Petersburg, Henryk and Sophia realized that there would no longer be room for their combination of socialism and Jewish nationalism, the Bundist movement, to flourish in the Communist state. They relocated to Warsaw.

But grandfather Simeon Dubnov would not abandon the "people." He tried to foster his approach to Judaism under the new regime; as an ideologist and as the most important Jewish historian of Eastern Europe, Dubnov had a large following. Yet eventually, in 1922, he and his wife had to flee as well, first to Lithuania, then to Berlin. Erlich remembers his grandfather as a "vital and significant presence, caring, involved, richly instructive, and enjoyably zestful. I feel fortunate to have known him as well as I did."

As Victor walked through the streets of Vilnius in the fall of 1939, he remembered his last visit here.

> In 1935, mother and I journeyed to Vilna to meet grandfather and to join him at the Second Congress of YIVO [the Yiddish-named foremost research institute on Eastern European Jewry, now in New York]. It was an unmistakably Eastern European Jewish festival—intense, tumultuous, occasionally abrasive, teeming with ideas and projects, with methodological and ideological controversies. The main reason I came to Vilna was to hang around grandfather and to see him in action. What I saw was consistently impressive. His impassioned speech at the beginning session, delivered in crisp, clear Yiddish, visibly stirred the large and attentive audience. The outpouring of affection for the doyen of Jewish historians must have been deeply gratifying.

As it turned out, Marc Chagall and his wife, Bella, attended the conference in connection with an exhibit of his drawings. Erlich recalls how "our breakfast routine was especially memorable. Each morning the pert waitress would confront us with a thoroughly ethnic choice—chopped liver or herring. I recall that whenever Chagall's turn came to answer the standard question, he would turn to his wife, his large blue eyes pleading helplessness, and say, 'Bella, what do I feel like today?'" His wife, Erlich remembers, "had no difficulty answering this query."

For the next year and a half after the NKVD took Henryk, the family would live in terror. They also worried for the well-being of Zeide (grandfather) Dubnov, who had moved to Riga. In the meantime, the Erlichs were part of a group of about forty Jewish Labor Bund activists from Warsaw "most of whom lived under constant threat of arrest," as Erlich says. The short-lived Lithuanian regime did its most to suppress Polish nationalism, driving many of Erlich's colleagues underground. Some Polish party leaders had sympathy for Bundists doubly victimized as Poles and as Jews. But as Jewish resistance fighters discovered a few years later, antisemitism endured even among some anti-Nazi Poles.

Soon, Victor and his family would again meet his sagely grandfather in "the Jerusalem of Lithuania." Thoroughly unexpectedly, in spring of 1940, Professor Simeon Dubnov came to Vilnius bringing great joy and encouragement to his many admirers and loving family. Victor remembers his grandfather, then approaching eighty, as "one of the youngest men I would ever know. He fully shared our intense worry about Father and viewed Hitler's westward advance with increasing dismay. Yet, characteristically, he refused to surrender to gloom, let alone despair. He was full of plans for further activities—as vigorous, involved, and energetic as ever."

Simeon Dubnov returned to Riga to be with the "people," as he always put it, meaning the ordinary, simple, vulnerable folk whom Dubnov, the intellectual and sagely leader, loved so much. On December 8, 1941, as the Nazis rounded up the Jews of that city to enter the ghetto, a drunken Latvian soldier shot the great man. The story quickly spread among the millions of Jews facing the same dangers that his last words were, "People, do not forget. Speak of this, people. Record it all." Had the sage remained with his family in Lithuania, he too might have been rescued by Sugihara.

Moe Beckelman: Other "New Eyes" in Lithuania

Moe Beckelman was both a spiritual heir of Dubnov and a partner of Sugihara. His uniqueness does not end there; of all the names that appear on Sugihara's list, he, number 1890, is the only American. Beckelman's story is full of surprises. He and Sugihara may have first crossed paths in mid-October, 1939, at Kaunas's Metropole Hotel. The vice consul's family were lodging there until the consulate was ready, and we might imagine the robust Japanese diplomat from Yaotsu and the six-foot-tall social worker from New York City nodding at each other in the lobby, but of course we cannot know whether they did.

Beckelman, thirty-three, was sent by the Joint Distribution Committee (JDC), an organization established by American Jews in 1914 to assist Jews abroad in distress.[26] Some local Jewish leaders greeted him with muted enthusiasm. They were "astonished" by alarming and exaggerated reports of refugees, acknowledging that there were only twenty-five "in Kaunas and the nearer vicinity." Beckelman claimed there were fifteen thousand.[27] His own organization had recently described "beautiful Lithuania" as that "island of peace." "Surrounded by Germany, Poland, and Latvia—countries where the Jews suffer from oppression—Lithuania today looms up as one spot in Eastern Europe where the Jews feel themselves at home and where the Government . . . is sincerely friendly towards the Jewish citizens."[28]

But Beckelman must not have believed all was well. Remember, in Sugihara's Manchukuo period, how he himself would go out to the provinces to survey flood damages and human suffering and only then write his report? Moe Beckelman, too, had to see with his own eyes. As soon as he arrives in Kaunas, a spate of memos and field reports begins. Beckelman realizes that the country has been inundated with Jewish refugees with nowhere else to turn. He informs New York; there are twenty-five thousand refugees, according to some reports, from Nazi-conquered Poland in the west and Soviet-conquered Poland in the east, converging on Vilna alone in fewer than two months. Since October 11, when the Soviets announced that Polish Vilna would now become Lithuanian Vilnius, the situation for Jews had darkened further. Hardly had the celebrations of "an independent Lithuanian State having its historic capital returned" quieted down when citizens began devising how to preserve "Lithuania for the Lithuanians."

Suddenly, some ninety thousand Vilnius Jews, besides the refugees, were also subject to disenfranchisement and economically restrictive measures—perhaps even deportation. The new masters of the city decided to grant Lithuanian citizenship only to those Vilnius citizens who could prove that they had lived there before it was annexed to Poland twenty years earlier. Many Jews and Poles had in fact migrated from other parts of the old tsarist empire shortly after World War I. Now, a generation later, they, their children, even their grandchildren were being threatened. There was nothing in Moe Beckelman's social work textbooks that remotely explained what to do in such situations, but he did have an idea: emigration.

On October 24, Beckelman cables headquarters in New York with his suggestions: "There may be something in this [an agreement with the

Lithuanian government to provide transit for desperate refugees backed by a firm commitment they will receive visas to elsewhere soon], for the first few months at least, though a checkup with the American consul and a canvass of other immigration opportunities would explode this idea."[29] Strong word, "explode." "On the other hand," he quickly adds, "the whole question may be academic because even if the Lithuanian government wants to expel those people whom it refuses to recognize as citizens, I do not see how it can do so if Russia and Germany which have taken over Poland refuse to accept them." Beckelman could demonstrate how the bad intentions of bad people could be thwarted by even worse people! "Unless this scheme for a Jewish State in Poland gets anywhere," he adds.

We look at phrases like a "Jewish State in Poland" now and cringe at the naïveté of believing that the Nazis had any such intentions. But at that time, it was one way of evaluating what did seem to be a Nazi "scheme" for concentrating Jews in southeast Poland. *Lebensraum* had not yet turned into the final solution. Beckelman was not the only Jew to want to see in the Nazis' isolation of the Jews a prelude to autonomy rather than preparation for mass murder. In those days, it was also Beckelman's job to report on what was going on in Nazi- and Soviet-occupied Poland, where the JDC was trying to sustain assistance.

The arrival of a Warsaw JDC employee named Jozef Szimkin—later, his special calligraphic talents would increase the number of Jews that Sugihara helped through forgeries—provided Beckelman with reliable updates. "The activity is conducted with German permission," Beckelman writes of the violence Polish Jews were suffering. But ultimately, he sees it as the Poles who are "taking the lead in stimulating the Germans to antisemitic measures." Beckelman, like many Jews, even fifteen years after the publication of *Mein Kampf,* could not quite grasp how the people of Beethoven and Goethe were doing such nasty things and not merely giving "permission" to Polish thugs.

As the months pass and Beckelman becomes increasingly overwhelmed by the desperate situation of thousands of Jews, he also becomes increasingly frustrated. Much as he tries to describe to his friends at the JDC what is going on, they do not quite grasp the growing urgency of the situation. Neither are they funneling him the money he needs to save lives, much as he believes that his reports "will be very useful for [the JDC's fundraising] campaign purposes in the States."[30] Surveying the "immigration opportunities," as Beckelman so delicately put it, he found more reasons to be frustrated. One of the consulates he might have approached, for example, was the Swedish consulate, down the block from the Japanese consulate. Beckelman may have partaken of herring and vodka at the same parties where Sugihara was seeking recommendations for a valet. But returning to discuss "immigration opportunities," Beckelman would have found an atmosphere as warm as the Swedish archipelago in February. The Swedes would not even allow male Jews, ages fifteen to fifty, to transit, because there was always a chance they could be military defectors. If the Swedes let them through, they believed, their neutrality would be in peril.

Beckelman did enjoy a working relationship with the U.S. diplomats in town, though. He dutifully kept the consul general, Owen J.C. Norem, apprised of his activities, enabling Norem to write better-informed reports to Washington. In spite of their different backgrounds (Norem was a Minnesota Lutheran), the two seemed to get along. Indeed, it was Beckelman who ultimately found a flight for Norem to Geneva when things got truly rough in that summer of 1940. Norem also got along with the Lithuanians—so well, in fact, that he was offered a decoration that he was "forced by diplomatic rules to refuse." In lieu of this, he accepted an honorary degree from the University of Kaunas. Shortly after his experience as a diplomat, he published a book called *Timeless Lithuania*. The "Jewish problem" in Lithuania is intractable, he claims. A "Palestine of their very own" is the only solution: "Let him carve out his own destiny against his own relatives, the Arabs. If he has enough of good arms, he can take care of himself."[31]

Apart from these pseudo-Zionist glimmers, and whatever his personal feelings may have been toward Jews, Norem was not oblivious to the antisemitism around him. During the three years he was in Lithuania, the consul kept the State Department reasonably well informed on the situation of Jews. He translated newspaper articles and analyzed positions of government and party officials. "There is good reason to believe," he indicated in a report dated February 1, 1939, "that certain people in Lithuania entertain antisemitic feelings." He is quick to add, however, that these are "inherited from the time when Kaunas was under the dominion of the Russian empire."[32]

And antisemitism back home in America? Beckelman had few illusions. Shortly before he left the United States, some Jewish congressmen made another try to open the doors to a few refugees. They did not even suggest changes in the restrictive quotas of 1924 but recommended the more efficient distribution of the few visas allowed by law. Now, articles with titles like "Hitler's Slave Spies in America" cast suspicion on Jewish refugees and their loyalties. Government officials such as Breckinridge Long and J. Edgar Hoover encouraged vigilance against the "fifth column," and émigrés from Europe were automatically deemed potential "fifth columnists." Long in 1940 would proudly write in his diary, "The cables practically stopping immigration went!"[33] Jews would know the effect of those cables.

Back in Lithuania, Norem's assistant, Bernard Gufler, set the tone for the situation. In his May 12, 1939, report to the State Department, entitled "Registration of Aliens at Kaunas, Lithuania," Gufler proudly announced his innovative efforts to create greater efficiency and financial savings by cancelling the rights of "nonpreference" Jews, those without family in America, to *apply* for the few available visas.[34] He even advertised this policy in the local newspaper. This was going too far, even for the State Department. Gufler was rebuked and ordered to reinstitute a sign-up list of sorts. Other measures that he instated included more rigorous standards for all character references, which visa applicants were required to file. Such standards only played into the hands of the local police, who wrote these reports and used them as an ideal opportunity to extort from those few Jews whom Gufler would even consider.

In making the rounds Beckelman was a quick learner. But it was hard to keep up, because events changed so fast. On October 24, Beckelman cables home: "Unless there is some last minute unexpected hitch, I now expect to be in Vilna Wednesday, October 25 or Thursday October 26. Until telephone and telegraph communications are restored, I shall try to come back to Kaunas each evening, keeping my headquarters at Hotel Metropole."[35] To ensure that there would be no "hitch," the chairman of his board, Paul Baerwald, sent a telegram to the State Department. Robert Pell, assistant chief of the Division of European Affairs, forwarded Baerwald's request to Pavilas Zadeikis at the Lithuanian Legation in Washington. On October 27, Consul Zadeikis notified Baerwald that "yesterday I cabled my Government requesting that permission be accorded Mr. Moses Beckelman to enter Vilnius at the first opportunity."[36]

He gets the go-ahead and quite soon everything goes bad. On October 31, as the Red Army was concluding its plunder of Vilnius before turning it over to the Lithuanians, riots broke out.[37] Beckelman, the Bronx boy, knew all too well what happens to a Jew who wanders in the wrong direction off the Grand Concourse. Still, he registered no small degree of shock in witnessing his first pogrom. This is taken from what he sent immediately after to New York with the heading "Memorandum on the Pogrom in Vilna":

"Bread, bread, zloty-lit, lit-zloty." I was awakened about 7:30 A.M. by the noise of a crowd outside the window of my hotel room. I observed from the window about 500 people, shouting and singing. In about ten minutes two friends of mine came into the room. They told me that they had been riding in a droshky [buggy] toward my hotel and that about five blocks away

Sugihara was born and spent his first years in a small town in central Japan. Japan at the turn of the century preserved much of its traditional way of life, but the world beyond that island empire was beginning to encroach even on Yaotsu. A remote event had a major impact on the young Chiune's childhood: in 1905 in Portsmouth, New Hampshire, Russia and Japan negotiated a treaty ending their war in Chinese Manchuria. President Theodore Roosevelt heralded the "lasting peace"—that rather left Japan and Russia with a sense of an "inevitable" new war. As an adult Sugihara became one of Japan's foremost experts on the Russian language and Soviet affairs.

Sugihara (right), his mother and two brothers circa 1905 *(Yuji Takechi)*

Yaotsu festival *(Heiichiro Furuta and Sumio Yokoyama, Yaotsu: Meiji, Taisho, Showa [Nagoya: Sobun Shuppansha, 1985])*

Postcard commemorating the Portsmouth Treaty *(Courtesy Portsmouth Athenaeum Photograph Collections)*

The Portsmouth Treaty also provided the first international recognition of Japan's emergence as a colonial empire. Sugihara's father became a colonial official in Korea. The Japanese began to increase their presence in Manchuria. Harbin, once a small Chinese fishing village, emerged as a meeting point of East and West. An important junction on the Trans-Siberian Railroad, the city developed commercially and industrially. A constant stream of Russian and Jewish refugees arrived. The small Japanese population became increasingly significant as Japan broadened its interests in Manchuria. The Harbin Gakuin, a Japanese college, was established shortly after World War I by Shimpei Goto, a theoretician and administrator of Japanese colonialism. Sugihara studied and taught there before entering the Japanese and then Manchurian civil service.

(Above) Sugihara in military uniform with his father, his brothers, and a sister in Korea, 1920
(*Hiroki Sugihara*)

Sugihara's mother's funeral, 1920
(*Yuji Takechi*)

A Harbin street scene
(*Yuji Takechi*)

Harbin Gakuin *(Alumni List of Harbin Gakuin National University)*

(Above) Shimpei Goto *(Alumni List of Harbin Gakuin National University)*

Sugihara's first wife, Klaudia Semionova Apollonov, from a prominent White Russian family. They were married from 1924 to 1935. *(Klaudia Semionova Apollonov Sugihara Dorf)*

After nearly two years in Helsinki, Sugihara was asked to open a Japanese consulate in Kaunas, Lithuania, at the end of August 1939. The Sugihara family arrived in Kaunas just as the Nazis attacked Poland, signaling the beginning of World War II. Many Polish Jews, escaping the Nazis, saw Lithuania as a safe haven in which they might wait for the war to end. In June 1940 the Soviet Union began to assert control over the Baltic States, and these refugees as well as other Poles felt increasingly trapped between the Nazis and the Communists.

(Above) Sugihara in his consulate (*Hiroki Sugihara*)

Sugihara helped high-ranking Polish intelligence and military officers to escape. Here he is seeing off one such officer and his wife at the Kovno railroad station. (*Stella Karninska-Kuza*)

Jews, hearing that Sugihara is issuing visas, gather outside the consulate in August 1940. (*Hiroki Sugihara*)

Sugihara was aware of the dangers that he and his family might face if he issued visas. Here he is in Kovno with his wife and sister-in-law and two sons. A third son was born while they were living in that city. *(Hiroki Sugihara)*

(Left) Moses Beckelman, American representative of the Joint Distribution Committee, helped organize rescue activities *(American Jewish Joint Distribution Committee)*

(Below) The Sugiharas in Berlin dining with a Nazi officer. *(Hiroki Sugihara)*

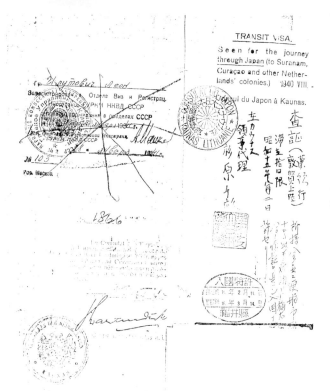

TRANSIT VISA.

Seen for the journey through Japan (to Suranam, Curaçao and other Netherlands' colonies.) 1940 VIII.

Consul du Japon à Kaunas.

(Left) One of Sugihara's thousands of transit visas *(Leon Ilutovich)*

(Below) A page of the list *(Japanese Foreign Ministry)*

Several thousand Jews received visas from Sugihara. It is not known how many actually were able to cross the Soviet Union and arrive in Japan. A small group of European Jews in Kobe organized relief efforts for Jewish refugees with the support of Japanese officials. Many Jews who possessed visas from Sugihara remained in Kobe for several months until they received travel documents to the United States, Palestine, Canada, or some countries in South America. By the fall of 1941, as tensions increased between Japan and the United States, most Jewish refugees who could not go elsewhere were sent to Shanghai or made it to other areas of the Far East where they lived out World War II. Sugihara had short postings in Berlin and Prague, where he compiled his 31-page list with 2,139 names. He was then sent to Königsberg and Bucharest, where he spent the last two years of the war. After internment by the Soviets, he and his family returned to Japan in 1946. He lost his job in the foreign ministry, and he lived out his life doing odd jobs and feeling humiliated.

NN	NATIONALITY	NAME	ENTRANCE OF TRANSIT	DATE OF VISA	SASHO	RIO	BIKOO
1862	Polnisch	Aleksandrowicz Maks.	Transit	17/VIII	2		
1863	"	Aleksandrowicz Ignacy	"	"	2		
1864	"	Lieberfrojnd Henryk	"	"	2		
1865	"	Lieberfrojnd Maroźn	"	"	2		
1866	"	Pecyna Motel	"	"	2		
1867	"	Tempelhof Mieczyslaw	"	"	2		
1868	"	Gringauz Izrael	"	"	2		
1869	"	Mendelson Manas	"	"	2		
1870	"	Gasner Hersz	"	"	2		
1871	"	Wolchajm Boruch	"	"	2		
1872	"	Pinkus Henryk	"	"	2		
1873	"	Pinkus Leja	"	"	2		
1874	"	Sobolewski Henryk	"	"	2		
1875	"	Fiss Szloma	"	"	2		
1876	"	Ofman Paulina	"	"	2		
1877	"	Wernik Hena	"	"	2		
1878	"	Kolanski Aleksander	"	"	2		
1879	"	Horodysz Mowsza	"	"	2		
1880	"	Federman Saul	"	"	2		
1881	"	Milrom Srul	"	"	2		
1882	"	Bernsztejn Zelda	"	"	2		
1883	Lithuanien	Adamaite Elena	"	"	2		
1884	Polnisch	Nelkenbaum Lejba	"	"	2		
1885	"	Kuperman Icchok	"	"	2		
1886	"	Cukier Majer	"	"	2		
1887	Tchecoslov.	Rsch Rudolf	"	"	2		
1888	Polnisch	Frydman Jakob	"	"	2		
1889	"	Frydman Boruch	"	"	2		
1890	U.S.A.	Beckelman Moses	"	"	10		
1891	Polnisch	Zelmanowicz Jenta	"	"	2		
1892	"	Zelmanowicz Froim	"	"	2		
1893	"	Tilinska Liba	"	"	2		
1894	"	Gister Ryfka	"	"	2		
1895	"	Gero Jakob	"	"	2		
1896	"	Roguski Stefan	"	"	2		
1897	"	Szwaroman Golda	"	"	2		
1898	Polish	Iwanicki Jerzy	Transit	19/VIII	2		
1899	"	Rozenberg Szmul	"	"	2		
1900	"	Liker Szyja	"	"	2		
1901	"	Liker Szyja	"	"	2		
1902	"	Fiszgendler Rubin	"	"	2		
1903	"	Grynberg Jankiel	"	"	2		
1904	Lithuanien	Zibavičius Liudas	"	"	2		
1905	Polnish	Wajnsstejn Nison	"	"	2		
1906	"	Wajnsstejn Jakob	"	"	2		
1907	"	Rubinsztajn Gilel	"	"	2		
1908	Canadian	April Tauba	"	"	2		
1909	Polish	Sztejnwach Pinchos	"	"	2		
1910	Polnish	Sapir Seba	"	"	5		
1911	Polish	Gabaj Sura	"	"	2		
1912	"	Kruk Sima	"	"	2		
1913	"	Kruk Roza	"	"	2		
1914	"	Szmid Basia	"	"	2		
1915	"	Fajgenbaum Ioko	"	"	2		
1915a	"	Wojlang Sara	"	"	2		
1916	"	Rudawski Chaim	"	"	2		
1917	"	Muller Izaak	"	"	2		
1918	"	Seroka Simon	"	"	2		
1919	British	Klein Manna	"	"	2		
1920	"	Klein Dawid	"	"	2		
1921	Polish	Bilgoraj Icek	"	"	2		
1922	"	Sztiglic Izrael	"	"	2		
1923	"	Pastag Dawid	"	"	2		
1924	"	Lipszyc Nuta	"	"	2		
1925	Lithuanien	Mazijas Azonas	"	"	2		
1926	Polish	Skalski Stefan	"	"	2		
1927	"	Gradje Majer	"	"	2		

The U.S. government and much of American public opinion exaggerated the strength of the connections between Nazi Germany and Japan and saw both countries as enemies. In reality, even after the Axis agreement was formalized, Japan did not share Germany's anti-Jewish policies. *(Captain Marvel Jr. #29, copyright © 1940 DC Comics. All rights reserved. Used with permission.)*

Kobe committee organizing rescue efforts *(Bill Craig)*

Many Kovno Jews who could not obtain visas from Sugihara were murdered at the Ninth Fort in the following years *(Yad Vashem Photo Archives, courtesy the United States Holocaust Memorial Museum)*

someone in the street had yelled: "Look at the Jews riding in the droshky." A soldier had run up and aimed a blow at one of my friends, who called out that he was a Lithuanian. The soldier then reversed his blow and rammed his gunbutt into my other friend's belly. My friends reported that similar scenes were going on all over town, and that anyone who seemed to be a Jew was being beaten on sight.

I went back to the window and saw that the civilians with the white armbands were now armed with stones and sticks of wood and were indiscriminately clubbing and hitting any Jew they saw passing on the street. The police made no attempt to interfere. I saw one man take a stone out of his pocket, put it in his fist and sneak up behind an old man walking on the other side of the street and knock him down with his fist. A woman standing by directed the attention of a policeman facing the other way, whereupon the assailant took a white armband out of his pocket, put it on and walked away. I saw two men driving by in a droshky dragged from the carriage and beaten up by civilians. Police came and arrested the victims. Reports continued to come in that the disturbance was spreading to fresh quarters of the city and that mobs were beginning to break into stores and dwellings.[38]

At first after the pogrom, the atmosphere in Kaunas was very bad. But a few days later, Beckelman dryly claims, "the mood is one of sweetness and light."[39] On November 3, he calls the JDC office in Geneva, expressing grave concern about Jews stranded on the Polish-Lithuanian border. In the weeks since the Soviets returned the Vilna district to Poland, the borders have grown more stringently guarded. Moreover, the Germans have annexed the Suwalki district in the northwest part of the country; the Wehrmacht simply moved in and chased Jewish residents out.

With the weather turning colder and thousands of refugees caught in the no-man's-land, Beckelman anticipated the worst. He alerted international relief agencies and Polish Quakers, then asked the JDC to give several thousand dollars to the Red Cross, presumably because they had connections that would be helpful to him in his rescue efforts. Those relief agencies might intervene with the German authorities to deliver assistance, as if cash would make a difference in the German attitude toward Jews. Beckelman's requests were used in a report from Paul Baerwald to the American Red Cross on November 14. Describing the emergencies arising out of the war situation in Poland, he indicated that the Joint had already spent $1,030,000 for refugee relief in Poland in the past weeks and that for the remainder of the year it would have to commit $275,000 for Lithuania.

By his end-of-the-year report, Moses Beckelman was voicing a growing concern that the idea of making of Lithuania a haven for Jews was possibly shortsighted. Lithuania was simply not viable. "There is grave concern that within a measurable period, Soviet Russia will take over the Baltic countries." Much as he was concerned to procure adequate budgets to feed, clothe, and house what he estimates to be more than one hundred thousand recent Jewish refugees from Poland plus other indigent Jews, emigration was the only alternative, he began to insist. But to where? America, as he painfully knew, was problematic. Western Europe was out; the Soviet Union was out. There was another place, though, as incredibly unlikely as it seemed: Japan.

The *Latke* Theory

In December 1939, Chiune Sugihara was celebrating Hanukah. Or so Solly Ganor tells me. Ganor is in his early sixties, short and muscular, and lives half the year in a house overlooking the sea in Herzelia, Israel, and half in one similarly sited in La Jolla, California.[40] He is nautically inclined, with a well-bronzed face and several decades in the Israeli merchant marine behind him. Five decades before, his parents decided, too late, to try to leave Kaunas. By the time the Soviets fully annexed Lithuania in late spring 1940, Lithuanians automatically received new citizenship in the Soviet "paradise," and it became virtually impossible for local Jews such as the Minkowitzs and the Ganors to leave. He and his family are not found on Sugihara's list, though Solly Ganor was eventually rescued by a Japanese man in 1945. By that time, however, he was an alumnus of several concentration camps, and was so weakened by a death march that he slipped into the snow, only to be pulled out of a deathly stupor by a man with a strangely familiar appearance. It was a member of the famous 522nd Regiment of the U.S. Army, a unit made up of Japanese-Americans who at the moment were on their way to liberate Dachau. He never tires of contemplating this blessed coincidence.

Solly Ganor well remembers his first meeting with Sugihara. His aunt, Anushka Shtrom, had a reputation all over Kaunas and beyond not only for her beauty and charm but for the fine chocolate and champagne she sold in her shop. One day in December 1939, eleven-year-old Solly headed to his aunt's store, too shy to ask but in dire need of a favor. The Jewish festival of Hanukah was about to begin and Solly had anticipated a lucrative season:

> "But this year I had to give up all the money I collected to the Jewish Refugee Fund," he tells me. "Ten lit was a lot of money. I immediately regretted it because I had lots of plans for the money. That week Laurel and Hardy were being shown in the Metropolitan Movie House. I was dying to

see the new movie, but I had no money left." His mother, feeling sorry, wanted to lend him the cash but his father put his foot down. "You must stick to certain principles. It was a noble gesture to give your money to the refugees, but then don't come whining to us for reimbursement."

The young Solly knew his father was right. But if his father's was the hard voice of justice, Aunt Anushka was softer and Solly knew "she would have mercy on me. She knew how crazy I was about Laurel and Hardy." His mother checked whether he was warmly dressed and warned him to return home before dark.

There was a war out there, somewhere, far away and the Nazis had captured Poland. But if it weren't for the Jewish refugees who came flooding into Lithuania, we wouldn't have noticed it. On the way to Aunt Anushka's shop, I saw menoras with candles in the windows of Jewish homes and here and there decorated Christmas trees in the homes of Christians.

When I walked in she was serving some elegantly dressed man with strange slanted eyes, he recalls. Anushka was talking to him in Russian. "Ah, my dear nephew came for his Hanukah money, I bet. Come here and meet his Excellency, the Consul of Japan, Mr. Sugihara." She said this as she noticed that I was staring at the man. I walked up slowly and extended my hand. "How do you do, Sir," I said politely. He solemnly shook my hand and then smiled. There was humor and kindness in those strange eyes. I took an immediate liking to this man. It reminded me of what my grandfather once told me: "Remember, the eyes are the windows to a person's soul. If you look close enough you may see what is behind them." I took this saying as many other inscrutable sayings of grandfather. But when I looked at this man I suddenly understood what he meant. There was something in those eyes that made me feel the man behind them. I sensed an aura of goodness and kindness about him, I couldn't explain.

But Sugihara, drawing on the richness of his tradition, gave his own expression to the encounter. Tapping Solly on the head, he said, "I like you. We must have been souls who met before." Anushka, not exactly focused on the sentimentality of the moment, wanted to return to the business of her nephew and the business of her customer. She quickly assessed the situation. Perhaps she had heard of Solly's act of kindness. "You want to go to the movies and you need a lit, right?" she said. "I nodded quickly, still looking at Mr. Sugihara," says Ganor. "While Anushka went to the cash register, he took out from his pocket a shiny lit and extended it to me. "Since this is Hanukah consider me your uncle." I hesitated for a moment then took from him the coin and said something totally unexpected: "Since you are my uncle then you should come Saturday to our

Hanukah party. The whole family will be there." In reflecting on that encounter with Sugihara so many years later, Solly Ganor is still mystified by what in that man drew out the child's boldness.

Aunt Anushka was not one to be flustered. But before she could regain her composure, Sugihara responded, "Come to think of it, I have never been to a Hanukah party. I would gladly come. But don't you think you should ask your parents first?" The arrangements were made and young Solly went off to Laurel and Hardy. "Precisely at six Anushka arrived with Mr. Sugihara, his wife, and her sister. His wife was dressed in a very elegant black dress and Mr. Sugihara wore a formal striped suit. They both looked very distinguished. The tables were laden with the best of food and drinks and mother even surprised the Japanese couple with some Japanese food that Anushka brought from her deli."

Yukiko Sugihara remembers that evening: "There was so much food that I couldn't finish it all. I was surprised that the family kept serving more and more food. What was more surprising was that after such a big meal, they served a huge cake for dessert. My sister, who was with me, and I were saying, 'What are we going to do?' My sister was even half crying."

Some refugees from Warsaw, the Rosenblatts, who had been staying with the Ganor family, began telling of their experiences. Sitting in the warm living room with the glow of the holiday and in the presence of the loving family and new Japanese friends, it seemed as if the Warsaw Jews lived on a different planet. It was painful to hear those horrible stories. But Sugihara listened to every word. Young Lea Rosenblatt, the daughter, joined Solly in lighting the Hanukah candles, Uncle Jacob took out his harmonica, and the Ganor family sang Hanukah and other Hebrew songs.

"Sugihara stood near me and looked curiously at the ceremony," Ganor recalled.

Later he told me that in Japan they had a similar ceremony of lighting candles. He wanted to know more details about the historical background of the Maccabees. He asked me many questions about my hobbies and when I told him that one of my hobbies was collecting stamps, he invited me to come and visit them. He could give me some Japanese stamps. The Sugiharas enjoyed the evening very much, especially the Hanukah songs we sang. He told my mother and Aunt Anushka that he was very impressed with the family spirit and unity he sensed in the room, which again reminded him very much of Japan. "One can sense the love and affection you all have for each other. I would like to meet more people of the Jewish community here," Sugihara declared.

Mr. Rosenblatt, the Warsaw guest, suddenly came up to mother and asked her if she would introduce him to the Japanese consul. He looked somewhat out of place with all the elegantly dressed crowd. Father had given him one of his suits but it was too big on him and he looked awkward in it. Father rang a servant's bell and asked for the family's attention. "I want you to meet Mr. Rosenblatt and his daughter Lea, who recently escaped from Poland. He wants to say a few words," Father announced. Everyone's eyes turned to Mr. Rosenblatt, who looked uncomfortable in front of all the people.

Mr. Rosenblatt spoke in German, either for the benefit of the Sugiharas, or because he spoke a Yiddish dialect which was hard to understand. In the beginning he spoke hesitantly, then he warmed up to the subject and described to the hushed audience the terrible things the Nazis did to the Jews in Poland and to him and his family. Then he became so emotional that he broke down and cried. All the time I noticed that Mr. Sugihara listened very attentively to Jacob Rosenblatt. I noticed that he was visibly upset by Rosenblatt's accounts. He wanted to know many more details about the conditions of Poland under the Nazi occupation.

Later I overheard Mr. Rosenblatt imploring the Japanese consul to issue him a visa. "Even a transit visa will help," he begged. Mr. Sugihara looked doubtful. But then he invited him to come to the consulate and he would see how he could help him. "I must do something for this poor man. I had no idea that the Germans were behaving in such a despicable manner," he later told Father. But it seems Sugihara, as usual, knew considerably more than he conceded. A few days later, when Solly visited his Japanese "uncle" to obtain some stamps, Sugihara sent the boy home with an unequivocal message. Tell your family and friends this, he said: "The time to leave is now."

Sugihara Studying Talmud: The Gorgeous Life in Kaunas

Sugihara had curiosity and an ability to sense quality in people whether drawn to them or not—useful professional skills for a spy. When encountering someone he liked, however, this man who in other ways was so Japanese abandoned all strictures of Japanese indirectness and discretion. He became—as we have seen with his upstairs neighbor and with young Solly Ganor—warm and personable, almost oracular in his pronouncements.

Hanukah celebrations were something quite new for the Sugiharas, but diplomatic fetes were all too familiar. Still, as they participated in the "gorgeous life," Lithuanian-style, our vice consul met people who launched him into new areas unrelated to borders and troop movements.

At one such party, Sugihara seems to have been introduced to the new consul general of Estonia to Lithuania, Dr. Jaan Lattik.[41] Lattik had studied in a theological seminary in his native Estonia and was not only knowledgeable about Jews but spoke Hebrew fluently. He had even visited Palestine. Several years before, when he was minister of education, Lattik gave support to the establishment of a Hebrew high school in Tallinn.

Lattik had a childhood Jewish friend named Moses Brauns who was a medical doctor in Kaunas and would one day save many lives in the Kovno ghetto. I met Brauns's son Jack, now a surgeon in Los Angeles, who also remembers that strange and wonderful houseguest:

> My father and Dr. Lattik were the closest of friends. When Lattik would come over to the house for dinner, the two men would go into the sitting room, smoke their cigars, and discuss fine points of Jewish law. My father, who had studied medicine in Germany, had fond memories of his childhood Talmud studies.
>
> One evening, when Dr. Lattik was visiting our home in Kaunas, he asked whether he could bring a guest with him. There was a new Japanese Consul whom he wanted us to meet. I was fifteen, but I had never seen a Japanese man before. He looked so very different. He was not very tall and his eyes were different. But he was so extremely polite. The men, as usual, retired to the study.

Dr. Jack Brauns, decades later, still vividly recalls overhearing a most unusual threesome in the study: his father, his father's close Christian friend, and a Japanese diplomat, all learning Talmud together! The first two were trying to explain to Sugihara how the Talmud presents its case law. This particular hypothetical case concerned a cow that ate rocks. Such a practice might have wounded the cow internally, which would render it unkosher, thus ritually unqualified to be eaten. But what if this cow were jointly owned by a rich man and a poor man? Dr. Lattik and Dr. Brauns reviewed the various logics that different rabbis might apply to protect the poor man's interest from the full stringency of the law and to shield him from still greater poverty. Sugihara smiled warmly when he understood the hidden compassion in Talmudic study. The men continued speaking until late in the evening. Their Talmudical discourses were interspersed with discussions of the Jewish tragedy and what could be done. "Sugihara listened intently," as Jack Brauns recalls.

"In the summers my family would vacation in Palangi," he continues, "a wonderful Lithuanian resort town. Dr. Lattik would often visit us." In the summer of 1939, a wealthy German Jewish family by the name of Balk was staying at the resort as well. "They had two lovely daughters. In hushed tones, they would tell us about how the Nazis were treating the Jews in Germany." Lattik convinced them not to return to Germany and helped them get visas to stay in Estonia. They had applied to go to the United States and received visas, but had no way of getting there.

> Some months later, the Balk family was again in contact with us. They had decided that it was too dangerous to return to Germany, but had nowhere else to go. My father raised the situation with Dr. Lattik who discussed the matter with his new friend, the Japanese Consul. Sugihara issued a transit visa to the Balk family enabling them to cross the Soviet Union and eventually make it to the United States.[42]

Sugihara, sent by his government to Kovno for reasons other than to issue visas, was becoming a real consul general!

Virtue and Virtuosity

While the road to Kovno seemed to involve Sugihara with Jews and spies, they were not Sugihara's first connection with matters Polish. There is one distinct memory of Sugihara shared by many of his friends from Harbin days and later on. It is nothing to "make a big deal of," as Yukiko would say of her husband's peculiar inclination, whether out of modesty or out of dismissiveness it's hard to say. It is a telling story about Sugihara, though, and it concerns music.

In addition to his ardor for baseball and his proficiency as a player of GO, Chiune had another consuming passion. In the corner of the apartment on the second floor above the consulate that he shared with Klaudia and her family, in the elegant chancery on the lake in Helsinki, in the house on Vaizgantas Street in Kaunas with Yukiko, and in other residences that he had through his last home near the Bay of Tokyo, Sugihara would sit for hours on end playing the piano.

Any passerby would surely be impressed by the diplomat's great virtuosity, the sure tone, and dexterity of tempo. But if one passed by often, it would soon become clear that this prodigy's repertoire was extremely limited. Thinking back to their Harbin years, Giichi Shimura recalls with astonishment that "Sergei Pavelovich Chiune Sempo Sugihara Sugiwara" constantly practiced, even taking lessons with a teacher for three years—but all to play *the same song*.

The name of this one song was "The Maiden's Prayer," and why Sugihara chose it remains an absolute mystery. Perhaps he admired it because of the way it combines sentimentalism with a scalelike logic and orderliness, perhaps because of its variations on a theme but without any development that might be confusing. Perhaps he liked it because he knew how familiar it was to many of the nationals he spied on, or perhaps he just liked the melody a lot. The song was composed by Tekla Badarzewska-Baranowska and published in Warsaw in 1856, and was printed in eighty editions, reaching several hundred thousands of copies all over the world. In its own country, though, the composer was "subject to abuse and parody" for being "absurdly sentimental," as Grove's *Dictionary of Music and Musicians* reports. The *Oxford Companion to Music* says, "The Maiden's Prayer" was the "most banal music, the source of bad taste the world over," which informs us of little more than its own disdain for the hoi polloi.

But his old friend Shimura tells us more about Chiune's attachment to this single piece: "Everyone, hearing Sugihara play 'The Maiden's Prayer,' thinks that he can play like Beethoven and Mozart. But this is, in fact, the only piece that he could actually play. Why, he couldn't even play the Japanese national anthem! He couldn't play children's music! He couldn't play anything!!!"

That he had this party trick—not uncommon among Japanese men—tells us less than we would care to know about the type of person that attains singular achievement with one act. And yet, this curious detail seems to mean something, I feel.

Sugihara perhaps embodies that quality of moral greatness to which the ancient rabbis of the Talmud alluded when they said, "There is a type of person who procures eternity in a single moment." What they were saying, I believe, seemingly renders our biographical approach of limited use. Those rabbis agreed that most acts require prolonged rehearsal and intense preparation to achieve perfection. But, they would add, there are some acts, so bold in their conception and significant in their impact, that they have no such roots. All Sugihara's musical acumen is poured into one song. All his compassion and powers of strategy are distilled into a few days of mass rescue.

Eternity in a single moment. I so much want to understand that moment!

Chapter 5

"Outside the Kovno Consulate"

Spring 1940

. . . outside the Kovno consulate . . . I saw a crowd of Polish
refugees behind the fences. . . . There were not only male
refugees, among them were women, old people and children.
They all seemed very tired and exhausted. I did not know
whether they had any place to sleep in Kovno in those days,
maybe they just slept in the station or on the street . . .
I finally decided that it was completely useless to continue
the discussions with Tokyo.

"Discussions with Tokyo"

On April 6, 1940, Chiune Sugihara sent cable No. 58 from Kaunas to
Tokyo:

To: Foreign Minister Arita

From: Sugihara in Kaunas

*About: the renewal of the contract for renting the building of the consulate. Sug-
ihara and the owner wish to renew the contract for one more year. They also plan
to lease the garage which will be a new addition to the house.*

The Vaizgantas Street lease was only half up, but Sugihara knew there
would soon be *no* new quarters left in Kaunas. He better make his bid
now. The city was thoroughly flooded with refugees, all needing a place
to stay. Most were Jews from Nazi-occupied western Poland and Soviet-
occupied eastern Poland. A few Jewish and Christian Lithuanians were

161

still arriving from Memel, northwest of Kovno, which Germany had annexed from Lithuania. There were even a few lucky Jews able to exit Germany, Czechoslovakia, and Austria, and other European Jews might soon make their way here, too. Perhaps Sugihara had some intelligence reports that Hitler's blitzkriegs against Denmark and Norway would begin within three days of Cable No. 58. Luxembourg, Holland, Belgium, and France would fall in a month. Who knows how many other refugees would push for Kaunas? Nearly all the other havens had been eclipsed. Best to telegram Tokyo now, even six months ahead of time; the wheels of bureaucracy turned slowly in the *Gaimusho.*

But that April day, it seems, Sugihara had not amassed enough intelligence from his network of informants and his own travel around the border regions to predict when the Soviets might move against Lithuania. Could he have known that from June 15, the Soviets would be so bent on swallowing the Baltic countries whole that any vestige of their independence, such as foreign consulates, would be closed?

While Lithuania was still free, it was one of the most desirable places in Europe for Jews and others fleeing the coming war. Consequently, the real estate market was hotter than hot. Any entrepreneurial burgher landlord could make a fortune on subdivides; the Japanese could conceivably be dropped from their lease if the lessor got a sweeter offer. Sugihara knew this, which is why his cables regarding leases and architectural plans are so copious. What seemed quotidian was really a matter of life—at least for 2,139 Jews and their families—or death.

I was amused to find in the Tokyo archives even the record of Sugihara's negotiations over how to divide the heating bills with the neighbor upstairs. It seemed trivial. But in his well-situated and heated home, Sugihara knew that other foreigners were not so fortunate. Many refugees had been undone by the cold of the last few months, the police herding them out of the city streets into crowded and cold apartments on the Slobodka side of the Neeman River, and out farther near German-occupied Poland. Sugihara on his countryside forays must have come across the type of open refugee enclaves that Moses Beckelman described seeing the previous fall—Jews spending the season in battle-charred and snow-covered ravines of the Bug River, trapped between Nazi, Soviet, and Lithuanian border guards, waiting until enough were sufficiently drunk so they could take a chance running across the Lithuanian border without getting shot.

By April, the ground was just beginning to thaw. But before Chiune got too busy with his spice garden, he needed to grapple with the lines of authority spidering out from Tokyo. This was easier said than done. During Sugihara's posting to Kaunas, from the summer of 1939 to the sum-

mer of 1940, the Japanese cabinet changed no fewer than four times.[1]
Even Togo, now stationed in Moscow and a far more powerful diplomat
than Sugihara, complained: "I began to feel some anxiety over our condition at home," as he writes in his unpublished memoirs.[2]

We do not know who first thought of sending Sugihara to be "new
eyes" in Lithuania. The initial arrangements, though, had been made
when Hachiro Arita was foreign minister. Sugihara himself believed that
he had been sent on his mission by the pro-German militarist faction, and
Arita was by no means a militarist. He was even alleged to oppose warm-
ing relations with the Axis powers and to espouse a more pro-U.S. stance.
But precisely because of his personal positions, Arita was forced to compromise with the powerful military factions. In the debacle that followed
the Nazi-Soviet Pact at the end of August 1939, he was told to resign.

Nobuyuki Abe became both prime minister and foreign minister in
September 1939, just as the Sugiharas were arriving in Kaunas. Abe was
an Imperial Japanese Army general who advocated an end to the Sino-
Japanese War and Japanese neutrality in the growing European conflict.
As an army insider, it was hoped that he would be able to reign in the
militarists. He handed over the *Gaimusho* portfolio to Admiral Kichi-
saburo Nomura of the navy by the end of the month. The transition was
apparently not smooth. Twice, Sugihara had to send the architectural
drawings of his offices to the newcomer, as well as repeat the terms of the
lease. And all for nought; by January 1940, the Abe-Nomura team was
out. Notwithstanding its broad military connections, it could not make
the military cooperate with the major political parties. Arita returned to
head the *Gaimusho*.

In addition to the intra-agency squabbles and the inconsistencies that
resulted, each of these foreign ministers and cabinets had its own foreign
policies. Sugihara's cables were always addressed to the foreign minister. In
itself, this designation is probably little more than a formality. Consular
administrative matters and even visa questions in a well-run ministry usually do not involve matters of state. They would likely be dealt with by
low- or mid-level bureaucrats. Ideological shifts at the top of the government should not have held much sway over someone in Sugihara's position.

But "the masterless man" rarely fell into a neat slot in anyone's organizational chart. In fact, he had a true knack for hovering between conflicting interests. Sometimes this was his undoing, but sometimes, under
certain circumstances, he was able to finesse both sides against each other.
The sensitivity of pro-U.S. and pro-German factions to information regarding Germany's true intentions toward the Soviet Union (which "our
man in Kaunas" was sent to provide) placed this low-level official more in

the loop than he otherwise might have been. Whatever "discussions with Tokyo" he was having, however, getting a decision was no simple matter.

Visa Policies

Housekeeping issues were not the only ones Sugihara struggled to coordinate with Headquarters. While it was true that he had more important tasks to perform in Lithuania than consular work, the fact that he opened the consulate at all took on a life of its own. Who could know it was mostly for show? People needed visas, and they figured the consul was the one to ask. He could not tell them he was too busy spying on Soviet and German troop movements, figuring out their implications for potential Japanese alliances in Europe, and thinking, at least for himself, how these developments would affect one faction in the Ministries of Foreign Affairs or Interior and another in the army or navy.

At the start of his assignment, it seems, visas fell low on Sugihara's list of priorities. Under normal circumstances, there would not have been much of the three s's—signing, stamping, sealing—that consumes so much of a "real" diplomat's time. Who could have predicted so many Lithuanians would want to go to Japan, of all places? And even among the many refugees flocking into town, few ever considered Japan at all. But these were not normal times. Japan looked better and better as the doors of so many other countries slammed shut.

Yet how did visa seekers find their way to the doors at Vaizgantas Street in the first place? To what extent did Sugihara have to consult with Headquarters, and by what criteria could he make decisions once they had? How do his early visa-granting activities bear on the mass rescue of the following summer? Perhaps we can trace things back to one Alfred Katz, the Kaunas representative of Metro-Goldwyn-Mayer. As coincidence would have it, Katz was the man who booked the Laurel and Hardy movie that young Solly Ganor watched, courtesy of Sugihara's Hanukah *gelt,* back in December 1939.[3]

Born in Poland, Katz worked out of one of the few MGM branch offices in Lithuania. The movies got him into Kaunas, and it seems the movies would get him out. "There was an entreaty from Berman, manager of Metro-Goldwyn-Mayer Co. in Tokyo, that he would like to summon his younger brother-in-law, Alfred Katz (Polish), who is taking refuge and living in your region, to our country for a month," Sugihara is informed by the director of the American Third Division of the *Gaimusho* in January 1940. Of course, this matter had already been discussed with the Ministry of the Interior as well. Sugihara is assured that advanced payment has been collected for the cost of the diplomatic cables. If Katz, in Kaunas, indeed files the application, "there will be no problem issuing an entrance visa to him."[4]

Simple enough. And yet there seem to have been lots of problems, as shown in Sugihara's cable No. 50 of March 21, 1940:

> According to the telegram you gave me in the middle of January, I issued the entrance visa to Alfred Katz who lives in Vilna in this country on March 21st and I will send the report about this visa and others. I gave the visa for the following reasons so please acknowledge. He has asked for the visa from us after finishing the departing procedure by "Nansen passport," and if we refuse to issue a visa on this passport, it will be actually impossible for him to leave the country. Regarding these actual circumstances, we conceded that this is an unavoidable circumstance.

Why so much bother over one visa? Why was Sugihara sending "reports," and even if this was standard procedure, why was he so demonstrative about it? Why was he seeking acknowledgment and why did he sound so concerned? Unlike most of the refugees in Kaunas, Katz had a good job and important international connections. And there were assurances he would be supported in Japan, and that he could move to another country shortly. His case should have been open and shut.

But it was not. The proceedings took on a decidedly surreal cast for poor Alfred Katz, so close to being rescued, and to his concerned relative in Tokyo. Katz's plight was similar to that of thousands of Jewish refugees trying to stay a step ahead of the Nazis and who were forced to reconcile bureaucratic demands of different governments if they wanted to save their lives. What was different in the case of Alfred Katz was but one factor, the involvement of vice consul Chiune Sugihara.

Let us parse the problem. Katz, as the Japanese records indicate, was a Polish citizen and carried that country's passport. Japan continued to recognize Poland through Pearl Harbor, and the Polish government-in-exile was represented in Tokyo. But for Stalin, as for Hitler, the Polish government no longer existed. Even German and Austrian Jews escaping from years of Nazi persecution and humiliation could travel on their national passports. Since last fall, when Germany and the Soviet Union carved up Poland, three million Polish Jews had become stateless. Sugihara, therefore, could not issue the visa on the Polish passport that Katz likely possessed, because the Soviets would not recognize Katz's travel documents.

But a remedy was seemingly at hand. The British consul in Kaunas, Thomas Preston, allowed representatives of the Polish government-in-exile to operate within the British consulate. And those officials were issuing "Sauf Conduit," safe conduct papers, or as Sugihara more precisely called them, "Nansen passports," named for Fridtjof Nansen, a League of

Nations official who first proposed them in 1922. Since then, millions of stateless people, often endangered, had been able to cross borders to safety with these "semi-visas." Katz could undoubtedly receive such a Nansen passport at the British consulate. But would Sugihara's government, so antagonistic to the League of Nations, recognize it?

Theoretically, the Sauf Conduit documents would allow Alfred Katz to gather needed transit visas for his trip, to leave Lithuania, to enter, traverse, and exit the Soviet Union, and to be perched at the Japanese entry point, where he could finally use the visa that Tokyo officials were asking Sugihara in Kaunas to issue to join his brother in Japan. But only theoretically. In this hornet's nest, we have a precious opportunity to observe Sugihara in action. The prepaid cable sent by Berman, the MGM representative in Tokyo, on behalf of his brother-in-law was but one of many cables that a busy consul would receive. It is possible Berman had special connections or procured special favors. But even if Sugihara sensed that this were the case, he might have chosen an easier course of action. Given all the uncertainty for an official in Sugihara's position as to what was really going on at any moment in Tokyo, he might have cabled back that Katz possessed no valid travel documents and be done with the matter. This surely would have been the safest response. He might have even tried to score some points by demonstrating his conscientiousness or play up to the militarists (with whom he allegedly had connections) by asserting his antagonism to the West and its bigoted League of Nations. He could have flaunted his "ideological purity."

But instead he did not ask permission; he created a precedent. "I issued the entrance visa to Alfred Katz who lives in Vilna in this country on March 21st and I will send the report about this visa and others." Sugihara protected himself—and his mass rescue to come—by upholding the authority of the *Gaimusho* to make such decisions, by registering awareness of the problem of Nansen papers, by defying with indirection challenges to their validity, but, most important, by taking the risk to act decisively and by raising the cost to anyone who would want to bother to challenge him.

We do not know what Sugihara wrote in his report, nor, for that matter, do we know what ultimately happened to Alfred Katz. But we do know, because of Katz's case, a bit more about how Sugihara operates. For one thing, he uses the neat bureaucratic formula of "unavoidable circumstance," an argument often used by officials in his position to legitimate inaction. He could have entirely avoided the conflict—among Japanese visa policy, the new realities of stateless refugees, and Japanese hostility to the League of Nations—by turning down Katz. But like Oishi and his *ronin*, Sugihara courts danger in trying to resolve incompatible debts.

And within this cunning strategy and cover-up, he hints around about "others" who were seeking visas at this time, but only hints. He seeks acknowledgment for his handling of the situation. Who were these "others" seeking visas at this time? Was he shoring up his defenses for later situations? What discussions did Sugihara have with Tokyo, ultimately deeming those discussions "useless"? What risks did he begin to take in acting with only the partial authority granted by rival factions who could not achieve consensus, and what risks was he taking in acting even with no authority at all?

Kristallnacht and the *Gosho Kaigi*

Plenty of other interminable and unresolved discussions were taking place in Tokyo besides the little case of Alfred Katz of Kovno. In recent years, Jewish visa matters were confined to speculative proposals of minor Jew hands such as Norihiro Yasue, who toured Palestine and wrote of Jewish conspiracies. Mostly, they focused on fears of Jews spreading communism to the East. But after *Kristallnacht,* the murderous riots in Germany and Austria in November 1938, pressures increased on making decisions. Allegedly, the question of Jewish immigration was discussed just about a month later by the *Gosho Kaigi,* the Five Ministers Meeting, which brought together the prime minister, foreign minister, and ministers of the treasury, army, and navy.

The number of Jewish refugees applying for temporary resident and transit visas in Manchukuo and Japan, or trying to make their way to visa-free Japanese-controlled Shanghai, was rising dramatically. After the dissolution of Poland in September 1939, that number skyrocketed. The usual rivalries between Japanese ministries, plus their lack of coordination with the Manchukuo ministries, also stymied Jewish immigration policy. No clear directive came from any line of authority. This is what made Sugihara's "discussions with Tokyo" so futile.

How Jews were perceived by other nations—not only the viciousness of the Nazis but also the anemia of the Americans and Europeans—exerted much influence on the highest levels of the Japanese cabinet and Diet. After the Evian Conference in July 1938, it was clear few places in the West would welcome Jewish refugees. *Kristallnacht* occurred in November, and the following spring, the British government issued its White Paper, which severely limited the number of Jews who could settle in Palestine.

In June 1939, the ship *St. Louis,* loaded with 1,128 Jewish refugees, found itself unable to dock anywhere in the United States or Cuba. No one would let the passengers come ashore, even though many had documents and adoring relatives who would accept financial responsibility. The ship returned to Europe, and many of the refugees eventually were murdered in the Holocaust. This floating prison became the ultimate symbol that the Jews were unwanted. In that light, the Japanese felt increasingly pressured by glowing Soviet propaganda on the "Jewish Autonomous Region" in nearby Birobidzhan to allow at least some Jews to settle in Manchuria.

Certainly the Japanese did not want to lose an image war to their old enemies the Soviets. At the same time, insofar as the Japanese government wanted to primarily exclude Jews, they preferred to smokescreen the policy by blaming such exclusion on the Manchurians. As the Japanese ambassador to Manchukuo instructed one of his officials: "So make the Manchurian Police take part in this [limiting the entrance of Jews] and defend yourself from being dragged into the international dispute."[5]

It is around this time in December 1938 that the most authoritative proclamation regarding Jews was made. Attributed to the *Gosho Kaigi*, it virtually dictated—though other proclamations would follow—norms of thought and action for the time to come:

No. 1 Outline of Responses to Jews: To maintain good will and close relations with both Germany and Italy is central to the diplomacy of the Empire at the present time. So on principle we should certainly avoid tolerating Jews in our Empire whom our allies so vehemently reject. But taking the attitude of shunning them completely, as do the Germans, does not accord with the spirit of racial equality which our Empire has insisted on for many years.

Not only that but we must consider the fact that we need to introduce foreign capital for economic construction to accomplish the war in this state of emergency which the Empire now faces. And also we must avoid making relations with the United States worse. It could cause disadvantageous results. So we should treat [Jews] in accordance with the Guidelines on the left [below]:

Guidelines: 1. We will treat the Jews living in Japan, Manchuria, and China at present with fairness, in the same manner as we treat other foreigners and we will not take special measures to reject them. 2. We will treat the newly arrived Jews to Japan, Manchukuo, and China fairly, generally within the regulations of controlling the entry of foreigners. 3. We will avoid making special efforts to invite Jews to Japan, Manchuria, and China. But this policy does not include people who are worth using such as capitalists and technologists.[6]

There is no indication who prepared these guidelines or which ministries enforced them, but it is safe to say they reflected a philosophy at the highest level of government. Jewish visas were justifiable within these stated, if somewhat equivocal, considerations. Finally, it seemed, Japanese field consuls had their marching orders. These guidelines were apparently not written for mere effect in internal bureaucratic wars. For example, Y. Miura, the Japanese consul in Shanghai, sent a cable marked "secret" to Foreign Minister Nomura in which he summarized the discussions taking place in regard to "establishing a special area for Jews and operations with the US."[7]

Koreshige Inuzuka, Yasue's counterpart as the Jewish hand of the navy—who would play a major role in establishing policies for twenty thousand-plus Jewish refugees who spent World War II in Shanghai—was also involved in this scheme to enlist foreign support for a Jewish haven in Manchukuo. He teamed up with Mitsuzo Tamura, a former liaison for the South Manchurian Railway in New York—where he might have met Jews in business circles—and now an Osaka steel executive with good *Gaimusho* connections. Through a Shanghai Jewish resident named Ellis Hayim, chairman of the Jewish Refugee Committee, Tamura was introduced to an American Jew named Frank Garson, president of the Long Island Machinery Company in suburban New York.[8]

In view of Japan's need for specialized steel and machinery for war preparations and the threat of an American embargo on Japanese military and civilian production, it is telling with which "Jewish leader" dicussions were initiated. While Garson was not exactly a steel magnate, Tamura must have assumed that Garson had clout in both the steel business and the Jewish community. Whatever the case, the cables they exchange lay out an intricate dance, each side circling the other. In one, Garson is ordered to send his representatives to Tokyo without further conditions and delay, there to begin negotiations, in typical Japanese manner, face-to-face. Garson's inquiries in the interim about how many Jews might be accommodated in specified parts of Manchukuo are rebuffed. Not until we get the steel, the polite cables from Tokyo and Osaka imply.

But the Japanese had other forms of payment in mind as well. The deal was clear: the Japanese would gladly give visas to Jews if Garson and Company would praise the Japanese in the American media. And that was only the first condition. At least one Japanese also demanded a $100,000,000 sweetener for the admission of thirty thousand Jewish refugees.[9] From the end of 1939 through the summer of 1940, negotiations proceeded, moving well beyond Garson. Indeed, the eminent Rabbi Stephen Wise of New York City, with his backstairs connections with FDR, grew increasingly worried about being exploited by the Japanese and deferred to the State Department rather than fully exploring the potential for rescuing Jews without harming America's interests. In the end, neither side got what it wanted, and the talks fell apart.

But the Japanese did not give up. Instead, they turned to another Allied power with "valuable" Jews, and tried to curry favor with Sir Victor Sassoon (1881–1961), a scion of the great Jewish family of scholars and merchants based in Shanghai, but with British ties. Sir Victor was born in India but educated in England, and even survived a plane crash in 1915 while in training with the Royal Naval Air Service. He moved his family banking business to Shanghai in 1931, where he quickly became a major player in real estate, erecting some of the city's most famous and beautiful buildings. His lavish parties contributed to the city's cosmopolitan reputation, and Sir Victor became a pillar of the local Jewish community. He also became the top philanthropist to his fellow Sefardim, Jews most recently connected with areas of Asia rather than Europe. His form of piety was altogether worldly. "There's only one race greater than the Jews and that's the Derby," he once said. In fact, his thoroughbreds won that Kentucky competition four times.[10]

Sir Victor seemed less remote and enigmatic than American Jewish entrepreneurs, and the Japanese made it their business to watch the power broker's every move and transaction, particularly as they increased their control over Shanghai. On January 17, 1939, Shanghai consul Miura informed Foreign Minister Arita that Sassoon donated $1,500,000 to help rescue and support Jewish refugees.[11] Three days later, Arita advised Miura how to behave at an upcoming meeting of various Shanghai-based diplomats concerning refugee policy. Miura was to "avoid taking (a) positive position of support [for continued immigration] but handle this so that we can realize the purpose of the Operations Department." This vague and delicate wording does not clarify exactly what "purpose" the foreign minister meant. What *is* clear is that Sassoon was considered too prominent to be antagonized.

On February 28, 1939, the *Japan Times* reported a discussion held during the budgetary debate of the House of Peers. Katsuji Debuchi raised the fact that "great concern has been manifested by some sections of the Japanese public threatened by the recent increase in number of Jews in the Far East, the result of the antisemitism campaign in Germany." Foreign Minister Arita declared unequivocally: "No discrimination will be made against Jewish residents or immigrants in Japan."

Nevertheless, by the time Sugihara was on his way to Kaunas later that summer, his government had imposed limitations on the acceptance of new Jewish refugees in Shanghai and ordered that Jews already there be registered. The German government agreed to this policy and made radio announcements that German Jews would no longer be admitted to the colony, but did not persistently enforce this restriction.

In the end, this "secret" proposal and other not-so-secret proposals to establish a "Japanese Birobidzhan" was stalemated, unsurprisingly, by conflict between Japanese ministries. Hitler's military successes in northern and Western Europe in the spring of 1940 strengthened the Japanese pro-Nazi faction, which paid greater heed to Nazi disfavor over the idea of a Japanese Jewish haven. But even this pro-Nazi faction was interested in Jewish capital and talent. No colonies and settlements emerged, but some routes remained open to Jews—if certain officials forced them open.

Saving Stella

As Japan grappled with policy issues, Sugihara was becoming an expert not only at working within the system but also at improvising around it. To quote the old Harbin Gakuin song, he certainly did have "guts and determination," also compassion. Each of these qualities flowered in the story of Stella Kominskaya, one of the non-Jews to have received a Sugihara visa in Kaunas. I spoke with Mrs. Kominskaya in February 1995. This spirited octogenarian still talks of Sugihara with a lovely kind of infatuation. "He was really a wonderful man, just a good man," she says, drawing out the vowels of "good" for emphasis.

Stella's memories of Sugihara were renewed in the late sixties, when he made a sentimental call on her in London, not long after penning his short "memoir" for the Polish scholar Korab-Zabryk. Perhaps the act of writing had stirred up the past, and he acted on an urge. At any rate, it seems to have been a poignant time for the old vice consul. He was nearing his eighth decade and working as a sewing machine salesman, based in Moscow. His life after the war was full of setbacks, which we will learn about later.

He was hardly the vigorous Sugihara she remembered, as captured in the 1940 photograph that both had held onto over the years. In the picture, there is a group of friends and family members standing at the Kovno railroad station. Stella is the beautiful young woman holding a large bouquet of flowers, donning hat and coat as if leisurely embarking on a luxury vacation. And there stands Sugihara, leaning just a bit forward as if he were organizing the event, in his suit and vest, umbrella in hand, and a fedora turned down at a fashionable angle. He exudes abundant self-confidence. For a man so blatantly spying against warring nationals who might assassinate him at any moment, a man constantly taking risks by playing off opposing factions at home, he looks mysteriously relaxed.

In the spring of 1940, Stella and her husband, Lieutenant Stanisław Kaspcik, turned to Sugihara in absolute desperation. Stella had grown up with her Belgian mother and White Russian stepfather on his estate in

Baranowic, in eastern Poland. The previous fall, when the Soviets annexed that area, the aristocratic, anti-Bolshevik stepfather, fearing the Soviet secret police, fled with his family to Vilnius. This may not have been
the best choice. His son-in-law, serving in a high position in Polish intelligence, had already been arrested three times by the Lithuanian police on
suspicions of being a Communist agent. Stella's husband also had reason
to fear the Soviets. She remembers their anguish as he was bluntly warned
by Lithuanian officials to "choose another country."

The Kaspciks felt trapped. They cast about for some safe part of the
world, despairing that, even if one existed, they could not get the papers
to move there. But Stella's mother suddenly remembered a strange friendship with a Japanese man from her student days in Brussels. Stella recalls
how amused she was by her mother's insistence that "there must be a consulate of Japan" somewhere around. It seemed so farfetched. She does not
know whether she was laughing or crying when she returned from the
consulate on Vaizgantas Street, telling mother that "a very nice gentleman" said, "Yes, of course I will help."

For what happens next, we actually have Sugihara's own words! In his
memoir for Korab-Zabryk, under the heading, "My Polish friends in
Kovno and Königsberg," he writes the following:

A few months later after my being a consul, a young European woman with
slight Asiatic features came to me. This woman had a Polish passport. She
said she was the daughter of the Japanese Kavagoe who lived in Japan and
she wanted to join him there. One day later this woman returned to the
consulate together with her husband, who was about 26–27 years old and
introduced himself as senior lieutenant in the Polish army. As I understood
it, he was a secret service man of the Polish general staff and interested in
eastern cultures and he wanted to accompany his wife to Japan to meet her
father.

I made some inquiries in Japan and after some time I told the couple
Kaspcik that I was prepared to help them to get to Japan via Germany. Stella
was born in Belgium as the daughter of Kavagoe who at that time was a student, and a Belgian girl. Kavagoe, however, obeying his parents, returned to
his fatherland breaking all ties with Stella's mother, who then married a
Russian tsarist officer Möller. They lived in Vilnius at that time. I found out
that Kavagoe had become the manager of a fashionable hotel and golf club
in Kavana, Japan, and he immediately answered that Stella was indeed his
daughter and that he wanted her to come to Japan. He asked me to give the
couple all the information concerning their trip to Japan, as well as means
for their travel.

Soon after, the Kaspcik couple openly traveled to Japan via Nazi Germany and Italy, with the certificates that I had issued. After a successful journey they arrived in the country of their father. After the war was finished, I heard that the husband Kaspcik had been killed in China under unknown circumstances. His wife Stella married for the second time and is now living under the name Kaminskaya in England.

This passage can only be called a tour de force. It seems the "Japanese father" was fictional, for a starter; Stella disclaims the Japanese lineage and indicates that this Kavana gentleman was nothing more than her mother's old college chum. (The photograph showing no "slight Asiatic features" seems to support her paternity claims.) Kavagoe, it would seem, readily agreed to let the Kaspciks use his name to qualify for Japanese visas. The vice consul even provided a résumé and study-abroad program for the lieutenant in Polish intelligence, underscoring his interest in "eastern cultures." Sugihara orchestrated the whole thing—but still kept up the pretense even twenty-seven years later!

At the time, there were two ways to get to Japan. They could travel overland through the Soviet Union, or proceed via Germany and Italy, where they could continue by ship. Neither choice was reassuring. Lieutenant Stanisław Kaspcik would probably have been arrested by both the Soviets and the Nazis. The Soviets would have deported him to Katyn, where that spring they shot 4,500 of his fellow Polish Army officers. If not the Katyn Forest, his fate would undoubtedly lie in the hands of one Nazi concentration camp commandant or another. Even with the visa, it seemed there was no way out for the young lieutenant and his beautiful wife.

Sugihara advised them to pick the lesser of two evils and travel west. "We will arrange something," he told them reassuringly and drew up the needed documentation. Stella remembers telling Sugihara stoically that, "Three days in fear until we get to the Mediterranean are better than seventeen days across the Soviet Union." They were sick with fright but had no choice except to trust him. He had gotten them this far, after all. On the eve of their departure, they sat down to a last dinner with family, friends, and the Japanese vice consul (how many consuls eat dinner with those to whom they give visas?!) at the Kovno railroad station. This was the setting for the photograph.

After the plates were cleared, Sugihara drew Stella aside and gave her a small package. "In this envelope is a pair of gloves," he told her, "a present for my Foreign Minister which you will deliver in Tokyo. Show this envelope at all border crossings. You will be like diplomatic couriers." So this was why he pointed them through the dangers of Europe! Their cover would work better in countries friendlier to Japan than the Soviet Union, and this envelope, therefore, would be their lifeline.

At each border crossing during those "three days in fear," Stella produced the envelope—as their train moved out of the Kaunas depot and they watched the fading figures of Sugihara and their dinner party waving from the platform, as they crossed the tightly guarded Lithuanian border with German-occupied Poland, as they left that war-scarred country for Germany, the heart of the beast, as Austria and Italy passed by their windows, and on to Naples, where a Japanese steamship waited to take them "home."

At each juncture, the door of their coach would open rather violently, the compartment quickly filling with more people than the Kaspciks thought would ever fit. The refugee couple would be accosted by Nazi and Italian fascist guards in a variety of uniforms, followed always by at least one plainclothes official who would pore over the documents, feel the paper, and check all the stamps. It was at that moment that Kaspcik, in his new civilian garb, would assume an intimidatingly official aspect and present the stamped, sealed envelope containing the gloves. The guards would take a last look at the Polish military intelligence officer— and his beautiful wife—smile, knowingly mumble *"Diplomatischer Kurier,"* and smartly salute.

Sugihara did a remarkable deed, yes, but he also got something in return. His "diplomatic courier" was a well-connected Polish spy who left behind some presents of his own for Sugihara. The Kaspciks seem to be just two of many of Sugihara's "Polish friends," as he benignly called the elaborate spy network that worked for him in the months ahead.

Whether Sugihara's assistance for the Kaspcik-Möller family was connected to his role as a consul, a spy, or just a "really wonderful man" is not clear. What is clear is that, given the climate of procedural uncertainty, he made up strategies as he went along, according to the case. The more I learned about Sugihara, the more I came to appreciate his creativity, his ability to improvise in endless variations.

The best way to "cover" yourself in the gray areas, it seems, was to pursue two distinct strategies of inquiry. With visa-seekers, Sugihara would ask as many extraneous, petty, self-evident questions as he could, then sift the answers for something, for some perfect detail. This would then spark a particular plan—a pretend father, a pair of gloves, it did not matter, as long as it was malleable enough to justify the visa. Then, in turning around to cope with the *Gaimusho,* Sugihara would simply *neglect* to ask any questions that might interfere with his various plans. This worked beautifully as long as Tokyo's leadership was at loose ends. It was hard enough to get any authoritative decision from the infighting *Gaimusho,* as all field consuls knew, and best for a "masterless man" not to bother asking at all. As Sugihara would write in 1967: "It was completely useless to continue discussions with Tokyo."

Springtime

On May 29, 1940, he received cable No. 14 in the name of Foreign Minister Arita, responding, finally, to his cable of early April regarding the Vaizgantas Street lease. "We will recognize the renewal of your contract [for your house]," it said.

But on June 15, the Soviets captured Lithuania as well as Latvia and Estonia, and within a month called for elections. The Lithuanian Communist Party, the only party listed on the ballot, not surprisingly won by a 99 percent margin. Within a few days, the new parliament petitioned the Soviet government to incorporate Lithuania within the Soviet Union. Sugihara, like Norem, Preston, and all the consuls in town, received notice that their governments would be represented in Moscow and that they were to close shop within thirty days.

We do not know where Sugihara stood with renegotiating the lease at that point. Whatever the case, his alacrity in this matter proved to be a waste. The Japanese consulate in Kaunas, like the cherry blossoms back home that the Sugiharas so missed, proved to be dazzling in its effect but so very short-lived. That said, Sugihara wasted not a second, though he does seem to have been caught at least somewhat unaware. Certainly he knew the Soviets were circling, but he did not guess their plans included annexation. Did the people to whom Sugihara reported in the Japanese government, with their embassy in Moscow and their extensive network of Polish and other spies, not realize, seventeen days before the Red Army marched through Lithuania, that it would be a waste of money to tell Sugihara to pay for next year's lease?

The spring of 1940 was full of astonishing twists on all sides. First the Soviets marched west, and then Germany let it happen! Who would have thought Hitler would allow Stalin some *Lebensraum,* annexed territory of his own in the East? Was Hitler throwing a bone to Stalin, so he could concentrate on taking the West? It seemed so at the time, though of course Hitler knew that Stalin's victory would be temporary. Precisely one year and a week would elapse, following Stalin's grab for the Baltics, until the Germans invaded the Soviet-annexed Baltics and the Soviet Union on June 22, 1941.

In that span of time, Germans were still most often willing to be rid of Jews even through immigration rather than through the murder and violence that later became the main thrust of their policy. This meant there were still a few escape hatches—one of them the Kaunas consulate, with its spice garden outside and its kind vice consul inside.

Perhaps now is the time to pick up the stories of others who had arrived when Sugihara came to Kaunas the previous fall, and were now experiencing their first Lithuanian spring. Before, we learned how they got to Lithuania. Now, we want to understand why they decided to leave Lithuania as we examine the role Sugihara played in that process. Let us return to Berek and Ruchel Zielonka, energetic and resourceful and now beginning to feel settled in Vilna. In 1985, Zielonka, now Zell, wrote about that vitality and false sense of security before the June 15, 1940, Soviet invasion of Lithuania. Spring of that year beckoned with promise, as it used to before fascism darkened Europe. In Lithuania, one allowed oneself to hope again, as Zell so wistfully remembers:

> Vilna was not only a beautiful city, but it was also a great center of Jewish culture. In fact, the old rabbinical literature used to call it the "Jerusalem of Lithuania." The city, which had been already swollen with refugees, now became choked with them. Our instincts told us this was not going to last.
>
> We didn't know how long we were going to be in Vilna, and I began to look for a way to make a living there. I was not one to just sit still and do nothing but go to a restaurant every day. Besides, the Polish currency we had with us was now worthless. We had some gold with us, which we kept hidden. But this was always in danger of being confiscated.
>
> I went into the business of flour, grain, and related commodities, which I knew better than anything else. In a short period of time, I made a lot of money from the business, the equivalent of thousands of dollars. We were doing well in Vilna. But the outlook was very bleak. There was only one way to get out—through Russia—and the chances were remote for Jewish refugees, Polish citizens, to get transit visas from the Russians. And, of course, even if we could cross Russia, we would need transit visas from those countries which had to be crossed to reach Palestine or the United States. Escape seemed far too complicated, and the odds very slim. But we did not give up hope.

Even for entrepreneurial sorts, Lithuania was beginning to feel like a gilded cage: Nazis to the west and north, Soviets to the east and south, no exit in any direction. One did what one could and, like Berek Zielonka, Zorach Warhaftig was also getting busy doing what he did best: organizing for the Zionist cause. People from Warhaftig's different worlds in Poland—the religious communities, the Jewish defense organizations, the political parties, the lawyerly professionals—were now reconstituting themselves in Lithuania. It was the only place left.

The culture of interwar Polish Jewry was so vibrant that, as it faced its last tragic moments in Nazi-occupied Poland, it magically began to recreate itself, if only for this short interval. Indeed, the new Jews in Lithuania experienced their own cherry blossom season that spring. As the Nazis began to imprison Jews in the ghettos that were forming in the larger cities of Poland, an underground leadership was established in places like Kaunas and Vilnius. Insofar as it was possible, Lithuanian-based Jews tried to maintain contact with their brethren left behind in Poland. Not only to the west but to the east, the shifting Soviet border provided new opportunities for communicating with Soviet Jews who had been largely cut off since the Communist takeover more than twenty years before. Then there was Palestine, America, and other parts of the world where Jews were not threatened; they might even be able to help. Suddenly, Lithuania was the hub of many spokes. It seemed for many to be the last best hope.

Surely for a leader of Warhaftig's ability and energy, there was much to do. However, "time was not on our side," he recalls. As the leader of Poland's religious Zionists, his only reasonable response was to throw himself "heart and soul into a life-saving program of *aliya* [immigration] to Eretz Israel," he says. This was not a simple or obvious conclusion. Lithuania was still viewed as a haven, the Switzerland of Eastern Europe. And though many Jews saw how frail and unreliable most international alliances were, they wanted to believe that the Nazis and Soviets had some shared interest in sustaining Lithuania's neutrality. Besides, it felt a bit like home here. For many Jews, especially those with aged parents left behind in their small towns, there was great comfort not to have to move too far away from the worlds they knew in Eastern Europe. Palestine seemed the far side of the moon.

Indeed, many Jews began to put down roots in Lithuania soon after they arrived. Schools and cultural institutions were organized and neighborhoods formed. This strategy was in keeping with the renowned spiritual leader of Vilna and head of the coordinating committee of the Yeshivot, Rabbi Hayyim Ozer Grodzinski: *"Shev ve'al taase,"* the patriarch ruled, "sit and don't do." When caught in irresolvable quandaries, sit, stay put, aggressively curb your instinct to act for the sake of acting, err on the side of omission, passivity is the better side of valor.

Others disagreed vehemently with this approach. Building schools and forming theater groups, they argued, deflected resources away from escape and resistance. Such optimistic activities lulled local Jews into feeling they had more control than they actually did. But as more war clouds gathered, the "stay put" Jews redoubled their efforts to forge ahead, undaunted. For most Jews in the spring of 1940, there was always another

Jewish joke whose punchline ended ". . . so we'll learn to live under water." In other words, no matter how bad it got, they would adjust.

Zionists like Warhaftig—he estimates there were about 2,500 in Lithuania that spring—did a bit of building, too, but along much different lines. Like the characters of a Devora Baron tale, they decided their fate lay in nature and homeland, and thus set about planting crops under the warm spring sun. As such, many regrouped in their *hakhsharot,* their preparatory programs, to be *halutzim,* pioneers in the Holyland, continuing the course of agricultural training that had flourished in rural Poland and was rudely interrupted by the Nazis.

Sugihara made frequent trips into the countryside to observe tank movements, check with local farmers about who was buying wool for winter uniforms, and find where various armies were stockpiling coffins for future inevitabilities—the type of intelligence gathering from which canny spies wove their predictions. Perhaps he had observed the odd sight of these formerly urban *halutzim* in their Saturday best, awkwardly trying to push plows through the rocky Lithuanian soil. Such activity, these *halutzim* felt, would bridge their old life in various Polish cities and their new life in a strange "Asiatic" homeland.

At the same time, some two thousand emphatically non–Zionist Jews, the teachers and students of the Yeshiva, were also busy regrouping. Some hailed from western Poland, like a few disciples of the Lubavitcher Rebbe, Joseph Schneersohn, who was already well established in Brooklyn. His emissary and son-in-law, Rabbi Shemaryahu Gurarye of Riga, Latvia, was busy getting his students settled in a new Yeshiva in Vilna and taking advantage of Lithuania's more fluid borders with the Soviet Union to try to pass some relief funds for poor rabbis in the Soviet Union, who since the Bolshevik takeover had had little contact with foreign Jews.

Rabbi Gurarye was particularly skilled at getting his allies abroad to pressure the international Jewish agencies, like Moe Beckelman's Joint Distribution Committee, to support his religious and educational endeavors. Beckelman said that the good rabbi did not understand the meaning of the word "no." Never one to sulk when meeting his match, Beckelman even suggested that the wealthy and powerful "uptown Jews," like Paul Baerwald—JDC leader of questionable effectiveness and FDR's choice for Jewish representative at the unsuccessful Evian conference— might learn a political lesson or two from the tough Polish rabbi.

During the winter months several academies, especially those from eastern Poland now under Soviet control, moved to Vilnius. Some students found themselves sleeping on cold benches and in chilly corridors of the synagogues around town. Then in the spring, as the Lithuanian government tried to weaken the Polish presence in Vilnius by forcing refugees into the countryside, some of the Yeshivot reestablished themselves again, this time outside the city. The process was terribly disruptive, but the Yeshivot would try, at all costs, not to lose time from their rigorous regime of prayer, study, and contemplation. As one chronicler of the Mirrer Yeshiva noted: "Even during the war when we wandered to escape the drawn sword, even then the spiritual condition of the Yeshiva did not weaken, not only did it not weaken but it reached new spiritual heights. . . . there was no change."[12]

If Sugihara was surprised by the Soviet's June incursion into Lithuania, then these diverse sets of religious Jews must have been, too. Some, though, including Warhaftig, had worriedly observed how the Red Army soldiers were becoming increasingly comfortable in their Baltic bivouacs. How would it be to live as religious Jews under the secular Soviets, they wondered? Was this a worse fate than Nazi persecution? Was it more likely? Some tried to probe the experiences of other religious Jews who had actually lived under Communist rule, on the other side of the Soviet border. Was this truly "living under water," or could it get even worse?

In summing up the short-lived Lithuanian Spring, Warhaftig offered me a little Freudian analysis: "The *halutzim* may have succeeded in allaying their fears concerning the future through their daily work and an extensive program of educational and cultural activities," he said. "The Yeshiva students, likewise, dispersed throughout Lithuania, may have drowned their sorrows in the bottomless 'sea' of the Talmud. The mass of refugees, mainly concentrated in Vilna, sought to relieve their anxieties through a variety of public and cultural activities."

One of those "public activities," I gather, for those who could afford it, was to linger in one of several establishments in town. The Rosemarin Restaurant, down the hill from Sugihara's consulate in Kaunas, catered to those who had refined palates, money, and better things to do with their time than wait on food lines at canteens. The intelligentsia and the well connected hung around the Café Metropole, where there was always someone interesting to see, always something interesting to discuss. The poorest made their way to the Alexander Restaurant. It was the best place for Jews to stretch their 1.2 lit-per-day food allocation from the JDC. Hungry refugees could afford a hearty *cholent,* the traditional East European Jewish spicy hot meat, potato, and beans stew.

But Zorach Warhaftig did not care for Lithuania's cafés or its verdant fields or its sacred houses of study. Each only distracted from the task at hand: getting himself, his beloved Naomi, and as many other Jews as possible out of Europe, preferably to Palestine. To that end, he and Naomi moved to Kaunas from Vilnius in the middle of November 1939, because with its consulates and government offices, he thought it would make him "more effective in regard to *aliya.*"

It was not an easy adjustment. Kaunas was a seller's market, and landlords could behave any way they liked, knowing there was an endless supply of refugees to replace each less-than-perfect tenant. "Our living conditions in Kaunas grew steadily worse," Warhaftig remembers. "My wife and I first occupied one room on Maironis Street but had to move elsewhere when our eldest child was born. His crying disturbed our landlord who slept in the adjoining room. Nor did we find life much easier in the next place where our landlady informed my wife that she would not allow any cooking in her apartment."

He had better luck finding a place for his work than for his home life. Taking advantage of the last days of British colonialism, Warhaftig actually managed to establish a "consulate" of his own. What he did was slip, ingeniously, through a tiny loophole, for it seems His Majesty's government accorded a modicum of recognition to Jewish self-government in Palestine, through the Jewish Agency. Warhaftig hit on the idea of getting his friends at the Jewish Agency in Jerusalem to designate what he decided to call the "Aliya Commission." The commission would represent the agency and the local British consulate, to distribute the precious few British-generated certificates for immigration to Palestine.

Warhaftig explains the particulars: "Our commission received full authority from the Jewish Agency in Jerusalem and was empowered to deal independently with the British Consulate in Kaunas where the local Palestine office was a party to this arrangement. My days were spent running to and fro between the Palestine office, the British Consulate, and the delegations of other countries.[13]

In the midst of all this "to and fro," Warhaftig also had to thread between the agendas of the different Zionist factions. This was no simple matter. Some of his colleagues promptly used their privileged positions to arrange for their own commission-sanctioned moves to Palestine and even the United States. They could better serve their followers, they argued, from the safer perches of New York or Tel Aviv. As Warhaftig bitterly reflected years later, "It was the old argument as to whether, and when, a leader could justifiably abandon his post and his duty."[14] But these defections weakened the local leadership and demoralized those Jews bereft of special connections.

Warhaftig has altogether positive memories of Moe Beckelman and the American social worker's distribution of food and living subsidies to thousands of Jewish refugees during these days. Beckelman makes no mention of the religious Zionist leader from Poland, but the two were kindred spirits. Like Beckelman, Warhaftig complains of colleagues abroad who just did not understand the gravity of the situation. For example, he would receive instructions on how to administer the funds or allocate the certificates that, under the dire circumstances, seemed wholly absurd. Henrietta Szold, the famous American Zionist leader, expressed her annoyance with Warhaftig from Jerusalem, chastising him for not granting certificates to children of specific ages in accordance with available dormitory space in Palestine.

Warhaftig and his colleagues responded with sardonic dismay. These Jewish leaders simply did not grasp the urgency of their situation, the real life-and-death issues they had to face daily in their rescue activities in Europe. Warhaftig, on his side, had his own reproach for Jewish organizations abroad regarding reserved space. "As a member of this delegation," he told me, "I complained about the preferential treatment accorded Jewish youth in Germany at the expense of Polish Jewish youth, insisting that our positions were one and the same."

Ruefully summarizing his rescue efforts in Lithuania, Warhaftig claims the following: "Unfortunately, the Jewish Agency did not realize the significance of this slender opportunity for the rescue of Jews and it was never fully exploited. In my numerous letters, cables, and telephone conversations, I tried to sound the alarm. But our cries for help were left unanswered."[15]

But if Warhaftig was trying to work miracles with scant funds and few certificates, he also had to dance around great geographic impediments. In the spring of 1940, escape route after escape route became dangerous, illegal, or both. He tried to negotiate for transit visas through the Soviet Union to Odessa, Istanbul, and on to Palestine. Just as he was succeeding with the Soviets, the British consul refused to issue certificates for Jews bound by way of Odessa on the questionable grounds, as he would put it, that "the Black Sea was dangerous." Warhaftig and colleagues were frustrated and unmoved by this British display of "concern." Subsequently, a few certificates were forged for Jews to escape via Istanbul. The British expressed even greater concern when they discovered that the Kovno Jews who forged these documents had apparently never seen a lion, and thus drew the symbol appearing on the seal of the British document more like a large, erratically maned house cat.

An American in Kovno

And what miracles was our American in Kovno attempting? Here we pick up the story of Moe Beckelman, who, lucky for us, enjoyed writing home and even kept a diary.[16] Here's one culinarily themed excerpt about life abroad:

> . . . beer (good) coffee (terrible—like coffee grounds that have been brewed for the fifth or sixth time). With three minute lumps of sugar and the palest of pale skim milk, herring salad (good but short on herring), lox (a slice so thin as to be transparent)—all of it frightfully expensive.

Beckelman was also impressed that "in Europe you can make noise eating your soup." Nonetheless, even the wife of his boss in Paris had to admit, grudgingly, that the Bronx-born Moe was actually acquiring some "savoir faire since he has been in Europe." Returning to Kaunas as soon as he could from his New Year's 1940 visit to Paris, he knew that this was where he wanted to be. Paris had been relief, yes, a place where one could forget, if only for a moment, that the world was falling apart (though of course it, too, would be occupied in barely five months). Sitting with his friends on the Champs-Élysées, he could talk with delicious detachment about conditions on strange planets called Germany, Lithuania, Estonia. On that last night "the orchestra played a medley of 1914 French and British war songs," Beckelman reminisces. "I was strongly tempted to call for 'Over There' but desisted out of respect for the Neutrality Act." Ever the conscientious rep.

He had gone to Paris to brief his JDC colleagues, an experience that turned out to be ragingly frustrating. They just did not get it. They did not comprehend the depth of the Jewish refugees' plight, how hard visas were to come by, how most escape routes had been shut off, how little money there was to feed, clothe, and house tens of thousands of Jewish refugees. The moment his presentation closed, he knew there was little he could do here in the City of Light. It was time to return east.

As Beckelman got ready to leave Paris, his colleagues expressed great concern for his safety. He was moved but would not be deterred, even realizing the drama of the moment could advance his last, most important request. He pulled out some budgets with a flourish and tried once more to explain just how dire the situation was. At that point, the JDC had spent about $2 million to get some seven thousand people out of Europe. With half that amount, he could do wonders. Surely they could help? But the moment deflated quickly; nobody was prepared to assure him more than a paltry $25,000 per month—even if that had to feed thirty-thousand mouths and more.

Back in Kaunas, he began to think that the real divide lay between himself living at the doorstep of purgatory and everyone else. He could *see;* the others could not. There were decent people on the JDC staff back in Paris, he conceded. But they demonstrated so little grasp of the opportunity presented by the "Switzerland of Eastern Europe." Here, their help could be most effective. Like Warhaftig, Beckelman began to believe that the Jewish organizations abroad were giving priority to the rescue of German Jews over their *Ostjud* cousins.

It was at such moments that Beckelman almost wished the antisemites were right about "conspiracies of Elders of Zion." *Halevay bay uns,* "would that for us it were so," as his grandfather used to say. A conspiracy would mean he could get some *help;* it might also mean he would team up with some real authority. Beckelman was not the sort who needed to go by the book, but his position was becoming untenable. He craved direction, organization—anything to get something done.

But the Polish and Lithuanian Jews with whom he worked on a daily basis were so alienated by centuries of tyrannical government that they would not bow to anyone's purported authority, including his. They preferred organizations that were responsive to personal needs—in other words, their needs—rather than detached efficiency. Complaints quickly began to come in from different quarters that Beckelman and his colleagues were trying to impose "an element of bureaucracy into the administration of the JDC which was foreign to its tradition and to the spirit of East European Jewry." Leveling this complaint provided leaders of the refugee organizations a rare moment of unity.

"All in all the situation in Vilna with respect to relief administration is not going to be exactly plain sailing for the next couple of months," Beckelman wrote on February 16 to New York JDC headquarters. He asked for support in trying to impose order in the allocation of funds and asked that "New York does not see bogeyman every time somebody sends them a telegram."[17]

But unruly *Ostjuden* and spineless bureaucrats were not his only problems. Attached to Beckelman's note of that day is a new order from the Lithuanian "Refugee Commissar" assuming control of refugee assistance from the different relief agencies and assigning administrative responsibility to the Lithuanian Red Cross. Beckelman would now have to cope with direction from a source that he did not exactly welcome. He sensed, however, that he would not have to worry about the meddling of this Lithuanian commissar for too long. The word on the street was that the "big push would soon begin," as he put it. Beckelman seemed to take rumors of Nazi or Soviet annexation of the Baltics more seriously than Sugihara, who was then preoccupied with next year's lease.

On February 19, Beckelman sent another report to headquarters announcing that "the honeymoon period in Russian occupied Poland is over." Even if the current standoff between the Germans and the Soviet were to hold, there is little reason for optimism, he insisted. "The position of the refugees has deteriorated." Again he requests additional funds for the refugees in Lithuania whom he can assist.

Beckelman spends all his days running between meetings with contentious Jewish representatives, high-level and corrupt Lithuanian government officials, diplomats, the Red Cross, and representatives of other relief agencies. At night, he writes reports, appeals, and increasingly frustrated entries in his diary. Of a meeting with British Consul Preston, he reports:

> We greeted each other more effusively than I would have expected from an Englishman and diplomat. I discovered later that he had a weirdo reputation as a dilettante composer (opera, ballet—both lousy) than as a diplomat. Anyhow, he started to fume at the Lithuanian temerity in wanting to control our funds and asked whether I intended to permit that or would join him in telling the Lithuanians where to get off. I tried to explain the viewpoint of the Lithuanian Red Cross which conveyed to me that the Lithuanians were afraid the Poles (many long settled in Lithuania with foreign contracts) would use the money not for relief, [but] for political activity.
>
> He pooh-poohed this in most undiplomatic language demanding to know where the Lithuanians whose government officials could be bought and sold for money got the nerve to suggest that a representative of His Majesty's government couldn't be relied upon to see to it that a piddling 4000 pounds a month was expended exclusively on the relief activities for which it had been intended. I calmed him down a little by telling him . . . that my understanding of the concern of the Red Cross was that it wanted to audit and check reports of expenditures rather than determine in advance what expenditures should be made.[18]

Combining detachment and anxiety—Humphrey Bogart in *Casablanca* would perfect the stance two years later—Beckelman, in Bogart style, diarizes the period around March 22: "Dropped in at Willie's for a few highballs and got some detective stories from Mrs. Willie." He sums up the suffering that he witnesses daily and his limited ability to do anything about it: "I'm almost a slave of bicarb now."

As much as Beckelman took pride in his refugee canteens and food coupons, he, like Warhaftig, knew that rescue was his real task. On March 11, JDC Paris reports to JDC New York that Beckelman is bearing down hard on the Lithuanian Foreign Office in Vilna to negotiate with the Soviets for transit visas for Polish citizens wishing to go to Palestine. In return, the Soviets will reap the monies from these same citizens, who will buy railroad tickets to Odessa, and steamship tickets to leave from there. If this proposal can be worked out, Beckelman wagers he can get several hundred people out.

Yet things are unraveling so quickly that before he can implement this, or any particular rescue scheme, the opportunities blow away. This is from his diary entry sometime around March 22:

> Then there was [sic] long negotiations with the German and Russian authorities about the possibility of transit visas for Polish refugees with Palestine certificates. The Germans finally consented on the basis of sealed cars with joint Lithuanian and German escorts but the British squelched that plan by announcing that no one would be admitted to Palestine who had made transit through Germany. Negotiations with the Soviets are still going on and it is reported that they have agreed in principle to grant visas to Polish passport holders for transit purposes but so far as I know nothing has come of it. If Italy goes into the war in the near future then the road out will be completely closed, facetious suggestion of months ago that I would come home through Vladivostok may become uncomfortably close.

The "Facetious Suggestion"

Beckelman's "facetious suggestion of months ago" still seemed ridiculous to many Jews that spring. Why would Beckelman, the big shot from New York, have to worry about transit west back home? He had a good-as-gold U.S. passport, whereas for most Jews, westward travel had become a thing of the past. The only real routes left pointed eastward, but anything having to do with the Soviet Union evoked a sense of dread. Many knew of Jews who had disappeared in the crevices of that vast country, never to be seen again. At the time, Stalin was as fearsome as Hitler, and so now it was a matter of choosing between fears. The situation in Lithuania was highly precarious, a fluttering "between the jaws of two lions," as Beckelman himself described it. To remain was risky, but to leave was just as problematic.

Newcomers like the Zielonkas, the Dynensons, the Malowists, the Warhaftigs, the Dubnov-Erlichs, and the Yeshiva student Ben Fishoff had found minimally safe and comfortable accommodations in Lithuania. Local Jews, like the Ganors and the Braunses, were still preoccupied with their businesses, professions—even their summer homes—and didn't want to leave. Many agreed with the aged Rabbi Grodzinski of Vilna, who advised following the principle of *"shev ve'al taase,"* do not flail around in unproductive action, do not be tempted by harebrain schemes. Stay—tenaciously, aggressively, cautiously—put.

Besides, what if they really did depart, who would help their families left behind in Poland? It was the power of the familiar. Why abandon such security for extremely dire risks, especially when they concerned the wholly capricious Soviet Union? And once they did decide to leave, what if permission were denied? They would have exposed themselves and their identification papers, perhaps of questionable validity, and their positions as refugees or citizens could be permanently jeopardized. Then there was the concern that, even if they made it through the Soviet Union, no place would take them afterward. Europe was impossible, the British had issued the White Paper placing severe limits on immigration to Palestine, and the U.S. Congress repeatedly failed to pass measures that would reform the quota system to admit more Jewish refugees.

Again we must ask, how did visa-seekers find their way to the doors at Vaizgantas Street? More and more Jews began to believe that salvation might be waiting to the east. After all, thousands of German Jews had already gone to Vladivostok in search of new homes, and ended up in Manchukuo or China, even in Shanghai, which until the summer of 1939 had no visa requirement and had welcomed Jewish refugees. But now, almost a year later, for "stateless" Polish Jews in particular, Beckelman's suggestion remained "facetious." It was still too dangerous, until people began to realize there was one safe road, from Kaunas to Vladivostok and beyond—and it passed through Chiune Sugihara's consulate.

"Extremely Risky"

"Now is the time to leave," Sugihara told Solly Ganor's father, just around the time that Moe Beckelman was first making his facetious suggestion. "I wouldn't worry about the business if I were you," Sugihara had added. Who else was Sugihara rescuing, in the spring of 1940, and what can we learn from his modus operandi, from his management of risks, that sheds light on how he made that road to Vladivostok safe? Sugihara's autobiographical fragment, plus new sources that I recently discovered in the German and Lithuanian archives, provide important snapshots of Sugihara in action. They *seem* to shed light on the man behind the smile and firm grasp, the man who was always a "step ahead," as his buddy Shimura from the days of the "wetties" remembers, the man who "was going a step too far."

Stella Kaspcik and her husband, the spy: Their story, a good example of Sugihara's going a step too far, does not end with a farewell party, posing for the lens outside the Kovno train station, nor with their frightening trip across Europe disguised as diplomatic couriers. Here is Sugihara speaking of some of his "Polish friends," as he politely referred to the spies who worked for him: "One day during the Spring of 1940, Kaspcik sent me two young Poles from Vilnius, George Kuncewicz and

Jan Perts (or Pelts)," writes the old vice consul. Ultimately, they had no small favor to ask: "They demanded my protection," he continues:

> I agreed and gave them both official national Japanese passports, as secretaries of the consulate and on the 20th of August I sent them to Germany in my consular car. We then agreed to meet again in Berlin. We all met in Berlin on the 3rd of September, and were mutually pleased about this new meeting which, that is true, was rather dangerous in a country on the verge of war. It was extremely risky for me and for my career. In doing this I went far beyond my power and the official discipline and rules.

Sugihara could be extremely accommodating, at times. Dr. Roman Korab-Zabryk solicited his memoir to shore up a thesis, it seems, and Sugihara, in his choice of emphases and omission, obliged. He was trying to prove how active, well organized, and effective the Polish underground had been. Its ties with the Kaunas vice consulate, and the Japanese in general, were fine pieces of evidence. This must be why Sugihara pays such attention to Jerzy Kuncewicz (alias Jakubianiec, or Kuba) and Jan Perz (alias Jan Stanisław Daszkiewicz).

Yet in this account, he never indicates exactly when or why his relationship with Kuba and Perz warmed up, or what grounds they used to "demand" his protection. He provides more detail on his Polish valet, cook, butler, and driver and speaks more warmly of his Lithuanian-German secretary. Had they actually worked for him first, or did he merely designate them to be secretaries, after the fact, to justify their demands? Why did he send them to Berlin and then renew contact in the Nazi capital if it was so dangerous? And why, in thinking back to the reunion in Berlin in September 1940, does Sugihara remember Nazi Germany, then bombing Britain nightly and having conquered most of Europe, as "a country on the verge of war" when it was definitively *at* war?

As usual, Sugihara has left a fairly cold trail. Perhaps even in 1967 he retained his habit of parceling out only the absolute minimum of information. Such was his tactic with Tokyo, after all, while he was courting or being courted by these "Polish friends." Who in the *Gaimusho* might have approved or disapproved of his relationship with these two Polish spies—who also had close ties to the soon-to-be-enemy British consulate? Clearly, Kuba and Daszkiewicz must have become more than occasional visitors to Sugihara's quarters. They contributed mightily to his being "new eyes" for Japan on new developments in Nazi-Soviet relations.

It was no simple matter for Sugihara to procure "official national Japanese passports" for them and to do what was "extremely risky" for himself and his career, going far beyond his "power and the official discipline and rules." However useful Kuba and Perz might have been, during chaotic days such as those accompanying the fall of Kaunas, why did he bring them to Berlin? Loyal as he was, Sugihara would not have been the first super spy to abandon an informant or two on the grounds that it was "extremely risky."[19]

Also, just how "extremely risky" was it, truly? The Israelis at Yad Vashem initially believed Sugihara did not qualify as a "righteous Gentile" because his life was not in danger. It was precisely his emphasis on "my career" that may have left them with that impression. The dangers for Sugihara and his family were not limited to the potential angry responses of Japanese military or Foreign Ministry factions, which at any point could have called him back and charged the "masterless man" with treason. Neither did the danger let up when he left Soviet territory, where diplomat-spies often disappeared—as in the tragic case of another mass rescuer, Raoul Wallenberg. That danger did not relent when he arrived in Nazi Berlin, retrieving his consular car from his "Polish friends" for whom he had provided a cover for some of the most effectively damaging spying that took place against the Nazis.[20]

Indeed, that spring, before rescuing too many Polish spies or Jews, Sugihara's risk rate rose upwards as Japan and Germany edged closer to an alliance. For suddenly Germany looked like the favored side in the brewing war, and the pro-German faction in the Japanese government and military, only yesterday deemed marginal, was growing in power. By May, when Sugihara was whisking the Kaspciks out of Europe and helping his British friends, serious alliance talks reconvened. The salient topics included finding ways to reconcile German and Japanese territorial ambitions, particularly in the Far East, and determining how the anticipated spoils of war would be divided.[21]

Even at an earlier date, the Nazis made more than occasional observations on Sugihara, as they would on any diplomat.[22] At first they considered him "very reliable" and active in "hostile and neutral diplomacy."[23] They not only spied on him but used him to gather intelligence. At the encouragement of German intelligence in Kaunas, as their records indicate, Sugihara organized an "intimate" breakfast with the diplomatic representative of another of Nazi Germany's allies, Mussolini's Italy. The Germans wanted Sugihara to ascertain how strong anti-German sentiment was in Italy. Given this contact and his own vast experience in espionage, Sugihara must have known that he was being watched and that his activities could be risky and draw dangerous attention to himself.

Within that framework, the Germans needed to know whether Sugihara was *"deutschfreundlich,"* friendly to Germany. The affable, exuberant, cooperative, smiling Japanese consul certainly seemed to be friendly.

On the other hand, by the spring of 1940, Sugihara was associated with at least two Poles—Kuba and Daszkiewicz—of suspicious background. He would arrange for them to receive Manchurian passports under the ruse of possessing White Russian roots. Over the next year, these "blood-lines" stood them in good stead: the two gleaned intelligence all over Europe on their Manchukuo diplomatic passports, which went directly to the Polish government-in-exile in London and from there, probably, on to both Washington and Moscow. Sugihara's role in this network hardly constituted *"deutschfreundlich"* behavior. He was acting more foe than friend.

What did the Lithuanians, Germans, and Soviets, in fact, know of all this? One snapshot of his activities in the spring of 1940 captures the images of Sugihara the spy, dissembler, and risk-taker.[24] It seems to be the only document left in the Lithuanian archives that reflects on his year spent there, and provides a rare and bountiful glimpse into his work style. The report is dated July 12, 1940, and concerns Sugihara's visit to what seems to be the Lithuanian Foreign Ministry building, the previous day.

At the time, the Soviets were about to officially take over the Lithuanian government. They had already installed Lithuanian Communists and others believed loyal, and were seeking to legitimate such actions through a rigged referendum to be held around July 15. Sugihara called on a Lithuanian official, P. Glovacko, for the purpose, it appears, of pumping him for information. He wanted to know the degree of indigenous support for the looming Communist takeover of Lithuania, even if, the official reports, Sugihara confidently predicts "99%" support, the usual results in Communist elections. Glovacko appears more restrained in his assessment of Communist support, and becomes suspicious of Sugihara. If this Japanese man is so sure, then why is he here?

Perhaps Sugihara was trying to ingratiate himself with someone whom he assumed to be a pro-Soviet official. Indeed, Sugihara uses the opportunity to register a complaint about the pre-June 15 Lithuanian government and perhaps to clarify policy about travel arrangements under the new regime. His grievance centers on an incident wherein a "high-level Japanese official" was asked to present a visa while driving from Moscow to Berlin, in May. Glovacko's language makes it unclear whether Sugihara was complaining about his own experience at the border or that of someone else.

Sugihara goes on to claim that the Lithuanian government exempted other diplomats from carrying such visas; it should also exempt Japanese. Glovacko successfully conveys Sugihara's indignation, and it is at *that* moment, of all moments, when Sugihara asks for a visa for Kuncewicz, one of his spy friends whom he identified to the Lithuanian official as a "consular official." Indignation followed by bold request; we sense the strategist at work! He also asks about the availability of packing boxes, perhaps to underscore that he was getting ready to close shop as the new Soviet rulers were beginning to demand. Reassuring a new regime of its popularity, complaining about the former government while ascertaining the new rules, indicating that one was following the rules while asking for a favor: transparent, perhaps, with a pseudocandor, an obliging but by no means a meek way of presenting oneself.

Who was going—as related in this report—from Moscow and to Berlin in May 1940? Was Sugihara propelling his black Buick along roads where vital war preparations were being made on the Russian and German sides? Was he driving between Moscow and Berlin with a "Polish friend," perhaps even Kuba, who was reporting back, as we now know, to British intelligence? Moreover, what might he have been doing in Moscow? What was he discussing with Soviet officials? We have no information on any of these questions. What seems clear, however, is that Sugihara was quite active behind the scenes.

Our curiosity is piqued when we realize that the Glovacko to whom Sugihara gripes in July might have been the same new Lithuanian Deputy Prime Minister Pius Glovacki with whom Warhaftig met a month later to discuss Jewish passage through the Soviet Union. This Polish Communist, who had lived in Moscow for many years, was typical of the advance party sent by the Soviets to facilitate the incorporation of Lithuania within the Soviet Union. Did he have some other mission in regard to Jewish refugees?[25] Again, we do not know but this gives us a window into the world of intrigue in which Sugihara successfully operated.

We discover another spying-on-the-spy record of this period, filed at the Berlin Foreign Office, precisely when the Sugiharas are passing through that city the following October 1940. The memo makes it apparent that Sugihara was observed all through his stay in "Kowne," as the Germans called the city. Indeed, the very consulate that Sugihara reassured Tokyo was "suitable for our special circumstances" because it facilitated efforts to "keep matters secret" did no such thing.[26]

The truth was, the Japanese consulate was alarmingly porous when it came to matters of confidentiality. This German Legation in Kovno complains that Sugihara seems to have "kept with the Legation a rather active, to tell the truth, almost exclusive administrative relation. His visits did not fail to show that his main interest was military forces, and this in such a measure, that gave birth to the assumption that his functions, as Consul, were solely disguised military assignments."

The report goes on to describe Chiune Sugihara as a spy-prevaricator: "He made himself appear to be *deutschfreundlich*. At the same time, howvever, he was taking care of two former Polish citizens, Jerzy Kuncewizc and Jan Stanisław Perz, who were given Japanese citizenship, but who are known by our Intelligence Services as pro-English." It concludes on an ominous note: "The Defense Division of Berlin has been informed. Under these circumstances, a definite holdback is recommended."

What this particular "holdback" implied for Sugihara and his family is not evident. Perhaps orders were being issued to German diplomatic and military personnel to "hold back" any confidential information that under different circumstances might have been shared with military attachés or diplomats of "German-friendly" countries. What is evident is that Sugihara's cover was blown—and that he was vulnerable.

Whatever Nazi operative was spying on Sugihara could easily watch him intensifying his ties with the Polish underground as the spring of 1940 progressed. Indeed, his efforts to rescue these agents of the Polish military intelligence became altogether brazen, a brazenness that he would demonstrate again a few months later. He none too discreetly smuggled them out of Soviet-controlled Lithuania by providing them with trumped-up passports and, as with Stella and Stanisław Kaspcik, provided them with a transparently rigged diplomatic mission—in their case, as drivers of his beloved black Buick. He did not insist their chauffeur duties be confined to Lithuania, either. These "Polish friends" roamed the Baltics nearly unimpeded, it seems, smuggling out much information. Sugihara even managed to get them safely through Berlin, of all places—a remarkable feat, given the tenor of the times.

And yet, while the German Archives offer firm evidence of his clandestine activity with the Poles, it says *absolutely nothing* about the visas he would later hand out to thousands of Jews. Long lines of people gather up and down Vaizgantas Street during the summer of 1940, yet no one in Berlin seems to take notice! Who was "holding back" this time?

To attempt an answer, let us examine Sugihara's puzzling characterization of Germany as "on the verge of war." Through the spring, summer, and fall of 1940, Nazi Germany was certainly embattled, and positively at war. Yet it *was* on the verge of one of the two wars Japan most cared about. No one knew whether Great Britain would soon crumble like other West European countries, or whether it would keep the Nazis at bay, and Japan had its eye on the British naval presence in the Far East and the British colonies. If their Nazi allies were successful in the battle against Britain, Japan might acquire colonies and control—as it was acquiring from the fall of France and Holland!

Given this hope, it was no minor prank for Sugihara to be helping Polish spies, with their strong contacts with Britain, get established in Berlin just as Hitler was on the "verge" of fighting the decisive part of that war. If he persisted, Sugihara's tendency to "go too far" could lead to sabotage of high Japanese interests. For German intelligence at that moment, a few Jewish visas to the Far East might not have been worth bothering about, whereas anything pertaining to Britain mattered profoundly.

But there was another war on the horizon, one with important consequences—to Japan and Nazi Germany for altogether different reasons. As Sugihara already mentioned in his reminiscences, it was this German push on the Soviet Union that would tie up Soviet forces, eliminating the threat of a Soviet attack on Japan or Manchukuo and giving Japan a freer hand in the Far East, even enhancing its negotation stance with Great Britain and the United States. Here, too, Germany was on the "verge." In fact, Hitler seemed to have the strongest emotional investment in this war on his eastern flank; it would fiercely cloud his judgment and lead to his eventual defeat. On June 22, 1941, the Germans began their Operation Barbarossa with an attack on the Soviet Union and the annexed territories of the Baltics. Many Jews in Lithuania who had not been fortunate enough to obtain a Sugihara visa were killed en masse by Nazi storm troopers (and their Lithuanian accomplices) that first day of the invasion.

This was the world in which Sugihara operated. Conditions certainly did make his activities "extremely risky." Was he taking advantage of his association with General Oshima, who until September 1939 and after September 1940 was Japan's ambassador to Nazi Germany, to smuggle proven un-*deutschfreundlich* "employees" into Nazi Germany? These sorts of spy tricks were ill-advised in a country "on the verge of war," but at the same time, he might have been acting in the name of another Japanese governmental faction that *wanted* him to assist these Polish spies, perhaps to undermine Oshima's pro-Nazi faction. Or was there no faction directing his moves at all? Was he exceeding his own "power and the official discipline and rules," making his own foreign policy?

Whatever Japanese faction Sugihara was supporting at the moment, in Kuba and Daszkiewicz he had found reliable and well-connected informants. These military intelligence agents were regrouping after their country's disastrous but—as we have seen from Colonel Rybikowski's preparations for a German conquest of Poland—not entirely unanticipated military losses. They were using Lithuania as a backdrop where they could disappear into the community of well-established Poles who had lived there for centuries before Lithuania was separated from Poland after World War I, and into the sizable ranks of Polish refugees as well.

There they could establish a base of operations contiguous with the lands and people of carved-up Poland annexed to Germany and the USSR. Activists like Michal Rybikowski, who were born at the juncture of Slavic and Prussian cultures, could use their knowledge of languages and mores of each of these cultural areas to "go native." In the costume of an affable Latvian businessman or whatever other cover he chose at any particular time, the "Pesky Pole" was most successful and dangerous. These Polish spies were some of the best informed when it came to the plans of Germany and the Soviet Union, insights that were vital to Oshima's man in Lithuania.

The Poles were learning to pay their way with Japan but also with Great Britain and, perhaps under deeper cover, the United States. In return, they advanced their own concerns: to get as many Poles of military age out of the danger zone so they could some day help liberate Poland. This aim became plausible only after June 1941, when the Soviet Union was attacked by Germany. The Soviets then offered to liberate thousands of Poles from the Gulag if they joined in the fight against the Nazis. It was then discovered that a few thousand Polish military officers, the friends of Kaspcik, Kuba, and Daszkiewicz, were "missing," as the Soviets put it, somewhere in Siberia. In reality, many had been murdered, we now know, by the Soviets in the infamous Katyn massacre in the spring of 1940.

In 1947, Jan Daszkiewicz wrote about that spring of 1940:

We continued our military intelligence work and kept in close contact with the Japanese Consulate, hoping that with its help we would be able to leave Lithuania. In the month of April 1940, on the orders of Captain Jakubianiec, I made my way one day to the Japanese Consulate in Kovno, where I was to meet in Captain Jakubianiec's name and report about Soviet preparations being made on the [German-Soviet] border and about the concentration of Soviet forces in numerous regions, all of which seemed like some kind of military preparations.

Besides giving the Japanese Consul news from the territory of the USSR, I was to receive from him an answer as to the decision to issue transit visas through Japan. A campaign was being mounted at the time to allow Polish refugees to transit through Russia and Japan to America and one of the islands near the coast of South America [Curaçao]. We were only interested in securing transit through Japan, because other difficulties with this action had already been taken care of. The Consul, named Sugihara Chiune, had been informed by telephone of my arrival by Captain Jakubianiec. He received me immediately and our conversation was in Russian, lasted a short time, and was limited only to the mentioned topics.

I received an answer from him to the effect that the matter of issuing visas was to take place in 10 days since the Japanese government's permission had already been given, and he was waiting merely for further instruc-

tions from the Ministry of Foreign Affairs. From that meeting—I went often to see the Japanese Consul on the orders of Captain Jakubianiec, taking
care of, among other things, the matter of issuing visas and who was to be
placed first in line and he gave me information, while I gave him information determined by me together with Captain Jakubianiec, and having to do
only with Russian matters.

He knew perfectly well that Captain Jakubianiec and I were doing military intelligence work. The Consul was willing in taking care of matters relating to refugees and did much in this area. Thanks to the suggestions of
Captain Jakubianiec, it was precisely the Japanese Consul who was one of
the first to propose the official project of having Polish refugees leaving
through Japan to one of the small countries on the coast of South America
(I don't remember the name of this island or the country). He also asked
other representatives to support this project. The Honorary Consul of this
country [Holland] in Kovno agreed to issue entrance visas for an appropriate fee, even though he knew very well that none of those leaving would go
there, and from Japan, with the help of the still existing Polish Legation
there, they will go to other countries. This is the way it was and that's what
we had expected. In this matter Mr. Preston [the British consul] did little,
and at the outset was even opposed to it.[27]

Daszkiewicz's words are corroborated by Colonel Michal Rybikowski.
In the following passage, which he wrote following the war about his
protégé Jakubianiec, Colonel R. claims that high-level Japanese officials
not only knew but actually approved of Sugihara's rescue efforts. Indeed,
the authorities even seem to have taken the initiative:

Today I know that in commencing their [Japan's] work with us, they did not
proceed from the level of a small consul or military attaché but from the
level of the Office of the Chief of Staff and the Ministry of Foreign Affairs.
The head of the Japanese Imperial Staff was at this time General Yamawaki,
a great friend of the Poles. . . . When he was told about what was happening throughout Europe, he ordered the establishment of closer contact with
us and it was he who managed to secure 600 visas for our refugees for passage to the West through Japan.

Rybikowski amended his undated report over the years, first to 900
visas and then to over 3,500, including Yeshiva students, numbers he
likely got from Daszkiewicz's memoirs. Though he visited Kaunas on several occasions while Sugihara lived there, Rybikowski, curiously enough,
never met the vice consul. In a letter to Dr. J. Chapman, a historian at
Sussex University, on January 8, 1986, Rybikowski identifies another staff
person in the Japanese Consulate in Kaunas, one Wolfgang Gudze.

Gudze's presence acted as a barrier, it seems. "Japanese Consul Sugihara had in his office [as secretary] a Gestapo man by name Wolfgang Gudsche," writes Rybikowski. "That is the reason that I never worked closely with Sugihara and never met him."

In Sugihara's own memoir, we have heard of the "ethnic German Wolfgang Gudze." He was "the only consulate secretary at that time . . . who [sic] I had employed from the beginning of my stay in the consulate, [and who] helped me with all these consular documents." Gudze "helped him" says Sugihara. Gudze was "the reason" why he and Sugihara never worked closely together, says Rybikowski. What role does Gudze actually play in Sugihara's rescue effort? Could it be that the "in-house" spy on the spy, Gudze, was the source of the German Legation's information on Sugihara and his level of "German-friendliness?" What is remarkable, if this is the case, is how Gudze seemed unconcerned by his bosses' "Jewish-friendliness."

One of those Yeshiva students mentioned by Rybikowski even remembers Wolfgang Gudze. Moshe Zupnik, now a rabbi, also runs a fabric shop on Manhattan's Eldridge Street, where the old Jewish Lower East Side meets New York's Chinatown. The shop is an offshoot of the business his parents had in Frankfurt, Germany, before the war. Rabbi Zupnik converses with his neighbors in the few words of Chinese that he remembers from his years in Shanghai. He escaped to there with the help of Sugihara (No. 1225). Notwithstanding difficult years, he has real *hadras punim,* a radiance of presence, both physical and spiritual.

We met in his shop one stiflingly hot August day, with customers coming and going all the while. Rabbi Zupnik remembered another August forty-five years ago, when he spent two weeks in Sugihara's consulate working as a secretary filling out 350 visas for the students and faculty of the Lithuanian Yeshiva of Mir. Sugihara made a deep impression on him. "It was the best days of my life sitting there in the Japanese consulate with Sugihara," as he put it.

But Wolfgang Gudze made an even greater impression on the young rabbi. "He was a *zaddik,*" the rabbi says in Yiddish, "*a groyse zaddik,*" a righteous man.

When our talk concludes, I walk out onto bustling Eldridge Street. Jewish bookstores bump up against Chinese groceries, all anchored by the famous nineteenth-century-gothic Eldridge Street Synagogue, which broadly shoulders the sky. All of a sudden, the familiar cityscape seems skewed and unreal, both from the August heat and this most astonishing revelation. Wolfgang Gudze, Gestapo operative, righteous man. *What* was going on in Sugihara's consulate in Kovno? For two and one-half years I have been spending most of my time in search of Sugihara, finally persuading myself that I am homing in on the real story. And now I find that Sugihara's "conspiracy of goodness" includes both Yeshiva *bukhurs* and Nazi spies? Astonishing, astonishing. Can this really be so?

My mind balks. I think of this perpetually elusive Sugihara and gaze up at the turrets and great stained-glass windows of the old Eldrige Street Synagogue. It reminds me of the synagogue in the old Harbin Gakuin song. Some of those menacing words come back to me here on the blazing August afternoon.

> *Wings of the wild eagles are losing strength.*
> *Evening casts its dark shadow at the Kremlin.*
> *Who can be a brave one . . . ?*
> *The tower of the synagogue is tall . . .*
> *The synagogue shows no shadow of opulent spring.*
> *Oh, now it is the time of confusion.*

"Dear Mr. Sugihara . . ."

Dear Mr. Sugihara:

Is it "Chiune" or "Sempo?" Should I address you as "Mr. Sugihara" or the proper Japanese "Sugihara-san"? Or perhaps you would prefer the "Sergei Pavelovich Sugihara" of the Russian culture that you so loved, a culture closer to my own background and the thousands of my people whom you saved? Would you be uncomfortable were we to honor you with the Talmudic title "Reb Sugihara," meaning beloved master? Inconsequential questions, I know, but it is easier to evade the real awkwardness of trying to conjure you up, bring you to life.

Had I known you in your lifetime, I might have gone with you to Kaunas. You would have taken me through your former consulate, pointed to where the long lines formed. You would have walked me through the door that you kept open, shown me the window from which you persisted in observing and where you gave out the visas. But those were pre-Gorbachev days; how wary the Soviets would have made us. It may have been too hard to convey the meaning of No.

30 Vaizgantas Street to them, like Mount Sinai of our tradition, significant only for what transpired, not for its humble form.

But if not for a walk in Kaunas, then perhaps Kamamura, your last home on Tokyo Bay. How happy I would have been strolling with you along the beach, the setting sun to the right of us. Mt. Fuji to the left, or would it be the setting sun to the left and Mt. Fuji to the right? Whatever, how badly I now feel and how much I ask your forgiveness; we shared this earth for forty years and I never came to see you.

I am feeling desperate and have nowhere to turn other than to you, directly. I have done everything I could to prepare for this time, when I must try to describe the moment you began to issue visas without constraints. And now I am riddled with anxiety. It is the feeling that those of us who are Jewish have at Neila, *the closing moments of our Day of Atonement, the brink of final assessment. We have tried to do everything right. And yet we are so distant from our goal.*

Since that day, several years ago, when I first stood in front of your consulate in Kaunas and imagined you starting to grant those visas, I felt this was a mysterious instant that must somehow be understood. Your act was so full of humanity, and so lacking in caution. To me, it has come to hold such profound meaning, a beacon of decency at a time when compassion was quickly disappearing from the world.

Suddenly, Jews were being pushed to the outside of the Western civilization they helped create—and then blamed for being outsiders! They were demonized as destructive outsiders, greedy and lecherous, who sucked the very marrow out of society, giving nothing in return. But you, you invited those outsiders in. You saw Jews as mothers and fathers and children, as people who cherished memory and harbored hope, you wondered where they slept and how they kept warm. You worried what would become of them. You worried! How rare this was in a world racked with hate.

I have traveled to the four corners of the earth in search of people who once knew you: friends, colleagues, your disciples and bosses, your sister and her family, your first wife, Klaudia, and your second wife, Yukiko, your sons, daughters-in-law, grandchildren. The image that emerges consistently was that you were a man of extraordinary kindness and warmth, a cosmopolitan with special gifts for language, a man who felt at ease with people from diverse backgrounds, yet was also so very Japanese. All heartening information. Yet none of it explains why you opened your door to Jews when so few others did.

Each time I discover a new document about you I live in dread. This is the secret of Sugihara, I think, here is the smoking gun, the hidden motive. Now I will be compelled to recognize that a solitary act, the Act that appeared so pure, so expressive of the best that we might discover in human nature, was initiated from other sources and prompted by other considerations. . . .

So tell me, Mr. Sugihara, Chiune/Sempo, Reb Sergei—again I stall with anxiety—tell me, what did you do and why did you do it?

There is no paucity of explanations, you know. In fact, there are many who wish to share credit, if not wholly upstage you. The Poles, for instance. Some contemporary Polish historians are trying to use the long-standing association of Polish intelligence with your country to challenge evidence of antisemitism, even in the Polish underground, which undermined Jewish resistance and rescue. One of your informants, a Polish military officer named Jan Daszkiewicz, wrote his memoirs after the war describing his contact with you and his involvement in your rescue activities. "This was a result of our doing," he said, meaning what I see as your Act. It was Polish military operatives, concerned for the safety of Poland's Jews, that made of you a rescuer, or so Daszkiewicz and others would have us believe:[1]

> When the process of issuing visas began, Jews began applying in droves. Few Poles were interested. Of those a number left (among them were a few officers), and quickly wound up in the Carpathian Sharpshooters' Brigade. The Jews dispersed throughout the world, America and Palestine. None reported to the Polish army, although in conversations with me, many stated that was their intent. The Japanese Consul had orders to issue 600 visas, but many more were eventually issued, around 900.[2]

Do his words ring true to you? The very tone betrays his efforts to emphasize Polish underground assistance to its Jewish citizens. I cannot help but see how Daszkiewicz affirms the antisemitic stereotype that Jews evaded the army. Jews were disproportionately represented in the Polish Army at the beginning of World War II and notwithstanding such discrimination, even in the officers corps. Yes, Jews grabbed up most of the available visas, but who could blame them?[3] Polish Christians in 1940 faced many horrors under Nazi and Soviet subordination. But they were not threatened with mass annihiliation, as were Polish Jews. Daszkiewicz does not explain why "few Poles were interested" in taking the risk of crossing the Soviet Union to rejoin the Polish Army.

You knew well why Jews should take that risk. You told the young Solly Ganor to tell his father not to worry about selling his business; "the time to leave is now," you warned. Was it your idea to begin issuing transit visas, encouraged by the "Japanese Birobidzhan" proposals that were circulating in your government? Did one faction or another actually give you orders? Or was it all the "doing" of your Polish friends? Daszkiewicz and associates were most useful to you in your intelligence-gathering activities, as were some of your Jewish associ-

ates and the visa-seeking refugees who came to your door. Were your spy and visa-granting activities more closely linked than we assumed?

Daszkiewicz may have shared information with Colonel Michal Rybikowski, whom he likely met in London after the war when he was writing his memoirs; those memoirs ended up in Rybikowski's hands. Rybikowski claimed that it was General Yamawaki, "a great friend of the Poles," with important connections in Machuria, who initially got you to issue visas:

> When [Yamawaki] was told about what was happening throughout Europe, he ordered the establishment of closer contact with us and it was he who managed to secure 600 visas for our refugees for passage to the West through Japan.[4]

In the years after the war, the late General Makoto Onodera, the head of Japanese intelligence in Europe from early 1941 and close partner of Rybikowski, corroborated this high-level initiation of your rescue activities.[5] But only the initiation. Once you got started, you did far more than issue visas to a few escaping Polish soldiers. General Yamawaki's high-level encouragement (if ever conveyed to you, for there is no hard proof it was) might explain why you believed your later visas would allow Jews to cross Manchukuo into Japan.

But Daszkiewicz tells another tale. He seems to feel you acted apart from your superiors:

> The Consul was willing in taking care of matters relating to refugees and did much in this area. Thanks to the suggestions of Captain Jakubianiec, it was precisely the Japanese Consul who was one of the first to propose the official project of having Polish refugees leaving through Japan to one of the small countries on the coast of South America (I don't remember the name of this island or the country). He also asked other representatives to support this project.

"Precisely the Japanese consul." The emphasis shows that even Daszkiewicz, with all the credit that he would like to claim, recognizes that your role as a rescuer involved more than just following orders. In that emphatic "precisely" he seems to express some greater initiative on your part.

And then there is Jan Zwartendijk, the honorary Dutch consul in Kaunas. He also rescued Jews. His "Curaçao visa" provided the fiction, the cover, perhaps even the catalyst for your swinging into action as a mass rescuer. This is from a letter that he wrote after the war:

> The Japanese Consul at Kaunas was entirely willing to issue a transit-visa to those who had my annotation for the Netherlands West Indies in their

passports. A Russian transit-visa, I heard, was obtainable after the Japanese transit-visa was procured.[6]

Like the Polish spy, the Dutch diplomat is sure in his emphasis though more modest in his claims. He, too, had some direct contact with you and attests to your alacrity. You were not merely willing, you were "entirely willing." Something that you said, something that you did seems to have made an impression on him. He "heard" about Soviet transit visas but his involvement in the rescue seems to be limited to the visas he issued. He charged eleven Lithuanian lit (approximately one dollar), you charged two lit. He dutifully closed his doors around August 3 when ordered to do so by the Soviets, while you insisted on staying open. What "credit" should Zwartendijk receive for this rescue?

And what about the Soviets—NKVD officials in Lithuania issuing their transit visas and Intourist "guides" who enabled thousands of Jewish refugees to traverse miles of Soviet wasteland without being "side-tracked" to Siberia? No such large-scale movement could have taken place in that centralized society without Kremlin approval. What evidence is there that you pierced walls and perhaps hearts of stone to involve Soviet officials in a "conspiracy of goodness?" What pressure from abroad, what opportunities to plant spies among the refugees, what high-level payments and low-level bribes reinforced your efforts to elicit Soviet cooperation?

Even your wife, Yukiko, takes significant credit—justifiably or otherwise—for the one chapter in your life that rescued you from obscurity. In her memoirs she quotes you as expressing great ambivalence, as well you should have, in regard to dangers and risks. Only she is able to assuage your reluctance, apparently.

"If I leave the Jews and get out from this country, everything will be fine. That's all." He repeated several times over the next two days as if he was trying to convince himself. I said, "No, we can't. It's impossible for us to leave them." "You're right," he said. "Yukiko, I will issue visas against the Foreign Ministry under my own authority as a Consul. May I?" he said. I answered. "Yes, please. I don't know what will happen to us, though." My mind was the same as his. Hundreds or thousands of lives depended on us.[7]

Was it she, then, who fully participated in your decision to save the Jews, mindful of the implications for the family? Recently, well-intentioned admirers of hers have engaged in futile speculation. Stories of her massaging your hand, sore from signing thousands of documents, garner our praise—but they hardly qualify her to share equally in your glory. Without any independent corroboration, they have claimed on her behalf that she is somehow responsible for 49 percent of the visas, or was it 51 percent? It is not clear whether Yukiko Sugihara sanctions these assertions. But claims about her direct involvement are somehow inconsistent with the image that I get of what went on in your consulate and the adjacent chancery. In fact, when I ask Mrs. Sugihara about your marriage, she scorns the possibility that there was dialogue and mutuality between you two. "These Japanese men, they are all the same. They never speak to you."⁸ She was certainly there to suffer whatever consequences there were or might have been to your actions. But did you act in concert with her? What "credit" does she deserve?

Even your elder son, Hiroki, under five years old at the time, insists on playing a bit part in the rescue. "Father, please help them because the poor little children need your help." he allegedly said to you, according to Yukiko.⁹

Again, Mr. Sugihara, what did you do? Do you mind going over your own words? Here are some you have to Roman Korab-Zabryk:

One August day, early in the morning, there was an unusual noise outside the Kovno consulate. There were people outside and they were talking very loudly. I went to the window of my apartment and looked out to find out what was going on. I saw a crowd of Polish refugees behind the fences. They had come via Vilnius from all parts of Poland which had already been occupied by the German soldiers. Each day the crowd grew bigger. With tears in their eyes they asked for Japanese visa, in order to be able to cross Japan on their way to another continent. The majority of them gave the usual destination: Latin America, USA and Israel.

As is customary when issuing transit visa, the visa or any other document issued by the authorities of the country of destination must be presented. However, only a few of them had documents issued by the US government, the majority had no documents, indicating that they would only transit Japan without causing hindrance when travelling to the other country. During a period of 10 months [or days?], I regularly had to send a telegraph to the ministry in Tokyo for advice [or permission?] regarding these visa for Polish refugees, since they did their best to convince me that once in Japan they would surely apply for visa at the consulate of the other countries and therefore they intended to proceed to Yokohama and Kobe. Tokyo, however, gave me negative answers.

All this happened during my last 20 days before the evacuation of Kovno. The number of refugees applying for visa increased. On the 10th of August I finally decided that it was completely useless to continue the discussions with Tokyo, I was merely losing time, as I had a lot of other things to do regarding the evacuation of the consulate. And on the 11th of August, I started to issue Japanese transit visa without official permission and on my sole responsibility. I gave visa to all who came to me, regardless of the fact whether or not they could produce some kind of document proving they were going to another country via Japan. The only consulate secretary at that time, the ethnic German Wolfgang Gudze, whom I had employed as from the beginning of my stay in the consulate, helped me with all these consular documents.

As from the 20th of August on I started to receive express telegrams from the Tokyo ministry, or from captains on the Japanese fleet which made regular courier journeys between the port of Vladivostok and the Japanese port of Tsuruga. They informed me about the increasing crowd of Polish refugees, striving to board a Japanese ship in Vladivostok as quickly as possible and producing visa issued by me. Furthermore they warned about the chaotic situation this would cause for the local authorities in Yokohama and Kobe and the forthcoming inevitable problems to organize and manage the refugee rush. By telegram they ordered me to stop issuing any more visa.

August 10, 1940.[10] *So that was the watershed—a Saturday, "I decided that it was completely useless to continue the discussions with Tokyo, I was merely losing time." I can feel your tension, your exasperation. You had already been stamping hundreds of visas—on July 30 there were 257 alone. "I started to is- sue Japanese transit visa without official permission and on my sole responsibil- ity," you write. August 11 was a Sunday and the list indicates the consulate was closed. But on August 12, you began Monday morning by issuing visa number 1,608 to Olgierd Pawlowicz and, perhaps, several members of his family. Until August 20, you would process 454 more.*

But about this assertion—"I started to issue Japanese transit visas without of- ficial permission and on my sole responsibility"—I am perplexed. From your own reports, we know of the Alfred Katzes and the Stella Kaspciks, not to men- tion the Polish military intelligence officers, the problems that you had been hav- ing with getting "official permission" and your resourcefulness in manipulating situations. Furthermore, whatever you did begin to do on August 10, it is most unlikely that anyone could get Soviet visas, make travel arrangements, leave Kovno or Vilna, and arrive in Vladivostok by August 20, in time to make themselves nuisances to Japanese sea captains on the Tsuruga run or to officials in the Gaimusho. "Started," Mr. Sugihara??? You had been issuing visas, ac- cording to your list, since July 19th and, there is reason to believe, even earlier.

This narrative voice of yours is a strange combination of precision and vagueness. "One August day" does not exactly evoke the fairytale voice of "once upon a time," but it is hardly concrete. In fact, it's abstract enough to show how the whole piece is laced with internal contradictions, the omission of some events, and the conflation of others. I cannot tell, exactly, how you meant to be under-

stood. Your old spy instincts are at work; I do not know what is the actual and what is the cover.

Could it truly be that you became aware of the conditions of Jews only "one day in August" while in fact you had observed such scenes—Jews living in Kaunas streets and railroad stations—since arriving the previous September? It makes no sense. You yourself write in your letter to Korab-Zabryk about a photograph that you took of the lines outside your consulate on August 3 or 4. And why do you write about the occupation of German soldiers in Poland but not the Soviet invasion and annexation of Lithuania? The latter influenced more of the last intense efforts of Jews to escape this last European "haven"; German soldiers did not arrive in Lithuania until nearly ten months after you left Kaunas. Many more thousands of Jews who did not line up outside your consulate, who did not get Lithuanian exit visas or Soviet transit visas, were lined up and shot by German soldiers and their Lithuanian accomplices from June 22 of the following year.

Was it really just these "ten days" when you were sending telegrams to Tokyo, trying to get an "issue" or "do not issue?" decision? We have versions of your letter in Russian, Polish, English, and Hebrew, Russian likely the original. The translations are cloudy; even phrases as seemingly clear as "ten days" can be construed as "ten months." This imprecision is compounded by what, exactly, you were asking of Tokyo. It's hard to tell whether it is "advice" or "permission."

But whatever special instructions you may have received from the Gaimusho *or high-level officers of the Imperial Japanese Army, you were certainly not the only Japanese diplomat issuing visas to Jews. This fact sheds new light on your actions.* There are other Japanese lists. *Recently discovered documents in the Diplomatic Record Office of the Japanese Foreign Ministry list the issuance of visas to Jews in 1940 and 1941, lasting through Pearl Harbor.*[11] *These Jews, among others, received visas in more than twelve European cities, particularly Vienna, Prague, Stockholm, and Moscow, in addition to Kaunas. The record keeping is as detailed as it is elaborate. At times, we can identify the visa recipient as Jewish only by name—a task made easier by the Nazis, who forced Jews to attach the names "Israel" and "Sarah" to all their documents; at other times the statistical summaries themselves indicate who is Jewish. These lists were compiled in response to an order, seemingly issued by the foreign minister at the end of 1939, demanding that each consulate make quarterly reports on past activities and provide projections of the number of visas he was likely to issue in the next period. Notes in the columns raise many questions. For example, the estimated number of Jews to whom visas were issued in Vienna was 20,000 while the actual number of recipients was 786.*

These lists indicate 2,132 Jews arriving from Kaunas, a number close to the one actually stated on your list. But it also mentions an additional 3,448 visas issued in Kaunas. This number may well reflect the reality; it is not at all clear, however, what the basis of this number really is. But what it does indicate is that at least after the fact, the Japanese Foreign Ministry had a full accounting of your visa-issuing activities, even with a sense of the magnitude. Why do you and your wife claim that you were working in opposition to your government? My dear Mr. Sugihara, could it possibly be that you are making false claims on heroism?!

Precisely at the moment we need your autobiographical fragment the most, we are having such serious problems understanding it. But we do have several other sources of information. Some provide conflicting perspectives, difficult to reconcile; others suspiciously confirm each other, harmonizing disparate versions. We have the memories of survivors, some who actually had direct contact with you both before and after the August 10 date you mention, some who even spent extended periods of time assisting inside the consulate. With the popularization of your story, an unfortunate standardization of memory is taking place.

And yet there are occasional words in those reports, similar to what we discovered in the writings of the Polish intelligence officer, of the honorary Dutch consul—often simple adjectives—that provide an outburst, an explosion of primary, perhaps even, primal emotions, that give us a sense that we are touching authentic memories. We have four cables that you sent to the Japanese Foreign Ministry and four cables sent in the name of the foreign minister to you in the period of July 28 to September 2, 1940, preserved in the archives of the Japanese Foreign Ministry. We have the observations of your neighbor upstairs. We have the memories of Yukiko Sugihara, not necessarily consistent with her memoirs, which have been published in several editions in the 1990s.

We have an additional source with which we must reckon, though: silence. "Every school child," it might be said, "knows that you just can't argue from silence." That we hear no testimonies about long lines on Vaizgantas Street may have causes no more significant than records destroyed or still awaiting discovery. Still, as we try to listen to that "unusual noise" that you hear on that day in August when, as you describe it, "I went to the window of my apartment and looked out to find what was going on," we simply cannot ignore what might have been even more "unusual" than the scene that you describe. Silence. Does it not call for some explanation? There were so many interested, concerned, worried parties who clearly had the opportunity to observe the long lines of refugees entering your consulate with gloominess and leaving with optimism. These observers viewed what was going on—with approval or disapproval—and yet seem to have remained silent.

Where was the irrepressible Moe Beckelman, who months before was predicting a "worst scenario" of escape, at least for himself, by way of the Soviet Union and Japan? He received visa no. 1890 on August 17, paying, for reasons that we do not know, ten lit—a bit more than the weekly per capita food allocation he was making available to thousands of Jewish refugees in his JDC soup kitchens—rather than the standard two lit. When Beckelman finally did leave Lithuania in February 1941, he took the same route that Jews now waiting outside of the Japanese consulate were to follow, and he traversed Japan on his Sugihara visa. Why was he silent about you?

His diary ends abruptly in May 1940; what is preserved of his generally ample reports and frequent correspondences tapers off during the early summer of 1940 when the Soviets are taking over, not a good time for record keeping and memo writing, perhaps even a time when he destroyed documents that could add to his troubles should he be arrested. We hear from him again from mid-August just as the point when the escape route via Vladivostok and Japan becomes the most viable. But what is most curious is that in the decade and a half of his professional life that followed, even to colleagues with whom he worked closely, he said absolutely nothing *about you!*

What did the Honorable Owen J. C. Norem, Envoy Extraordinary and Minister Plenipotentiary to Lithuania at the U.S. Consulate, with his exquisitely detailed reports, now focusing more on the transport of consular files and furniture, budget, and personnel and, of course, himself getting out of Europe—what did he have to say about you? Several years later and after completing a stint with the OSS as a Lutheran minister back in the States, he writes of his involvement from September 1939 through August 1940 with relief work through the American Red Cross, Lithuanian, Polish, and British relief organizations, as well as the JDC. How is it that Norem has nothing to say about how you, his Japanese colleague, were spending his *last days in Kaunas?*

And what about British Consul General Thomas Hildebrand Preston, who was even more worried about where these Jewish refugees to whom you were offering transit might indeed transit, lest it place more pressure on his colleagues administering Palestine? What did Zorach Warhaftig, so imaginatively contriving escape routes—sealed trains through Germany and Italy, safe boats on the Black Sea and the Mediterranean—what did he report to his colleagues in Jerusalem, Geneva, or New York of Sugihara's activities? Your own sister-in-law took a photo of him outside your consulate gate, and you gave him one of your visas. In a 1986 interview you tell of a 1940 meeting that you convened with Dr. Warhaftig and four of his colleagues to inquire, as it were, into the situation of Jews under the Nazis.[12] The hounded refugee who, because of you, survived to become a prominent minister of a sovereign Jewish state, who seems to remem-

ber every meeting and to have preserved every memo, writes nothing about this interaction; when pressed about it, Dr. Warhaftig has only the vaguest recollection that some meeting did take place but cannot recall who accompanied him.[13]

The Soviets at this time were making their sweeps and mass arrests. And yet, according to you and the thousands who received your visas and did survive, even they seemed to be relatively cooperative. How did they view what was going on? Will the more publicity minded successors to the commissars claim credit too?

And finally the Germans who were so curious to know whether you were indeed "deutschfreundlich," whether you were sincerely friendly toward them as you appeard to be. They may have had the "best seats in the house" to observe what was going on outside as well as inside the Japanese Consulate. There is some evidence to believe that one of your assistants who had won your most enthusiastic trust was a Gestapo agent! You who spent your professional life as a spy, who everywhere you went recruited informants, who knew every trick in the book, who surmised the strong ties between Baltic ethnic Germans and their "Vaterland"—why did you not suspect your trusted personal secretary? What were the Germans thinking about your helping thousands of Jews to escape? In the many pages of reports and records that they kept on you, how is it that there is no mention of your contact with Jews and your visa-issuing activities?

To compound mystery upon mystery, with the exception of Warhaftig's rather brief account of the goings-on in your consulate written many years later, these interested parties seem to have nothing to report. You cannot argue from silence, perhaps. But you certainly must be curious about silence and what that silence might suggest.

To anticipate what might have gone on within your heart and soul and to understand what really happened inside the Japanese Consulate in Kaunas in the summer of 1940, we must try to understand what you observed going on "outside the Kovno consulate" beyond the long lines and the small huddles of anxious and unkempt men, of women dressed in frayed elegance, clutching children that once had been so neat and now looked like abandoned urchins, what did you see and hear from your window? What triggered this mass rescue effort? Initially, at least, was it supply or was it demand, was it your greater willingness to consider visa applications or the increasing assertiveness and scheming of various Jews, such as Zorach Warhaftig and Moses Beckelman, or was it the cooperation of Japanese and Polish intelligence agencies that created the long lines on Vaizgantas Street? What prompted thousands of Jews to seek Japanese visas and how did this enable them to organize their escape? How and why and when did you, by your own description, alter your modus operandi? What can we piece together from your's and others' selective memories that will *give us some sense as to how one of the largest rescue efforts of the Holocaust succeeded?*

Did hearing the unusual noise of desperate people lead you to try, directly but unsuccessfully, to change your government's policy? Did these cries and pleas and silent anguish lead you to a deep personal crisis, a moment of intense conflict, risk weighing, moral decision making, followed by sheer defiance of your government? Or did something even more unusual—might we call it "uncustomary"—occur, choreographed and executed by you yourself, but alas, somewhat forgotten when you wrote about these painful experiences twenty-seven years later? What made you believe that the Jews to whom you were issuing visas would be able to make it to and through Japan, given the severe breakdown in your communications with Tokyo that you report? Did you issue visas as a desperate and principled moral act, or did you organize an escape route? Did you merely enable a few individuals to take some long railroad trips, or did you organize, in cooperation with others, what was in fact an "underground" railroad? And, most important, of the many questions that we must ask, what, indeed, enabled these refugees to escape?

In your efforts to recover memory, twenty-seven years after the events, you present us with a crafted but elliptical narrative, highlighting some events, deleting others. Embedded in those memories—for us who are trying to recover from them the events even so many more years later—are your powerful emotions. These are best expressed, perhaps, in the words of your old Harbin Gakuin alma mater, which you might have sung during those long, tedious days while sitting at your desk in the consulate, issuing visas—"now is a time of confusion."

My dear Mr. Sugihara, could you please help me understand that confusion?

Chapter 6

"As Is Customary When Issuing Transit Visas . . ."

One August day, early in the morning, there was an unusual noise outside the Kovno consulate. . . . As is customary when issuing transit visas, the visa or any other document issued by the authorities of the country of destination must be presented.

—Chiune Sugihara

If you stand firm and start hitting back, the American will know he's talking to a man and you too can then talk man to man. . . . It is my America and my American people that really exist. There is no other America; there are no other American people. . . . My idea is to ride on the military away from war. . . . I admit people will call all this a tricky business.[1]

—Yosuke Matsuoka

Unusual Noise

What was this "unusual noise" that Sugihara heard on August 10? First, I imagine it sounded like a huge audition, with hundreds of actors rehearsing their life-or-death lines. Each visa seeker assumed he had to get the words and emphases just right, had to anticipate the promptings of the director, as it were, on the great "stage" of the consulate. There would be questions on country of origin and destination, questions on documents and certificates, questions about the status of family and finances. The din of so many anxious souls pushing in one direction or another would be punctuated every few minutes by the cries of someone cutting in line and the indignant protests of those closing ranks against him. Maybe the early morning fog heightened the clamor, so the voices spun and rose into a near oratorio of worry. It must have sounded unusual indeed.

On the other hand, variations of this noise had been playing at least since the middle of July. The noise seems to have actually been *usual,* one might say, for weeks now. The Jews weren't the only actors in the streets of Kaunas; the Soviets were providing quite a bit of their own theatrics. The nights were so full of movement there seemed no room for shadows. The church bells of Kovno—as the city was now called—no longer pealed their comforting chimes. The warm lights on the gold dome of the Sobor, the Russian Orthodox church at the center of town, no longer danced. One could hear cars coming to a screeching halt, house doors banging open, muted screams, occasional gunshots. Around the railroad station in particular it was dangerous to appear without well-demonstrated purposefulness. Yet Jews were flooding into Kovno from all over Lithuania, breaking curfews, risking the inspection of their documents, the interrogations, the searches.

"Customary When Issuing Transit Visas . . ."

It started almost politely, with a steady trickle of individuals making inquiries, and it ended with long lines of agitated people standing there day and night, pressing against the wrought iron gate, pounding on the consulate door to get in—with the desperation of those who knew this might be their last chance to get out. To understand what sparked the change in Sugihara, it is necessary to consider the changes going on "outside the consulate," and not only right outside but very far outside. To appreciate what was truly significant in Sugihara's issuing visas, we must more fully understand what was, in Sugihara's words, "customary when issuing transit visas."

Let us listen to some survivors who remember what went on inside and around the consulate before there were long lines—and as those lines became lengthier. Ludvik Salomon, number 22 on Sugihara's list, received a transit visa to Japan from Sugihara on July 26, 1940. "Closing my eyes I can still see the villa on the hill where the consulate was located, but when I went there nobody was in sight," as the man now known as Lewis Salton told me one crisp autumn day in 1994, when he was visiting Boston. "I must have been one of the first to receive the Japanese transit visa. Sugihara received me very nicely. He offered me tea. He looked at my passport. 'American visa,' he noted. 'No problem.' He sat at his desk and wrote the visa in long hand."

Salton likes to take charge of everything around him. At eighty-three, he still has an athletic energy, quick eyes, and an aura of success. Recently, he sold his small-appliance manufacturing company and is quite happy to be retired in rural Connecticut, with an apartment in Manhattan. But in September 1939, this can-do attitude mattered not a whit. In his efforts to stay a step ahead of the Nazis, Salomon was arrested by the Soviets while escaping east from his native Cracow, Poland, as he crossed the Carpathian Mountains. At several junctures, he and his traveling companions could not decide which direction to take. "They went one way and got killed," as he recalls. "I went the other and survived." A Hungarian border guard, who happened to be Jewish, saved him from walking into a massacre and a drunken New Year's revelry among soldiers on the Lithuanian border.

He made his way to Kaunas but soon decided he had to keep moving. A young Swede and his German cousin whom Salomon had befriended helped him get a German transit visa to Holland. But before he could make good on his latest escape, the Nazis conquered the Netherlands, at which point he found out the Swede was an SS agent and his cousin was in the Wehrmacht. Perhaps there was a better alternative. Before he left Poland, Salomon had obtained an American visa, but by the time he decided to use it, the visa had lapsed. He was comfortable with English from his childhood education in Cracow though, and shortly after he settled in Kaunas, he began to hang around the U.S. Consulate. He thought he might be able to butter up whatever official seemed likely to renew the old visa. Salomon's efforts went well for a while, for he even became an occasional drinking buddy to one of the consular officers (whose name he no longer remembers). As he told me:

> There was a woman whose husband and children were already in New York. She was trying to put her documents in order to complete the visa application process initiated by her husband but was having a difficult time. She asked for my help. I went drinking with the consul and I said, "Look here, why don't you give her a visa, for God's sake? Here she has all the papers and everything." He said, "Remember one thing. My country has laws. In accordance with those laws, foreigners are entitled to receive visas under certain circumstances and to enter my country. It is my job, as the American consul, to find the reasons why not to issue visas." He was a little drunk when he said this but he did say this!

The American consul, true to his role and in spite of his conviviality, was unwilling to renew Salomon's visa. So he came up with another idea. He simply decided to try all the other consulates, including the Japanese. Salomon himself might put the process in blunter words: "Twenty per-

cent thinking, eighty percent shit luck," as he told a *Wall Street Journal* re-
porter who wanted to know the secret of his success. This "eighty percent" seems to make him uncomfortable even now, knowing how little
control he had over his own fate. He is not prone to obsessing over the
past and once had little interest in remembering Sugihara. "When I saw
the list and my name on it, it really gave me a shock. 'My God,' I said to
myself. 'This is the guy who gave me my visa.' After reading your story
about Consul Sugihara (published in the *New York Times* on September
20, 1994), I began looking through my old, yellowing papers to refresh
my memory."

Salton shows me the visa he received on that day from Sugihara as he
closes his eyes and reminisces. "That evening I met with my friends in
Café Metropole. I told them about my visit to the Japanese consulate.
Soon, a line formed in front of the Japanese consulate. The rest is history."

Salton makes the transaction with Sugihara sound very simple, even
mundane. "American visa? No problem," Sugihara said. "Customary
when issuing transit visas," indeed. But Salton was presenting a *lapsed*
American visa and the Japanese consul did not seem to mind. Such sim-
plicity is all the more shocking, Salton realizes, when he compares it to
the actions of his American consulate "buddy." Sugihara offered him tea
and a visa, the American diplomat, liquor and no visa. Besides that, there
was no way Salomon could have anticipated the ease of his encounter at
the Japanese consulate. Asking *anyone* for a visa, at that stage, was inher-
ently dangerous. If it was denied and the Soviets got wind you were trying to quit Soviet territory, the tactic could backfire, sometimes fatally.
"Telling a Soviet official that you want to leave the Soviet 'heaven on
earth' meant that you are obviously anti-Soviet," Salton explains to me.
"And those officials did not necessarily give rewards to people with such
criminal attitudes."

The Soviet Annexation of Lithuania

"People with such criminal attitudes" were rife all over Kaunas, beginning June 15, the day the Soviets marched into Lithuania. On that day,
Moses Beckelman was sitting in a meeting with representatives of the different Jewish groups that the Joint was supporting. He was beginning to
kvell, as they say in Yiddish, to feel the pride of serious accomplishment,
for after months of struggle, he had actually gotten them to meet in the
same room, to discuss their shared plight, and to agree on a process for
distributing scarce resources. It was a cease-fire in what had become non-
stop kvetching. At last, the endless rivalries—between the Religious
Zionists and Yeshivas, the different Yeshivas against each other, the

Bundists versus other Polish Jewish Socialists, and everyone against the Revisionists—seemed to be softening.

On that same promising morning, Beckelman looked out the window and saw Soviet tanks, appearing toylike from the heights where he sat, gliding down the street. His first thought was sardonic: "We won't have to go through these arguments anymore."[2] It was a surprise and not a surprise. With all the distrust of Soviet intentions, the belief somehow prevailed that they and the Nazis would keep each other in check over the Baltics. At least, that's how it looked last October, when the Soviets restored Polish Vilna to Lithuanian Vilnius. But throughout that winter, the Nazis were encouraging ethnic Germans to return home to the "Fatherland," though some of their families had resided in Lithuania for centuries. The Nazis seemed to know about something. . . .

By the spring, the Soviets were complaining about anti-Soviet conspiracies and other violations of neutrality in Lithuania. Red Army soldiers were allegedly harassed, even kidnapped by the Lithuanians, who were out of control under an incompetent, corrupt, and anti-Soviet government, as the Soviets tried to portray these "incidents." Perhaps they were taking lessons from the Japanese-rigged Manchurian incident a few years earlier. Since May 10 and the opening of the Nazis' spring offensive, borders across Europe were being blurred by Third Reich conquest. The more politically savvy Jews, the more paranoid Jews, those who dared to confront their specious equanimity, wondered about the quid pro quo that Hitler had to allow his ally Stalin for Germany's new acquisitions in the west. To their mind, the Baltics were in jeopardy as territories of potential compensation. Signals indicated that the Lithuanian "haven" was not so secure. On the other hand, it was still better than almost any other place in Europe—and certainly safer than the land of Tolstoy itself. For many Jews, the thought of entering the vast Soviet prison was the most frightening of all propositions. Better to get to Lithuania, in spite of its flaws.

Throughout the spring these mostly self-inflicted "anti-Soviet conspiracies" continued, justifying bouts of increasing ferocity against Lithuania. Soviet Foreign Minister Vyacheslav Molotov even fatuously claimed "that Lithuania's fate was threatened by no one else but its own provocateurs." The scale of these doctored acts spiraled upward until finally, on June 14, the Lithuanian ministers were given until 10 A.M. the following morning to accept a series of proposals that involved a virtual endorsement of Soviet occupation. Their Latvian and Estonian peers were confronted with similar faits accompli. On June 15, 300,000 to 400,000 Soviet soldiers began to move into the cities, towns, and airports, and Lithuania's president, Antanas Smetona, escaped across the German frontier.[3]

While Moses Beckelman was looking out the window, Ruchel Zielonka (Zell) was walking down a narrow alley with her three-year-old daughter, Julie. "Coming our way were tanks," Julie Zielonka Zell Baskes so vividly recalls. "As they passed us on the narrow street, we were forced to press ourselves against the wall of the building. Even today after 56 years I can close my eyes and see them."[4]

Other Jews who would soon appear on Sugihara's list tell their own tales. Chaya Liba Szepsenwol (now Lucille Camhi), sixteen, and her sister, Fejga, eighteen, sharing No. 1609 on the list, were also in Vilna when the Soviets made their conquest. The two sisters were "attending a Betar rally, the more nationalistic of Zionist organizations. One of its leaders, a young lawyer from Warsaw named Menachem Begin (years later, Israel's prime minister), was addressing the crowd of two to three hundred. "He was a fiery speaker, tremendously effective," remembers Camhi:

> Suddenly, someone came on stage and handed Begin a note. We immediately knew that there was something wrong and we felt scared. People looked at each other and asked, "What's happening?" He became even more fiery. As he ended his speech, he asked everyone to stand up and to sing "Hatikva," the Jewish national anthem. When we finished singing, he told everyone to go home. As we walked out into the street, there were Russian tanks and soldiers all over the city. The leaders had handed him the note because they wanted him to leave the hall immediately, thinking that he would be arrested. But he would not stop his speech. As it turned out, he was not arrested until several weeks later. We were bewildered and scared. The atmosphere of Vilna soon became hostile with soldiers all around, bread lines, and food shortages.[5]

Here is how Lewis Salton (Ludvik Salomon) remembers the first days of the Soviet occupation in Kovno:

> I worked for a radio store fixing radios. Whenever I could, I would listen to Berlin, Moscow, and London to figure out what was going on. On June 14th, they were playing the "Internationale" for many hours. Soon they began to tell about all the awful things that Lithuanians were doing to Red Army soldiers. I knew that something was up. On the next day, Radio Moscow described how the population was greeting the Russian tanks and soldiers with flowers. The main street in Kovno, Laisves Alejea (Freedom Avenue), was empty. The Soviets soon re-named it in honor of Stalin."[6]

The streets may have become empty. But Café Metropole, the "telephone switchboard," was full. The Metropole, café and hotel, has survived a full array of regimes representing the political vicissitudes of the twentieth century. The red velvet upholstery has seen better days.

Through the epochs, the *karaliske kave,* the Lithuanian version of cap-
puccino, may have been enriched with more or fewer whipped eggs, the
napoleonas may have had thicker or thinner layerings of whipped cream.
The borscht had its optional supplements of potatoes, meat, or sour
cream in accordance with different ethnic traditions; what you might find
in your serving was usually a reliable indicator of power relations. The
bocin, however, the local honey liquor dubbed in Lithuanian "our old
folks" was always strong no matter who was in or out.

This is the place where, in 1940, anxious refugees would sit around enjoying the deceptive tranquility. Rumors and advice flew as the *bocin*
flowed—how to extend resident permits, where to find food, how to find
work, what was happening to the Jews east and west. Half-overheard conversations of half-recognized people sitting at the next table would encourage speculation about rescue activities of the Polish underground,
about American Jewish representatives passing through town on their way
back from cutting a deal with Stalin. But the most important informa-
tional tidbits concerned visas, visas, visas. . . .

During those warm summer days of 1940, Jewish patrons of the
Metropole would compare notes on the geopolitics of life-saving scraps
of paper. They were kept busy evaluating the value of rumors and of currencies, both circulating at great speeds. Ludvik Salomon and others in
the past months had become experts on occupations—the Nazis in
Poland, the Soviets in Lvov, in southeastern Poland. They knew their situation was bleaker than ever. But suddenly word got out about the Japanese Consulate. After knocking on so many dispiriting doors, Salomon
found the right place. Indeed, he and others returned from the hill filing
unbelievable reports. Many glasses of *bocin* were left half-filled as excited
Jews, learning about what was going on there, ran off to get in line.

Those days, one would also have seen a sad and exhausted Moe Beckelman, sipping borscht in the corner. By mid-July, he had no illusions
about what it would be like to manage refugee relief under the Soviets.
In the nine months since his arrival in Kovno, he had seen enough of Soviet rule to realize how little the commissars cared about cooperating
with the local capitalists. Beckelman had been rendered ineffectual; he
decided to pack his bags for New York.

But at the last minute, he changed his mind. He recognized that the
commissars cared nothing for capitalists, true. But they were keenly interested in capitalist dollars. Dollars into Soviet coffers—and perhaps a few
into commissars' pockets—would enable Beckelman to stay behind and
run his refugee relief projects for a while longer. But as he got to know
those commissars and began to hear about the strange goings-on in the
Japanese Consulate, Moe Beckelman began to think that escape by way

of Vladivostok might not be so "facetious" after all. Vaizgantas Street could be the first leg of any eastern-facing escape.

"Ah! It's a money world," as the old song used to chirp, back in the Japan of Sugihara's childhood. Or as Mojsze Grynberg liked to say: "Follow the money."[7] In 1940, Grynberg, a Bundist, or Jewish Socialist, from Poland became No. 691 on Sugihara's list. After the war, he and his wife, Sara, made their way through Asia all the way to Mexico, where he managed a few successful businesses. We spoke in their posh Boston hotel room on October 26, 1994, on their way to visit their grandson in a New England college. "In situations such as this," he tells me, referring to Lithuania that summer, "to understand what was really going on, you just have to follow the money."

They have vivid memories of the Soviet invasion. "First the soldiers on the tanks began to steal our watches," says Mojsze Grynberg, "but then it became much more 'orderly.'" He pauses, amused by the irony. "Soviet officials came around and confiscated bicycles and radios, they took over small stores." Clearly, Stalin's henchmen were following the money; the rate of confiscation skyrocketed those first weeks. "Then they appointed a Refugee Commissar," Grynberg continues. "He was a Jew, a drunkard, a school teacher who had been a Communist. *Him* they made Refugee Commissar! At the same time they said that there were no refugees in Lithuania. They tried to force us to accept Soviet citizenship and to vote for unification. At a certain point, you had to prove that you voted even to buy food. Most Jews resisted. We refused to turn in whatever papers that we had to become Soviet citizens. We were scared and did not know what to do."

Warhaftig was as scared as Grynberg.[8] The Polish lawyer and Zionist leader was more comfortable making arguments and processing papers than raising funds. But Warhaftig, too, was beginning to realize "it was a money world," even under Communist rule. "The Jewish community was aghast," he recalls, speaking of those early days of Communist rule. "We were organized as a refugee community with a relief committee receiving funds from abroad." Those funds, more than the certificates for *aliya,* "going up" to Palestine, that he cajoled out of the British were now his lifeline for negotiating with the Soviets.

The recent Soviet takeover would certainly put an end to his Aliya Office and his peculiarly official position representing, simultaneously, the "Zionist-Jewish conspiracy" and British imperialism. The commissars roaming the streets might put an end to him as well. Warhaftig tells that in those days, he could not stop thinking about Rabbi Akiva, the great scholar who lived after the destruction of Jerusalem in 70 C.E. The sage supported a political rebellion with messianic overtones and then himself was martyred. Warhaftig had lived in the great Jewish communities of Eastern Europe; another destruction seemed imminent.

"I felt the noose tightening around us," as Warhaftig puts it. "It was evident that our activities were being monitored." As such, he tried to follow the advice of the Talmud. "Take counsel only out in the fields."[9] And so, Warhaftig recalls, "we began holding our meetings in the street or in the municipal garden. I would sit down on a garden bench with *Izvestia* spread on my lap. Next to me would sit two or three of my colleagues similarly perusing the paper, and in this manner we would exchange information and plan our activities. I had been informed that Russian detectives were eager to learn who was in charge of *aliya*. Those who were approached would answer evasively that there was no organization behind these activities, and that everybody was fending for himself."

The NKVD did not arrest and shoot him first thing, as one might have expected. Still, it would be extremely dangerous for Warhaftig to maintain his international connections, plus his ongoing contact with the British Consulate. Within a few days of the annexation, it became clear that the Soviets would shut down the British Consulate and all the other consular offices in Kovno to isolate the new Soviet citizens of Lithuania. Warhaftig and his fellow Zionists would have to "long for Zion" underground, in an embattled country with hermetically sealed borders. The Soviet Union would not allow them the faintest hope of ever marching up to Zion.

Here is how Warhaftig saw the predicament: "Reports of the impending closure of the British consulate struck fear in our hearts that the British consul would take with him the entire batch of certificates earmarked for us and thus eliminate our last chances for *Aliya*. As the British consulate in Moscow had already declared that it would refuse to endorse the Palestinian visas, we brought even more pressure to bear upon the consulate, but to no avail."

June 15 was awful enough, as Soviet tanks rolled into the streets of Lithuania. But July 15 dawned just as bad. In the bogus referendum held on that day, 99 percent of Lithuanians voted to be taken over by "Mother Russia." Now, decidedly nonmaternal Soviet troops and artillery were everywhere, as well as phalanxes of secret agents, and long strings of railroad cars full of victims of mass arrests and deportations. These facts finally galvanized Lithuania's Jews to action. "When people have a roof and a meal, no one is pushing them, they are not going to take risks," as Berek Winter, a Sugihara survivor living in San Francisco, explains the initial sense of paralysis.

Bernard Zell felt a most uneasy sense of *déjà vu;* he had seen how denial had turned to desperation back in his native Poland the previous September: "The same situation could have developed in Lithuania, and the same mentality," he writes in his memoir. "So I tried not to forget for one moment that we were refugees, and we were determined not to be trapped by the old complacent thinking: 'It's not going to happen here. We will live safely here through the war. This is the best place to live out the war.' Many of the Jewish refugees in Lithuania at that time did fall into that trap of the mind, particularly those who had no problems in making a living there."

The haven had ceased to be such. Enlisting informants and expanding their spy networks by leaps and bounds, the Soviets did all they could to inculcate the sense they knew everything about everyone. The more uncertain things got, the more risks Jews began to take, and by mid-July, they were running from consulate to consulate, standing in lines where, at any moment, they might be arrested for voting with their feet against the Soviet "Paradise."

The ultimate irony was that, with all points west closed, the only way to get away from the Soviets was to go east, *through the Soviet Union*. Bernard Zell explains the threat of this catch-22:

> We had another good reason to be scared, apart from the general reputation of the Soviets. By that time we had heard about what the Russians had done to Polish refugees in Lvov in June of 1940. The Russians had asked all of them who wanted to go back to Poland to register—so they had all their names and addresses. Then, on a certain night in June, they rounded them all up. They took them right to freight cars they had waiting and shipped them to Siberia. Those of us in Vilna were afraid the Russians were playing a cat-and-mouse game, letting us apply for visas to leave their control, and then rounding us all up. We were so afraid that we had the warmest clothes we could find for all of us, including the heaviest Russian boots, hidden under our beds in case they suddenly came for us and sent us to Siberia. It was a very fearful way to live.

One more development raised the bar on the situation's absurdity: in those very days of pervasive panic over one-way trips to Siberia, the Soviets actually opened two Intourist branches, one in Kovno and one in Vilna. I like to imagine the commissars moving into their confiscated storefront offices and touching up the ex-capitalist premises with a fresh coat of paint. Perhaps they pasted up a few sunbleached travel posters: "See Moscow in the evenings," "It never rains when you tour the Ukraine," "Go fishing on Lake Baikal." Many Jews were, of course, utterly scornful. "Do these Communists take us for complete fools?" they asked. Perhaps it was some sort of bureaucratic imperative. If one Soviet agency, such as the NKVD, opens a branch in a newly annexed area, all Soviet agencies must follow. Who could tell?

In Lithuania in mid-1940, the Nazi menace was not as immediate as the specter of the Gulag. With the long, dilapidated trains waiting at the sidings for the latest sweeps of the Red Army and the arrests of the NKVD, with a few million Lithuanians and many thousands of refugees, hiding as best they could in the cities and countryside, it was easy to feel absolutely terrorized about the threat of deportations to the East. The only thing to do, it seemed, was to play upon communism's "entrepreneurial" side. Hard currency gave off a particularly sweet fragrance for the commissars![10] A spate of bribes followed, some under the condition that, once these refugees were settled in their Soviet homelands, they would become spies for their new hosts![11] Just as lines formed outside the Japanese consulate in Kovno, so they gathered outside the Intourist offices. People on the way to the Intourist offices were easy to distinguish; their pockets and purses bulged with any currency, as the commissars demanded, other than rubles.[12]

What did Chiune Sugihara think of all this? At age eighteen, with his father in Korea, he had witnessed what occupying forces do to vulnerable populations, and had had sufficient glimpses of Soviet brutality to anticipate what might await Jews in Kovno. Perhaps these experiences made him more willing to allow "what was customary in issuing visas" to become "uncustomary." Certainly, the Soviets had left the realm of the customary in opening their ersatz Intourist offices. How did they hit on the idea of selling Jews transit visas rather than "selling" Jews themselves into slave labor? Clearly, they realized there was much more money to be made the former way, rather than the latter. Sergei Pavelovich Sugihara "understood Russian people" so very well, as Klaudia, his first wife remembered. Did he have anything to do with the Soviet's Intourist strategy?

"Missing the Bus . . . ": Japan Between Allies and Axis

As Intourist offices bloomed and consulate lines sprouted, what developments were growing back in Tokyo? The pro-Nazi faction was gaining considerable power. Talks in the spring and summer of 1940 would culminate on September 22, 1940, when Japan signed the Tripartite Pact with Nazi Germany and Fascist Italy, which cemented the Axis alliance.

Before Hitler's May 10, 1940 blitzkrieg, the Japanese Army General Staff had come to a secret decision on their intractable war in China. If they finally did not achieve total victory, they would cut their losses and withdraw but bolster their position in the north, in Manchuria. Manchukuo would be retained as a defense against communism.[13] But after the blitzkrieg, as more and more European countries fell, the Japanese

military leaders quickly regretted that decision. Hitler had opened up un-
foreseen opportunities for Japan. The same generals who had just advocated a withdrawal from China were now recommending an immediate
suprise attack on Singapore, plus a bid against the fallen Western colonial
powers (especially the beleaguered British Empire) for the resources of
Southeast Asia.[14] "Don't miss the bus!" became the new motto.[15]

Hitler and Ribbentrop knew Japan was newly enthralled, and reconvened efforts to court the Japanese government. Their "man in Tokyo,"
Japan's former and future ambassador to Nazi Germany, was altogether
busy that summer ferrying messages back and forth, and urging negotiations for a strengthened German-Japanese alliance. General Hiroshi
Oshima, we remember, was also patron and client of Chiune Sugihara, a
lanzman, as the Yiddish-speaking refugees on Vaizgantas Street would say,
in regard to the two men's shared birthplace of Gifu Prefecture.

All spring, Oshima had been reading a steady stream of reports from
Sugihara—culled from excursions in his black Buick and talks with Polish and White Russian spies—on Nazi and Soviet military deployments.
But by August, word began to arrive about all sorts of people flashing
documents with Sugihara's signature. In the who-knows-whom politics
of Tokyo, did Oshima's good word, at the right moment, protect and
work wonders that we can only imagine for Sugihara and those on his
list? If Sugihara had no masters, did he at least have some patrons?

"Tricky Business"

Some of that "unusual noise" that Sugihara was hearing in Kovno had to
do with U.S.-Japanese relations; Sugihara's old colleague and new boss in
the summer of 1940, Foreign Minister Yosuke Matsuoka, was enamored
of "tricky business," as he called it. While Japan was edging toward the
Tripartite Pact, the United States was frantically trying to find out its
aims. Japan's ambitions for territory in China and control over former European colonies in Southeast Asia, now encouraged by the Nazis, did not
lead to an improvement of Japan's relations with the Allies. The United
States had its own bag of tricks: outright reproach, abrogation of trade
agreements, the threat of embargoes, and actual trade sanctions. When
the Tripartite Pact was announced, Japan was summarily dismissed as pro-
Nazi. Whether the Allies could have contributed to the political success
of the Japanese pro-U.S. faction is still a question for debate. Who, indeed, "missed the bus"?[16]

Whatever the circumstances, Allied policy decisions, coupled with the
tenor of diplomatic negotiations—the Japanese were extremely sensitive
to perceived Western snubs—made the breakdown seem inevitable.

Joseph Grew, America's ambassador to Japan, warned that a blatantly dis-approving approach would accomplish little more than to alienate the Japanese. "We are here dealing not with a unified Japan," he stressed. The Japanese government is "endeavoring courageously" in "battle which happens to be our own battle" against the Japanese Army.[17]

Indeed, oversimplifications were responded to with more oversimplifications. Back in Washington, rivalries among State Department factions, China hands, and budget-conscious officials in the Treasury Department impeded the development of nuanced policies to deal with Japan more effectively. Those advocating confrontation and those espousing concilia-tion competed for the ear of FDR. He seemed to lean toward the hard-liners, whose position was best expressed by Henry Stimson, soon to be appointed secretary of war: "The only way to treat Japan is not to give her anything."[18]

On July 2, 1940, President Roosevelt signed Proclamation No. 2143:

> Now, therefore, I, Franklin D. Roosevelt, President of the United States of America, acting under and by virtue of the authority vested in me by the said act of Congress, do hereby proclaim that the administration of the pro-visions of section 6 of that act [strengthening American national defense through limiting exports] is vested in the Administrator of Export Control, who shall administer such provisions under such rules and regulations as I shall from time to time prescribe in the interest of the national defense.[19]

The United States was about to realize one of Japan's worst fears: the lessening of exports of "arms, ammunition, and implements of war" from a country teeming, unlike Japan, with vast natural resources. As the summer progressed, Roosevelt announced more limits on trade. Then ameliorated those limits, perhaps as a way of compromising between the hawks and doves among his advisers. It would be tough to say whether Roosevelt could have controlled Japan's expansionism by using more car-rot than stick. I wonder if he thought of his presidential fifth cousin Teddy, whose Nobel Peace Prize, bestowed for negotiating an end to the Russo-Japanese War, arose from his "speak softly" technique more than the concomitant "big stick." TR dismissed the Yellow Peril outright, but FDR took it to heart.[20]

FDR did not trust the Japanese—for what he believed were good rea-sons. In the thirty-five years since Portsmouth, Japan had gotten a repu-tation for aggression. Its brutality in China particularly had created a severe deterioration in support in the United States. Thus FDR felt justi-fied in peppering his speeches with condemnations of Japan's behavior, freely advocating a "quarantine." Roosevelt exaggerated for effect, in or-der to transform American majority opinion from isolationist to interventionist. But such rhetoric inflamed the Japanese, nonetheless. When this kind of talk was backed up by an actual embargo, tensions neared the breaking point. The general feeling throughout Japanese society was that the embargo pushed Japan to increase its control over Southeast Asia as a form of insurance. The more the United States accused Japan, the lower the pro-U.S. faction in Japan sank. The embargo was an attack on Japan's very dignity; and thus it, among other factors, contributed to driving Japan more closely into the camp of Nazi Germany and Fascist Italy.[21]

Circumventing or Canceling the U.S. Embargo

We have seen how some Japanese advocated increased confrontation with the West, while others sought accommodation. Still others chose a middle ground, in which the embargo was not so much disobeyed as evaded through economic or political means. The remarkable thing about this approach—and the aspect that most affects Sugihara and those on his list—was that these evaders saw Jews as particularly useful for their purposes!

In the summer of 1940, along the corridors of the *Gaimusho* and in the chambers of the Diet, there was a surge of interest in the state of "world Jewry." In anticipation of Roosevelt's announcement of the embargo, a particular political faction circulated a proposal whose message reflected two years of planning for precisely this sort of crisis. Document S 9460-3 2248-2252 was issued on July 1 on the stationery of the foreign minister. It was classified "secret" but was reviewed and signed-off by several lower officials. Only on July 5 was it finally released:

> In order to strengthen self-sufficiency of the empire economically, we must be independent, we must make use of the Sassoon *Zaybatsu* [the multinational corporation run by Victor Sassoon, the Shanghai-based mogul]. We are facing worldwide changes and we are trying to unify Japan, Manchuria, and China. Our standards of technology are still low and we must develop them to meet the standards of a modern nation that can defend itself. To become capable of self-defense, we must have an economy that is self-sufficient.[22]

Because of the war, those behind this proposal argue, Japan's capacity to import and export had been seriously hampered.

> We have imported the most important material from the U.S. In the American *zaybatsus,* there are many Jewish people and we are sure that Sassoon has connections with many of them. And, also, Jewish *zaybatsus* tend to expand their activities worldwide, across national boundaries. The Jewish *zaybatsus'* pursuit of money worldwide is a good point for us to make use

of to attain our nation's self-sufficient economy. According to recent information, Sassoon possesses US $100,000,000 in capital and it is not impossible for us to use that according to how we act.

Some Japanese, the report confides, already have been dealing with Sassoon and have "manipulated" him into offering to do business on certain types of machinery, whose export is perhaps already or will soon be banned by the United States. The advocates of this proposal suggest, with great confidence, that Sassoon will "deal with whatever we don't have access to and we need to get."

Sir Victor, as we have seen, was the scion of an old Sefardic Jewish family. His vast wealth and international connections quickly became of interest to the Japanese as they consolidated their foothold in Shanghai. In the late 1930s, they began observing Sassoon wherever he traveled. The Diplomatic Records Office of the Japanese Foreign Ministry contains an astounding number of documents from Japanese diplomats the world over, reporting back to Tokyo on Sassoon's visits, what business he conducted, what he said, and with whom he met. Many proposals tie him to Japanese schemes for military preparedness, increasing national, political, and economic power, strengthening territorial claims, and controlling eastern Asian economic blocs.

Another memo of July 3 indicates further discussion of this most recent proposal:

> In "Koain" [the finance and economic] committee, we discussed our two projects—one is on making use of Sassoon in Shanghai to obtain our Imperial state's self-sufficient economy and the other is on the importing of American machine tools through a neutral country. We listened to various opinions and concluded that we did not have to make a decision right now on these principles. Finally, we decided that we will not put this into action. About the second, at the moment we all agreed that we will try to realize this. In order to accomplish this, we must organize a committee and clarify the tasks. But we will leave it to the Ministry of Commerce.

Sassoon had a certain amount of clout with the Japanese and was able to use it effectively against the Nazis to help Jews settle in Shanghai. But it is not clear what relationship he had with the Japanese Army or the government, nor can we gauge how much he convinced anyone to rescue Jews. It certainly seems plausible, but there is no corroborating evidence that Victor Sassoon actually ever helped the Japanese circumvent U.S. trade embargoes. In fact, he did not muffle his criticism of Japanese foreign policy, to the chagrin of those Japanese officials who saw the Jews as "useful."[23]

Little appears to have come from these schemes, probably because de-cision making was nearly impossible, owing to divisions within ministries, rampant factionalism, and secret affiliations. This was the case even with less brazen proposals to use Jews, so vested with mysterious powers and exaggerated levels of influence, to bolster the Japanese economy. All seem to have dwindled to nothing. There are no direct connections known between those who sought Sassoon's assistance and those who were connected to Sugihara. But Sassoon's concern for the plight of Jewish refugees certainly was common knowledge among Japanese officials.

Might they have tried to accommodate Sassoon by allowing Sugihara a certain amount of leeway in signing dubious visas in Kovno that sum-mer? Or perhaps their tacit endorsement was enacted on the other end, in not stopping those Sugihara-visa-carrying Jews as they arrived late at night at desolate Soviet-Manchurian border crossings and the Port of Tsuruga. Inflated notions of Jewish influence—men like Sassoon or other Jewish industrialists, media moguls in New York City and Hollywood, Washington actors like Secretary of the Treasury Henry Morgenthau Jr.—may have created a favorable environment in Tokyo for dealing with Jewish refugees. Perhaps Japanese officials, more than most others, were liable to wave those Jews across.

Here is an example of how the Japanese took quite seriously the idea of utilizing Jews to their advantage. In this proposal, one of many adum-brated in these July days, the author wonders how U.S. and world Jewish political power can be harnessed to the interests of the empire and the Imperial Way:

> To gain power, it is said that having trade relations with the United States is most important. But day by day, relations have become worse. There is no way of having a good trade relationship with the US without taking advan-tage of Jews. Since China became a colony of Japan, it has been inevitable that we face the issue of thousands of Jews. Jews at first were anti-Japan be-cause of their ignorance about our country and the success of Chinese tactics. But now they recognize our true power and they have many opportunities to recognize our spirit of equality. So they are becoming pro-Japan.[24]

This author has a keen sense of the threatened position of world Jewry and the strength of antisemites. He realizes that Japan can take advantage of this development:

> Since the war has begun, five million Jews have been expelled from their countries and sixteen million Jews have been living under severe conditions. In the US there are organizations that try to rescue Jews but no country has offered them land other than Japan.

The author concludes by advocating the use of Jewish refugee issues in maneuvering against the United States.

> In the field of politics, business, finance, and the press in the US, Jews have much power. They are anti-Japan because of our alliance with Germany. We have gained the wrong reputation among them. But as Jews in America face the persecution that European Jews are enduring and the problem of so many refugees, our country has a great chance to negotiate with the United States by sharing our land with Jews.

There was little new in such proposals. Over the past years, as we have seen, various Japanese "Jew experts," such as Colonel Norihiro Yasue, voiced similar plans to link Jewish "leverage" to Japan's international aims. In Harbin, Japanese and Manchukuo officials convened three annual Far Eastern Jewish Conferences from December 1937 to late 1939. In each, they tried to elicit statements from Jews about Japanese generosity to European Jewish refugees—which were calculated to mobilize American Jews to lobby Washington on Japan's behalf.

These memos, swirling around in the first days of July 1940, indicate that these proposals were real and not meant to accumulate dust on the shelf. Many political and bureaucratic operatives backed these ideas— even risked their careers to voice them—in the belief that the "right Jews" would help the war effort as much as adequate scrap iron and rubber. They thought it might be worth "sharing our land with Jews" if, say, "making use of Sassoon in Shanghai [could] obtain our Imperial state's self-sufficient economy." Either way, Jewish support was worth courting.

"Regarding Visa Requests . . ."

In the summer of 1940 in the major cities of the world, deliberations over how to rescue Jewish refugees were minimal. With all the "influence" of "world Jewry," the threats to their well-being were tragically marginal to the serious policy discussions—*except* in Tokyo, of all places. Here, debates on Jewish immigration policy occurred near the center of the national discussion. This did not mean, however, that policy issues were actually resolved. In the intrigue-besotted atmosphere of Tokyo, it was safer "not [to] have to make a decision right now on these principles." Not acting seemed to be the most common approach—though such a luxury was unavailable to those in the field, like Sugihara.

Indeed, Sugihara was not the only Japanese diplomat having difficulty detecting clear signals from Tokyo. Japanese consuls throughout Europe were confounded as to what to do about issuing visas to Jewish refugees. Since September 1, 1939, their plight was further complicated by new political divisions in Europe and by the changed legal status of old citizenships in annexed countries like Poland and Czechoslovakia. The *Gaimusho's* instructions were so contradictory, as were instructions from elsewhere in the Japanese government. Consuls were told the following: (1) Visas for Jewish refugees are important in courting American favor and improving trade relations. (2) At the same time, Jews, like all foreigners, may bring dangerous influences. (3) Therefore, particularly in regard to Jews, extreme caution must be exerted to avoid antagonizing the Nazis, who soon might be Japan's allies.

On July 3, 1940, the Japanese ambassador in Peking, Nobuyuki Abe, cables Foreign Minister Arita for guidance "regarding visa requests from the people under German and Soviet influence."[25] Twelve days later, Arita replies to Peking with copies sent to many other legations, though, curiously, not to Sugihara in Kovno:

> At the moment, to those people who are in areas occupied by Germans and the Soviet Union who want to come to Japan, we will issue visas in accordance with the rules applicable for other non-Japanese foreigners. You will check applicants' background, thoughts, and their purpose for coming, etc. And if you find no grounds for suspicion, you may give them entry and transit visas. But for those who are coming as refugees to the US, they must complete the procedure to get the transit visas to their terminal countries. Only those people can get their transit visas. Other than these, you may not give any visas. It is the same thing for the Lithuanians and the Polish at the moment.[26]

In other words, consuls in the field are to interview and check the backgrounds of visa applicants, even those merely in transit. Why Arita expresses special concern in regard to refugees who claim that they are headed for the United States is not clear. Perhaps Arita recognized that the United States was not so favorably disposed to issuing visas to refugees, and often such applicants were subject to one obstacle after another. This discredited the complicated stories that so many refugees presented about visas awaiting them here or there. Japanese representatives were warned; those refugees claiming the United States as their "end point," even those who claimed they had family or friends there and therefore stood a chance of being able to immigrate, were to be rejected—unless they actually had valid United States visas affixed to their travel documents. If they did, they would be allowed transit through Japan.

On July 5, a cable to Arita from his consul in Vienna, Masayuki Tani, points to just one of many thorny problems incurred in making these visa decisions:

I have the following questions: 1—There is a Swiss woman who wants to visit her Jewish husband in Shanghai and requests a transit visa. Since she has Swiss nationality and is not Jewish, should we give her a transit visa? 2—In general, if one of a couple is Jewish and the other is Aryan, should we treat them as a Jewish couple?[27]

Though the Japanese government had made public pronouncements that Jewish visa applicants were to be treated as any other applicants, it had been trying to close Shanghai to further Jewish migration since the previous summer. The Viennese consul essentially was asking his minister whether there was a Japanese counterpart to the Nazi Nuremberg laws familiar to him because of his posting in German-annexed Austria, which would help him conveniently define who a Jew is.

Matsuoka

In mid-July, a political shuffle took place in Tokyo. Yosuke Matsuoka, an erratic personality and an acquaintance of Sugihara who knew him from Harbin and Chinese East Railway negotiations days, now emerged as foreign minister, and thus Sugihara's boss. Matsuoka's mystifying statements and paradoxical actions led many of his closest colleagues to believe that he was absolutely insane. "Mr. 50,000 Words," they called him, "The Talking Machine." As the historian John Toland said: "He left a wake of confusion behind him; even those who thought him one of the most brilliant men in Japan watched anxiously as he nimbly played his dangerous diplomatic games."[28]

Sugihara may have had additional personal connections in high places precisely at the moment that he needed support, or at least noninterference. The new war minister, Hideki Tojo, had spent part of the early 1930s in Manchukuo commanding the *Kempeitai,* the branch of the secret service related to the Kwantung Army with which Sugihara undoubtedly had some affiliation.

We have seen how difficult it was for Sugihara to receive the authorizations he needed, even in the ministries of Matsuoka's relatively mild-mannered predecessors. To survive, therefore, he, too, had to be "nimble" like "Mr. 50,000 Words." Indeed, it seems Sugihara may have been a player in one of Matsuoka's "dangerous diplomatic games." Whatever the case, attempting to navigate between Matsuoka's contradictory policies, Sugihara found himself once again in a familiar role: the masterless man.

Matsuoka, on assuming his new position, minced no words about his goals and the determination with which he would pursue them:

Accordingly, the immediate aim of our foreign policy at present is to establish, in accordance with the lofty spirit of the *kodo,* a great East Asian chain of common prosperity with the Japan-Manchukuo-China group as one of the links. We shall thus be able to demonstrate the *kodo* in the most effective manner, and pave the way toward the establishment of an equitable world peace. We should be resolved to surmount all obstacles, both material and spiritual, lying in our path. Furthermore, in concert with those friendly Powers which are prepared to co-operate with us, we should strive with courage and determination for the fulfilment [*sic*] of the ideal and the heaven-ordained mission of our country.

Matsuoka may have put a "heavenly" gloss on Japan's aims, but there were others who desired the same ends, for decidedly unspiritual reasons. Hitler's gains spurred them on; such an ally could help Japan advance their control over Asia, as long as Stalin remained outside the picture. The Japanese government knew it had to be mindful of developments on the long northern and western borders with the Soviet Union. Manchukuo, rather than providing that impervious defense of Japan, was proving to be altogether vulnerable. As recently as the summer of 1939, the Soviets had disastrously defeated Japan in the Battle of Nomonhan, in northwest Manchuria. There the Japanese had underestimated Soviet military abilities and will, while overestimating the Soviet level of fear of war against Germany. They found out the depth of their miscalculations in August 1939, when news arrived of the Nazi-Soviet Pact.

In the year that followed, the Japanese cabinet turned over four times. In spite of these changes, Sugihara's original mission did not alter; he was still supposed to gauge the degree to which the Soviet military was tied up in the West, which would then auger how much military elbow room Japan had in the Far East. Hence his involvements with Polish military intelligence, the frequent cocktail parties, and the black Buick "tours" along the borders. Each of these activities contributed to the search for evidence that Hitler was, or was not, going to keep the Soviets inextricably busy.

The end of an independent Lithuania proved to the Jews they would find no safety in the stalemate between the Nazis and the Soviets; such insecurity created the lines outside Sugihara's consulate. In less than a year, on June 22, 1941, with Hitler's attack on the USSR, for those Jews who did not stand in line and for the many more Lithuanian Jews who could not receive an exit visa from the Soviets, the shrinking haven became an expanding killing ground.

What did Sugihara report back home on the Baltic dance between Hitler and Stalin? What did his findings say about the future of Nazi-

Soviet relations and, by extension, Japanese-Soviet and Japanese-U.S. relations? Could he and his network of Polish spies advise Yosuke Matsuoka—University of Oregon, class of 1900—how to behave with the Americans based on his intelligence gathering? Matsuoka believed he could play better poker than—plus outdrink and outtalk—any American he ever met. But he would need the assistance of field representatives like Sugihara. By getting precise information from them, he could plot how to *appear,* at least, a bit more accommodating to these Americans and their "powerful" Jewish community.

Matsuoka, who saw himself a master of "tricky business," seems to have actually convinced himself (if not others) that a "stand firm and start hitting back" strategy was the best way to combat FDR's trade sanctions. In other words, courting Hitler was ultimately the way to gain Roosevelt's attention, perhaps even his respect! Matsuoka's tactic was to deploy paradoxes; he would "ride on the military away from war," as he put it. In a certain way, this theory made sense in that Matsuoka had no choice but to follow a military path. The new foreign minister owed the military his position, after all, and could not afford to alienate them. His choice, therefore, was not whether to prepare for war but *which* war to choose.

The army was lobbying for an alliance with the Axis powers. Some high-level officers had spent years in Germany and were fond of the country. Like Matsuoka with his lingering, painful memories of American snubs, these officers could not quite dispel doubts, though, over how the Nazis truly viewed them. Were they "honorable Aryans" or "lacquered monkeys"? The navy was allegedly pro-U.S., though they resented the treaty limits imposed by America in the past on Japanese naval tonnage; such curbs had inhibited their career advancement and made them averse to tangling with the British Navy—until May 10, that is, when the Germans began tying Great Britain up in battle. But by the summer of 1940, with Britain no longer much of a threat, the Japanese Navy was eager to establish control over Southeast Asia. They wanted to do this, though, without encouraging the wrath of the now-isolationist United States, which might lend Churchill more battleships to defend Britain's crumbling colonial Asian empire and those of its fallen European allies.

The new Japanese foreign minister, by nature more blunt than diplomatic, had much delicate work cut out for him. His diplomacy would not succeed unless backed by comprehensive, first-rate intelligence gathering. This is where Sugihara came in. The "new eyes" in Lithuania had to confirm that German war preparations were taking place on the Soviet border. Paraphrasing Matsuoka, he could have claimed: "It is my Soviet Union and my Soviet people that really exist." Sugihara—so at ease with

Russians, so fluent in their language that his "eyes grew large" when speaking Russian—could raise vodka toasts with his Russian friends as convincingly as Matsuoka, the American hand, could deal out the poker deck. His vast contacts, his reliable information was of great value to Matsuoka.

But in the summer of 1940, Sugihara may have been plying his Soviet buddies with vodka, as much to find out about "tourism" as about troop movements.

Getting to Curaçao

While Sugihara and Matsuoka were furiously trying to determine which moves the Germans and Soviets might make, twenty-four-year-old Nathan Gutwirth was busy studying Talmud in the world-famous Telse Yeshiva in eastern Lithuania. "We were more afraid of the Russians than of the Germans," Gutwirth recalls, astonished to remember how Jews viewed the situation in the summer of 1940.[29] "Everyone used to feel that the Iron Curtain *was* an iron curtain."

Now he is an elderly diamond merchant from Antwerp, his velvet skullcap slipping out from under his black hat on this June afternoon in 1994 in Amsterdam, where we spoke. He does not exactly evoke associations with the archetypical Dutch rescuer, the young lad in wooden shoes who stuck his finger into the punctured dike wall to prevent the sea waters from flooding in. And yet, Gutwirth can be seen only as an agent of serendipity, or, as he would prefer to call it in Hebrew or Yiddish, *hashguha,* providence. He had not set out to be such an important catalyst of mass rescue; he merely wanted to go home to visit his parents. But after May 10, when the Nazis conquered Holland, that was impossible. He tried to contact the local Dutch diplomats but they were rudderless until the Dutch government-in-exile could effectively regroup. Rudderless and then, after June 15, when the Soviets annexed the Baltic states, even more unrestrained. Indeed, the Dutch and the Japanese would soon match bold move for bold move.

Realizing that he couldn't travel west, Gutwirth thought about what lay east. He did have relatives in America, but he despaired, knowing that Jewish refugees had to jump through impossible hoops to get there. Requirements had become thoroughly Kafkaesque; many applicants were told to visit the American Embassy in Nazi Berlin or, equally inconceivable, Tokyo, to pick up their visas. But proud Dutchman that he was, Gutwirth remembered the colonies his country, once a great maritime power, still possessed in the Caribbean. Curaçao, Suriname—why not?

The subject of geography was pretty much anathema to devout

Yeshiva students. They had spent their lives zealously rejecting worldly sciences in favor of books such as *Mesilat Yesharim* (*Path of the Righteous*), yet now were assiduously plotting actual, physical paths. For they had no choice. As the Soviets tightened their control, staying put ceased to be an alternative, and though the Intourist offices tried to make the Soviet Union enticing, most were not persuaded. As Gutwirth tells me, "There were a lot of Jews in Lithuania who had relatives in Russia and never heard from them because there were no connections at all. Nobody wanted to stay and to become a Russian citizen. Everybody tried to get out because once you were a citizen it would be impossible to get out."

Several wealthy Jews in Lithuania had already purchased visas to Latin American countries at exorbitant prices from local consuls. But the young Yeshiva student had his own connections. "I knew him already," says Gutwirth, speaking of the honorary Dutch consul, Jan Zwartendijk. "In all of Lithuania there were five Dutch people. Whenever I came to Kovno I visited him. He all the time sent me Dutch newspapers to the Yeshiva in Telse. So I had a certain friendship with him."

As with Sugihara, Zwartendijk was remembered by those he rescued more as an angel than as a flesh-and-blood individual. It was only in 1963 that a California Jewish newspaper wrote about his deeds:

> No one seems to remember the name of the Curaçao angel, in their anxiety they forgot to ask. He may be alive today, someone ought to find out who was the Curaçao man in Kovno, Lithuania in 1941, and make him King.[30]

In the years after the war, even the Dutch Department of External Affairs had no file on the activity of their honorary consul; the German occupation had rendered record keeping a low priority. Zwartendijk was appointed by the Dutch ambassador to the Baltics after the fall of Holland. At that time, it became apparent that Dr. Tillmans, the current Dutch consul general in Kovno who had a German wife, harbored pro-Nazi sentiments. The dutch Ambassador in Riga, L.P.J. de Decker, sacked Tillmans and replaced him with Zwartendijk, who was a representative of the famous Dutch company, Philips Electronics, and was then peddling radios and light bulbs in the Baltics. He had no diplomatic background whatsoever.

In response to the 1963 newspaper article, Zwartendijk was discovered in retirement near Rotterdam. Later that year, Zwartendijk wrote of his activities in Kovno (he died in 1976):

> The idea to issue them was suggested by a visa request from the Netherlands East Indies made by a gentlemen whose name I have totally forgotten. I was not authorized to comply with this request.[31]

Another desperate refugee denied a visa; nothing unusual about that. But the "gentleman," Nathan Gutwirth, persevered and Zwartendijk wanted to help. Zwartendijk writes:

> The same gentleman a few days later asked a visa for the Netherlands West Indies. Not being able to issue such a visa, I asked Her Majesty's Ambassador, His Excellency LPJ de Decker at Riga, if the gentleman in question could be perhaps helped in some way to go to the Netherlands West Indies. His Excellency authorized me to make an annotation in the gentleman's passport, the text of the annotation was indicated by letter. I do not remember the text, but it differed from the text of an ordinary visa.

It was the way in which the Curaçao visa "differed" that made it usable as an "end-point visa," indicating that a refugee truly had somewhere to go. The ordinary visa that Dutch diplomats issued read thus: "For Curaçao [and other Dutch West Indies islands as well as Suriname], no visa is required. Only the local Governor has the authority to issue landing permits." If that governor hesitated or refused, shipping companies and countries along the line would get stuck with a sort of "permanent passenger." Consequently, they learned to root out potential rejects. The Dutch ambassador in Riga suddenly agreed that his consul in Kovno simply had to delete the second sentence; from now on, no governor had to give authority. The deletion of these eleven words saved thousands of lives.

Who convinced de Decker to do this? Was this an impulsive response to a desperate refugee, or was there some behind-the-scenes coordination? Zwartendijk's report is elusive:

> The Japanese Consul at Kovno was entirely willing to issue a transit-visa to those who had my annotation for the Netherlands West Indies in their passports. A Russian transit-visa, I heard, was obtainable after the Japanese transit-visa was procured.[32]

Again we feel Sugihara's assertiveness from still another source. Similar to Daszkiewicz, the Polish spy, who records that "it was precisely the Japanese Consul," Zwartendijk, too, captures Sugihara's alacrity, enthusiasm—perhaps his leadership and initiative—in doing more than enabling Gutwirth to leave. In developing an escape route. Sugihara was not merely *willing* but *entirely willing*.

According to the honorary consul's son, Jan Zwartendyk Jr. (so he spells the family name), a geologist who has lived much of his life in Ottawa and Pennsylvania, the Zwartendijk family arrived in Kovno sometime in 1938 when Jan Jr. was eleven years old.[33] The foreign community of Kovno was small enough that Zwartendijk might have known Sugihara even if the new consul was not invited to the diplomatic parties during the winter and early spring of 1940. But there is no record of any Curaçao visas being issued before this change in guard or, for that matter, before the May 10 conquest.

Whatever his relationship with Sugihara had been heretofore, it is clear that at the height of his rescue activity, Zwartendijk was running a "joint venture" with his Japanese colleague. "He called me repeatedly in a panic to ask me if I could not work so fast because he could not keep up with the brush work," Zwartendijk writes about his colleague's calligraphy. "At his office the street was full of waiting people." By this point the Dutch consul had acquired a stamp. Soon Sugihara also would take on assembly-line principles.

Gutwirth claims that he himself wrote to de Decker after the Soviet invasion asking for a visa. Indeed, other Dutch Jews in Lithuania had the same idea at about the same time. Apparently, de Decker then authorized Zwartendijk to issue visas for a small administrative fee of eleven lit. The honorary consul obliged.[34] "Within a few days, no, hours even," Gutwirth quickly corrects himself, "so many Jews stood at his [Zwartendijk's] door asking for a visa." Zwartendijk himself described it as "a chain reaction."[35]

By mid-July, word got out the Japanese would accept the visa issued at the Dutch consulate as an "end point" visa in order to qualify for a Japanese transit visa. Suddenly, escape through the Soviet Union became a reasonable risk, rather than a flirtation with the Gulag. Once the Soviet border was crossed into Japan—an obscure place best known as the home of "Madame Butterfly" to most Lithuanian Jews—one was home free to continue on to even more obscure Curaçao. It was really too fantastic. "No visa required." What lovely words, so many Jews were thinking.

A friend of a friend of Gutwirth's told Warhaftig of this remarkable Dutch-Japanese scheme, and the Zionist leader quickly passed the word around. "It got to Warhaftig," says Gutwirth. "He urged everybody to get Japanese visas. Lots of people didn't want to take it [visas]. They were afraid that if you express yourself that you want to leave Russia, you will be seen as an enemy. Then you will be deported. That did happen."[36]

Soviet Consolidation and Closing Consulates: "Missing the Boat"

When Warhaftig heard of the Dutch-Japanese connection, he was busy trying to organize orderly departures from Lithuania, mostly for those few who managed to get visas to Palestine. "Missing the boat" was the greatest fear in those last days of an independent Lithuania, as Kaunas and Vilnius fell into Communist hands. The Soviet takeover seems to have induced "an altered state of mind" even among His Majesty's staunch officials.

For nearly ten months, the Aliya Commission and the local British diplomatic corps had been enmeshed in an adversarial relationship. But now, Consul General Preston and his staff, along with Warhaftig and his colleagues, showed signs of cooperation, perhaps even a measure of identification and compassion.[37] Suddenly there was a new and brutal "them," which redrew new parameters of "us." Preston and his staff began offering unanticipated assistance to the Jewish refugees. Decades later, even the abundant evidence of lives saved did not spare Warhaftig, the pious and proper Jew, the cautious lawyer, a nagging conscience:

> Unfortunately only four days were left before the consulate was to close down. Normally the consulate would issue only 20–30 visas a day. As we knew what would happen once the files were transferred to Moscow, I offered the envoy our help in clearing the backlog and he concurred. I appealed to the consul that he might issue written confirmations endorsing the fact that an entry permit to Eretz Israel was on file for the applicant in question. The consul provided us with official stationery, which was duly inscribed by the members of our commission and by the consul. Time was running short. Not enough days were left to finish the entire procedure. On Sundays the consulate did not function and they also needed time to pack and organize their move. We took the liberty of transferring into our possession part of the stock of the consulate's official note paper which we proceeded to fill in as required. We even appended the signature of the consul, Mr. Gent—may he forgive the impertinence!"

Altering and forging documents undoubtedly became a cottage industry in the British, Dutch, and, as we shall see, Japanese consulates. All three invited refugees—civilian and military, Christian and Jewish—to assist in expediting the processing of applications. Some, such as Berek Winter and Berek Zielonka, provided rubber stamps, even potato carvings of the visa in the Dutch consulate. "So we had a stamp made for him [Zwartendijk] in Vilna, a green stamp, embossed with the Royal Dutch crest, as pretty a stamp as you will see anywhere, and he used it to issue to us the 'non-visa visas,' as we called them," Zell recalls. Daszkiewicz reports about the copies of these stamps circulating in the underground. Jozef Szimkin, Moe Beckelman's JDC colleague from Warsaw who was around Kovno that summer and who helped refugees along the escape route to Vladivostok, was particularly skilled in such forgeries.

"Time was running short," as Warhaftig recognized. It was not the moment to consider "impertinence" and improprieties. Mojsze Grynberg recalls:

One day my wife Sarah, who served as a nurse in the hospital, heard about a Dutch consul giving out visas. I quickly went there. There was a long line leading to the front door. On the side of the house I noticed a water pipe that led to the second floor. I quickly climbed up the pipe and entered the window. The consul looked a bit surprised but quickly issued me a visa. Café Metropole was the place to discover information. It was situated on the largest boulevard in Kovno, Laisves Alle. The café became the switchboard of Jewish Kovno.

One day I saw a tall, good-looking man sitting in the Café. He was Moses Beckelman, I believe, the Joint representative. Around the café people were saying that Beckelman had been to Moscow where he made a deal with Stalin. The Soviets will open an Intourist office in Kovno to make it possible for Jews to escape across the Soviet Union. Beckelman and Stalin even agreed that religious Jews will not have to pay in advance 12 dollars a day for food that they cannot eat and will be allowed to bring along their own Kosher food. Beckelman also helped make deals to get out money.

It was, in fact, only for a few days at the end of July that Soviet, Japanese, and Curaçao visas were all available for the most resourceful people. Jan Zwartendyk Jr. claims that his father issued 1,200–1,400 visas. With the unauthorized versions in circulation, it is likely that even more Jews attempted to escape using this "non-visa visa." However long-lasting his actions, Zwartendijk's career as a diplomat was rather short-lived: "After the annexation of Lithuania was formalized on August 3rd, my father closed the consulate and we went into the countryside." By then, the butchery had begun. "In Kovno," Zwartendyk Jr. remembers, "someone was hanging from every tree."

"Daily, Hundreds of Jews Are Thronging Our Building . . ."

By the end of July, the Soviets were pressing to close all foreign delegations in Kovno; the new citizens of the Lithuanian Soviet Socialist Republic, after all, would now be represented in Moscow. On July 28, as the Dutch honorary consul was winding down, and as his impressionable son was noting bodies hanging from trees, Sugihara conveyed his own report of local horrors. His cable is extraordinary in its comprehensiveness as well as in its vividness, capturing, among other things, the desperation of Jews in Lithuania. Understandably, the cable is marked "secret" and sent directly to the new foreign minister, Matsuoka. At the same time, he keeps his colleagues, Ambassador Togo in Moscow and Ambassador Kurusu in Berlin, informed:

The Communists' power in this country is rapidly exapnding. Under the influence of the GPU [intelligence agency], many acts of terrorism occur. At first, the GPU, arriving with the Red Army, attacked the headquarters of political parties of the Polish and White Russian people of this country, and Jews. They confiscate membership lists. During the three days that preceded the elections, they began to arrest those members on the list and they continue to do this. From Vilna they have imprisoned 1500 to 2000 from other areas. Most of them are members of the Poland military government, White Russian military officer, and members of the ruling party of the old administrative power of this country, Socialists, Bundists, Zionists, and other Jews.

The former Prime Minister Merkys and Foreign Minister Rupischitz, with their families, were all sent to Moscow. And in the past week, 1600 Poles have been sent to Samara. Because of this, the British government here has been protesting to the Russians. As this has been happening, many have felt the danger and have escaped to rural areas but only a few have been successful in reaching German territory. The number of people who have escaped to German territory is said to be several hundred. Daily, hundreds of Jews are thronging our building asking for visas to go to the US via Japan.[38]

There was, indeed, an increasing number of Jews standing outside the consulate during those days. But was it accurate for him to report that they were "thronging"? Ludvik Salomon (Lewis Salton), from Cracow and Connecticut, visited the consulate on July 26, and described the situation thus: *"Nobody was in sight."* Two Dutch Jews, Levi Sternheim and his sister Rachel, numbers 18 and 16, also were among the first to receive Curaçao visas on July 26. Rachel had special problems; she lost her Dutch citizenship by marrying Isaac Lewin, a Polish Jew, but de Decker had been kind enough to renew her documents and now all three had transit visas to Japan.[39] When did this thronging begin, then? On July 26, Sugihara—on his list compiled several months later—records issuing only seventeen visas. On July 27, that number of visas rises to forty-one. On July 28, a Sunday, he takes the time to write his letter to Tokyo since the consulate was closed.

We do not kow how many were lined up outside when the doors opened on July 29, Monday morning, but by evening, Salomon and others around the Café Metropole were talking excitedly about the Japanese consul and what was going on up the hill. On the day after Sugihara wrote the first of his three letters to Matsuoka and staff, allegedly asking for "permission" to issue visas to Jews and before he possibly could have received any kind of response—on that day he issued 121 more visas for an unspecified number of refugees, Jewish and otherwise.[40] On July 30, at least two days prior to any recorded response from Tokyo, Sugihara gave out approximately 257 visas. The issuance rate had gone up fifteen-fold in four working days. But this "thronging" took place *after,* not before his letter to the *Gaimusho.*

Warhaftig himself may have been part of that Monday crowd. He had his pile of "Certificates," the quota of entry visas to Palestine, issued by the British Mandate officials in Jerusalem, which he was distributing among the members of the different Zionist groups. The catch was there seemed to be no plausible way to get from Lithuania to the Land of Israel. Thousands of Jews had been escaping to the east by sailing to Shanghai via Italy, a route now closed, while a few made the trek by rail, taking a chance that a Soviet transit would let them in and out. Warhaftig had negotiated with Lithuanian and Soviet officials to allow some Jewish refugees transit across the Soviet Union.[41] But such negotiations did little toward meeting the vast need for more visas.

The "thronging" that Sugihara described might have begun earlier, though it took awhile before wary Jews could believe the Soviets and Japanese would issue thousands of visas, and legitimate ones at that. Until they could trust what they heard, many decided the risks of arrest and deportation were not worth it. Warhaftig was trained as a lawyer and had not lost all faith in signatures and stamps, maintaining that some laws, at least, might still be observed. It was näiveté, to be sure. And among Jews in 1940, in Lithuania and elsewhere, there was abundant and catastrophic näiveté, but Warhaftig's turned out to be the winning kind. By the end of July, he and others were urging Jews to hurry quickly up the hill to Vaizgantas Street, before the Soviets shut down all consulates. The Aliya "Commissar" took his own advice; on Tuesday, July 30, "Nauma and Zorach Warhaftig," numbers 454 and 455 on Sugihara's list, described as "Polnisch," paid two lit each and received their Japanese transit visas.[42]

Sugihara's cable of July 28 is so detailed and direct in tone, yet it dissembles. First, why should he assume that his new foreign minister, Matsuoka, and his staff, who are identified with the pro-Nazi faction, would be eager to hear reports of "Socialists, Bundists, Zionists, and other Jews" when they were so much more preoccupied with the Soviet threat? Second, why does he describe the circumstances ("Daily, hundreds of Jews are thronging our building asking for visas to go to the US via Japan"), even hint at his emotional response to this, yet not concede the reason behind those circumstances, namely, that the more visas he granted, the more the crowds grew? Third, if he suspected there was danger of strong disapproval from Tokyo, why tell his superiors *anything* about his activities? Was he really asking permission, as his wife and others, years later, would claim? Could it be that Sugihara was playing down or concealing his action, constructing a cover-up in response to contradictory messages coming from Tokyo?

The Japanese have a well-earned reputation for being masters of indirection. And Sugihara, in spite of his cosmopolitanism, linguistic fluency, and ease with foreign cultures, was still Japanese to the core. These letters are all masterpieces of indirection. The confounding thing, though, is that this indirection was always laced with generous amounts of directness. For instance, when he had something forthright to ask, such as his exchanges a few months earlier about renting garages or renewing leases, Sugihara was also forthright. Even when he was trying to ascertain how to handle the questionable document of Alfred Katz, the MGM representative in Kovno with his Nansen papers, he was direct. The same goes for his colleagues in Peking and Vienna who had earlier asked for clarification of their government's latest policy on Jewish refugee visas. Other than providing Headequarters with basic information, what was he trying to accomplish with this missive? Whatever he was doing, I maintain, *he was not asking permission to issue visas.*

In his July 28 letter to the Japanese Foreign Ministry, Sugihara confirms that Jews had good reason to fear the worst from the Soviets. The Russians were making determined efforts to siphon off leaders, as they had done months earlier with Henryk Erlich, Victor's father, the leader of the Socialist Bund. They immediately began capturing membership lists to settle old scores; former activists and aging fighters for the wrong faction were the highest priority, though they also liked to intimidate young leaders. These moves were mere prologue, though, to using random violence to crush dissent and "smooth" the transition to Soviet rule. None of this, we may assume, was new to Sugihara. His network of informants probably kept him abreast of Katyn-like situations. Plus, he had traveled through Siberia on a few occasions and knew all about the Gulag.

"A Veritable Pall Has Descended Over the Country . . ."

On about the same late July day as Sugihara was reporting on developments in Kovno to Matsuoka, Owen J. C. Norem, the American consul in Kovno, was briefing Cordell Hull, the U.S. secretary of state. Norem kept Washington well informed on the situation in Lithuania, including the plight of local Jews and Jewish refugees. The National Archives in Washington hold Norem titles like "Antisemitic Actions in Lithuania, Policy of the Lithuanian Government towards Jewish Importers" or, more generally, "The Jewish Question." These reports provided gleanings from the Lithuanian press, in translation, that detailed everything from indigenous antisemitism to discriminatory policies by the Lithuanian government, to the troubles of Lithuanian and Polish Jews in areas ceded to the Germans, and more. Norem consistently sounded the alarm during his two-year stint as U.S. consul general to Lithuania. Even as he was preparing to leave his post following the Soviet takeover, he managed to transmit reports about the Jews, as they were victimized in the first days of the rule of the Soviet commissars. This dispatch dates from July 25:

> [The] Sovietization process is being intensified. Gestapo, police, and workers' militia are active. Yesterday all jewelry stores were relieved of their valuable gold and silver stocks and precious stones. Estate owners, former leaders, and wealthy people are receiving attention. Arrests are being made consistently and so silently, usually under cover at night, that a veritable pall has descended over the country. The deposits of all Americans have been frozen as an answer to our action. It is difficult for local people to obtain visas or other attention since such confusion obtains from the state of disintegration and division of authority.[43]

Frozen assets notwithstanding, none of this concern was translated into actual U.S. assistance for local Jews. Secretary of State Hull froze Lithuanian assets in retaliation and imposed special license requirements on the transfer of U.S. dollars to that formerly independent country. This may have hurt the Soviets, but of course it wounded now truly desperate Jews even more. The Soviet's "answer to our action," as Norem describes it, considerably complicated Moe Beckelman's current refugee assistance work, not to mention any potential activities in the coming months. In one poignant cable after another, Beckelman begged Joint officials to convince Washington to thaw assets, as well as transfer additional funds to help him save other refugees.

But Beckelman's pleas were to no avail. Even more tragic, however, was Owen Norem's response to the "thronging" of *his* consulate. Almost from the very beginning of his tenure in Lithuania, the consulate was beseiged with visa requests. But these urgent pleas repeatedly fell on deaf ears. On May 12, 1939, for instance, a vice consul named Bernard Gufler, in a letter entitled "Registration of Aliens at Kovno, Lithuania," responds to what seems to be criticism from Washington. The Kaunas consulate had established a reputation for making it onerous for refugees to receive a U.S. visa; the State Department, not particularly generous with visas, orders Gufler to change procedures.[44] Here is his rejoinder to the order:

> Registration of persons chargeable to the nonpreference category of the Lithuanian quota was discontinued temporarily because of the great increase in the visa work of this office. With the quota filled for a very long

period in advance, it seemed preferable to free the office from the burden of registering numerous persons, who could not hope to receive visas until some indefinite time in the distant future and who were in many cases, insofar as could be judged from indications given by them, registering out of panic and not because they had a fixed desire to emigrate.

"Registering out of panic"—clearly this was not a good enough reason to be awarded a visa. The tone of the letter makes it seem such "panickers" were all but bothersome! In defense of the policy not to even register for the wait-list "nonpreference" immigrants—a policy that he was forced to cancel "in accordance with the Department's instruction under acknowledgement"—Gufler explains his reasoning: in the past month "not more than five persons" had applied for visas. Though "a notice was placed in all Lithuanian newspapers," Gufler concedes, which announced the consulate would not issue visas to applicants without families in America who issue invitations, Gufler does not underscore this notice as a reason for the small number of applicants. Moreover, he argues with his critics in Washington that not registering aliens would be "a source of saving to the Department" and then implies that those who are registered, anyway, do not actually need to be. "Their American relatives apparently are more alarmed over the situation here than they are" is how he puts it.

In Kaunas at this time, the American consul also proposed a new format for the "moral certificate" that visa applicants had to obtain from their local police, generally for a hefty bribe. The consulate now required much greater detail than before in attesting to the good character of visa applicants. This simply meant the police would now have greater opportunities to extort, and in more creative ways.

Shortly before the beginning of the war on September 1, 1939, the American consul in Kovno conceded that "only about 49% of the Lithuanian quota was actually used to issue visas." Six months later, a man identified only as "Bernstein," likely Dr. James Bernstein, the European representative of the New York–based Hebrew Immigrant Aid Society (HIAS), arrives in Kaunas. On March 6, 1940, he calls at the American Consulate and is referred to E. Tomlin Bailey, the vice consul and third secretary. Bernstein asks Bailey about the distribution of visas from the quota allocated to Polish Jews for immigration to the United States. Bailey's response is "very formalistic," Bernstein reports. His dispatch home indicates that there is little empathy for the applicants. For obvious reasons, many cannot fulfill certain requirements such as presenting documents "coming from parts of Poland from where it is impossible to get those papers," he writes. Neither are the consular officers moved by

the serious dangers and insurmountable handicaps faced by these applicants.[45]

On March 13, perhaps in response to Bernstein's visit, a "very urgent"
letter—"Re: Polish quota for 1939/1940"—is sent "by clipper," likely
from the HIAS office in Paris to Isaac Asofsky, a HIAS official in New
York[46]: "there was lately hardly any direct emigration from Poland to the
United States," the unidentified writer notes; "what happens to the thousands of numbers on the Polish quota which thus become available?" The
American Consulate is dragging its heels unmercifully. Even under the
terrible circumstances in Europe and with only 6,524 U.S. visas allowed
by law for Poles, 5,000 of the quota allowed for 1939–1940 remained
unissued. Asofsy turned to Isidore Hirshfield, the HIAS counsel in Washington, who inquired with the chief of the Visa Division of the Department of State. Hirshfield responded to Asofsky on March 21 that he was
told no visas were being withheld. But there was no discussion as to how
the remaining visas might be parceled out.

The same level of imagination that led Sugihara to give out visas was
duplicated at the American Consulate, except here it was used *not* to give
out visas. From 1938 to 1940, sorry document after sorry document indicates that whatever restrictions on immigration were ordered from
Washington, the local consulate chose the most extreme interpretation.
On August 17, 1940, as the American Consulate was closing its doors,
the same Bernard Gufler cabled to Washington the following message:

> Visas issued by American representatives at Kovno are useless to 99% of the
> applicants despite the demand for them since few can obtain proper travel
> documents and fewer can obtain exit visas or arrange transportation.

By that late date, having made it so difficult for Jews to obtain visas,
Gufler's report may have been close to accurate! They were useless because Gufler and his men had helped make them so. During the month
prior to Gufler's discouraging announcement, Vice Consul Sugihara had
distributed 1,861 visas. We do not know how many of these were heads
of households or individuals, or how many of them actually survived. We
do not know how much Sugihara helped Jews once they had left Vaizgantas Street; but there is mounting evidence that granting Japanese visas
is only part of what Sugihara attempted.

What we do know is that, unlike the American diplomats, Sugihara responded. He took initiative beyond his government's policies, beyond his
responsibilities to carry those policies out, reacting as a human being first
and an administrator second. His American colleagues acted one way,
when "much confusion obtain[ed] from the state of disintegration and

division of authority [in Kovno]," as the Honorable Owen Norem described it. They used that "veritable pall" that descended over Lithuania to conceal American unresponsiveness. Sugihara used that same pall to shield his activities—activities that saved thousands and thousands of lives.

"Japan Is More Civilized . . ."

"The world says that America is civilized," said Sugihara to the rabbi. "I will show the world that Japan is more civilized." It was late July, perhaps early August, 1940 and Sugihara accompanied the rabbi to the door of the consulate.[47] The vice consul had seen such strangely garbed and bearded gentlemen in his old Harbin days and met a few more this past year, but it is unlikely he had ever had such an intense discussion with one. Sugihara ended their talk with a handshake and his usual smile. The rabbi was more than a bit flustered.

Rabbi Eliezer Portnoy, age thirty (No. 1099), was better known to his friends as Laizer. He had just received two tongue-lashings in the past few days: from another rabbi, more venerable than he, and from an impatient American consul. How relieved Portnoy was to walk out of *this* meeting with his dignity intact. And not only with dignity, he thought, but with real visas. Portnoy could not quite absorb the meaning of what had just happened. He had worked up his nerve to ask for three hundred visas, knowing the request was probably futile, yet this Sugihara, miraculously, seemed to have said yes. Maybe he had not heard correctly. But even if Sugihara understood Portnoy's less-than-perfect German and took seriously the whole idea of issuing visas to the entire Mirrer Yeshiva, how would the students, teachers, and the families ever make it to Japan, even with these visas?

Then again, emissaries of good deeds, the Yeshiva students would darkly joke, never sustain harm, as the Talmud states. And who were greater emissaries of good than the next generation's rabbis and teachers? And what was a greater deed than to enable them to survive? But try telling this to the now ubiquitous emissaries of evil, who are not acquainted with the Talmud's assurance to the perpetrators of good deeds and might negate these visas as they pleased! Try also telling it to the rabbi who most disagreed with Portnoy and his friends' actions. Rabbi Hayyim Ozer Grodzinski was the esteemed head of the council of the world's greatest Torah academies, and he was adamantly opposed to such speculative schemes.

Four decades later, as he told his son Moishe, Portnoy still prefers not to remember the "worst Shabbos of my life." As he was getting off the train on that Friday afternoon in Kovno, whom should he bump into on the platform but Rabbi Aaron Kotler, the head of another of the world-famous Lithuanian Torah academies. Rabbi Kotler supported Rabbi Godzinski's position on *shev ve'al taase,* on staying put.

Rabbi Grodzinski, shouted Kotler, had not issued his opinion in the usual responsum in which significant points of Jewish law are clarified, but in a *kol korai,* a "calling voice," a public proclamation issued to the broadest audience. And who was he, Portnoy, a brash "putrifier of Israel," to go against his word? Did this *bukhur* not know what the Talmud said of those who defy the opinion of the scholars? The great Rabbi Hayyim Ozer had ordered the Yeshiva students to gather in Vilna, to await God's mighty and inevitable redemption. Yet he, Portnoy, and some other hooligan-*bukhurs,* did not trust in the great Rabbi—even worse, in God himself—but had the vanity to think he had a better plan! Kotler was livid. Portnoy was trembling, stunned by the rabbi's fiery invective, but he stood firm in his position.

Yeshivas were not institutions known to foster young turks. But the decision that the *shtarke,* the strong-willed Reb Leib Mallin (No. 936), and some of the older *bukhurs* had made to move the Yeshiva far away from Nazis and Communists, as far away as Curaçao or Japan, was the closest this particular Yeshiva had ever come to a youth rebellion. Reb Leib Mallin was the general, the chief of operations; he knew how to choose the right lieutenants for the right task. Why pick Laizer? He spoke some German, dressed well, was mild of manner, and seemed to have the natural abilities of a diplomat.

Laizer Portnoy had a friend at the Telse Yeshiva, the young Dutch *bukhur,* Nathan Gutwirth. Gutwirth told Portnoy about the Curaçao visas being given out at the Dutch Embassy. But sunny Caribbean beaches and wavering palm trees seemed all too foreign to the black-overcoat-clad Yeshiva students. They were hoping for Brooklyn or Manhattan's Lower East Side, which meant the American Consulate had to be consulted. So that's where he headed after his unpleasant encounter on the railroad platform.

It's unclear just when Rabbi Portnoy visited the American Consulate. Perhaps it was around those last July days when Salton was there, charming his way around—unsuccessfully—with select officials. Whatever the case, the consulate was on an accelerated moving schedule; by the end of July, Owen Norem, with Moe Beckelman's good advice on the safest travel routes, was on his way out of town.[48] Whomever Portnoy did meet with, it was not long before their meeting broke down into a shouting match. And it continued from bad to worse. Portnoy's well-tailored suit and mild manners were working to no avail. "I have my orders," one of the consuls said to the young man. "The quota for visas to America has been used up. There will be no more visas issued here." Assistant Secretary of State Breckinridge Long would have been proud of his men. Now it was Portnoy's turn to be livid.

Following two such rebukes, the rabbi felt his confidence ebb as he arrived at the portal of Sugihara's consulate. But perhaps his excessive candor—prompted by desperation—charmed the Japanese vice consul. Sugihara asked the rabbi whether he had visited other consulates, and Portnoy poured out the story of his maltreatment by the Americans. It was a move that could have backfired badly. If the Americans had turned down this Portnoy fellow, then other consulates could follow suit; most seemed to fall in lockstep these days.

Portnoy could not know that the Japanese vice consul's colleagues, back at the *Gaimusho* and in the field, were constantly gathering information and impressions on how other governments were treating their Jews and Jewish refugees. To this day, the archives of various Japanese government agencies attest to these inquiries.[49] For several years now, Sugihara was hearing from Tokyo that helping Jews might help Japan. Jews controlled the American press and public opinion, they influenced Roosevelt, and such Jews could also assist Japan economically and politically. Sugihara was savvy enough to notice that these Kovno Jews had little of the clout of their wealthy American cousins. Besides, if Jews were so important to America, why would the American consulate dismiss them so summarily? Tokyo may have believed Americans would be impressed by Japanese efforts to rescue Jews, but Sugihara must have had his doubts.

Laizer Portnoy's candor might have been appealing to Sugihara yet ultimately most damaging. The unhelpfulness of the American Consulate in Kovno called into question the claim that Jewish refugees themselves were making to Sugihara: "Just help us get away from here! In Tokyo, in Moscow, we will straighten things out. The Americans will give us our immigration papers. After all, we have a cousin here, a sponsor there. Wealthy. Well connected. What happened to us at the American Consulate in Kovno? It's a mistake. It will be straightened out. You will see. Just help us now . . ."

Could Sugihara have believed, after what he heard of Laizer Portnoy's experience in the American Consulate, that helping those Jews would be anything but dangerous, and maybe even futile? Portnoy's candor, in this sense, was a burden for Sugihara. However the Americans would act, though, he knew what he must do. This child of the "post-Russo-Japanese War" suddenly had a fierce desire to compete with the Americans, to demonstrate who was, indeed, more "civilized."

While the Yeshiva's "Foreign Minister" Portnoy was on his diplomatic mission, Leib Mallin, the chief of operations for the Yeshiva's conspiracy, was busy gathering travel documents. The group had convinced the British consulate—representing the Polish government-in-exile—to issue a few hundred "safe-passages." At the last moment before the Dutch consul closed his doors, they also obtained Curaçao visas. Portnoy's meeting with Sugihara must have taken place around the time that Salton received his visa; the demand was light enough that he still had time to offer a cup of tea to his applicants. By the time the Mirrer students were ready to return to Sugihara, the lines on Vaizgantas Street were snaking around the corner and beyond. This is the point when Moshe Zupnik, later the proprietor of the fabric store on Manhattan's Lower East Side, was brought in to help process the now voluminous visa requests. Zupnik was also the one chosen to take the precious package of three hundred travel documents that Mallin had assembled to the Japanese Consulate for stamping.

Like Portnoy, Zupnik had what people in the Yeshiva recognized to be the stuff to make it in the outside world. He had grown up in Frankfurt, could recite Goethe, and his second language of Yiddish had little impact on his *hoch deutsch,* his more refined German. He also could speak English, should that be needed. Zupnik was assigned the next part of the operation. Leib Mallin had learned that Sugihara had a most trusted secretary at the consulate, of ethnic German descent, and it would be Zupnik's job to humor that secretary.[50]

Though it was hardly dawn when Zupnik arrived, the line was already quite long. No matter, he was determined to wait his turn and make good on the consul's promise to Laizer Portnoy. "On the day that I first tried to go in, they didn't let me in," Zupnik recalls with the same frustration he experienced then. "A Polish doorman—he was standing there, maybe there were too many people inside, I couldn't get in. The next day, we gave the Polish doorman 10 lits and he took me around to the back door." Zupnik would remain in that consulate for fourteen days helping to issue visas, even reporting for work on August 9, a day of great significance to his fellow Yeshivots. On that day, thousands turned out for the funeral of the Great Chief Rabbi Hayyim Ozer Grodzinski—the advocate of staying put. Zupnik decided he would pay his respects not by attending but by remaining at the consulate, trying to save lives with scraps of paper and hastily applied stamps. He remembers how it was those two critical weeks:

When I came in, I couldn't talk to the Consul yet. I spoke to that Wolfgang Gudze. He was the secretary. Gudze asked me, "Who are you?" So I told him, "I am a member of the Mirrer Yeshiva. I have three hundred passports with me. We will go to Curaçao. Help us to get there." He looked at me, "Three hundred people? The Consul gave visas to some people, but how will he give visas to three hundred? The Consul will never allow this." So I told him, "Let me talk to the Consul." He looked at me and looked at me and said, "Alright, talk to the Consul." I came in to the Consul and I could hear Gudze tell him, "The man came with three hundred visas, what should we do?" So he, Sugihara, asked me, "Who are you?"

So I told him: "We are a rabbinical seminary with over three hundred people and we want to go to Curaçao." Sugihara responded: "Russia did not let out anybody the whole twenty years of Communist rule. But lately, some people came to me saying that they want to leave Russia and they need a visa to show that they want to go out. I don't think they will be able to go out. Nobody ever goes out of Russia. I gave them the visas anyhow. But you want so many visas. And I am afraid you will come and you will stay in Japan and you won't be able to get out. How could I be responsible to my government giving out so many visas at one time?"

At this point, Zupnik told a white lie: "We have a Rabbi Kalmanovich in the United States. He promised us that we don't have to worry." Zupnik remembers Sugihara then said: "But there are no ships going at the moment?" The rabbi quickly retorted:

"He promised us that he has ships and the money and everything. Don't worry." Sugihara looked at me and looked at me and said, "Show me proof." I couldn't show him anything, of course. So I said something I still remember, which was very risky to say, "You know we are enemies of Russia. We are religious. So we can't do everything in the open. Everything we do, we have got to do in secret. So we sent secret cables with our own codes and that's how we know about Rabbi Kalmanovich's plans." He looked at me and looked at me. He said, "Alright, I believe you. But I have to make sure for the government that you go out. And I have to make a special stamp in Japanese that says that it is only a transit visa and you will go out." And for this stamp we had to wait a couple of days till it was finished. I had no other priority so I agreed to it. And all of a sudden people came in droves for the consul to make visas for them, too.

The German secretary said, "How can I handle such a crowd?" I said, "You know what? I will help you." The Consul, he looks at me and says, "He's alright, let him help." He was very friendly, he was a small man. The helping him was done in the corridor. From that day on, for the next two weeks, I used to come in the morning and sit in the room, not with Sugihara but with Gudze. I was stamping and he was stamping. I don't have the list in my memory, I don't remember it. But there were applications that people filled out.

Gudze spoke German, Russian, and Lithuanian. He was the translator to communicate to the Lithuanian government officials. I think he was a wine salesman, born and brought up in Kovno. I brought a package for Gudze every day because things were scant in wartime. One day Sugihara observed me giving him cigarettes. "No monkey-business here," the Japanese diplomat warned. I saw Mrs. Sugihara in a kimono with the children. But I never saw her in the office working and I never saw her stamping passports. I saw Sugihara often during the two weeks that I worked there.

At that time, while I was still stamping visas, we had conversations. Gudze told me that he would go back to his Fatherland to fight for Germany, but on one point he is against Hitler. He has respect for Jews, particularly religious ones. He told me a story that before he married his German wife, he had some connection with a Jewish girl. He did not marry her. But since then, he has respect for Jews. I saw his German wife later on when the consulate was closing up. She was a teacher in a German gymnasium in Kovno.

When I left, I said, "Wolfgang, how can I thank you?" He said to me, "Remember, the world is like a *rad*." He used the German word for wheel. "Whoever is on top today tomorrow might be down. Don't forget what I did for you." Those were his last words to me, exactly. He was thinking of Hitler and his successes but what yet might happen to him. I had one thing on my mind: how to get out. I still can't understand how Sugihara let me in, a boy. He didn't have any records or anything on me. He simply handed over the consular stamp and allowed me to make visas! He wanted to do good. He told me, "I do it just because I have pity on the people. They want to get out so I let them have the visas." He had a good heart and he was very outgoing and saved people. I don't know how much he knew that he was in danger to do it, but he did it. And he did it wholeheartedly. And he was not formal. He listened to us and he knew that we were in danger and he did it.

What are we to make of this Wolfgang Gudze? Zupnik finds it hard to believe the postwar reports from the Polish underground that Gudze was a Gestapo agent. Did he truly respect Jews, "especially religious ones"? Had he actually loved a Jewish woman? Did he shrewdly forsee Hitler's downfall and want to protect against the future, and thus helped Zupnik and others? I have not found any documentation on him in the German archives; it's impossible to say. In view of Nazi ties to Baltic ethnic Germans, it's certainly plausible he was a Gestapo agent. On the other hand, we have the German secret service files on Sugihara—files that say little of the Kovno period and *nothing* on the issuing of visas to Jews. Surely, a Gestapo mole would have smelled a promotion and reported such bald misdeeds. Given Sugihara's own vast experience with spy networks and the planting of moles, it would be strange for him to slip so badly as to employ someone of German descent without being sure of his loyalty.

Whatever Gudze and Sugihara were finessing in the consulate that summer, Moshe Zupnik watched, minute by minute, lives being saved. As he says: "These were the best two weeks of my life!"

"Tokyo Gave Me Negative Answers . . ."

On August 1 or 2, Sugihara cables Matsuoka. His cable of July 28—on "Socialists, Bundists, Zionists and other Jews . . . thronging our building asking for visas to go to the US via Japan"—had still not received a *Gaimusho* response. But Sugihara does mention receiving "Cable no. 22 regarding the way of treating refugee cases." There is no record of the contents of this cable. We can infer a bit about it, though, from Sugihara's response:

> Among refugees in this country who request our visa which is the only country left to transit because there are no representatives of Central or Southern America countries in this vicinity and also anticipating the evacuation of this consulate, there are many applying to me to issue to them our visa. Moreover, our visa is the necessary condition required by the Soviet Union for leaving that country and transit to the United States and that area.
>
> We have to consider these facts. Only the person whose background guaranteed by a reliable introduction, before they leave from Vladivostok, must have reservations on ships to our country and have permission to land, thereafter, in a destination country. Also, they need to make advance arrangements for the forwarding of money to cover their expenses due to strict currency exchange rules. Should relief funds from outside be offered, prior notification to Tsuruga [the Japanese port city] must be given. Since I am issuing visas contingent upon the compliance with all of the above-mentioned conditions, I demand that you refuse boarding the ships at Vladivostok to those who have not completed these procedures.[51]

From the mention of this missing cable number 22, here, and in other available cables, it might be assumed that this was a directive that the new foreign minister sent out. Basically, Sugihara seems to be mouthing back the rules he had been given. The directive likely reaffirmed what Arita and others in the Japanese Foreign Ministry had stated over the past years. Jews who had the proper documentation should be treated as all other foreigners, no better, no worse. They would be required to produce a visa to an end point, transportation tickets, and money to cover living expenses while in Japan. There is no indication here, as there was on July 15 in Arita's directive, that cable number 22 urged consular officials to check applicants' "background, thoughts, and their purpose for coming." Was Matsuoka, the new foreign minister, easing up on the requirements?

At about the same time that Matsuoka might have issued this now-missing cable number 22, we have another cable dated July 23 that he forwarded to his ambassador, Saburo Kurusu, in Berlin. This cable I discovered among 115,000 secret Japanese documents stored at the National Archives in Washington, D.C., recently declassified. In the summer of 1940, Allied intelligence, particularly the U.S. Signal Intelligence Service, using what was called Magic, broke Japan's most important diplomatic codes. They began tapping Japanese messages. Thereafter news of Sugihara's consulate—I was astounded to realize—could reach Washington at the same time that it reached Tokyo, and certainly sooner than it might have gotten through to Berlin via the Gestapo's *"groyse zaddik"* in residence, Gudze, sitting with a Yeshiva *bukhur* in the corridor.[52] Matsuoka cables:

> Lately a large number of Jews and other refugees from Europe have gone to the various nations of the American Continent via Japan. At present the Berlin branch of the N.Y.K. (a Japanese shipping company) alone is undertaking to transport about 600 of these people between Japan and the United States. More and more requests are coming in and unless all arrangements have been completed concerning destination and entrance permits, I want you to be careful not to grant any visas for passage through our country. For your caution. Please transmit as an ordinary report.

Aware of the obstacles U.S. consular officials placed before refugees, Matsuoka had good reason to express such "caution." His warning was not sent directly to Sugihara though it well may have been forwarded to him; reports to Kovno did sometimes arrive via Berlin. The question, then, is whether Sugihara was following those rules or ignoring them. Either way, what were his intentions in his cables of July 28 and August 1 or 2? Why did he review what was commonly agreed upon—and why in such emphatic language?

On August 7, Sugihara issued 210 visas, taking time out to send cable number 58 to Matsuoka: "I am sending this telegram to let you know that I am issuing a transit visa on a Czechoslovakian passport. A German transit visa might be provided for this passport at the German embassy here as an exception." Why did this particular case merit a cable, and not others? To give some context, Czechoslovakia was now a German protectorate, and the status of a Czech passport was complicated, to say the least. It was issued under a different regime, for one, and Sugihara would not want to hurt his country's relationship with Germany by doing anything that might be taken as recognizing the autonomy of a nation now absorbed by Hitler.

It was an interesting political and legal question, surely, for a conscientious diplomat to put to his superior. It's not odd that Sugihara would ask for advice from Tokyo on this question. Sugihara did issue visas to twenty-one Czechs later that month. But something else is odd. What procedures, regulations, hidden understandings might he have violated in issuing all those *other* visas on August 7 at the same moment he was making appearances of scrupulous attention to detail and unwavering obedience to his superiors?

On August 10, Sugihara receives cable number 18 from the *Gaimusho* in response to his cable number 58 on the Czech question:

> If the Czechoslovakian passport was issued before March 16, 1939, or was extended, you may issue a visa within the effective date of the passport. However, in the case of refugees, you need to be careful that you can issue transit visas only to the ones who already have permission from the countries of their destination. [They must have entrance visas for the terminal countries.] But if they do not have that, please do not issue the visas and please be careful about that.

That same day, when Sugihara received this severe warning—not in regard to *whether* to issue visas but *how* to issue them—he sent cable number 59, setting off another futile exchange:

> Mr. Bergman and fifteen others are powerful figures in Jewish industrial families in Warsaw. They want to immigrate to South America and they have the visas issued at this consulate to pass through Tsuruga for ten days only. But on their way through Tsuruga they would like to consult with Japanese industrialists regarding the capital and experience that they have to offer. Consequently, they would appreciate a visa valid for a month. I see no reason to hesitate about these things and so I want to give permission. Please respond promptly as to whether you agree or not.

Sugihara does not make clear whether Bergman and company have successfully completed their application for "terminal countries." But he, on behalf of these "powerful figures in Jewish industrial families"—precisely the image of Jews Tokyo found so compelling—is testing whether the rules can be stretched to let them in for longer than the usual ten days.

We recall that August 10 was the day Sugihara claimed, in his 1967 memoir, he began issuing visas. And yet we know—from documents in the Foreign Ministry archives, from the testimony of others, from Sugihara's own cables—that he had been handing out visas for some time before then. Why did Sugihara choose August 10 as the beginning, when it clearly was not?

"To All Who Came to Me"

August 10, 1940, well may have been an agonizing day for Sugihara, but it was not necessarily the turning point he describes. In his recent cables, he was probing, writing for the record, flaunting his conscientiousness, concealing the manner in which he was stretching the rules far more than he was directly asking for "permission" from the Foreign Ministry or any official.[53] He believed himself to be fully authorized to issue transit visas under the repeatedly specified conditions that guests would be self-sufficient and that—as all good guests—they would leave in due time. The messages from the *Gaimusho* to him and to other Japanese diplomats around the world corroborate this belief. It was a well-worn path; thousands of German Jews already had passed through Manchukuo on their way to Shanghai and elsewhere. Permission to issue visas was not what he needed nor what he was seeking. So what did take place on that day and why does he remember it as so troubling?

It could be that Sugihara was exaggerating the boldness of his act, overstating his personal risk, and taking credit for initiative when in fact he was merely executing the policies arrived at by others. Or there could be false modesty at work here; it could be he was understating the significance of that moment of moral decision making. Which is it? We must consider very carefully what did take place on the day of August 10, 1940.

On that day, as he looked out the window at the interminable line of refugees, so many that the individuals blurred into an indistinguishable mass, there must have been at least three questions on his mind: (1) Was he actually authorized to issue *as many* visas as were being requested? (2) Under the circumstances that he so movingly described in his cable of July 28, was he authorized to cut some corners? (3) How could he know Matsuoka's *real* position on refugee visas, given the foreign minister's alliance with Japan's pro-Nazi faction, but also his espousal of Japan's abhorrence of racial prejudice, plus his strangely positive attitudes toward America?

Whatever change took place around August 10 did not have to do with issuing visas per se. Sugihara had already given visas out, in accordance with the rules. What I think happened was that on August 10, he realized those rules no longer made sense and whatever the circumstances, he, Chiune Sugihara, could no longer enforce them. This passage, from the 1967 memoir, seems to bear out his change in attitude, given what he was seeing in Kovno that summer:

However, only a few of them had documents issued by the US government, the majority had no documents, indicating that they would only transit Japan without causing hindrance when travelling to the other country. . . . There were not only male refugees, among them were women, old people and children. They all seemed very tired and exhausted. I did not know whether they had any place to sleep in Kovno in those days, maybe they just slept in the station or on the street.

In other words, once reports spread about the generous Japanese consul, not only did more refugees appear, but a different *kind*. Suddenly not just men, but women, children, and old people were squatting along the curb and in the lot across Vaizgantas Street. If Sugihara had been agonizing over what to do, this sight galvanized his resolve. It was too much to bear; it was now his moral duty to act. The most vulnerable, the most miserable had arrived at his doorstep, and he could not turn away his eyes.

Sugihara's colleagues over at the American Consulate had their "bureaucratese" to handle these situations. "Registering out of panic" it was called, and the "women, old people, and children" that Sugihara could not forget, even so many years later, were drily termed "nonpreference." For Sugihara, as he made clear to the suave Ludvik Salomon on July 26, there had been "no problem" in issuing transit visas to the select few who already had one of the rare American visas. In accordance with his *Gaimusho* instructions, Sugihara could issue the Japanese transit visa, taking care not to ask too many questions about the real validity of a Curaçao visa, the approaching expiration date of an American "destination point" visa, or the authority of suspicious-looking telegrams from the U.S. Embassy in Moscow in which the "not" from the message "US visas will not be issued in Moscow" was clumsily effaced.

These were the easy cases. Most refugees had far more flimsy documents, bad forgeries, old Polish passports, new Czechoslovak passports, League of Nations Nansen "sauf conduits"; some had no papers whatsoever. Each was seeking an opportunity to plead his or her special case before the consul. And why not? At Moe Beckelman's Joint Distribution Committee canteens or the Café Metropole, wherever refugees were gathered, rumor had it that Sugihara was a "mensch." Others said better than a mensch, a *"malakh,"* an angel/emissary sent to help God's people precisely at times like these. He was Elijah the Prophet, ever reliable to help "women, old people, and children," who comes in times of trouble in strange disguises, this time appearing in the garb of an affable Japanese diplomat. Eliyahu from Yaotsu . . .

As word got out, the composition of the Vaizgantas Street line changed from relatively upper-class, well-orgainzed, and resourceful such as Ludvik Salomon (with his ingratiating ways and "shit luck") or the Zielonka family (grain brokers, valuables sewn into the lining of their clothes), to those in far worse shape. Now most bore the signs of some personal experiences with Nazi "special" treatment of Jews. They had spent the winter foraging for food, they had no shelter, no money to bribe the Soviets. They knew Sugihara's door might be the only means of escape and that their lives depended on leaving Europe.

But surely Sugihara had seen other "women, old people, and children" who were "tired and exhausted," and maybe have "just slept in the station or on the street"? Lithuania had been swarming with tens of thousands of refugees, many indigent and homeless, since he arrived at the Kaunas railroad station around September 1 of the previous year. Why did this one scene make such a deep impression? Let us zero in on the phrase "women and children" for a moment. There are moving photographs taken at the time of the Sugihara family, with Yukiko beatifically nursing their newborn baby, Haruki, with their two cherublike children, Hiroki, five, and Chiaki, barely two, alongside. Here are Sugihara's links with immortality, the reasons he gave up his beloved Klaudia only five years earlier.

It seems someone in Sugihara's predicament could have chosen two paths. Gazing at the loving scene of his family *inside*, he might have decided he could not save those families *outside*. There was too much risk. Or he could have yoked his family and the families outside together, bracing them with empathy. Which would it be? His family alone or humanity together? "*I did not pay any attention and just acted according to my sense of human justice, out of love for mankind*," he writes. The intriguing question is, was this a moment of sacrificial idealism—like the forty-seven *ronin*, prepared to pauperize mothers, even to sell sisters into prostitution—to uphold an abstract principle? Not the honor of one's lord, this time, but the honor of one's country? Or was Sugihara, the masterless man, actually being realistic? Did he know that, in helping the families outside, he would *not* be jeopardizing his own family?

Let us turn to his own words, again from the 1967 memoir:

> Of course a dismissal from the ministry could be expected, but anyhow I was to take the train to Berlin together with my family in the morning of 31st August 1940. So I went on issuing visas to any Pole who would ask for one.

His career might have been uncertain, but not his family's safety, it seems, and that was what mattered. The risks Sugihara faced, then, were probably threefold: First, he might have antagonized the Nazis by proving that he was even less "German-friendly" than they suspected. He seemed to believe that the Nazis posed no special danger, which may have been accurate, since even as late as the summer of 1940, the Nazis were primarily concerned with being rid of the Jews, whether through immigration or terror, whichever came first. Sugihara knew his visas were actually helping with the "riddance" process. Plus he was associated with Oshima, who was valuable to the Nazis, and furthermore, Hitler was close to getting the Axis agreement with Japan that he had been seeking before beginning *the* war against the communists and Jews. Perhaps Sugihara believed that provoking the Germans was not that risky after all.

Second, he could have provoked the Soviets, and this was a more dangerous and likely possibility. Sergei Pavelovich Sugihara well knew the dangers of Soviet occupation; he had seen them before, close up. But he seems to have covered himself by getting the Soviets to agree to "sell" rather than exploit and enslave Jews. "I applied for information regarding Soviet transit visas for their journey through the USSR," he writes. "The Soviet consulate made it clear that they were prepared to issue transit visas provided they had the correct Japanese visa." But the exit visa to Japan was only the beginning. The Intourist deal for thousands of Jews, payment in dollars, proved to be quite profitable to the Soviet Union in doing something that some Soviet officials might have deemed advantageous anyhow—ridding Lithuania of Jews particularly difficult to absorb. Yet even if "the Soviet consulate made it clear," surely Sugihara knew that was no guarantee. He was a keen student of Soviet capriciousness, poor coordination, and rivalries. What appeared to be a superb idea to one security agency such as the NKVD might have been deeply resented by another such as the GPU.

Add to that capriciousness the fact that Soviet-Japanese relations were so stormy that it was not beyond the pale, for instance, to think some Soviet agent might be authorized to dispense with that irksome Japanese diplomat. He corrected their Russian, drank them under the table, thwarted the Soviet Union back in 1934–35 when it tried to make a profit on the North Manchurian Railroad, and now was consorting with Poles and White Russians who undoubtedly had ties to London. Sugihara knew how these things worked, particularly under the anything-goes chaos in Kovno that summer. He understood enough to be scared, probably, but also wagered time was on his side. He and his family would be leaving for Berlin, as initially planned, and it was unlikely the Soviets would target him by then.

Third, and most powerfully, there was the question of back home; how would his act be received in Tokyo? More to the point, how would Matsuoka react? He was known to show leniency in some areas, but granting visas "to all who came to me . . . ," as Sugihara put it? Surely this bit of rule stretching made for real insubordination. And at that time, insubordination was not met with mere reprimand, or even dismissal. Usually, there would be a summons to Tokyo on "diplomatic" business, a pretense for an investigation, a trial, and then an execution. In the environment in which factional rivalries and espionage debacles like the famous Sorge Affair (in which a German journalist named Richard Sorge was in fact spying for Stalin) were unfolding, there would be little tolerance for any Japanese unduly chummy with the Soviets.

Sugihara seems to have calculated the risks—Nazi, Soviet, and Japanese—and decided to go forward. August 10, therefore, marks the date he threw caution to the wind, but not strategy and not good reasoning.

Also, if he were looking to make others see "Japan was more civilized," here was his golden opportunity. Owen J. C. Norem, E. Tomlin Bailey, and company would never consider these poor refugees for immigration. They hailed from a nation that had also imposed the 1924 anti-Japanese immigration act, so hurtful, so humiliating to Sugihara's own country. Sugihara would give out visas—and with a vengeance.

On Tuesday, August 12, sixteen-year-old Lucille Camhi (then known as Chaja Liba Szepsenwol), who told us of Menachem Begin's imperviousness to Soviet tanks, received her visa from Sugihara. A few years back, her relatives, also refugees, had emigrated to New York City. They were workers and small shopkeepers—not exactly what Japanese officials had in mind when calibrating American Jewish wealth and power. At great trouble and expense, they had collected the thousands of dollars necessary to pay for the transportation of the Szepsenwol family to safety in America, even to post bonds with the U.S. government ensuring that these immigrant-relatives would not become public charges. Chaja Liba had received immigration visas for herself and her older sister, who was eighteen, but they could not obtain a visa for their mother. Lucille Szepsenwol-Camhi remembers that August day:

> There were a lot of people waiting in line at the Japanese Consulate. Everyone had a story, everyone was trying to get somewhere, but most people did not have a definite destination and did not have money. [Sugihara] asked us where our parents were, and we replied that our father was not living and our mother had no papers. After we told him, he looked very sympathetic, he looked like such a kind man. He nodded his head and stamped our passport. We were terribly frightened of all authority figures, and we were very nervous and scared the whole time we were there. We kept on saying "thank you" "thank you" in Polish, and he raised his hand to let us know it's okay and smiled at us. We were crying and shaking when we left his office. The people outside who did not get in jeered at us, but some people patted us on the back and wished us good luck.

And then she adds, as if finding her own story difficult to believe even now, "the Japanese man just nodded his head and stamped our passport."

For those who did not have money or, like the Szepsenwol sisters, generous relatives abroad, there were risky alternatives. Forgeries abounded, with forgers often gouging their clients exorbitantly. According to Moshe Zupnik, a Russian Jew by the name of Schlossberg was the NKVD representative in Kovno issuing Soviet transit visas.[54] A visa applicant once presented Schlossberg with obviously bogus documents, which under Soviet rule was sufficient reason to be carted off to Siberia. "You are not ashamed to give me such bad work?" said the Jewish NKVD officer. "I have *rahmunis* [pity] for your children." Twenty years of Soviet living did not eliminate his compassion for a fellow Jew in distress. Another Jewish special agent turned with violent anger on a visa seeker. "How much did you pay the *Polak* for the forgery?" When the applicant was palpably scared, this Jewish commissar looked to the right and looked to the left to see whether he was being observed, moved closer to the frightened refugee, and whispered, *"Fur gezuntihait"* (have a good trip).

"The *Polak*" may have been a reference to Warsaw-born Jozef Szimkin, the Joint Distribution Committee representative who worked with Moe Beckelman. He was quite active in both the visa and the money "transfer" business. These schemes became rather elaborate, with financiers such as Joseph Gruss helping Jews with surplus cash in Eastern Europe transfer their funds abroad while financing the travel expenses for other refugees.[55] In 1985, Szimkin described his well-organized refugee assistance:

> I never knew Sugihara personally but it seemed so because we copied so many of his visas. It wasn't hard for us to duplicate them. We made a rubber stamp and, since he didn't care whether or not people had passports, we actually stamped whole lists of people on a single sheet of paper. And it worked.
>
> I think most outsiders thought that our money came from the United States or other governments. Actually, most of it came from the refugees themselves. They turned all their money over to the agency with the arrangement that they would be paid back in full, in US currency, after the War. It turned out that ninety percent of them didn't make it—they were lost. But at least their money went to help other Jews.[56]

On August 14, Sugihara receives cable number 21 from the *Gaimusho* in response to his cable number 59, which had mentioned the "powerful Jew" Mr. Bergman and his "fifteen others" who wanted advance permission to stay a bit longer in Japan in exchange for some helpful advice:

We will decide after they have arrived. But henceforth, those who want to have transit visas through our country . . . must complete the procedure for obtaining the entrance visa to the terminal country. Someone who has not finished the procedure we will not permit that person to land. Please consider that.

If rules are to be bent, Sugihara is essentially told, the *Gaimusho* will do the honors. Again, Sugihara is warned about procedural irregularities, but not about actually issuing visas. On August 16, though, the tone becomes harsher:

Recently, we discovered Lithuanians who possess our transit visa which you issued. They were travelling to America and Canada. Among them there are several who do not possess enough money and who have not finished their procedure to receive their entry visas to the terminal countries. We cannot give them permission to land. And in regard to these cases, there were several instances that left us confused and we do not know what to do. . . . you must make sure that they have finished their procedure for their entry visas and also they must possess the travel money or the money that they need during their stay in Japan. Otherwise, you should not give them the transit visa.[57]

The missing cable no. 22, "How to handle the refugees," is cited again in concluding these instructions. There are cases in which Sugihara issued visas that "left us confused," the *Gaimusho* notes, but they have not outright condemned the fact that he is issuing visas. Given that as early as August 16, refugees from Kovno were already arriving at the Japanese port city of Tsuruga—under the best of circumstances, at least ten days away—with ambiguous documents, it seems likely that Sugihara was neglecting the "customary" even before the August 10 date, at an earlier point than we thought.

On August 24, Sugihara again applies to Tokyo for clarification, in keeping with his Czech passport question of August 7: "A Polish refugee, a manufacturer, by the name of Leon Polak, aged 54, had completed procedure just before going to the United States through his cousin in New York," he writes. It seems Polak's wife and child received a visa at the U.S. Consulate and Sugihara had already given them Japanese transit visas as well. But Mr. Polak was unable to complete the procedure for his own American visa before the U.S. Consulate in Kovno closed. "He is eager to get a Japanese visa as soon as possible so that he may at once leave this country and go to Japan where he will wait for the visa for entering the United States," Sugihara continues. "He now asks us to grant him a special visa to make this possible. I would like to know whether it would be permissible to grant him a visa."

What is Sugihara up to now? Since August 10, when, as we believe, he began issuing visas without any regard to restrictions, he had issued an additional 549 visas to enter Japan. Yet he decided to ask "permission" only for this one? Here, perhaps, we see none other than "Sugihara the strategist" busy at work.

The last preserved cable, number 24, Matsuoka to Sugihara, was composed on September 2 but not sent until September 3, late in the afternoon. If Sugihara did receive it, then he had left Kovno several days later than the August 31 date he claimed in his 1967 autobiographical fragment. American intelligence tapped this cable as well:

> The shipping company cannot deny the person who holds our transit visa at Vladivostok and they cannot deny them against the Russian police. And also, it is the matter of the confidence of our visa issuing work. There are refugees coming over to us as you have said in the telegram. We have difficulties solving problems. From now on please keep under the conditions of telegram No. 22.

Here we have echoes of the Foreign Ministry and the ship captains on the Vladivostok-Tsuruga run complaining about unanticipated extra passengers, that Sugihara himself tells us about in 1967:

> They informed me about the increasing crowd of Polish refugees, striving to board a Japanese ship in Vladivostok as quickly as possible and producing visa issued by me. Furthermore they warned about the chaotic situation this would cause.

Once again, the emphasis falls on the terms of the visas, not that they were issued at all—plus, Sugihara's authority to grant them is in no way questioned.[58] We also sense the quandary Sugihara had placed the Japanese government in. He was concealing the fact that he had issued thousands of visas but slipping in red herrings as necessary. Indeed, with statements like "I demand that you refuse boarding the ships at Vladivostok to those who have not completed these procedures," by studiously following up on a few errant visas—the Bergman and the Polak—he could appear diplomatically pious.

But his disingenuousness meant the Japanese had to contend with the Soviets, something they were loath to do. If the Japanese would not recognize their own visas issued by their consul in Kovno, what propagandistic use would the Soviets make of this and what "face" would Japan lose? Was Sugihara Machiavellian enough to be forcing his own indecisive, intrigue-ridden government to appear more "civilized" than it was? And whatever convinced him this would work?

From "Masterless Man" to "Tragic Hero"

About a year before his death in 1986, Sugihara spoke to a visitor in his home close to Tokyo Bay. Toward the talk's conclusion, Sugihara spoke of what led him to take such enormous risks and why he thought he might get away with it all:

> You want to know about my motivation, don't you? Well. It is the kind of sentiments anyone would have when he actually sees the refugees face to face, begging with tears in their eyes. He just cannot help but sympathize with them. Among the refugees were the elderly and women. They were so desperate that they went so far as to kiss my shoes. Yes. I actually witnessed such scenes with my own eyes. Also, I felt at that time, that the Japanese government did not have any uniform opinion in Tokyo. Some Japanese military leaders were just scared because of the pressure from the Nazis; while other officials in the Home Ministry were simply excited.
>
> People in Tokyo were not unified. I felt it kind of silly to deal with them. So, I made up my mind not to wait for their reply. I knew that somebody would surely complain to me in the future. But, I myself thought this would be the right thing to do. There is nothing wrong in saving many people's lives. If anybody sees anything wrong in the action, it is because something "not pure" exists in their state of mind. The spirit of humanity, philanthropy . . . neighborly friendship . . . with this spirit, I ventured to do what I did, confronting this most difficult situation—and because of this reason, I went ahead with redoubled courage.[59]

Surely, Sugihara's act can be compared to Oishi's strategizing in the story of the forty-seven *ronin*. The vice consul acted just as boldly, behind his own scrim of false leads, calculated risks, and crucial loyalties. In preparing to stretch the rules, even to break some, what appears to be the uncharacteristic behavior of an obedient Japanese civil servant is actually, more historically and profoundly, quintessentially Japanese. In the end, Sugihara acted in the name of a great national tradition. So much so, he even keeps up the game until the end of his life! In 1967, at age sixty-seven, he continues to project the careful falsehood of himself as groveling, asking for permission that he would not receive, and ultimately defying and suffering the consequences. He portrays himself as that "tragic hero" deep within the coordinates of his own culture.[60] He never touches on his own astute powers of strategy, subterfuge, and heart: how he might have protected himself from the Nazis by inviting a "Gestapo agent/*groyse zaddik*" in, how he might have bought off the Soviets, how he might have maneuvered between his country's pro-American and pro-Nazi factions.

"American visa? No problem!" as Sugihara said to Lewis Salton on July 26, 1940. He may as well have said "No American visa? No problem! No visa whatsoever? No problem!" Whether it was Warhaftig's 300 certificates or Zwartendijk's 1,200–14,000 Curaçao "non-visas," or the Mirrer Yeshiva's 300, or the assortment of forgeries that came across his desk, it did not matter.

On August 26, Japan's ambassador to Berlin, Saburo Kurusu, in a cable sent across Europe—and, courtesy of U.S. intelligence, to Washington as well—warns his colleagues in Europe: "Travel going east on the Siberian line is very crowded" and return trips to Tokyo should be scheduled accordingly. Something inexplicable is about to happen. On September 6, Kurusu conveys the following message that he received from Kovno, seemingly from Sugihara, on to Tokyo; it, too, was intercepted by U.S. intelligence.[61] "I closed my office on the 4th and left the country bound for Berlin."

As Sugihara moved West with his young family, one of the largest and most successful rescue efforts of Jews had been set firmly in motion. Even as he was about to board the train for Berlin, even from the train window, even as his train began to move—as so many Sugihara survivors will tell you, but few actually observed—Sugihara continued to issue his life-saving scraps of paper. Thousands of Jews with Sugihara's visa were packed on trains bound not for forced labor camps and gas chambers but for freedom. The tracks spirited them away from the ghettos now being built, away from the "ordinary people" who succeeded in perpetrating unfathomable brutality, away from the murderers-in-training, of the *Einsatzgruppen,* the "special" units who ten months later would begin killing one and one-half million Jews, away from the death camps now moving from blueprints to fresh construction, away from the prototypes of the gas chambers and crematoria that were starting to be tested. Away from almost certain death.

As the conscience of civilization was being probed and found so wanting in what soon would be the destruction of six million Jews, one Japanese man refused to "stand on blood." We learn his story, in all its artful complexity and simple humanity, and realize its eternally wrenching power.

Sugihara shows us history as it could have been.

Conclusion

Roads Away from Kovno

Rescuers and Survivors

On September 27, 1940, nearly all of those with Sugihara's Japanese visas were still in Lithuania. On that day, in Berlin, years of diplomatic negotiations culminated in the signing of the Tripartite Pact among Nazi Germany, Fascist Italy, and Matsuoka's Japan. What Sugihara's patron, General Oshima, had not been able to do since 1936 in strengthening the ties between Japan and Germany, another acquaintance of Sugihara, Yosuke Matsuoka, now accomplished. He successfully pressured the different Japanese factions into supporting this pact. We do not know to what extent Japan's "new eyes in Luthuania," Chiune Sugihara, his reconnoitering in his black Buick along the borders with the Nazis and Soviets, and his reports lent support to this development in Japan. Matsuoka somehow saw this "tricky business"—siding with the pro-Nazi faction of his army and with Nazi Germany—as a way to "ride on the military away from war" even if that "ride" antagonized the Allies.

The "tricky business" of the Axis agreement might have put an end to Sugihara's mass rescue. All the smiles and cups of tea, the Curaçao "non-visa" visas, the Intourist tour-and-survive packages, the thousands of hard-to-come-by travel documents, and the scraps of paper with the Japanese visa—all of these might have been rendered worse than worthless had the Nazis pressed the Japanese to close this escape route. With the increasing Soviet terror in Lithuania, they would have proven to be absolutely dangerous.

Yet developments in the fall of 1940 did prove to be momentarily auspicious for possessors of Sugihara's visas. The Nazis seemed to continue to support emigration. A sizable number of Austrian and German Jews were receiving Japanese transit visas from Sugihara's colleagues in those countries—1,477 Japanese visas were issued in Vienna and Berlin alone between January 1940 and April 1941.[1] And the Soviets and Japanese now, at least formally, were on the same side through their separate treaties with Nazi Germany. By mid-April 1941, the Japanese and Soviets successfully concluded negotiations for a nonaggression pact of their own, completing what had not been completed at Portsmouth thirty-six years earlier. It was precisely in this period between September 1940 and April 1941 that most of the Jews with Sugihara's visas made their way across the Soviet Union. This delicate web of treaty relations might have provided extra incentives to the Soviets and Japanese to cooperate, even when it came to the passage of hapless Jewish refugees.

In the months to follow Sugihara's visit to Berlin, it was not only frequent travelers on the Trans-Siberian Railway—such as the Japanese diplomat that we have encountered, puzzling over the unusual problems of getting reservations—who sensed that something extraordinary was happening. In Tokyo on December 27, British Ambassador Robert Craigie wrote that infamous letter to Foreign Minister Matsuoka about the "dangers of personification," whatever Craigie meant by this equivocal phrase. He warned the Japanese foreign minister of the consequence of Sugihara's rescue efforts "at once so as to avoid the risk of such persons being stranded in Japan."

What was happening to the Jews in Lithuania with Sugihara visas?

• On just about the same day the Sugiharas were headed west, Chaya Liba Szepsenwol (Lucille Camhi) and her sister Fejga were headed east. The ardent young Zionists, daughters of Devora Baron and Josef Trumpeldor's struggles, seeking their *har zel*, their protective mountain, would have liked to head southeast to Palestine. That road was blocked. Relatives in America, those "capitalists" of candy store and gift shop stature, had placed family savings and loans on life insurance in the hands of Cooks Travel to ensure that the two young sisters would be able to leave, first class if necessary, without delay. With their Sugihara visas, they headed to Japan. "When I think of it now, I can't imagine how we managed," Lucille Camhi exclaims. "When we arrived in Tsuruga the officials detained us when they noticed that we didn't have visas to go anywhere. We told them that we expected to get a visa to the US. They said they would call the US Embassy to check. Unfortunately, the embassy was closed because of a holiday and they did not know what to do with us. Somehow they got in touch with the Jewish community in Kobe. Two men arrived and convinced the authorities that they would be responsible for us and to let us go." She recalls other golden stories of human concern. Some twenty or so Jewish families in Kobe, largely themselves East European refugees from an earlier period, provided extraordinarily generous assistance to the thousands of Jews who passed through in the three years between *Krystallnacht* and Pearl Harbor. As with the German Jews of the "Jewish Consulate" in Tokyo, the Japanese officials assumed that the "Committee for the Assistance of Refugees of the Jewish Community of Kobe (Ashkenazim)" would take care of their own. Low-level Japanese police and immigration officials were often considerate, particularly when it came to extending Sugihara's ten-day transit visas. There is evidence that the old South Manchurian Railway Jew hand and Hebrew scholar, Dr. Setsuzo Kotsuji, intervened personally with Matsuoka and used a significant part of his family fortune in payments to officials to ensure this helpfulness to Jewish refugees. So impressive and moving was the response of many ordinary Japanese in Kobe who greeted people like the Szepsenwol sisters with baskets of fruit; this spontaneous outpouring of kindness was matched only by curiosity about the strange-looking foreigners. International Jewish relief organizations, such as the American JDC, soon helped fund the Kobe Committee in providing food, clothing, shelter, and medical assistance, and in paying for transport out of Japan. Fejge and Chaya Liba had to stay in Kobe for two months until their American visas came through. On November 8, they set sail on the President Coolidge for San Francisco. "I think of Mr. Sugihara as my savior," Lucille Camhi, in her comfortable suburban New York home, adds.

• On the very same day that Craigie warned Matsuoka regarding the "serious danger of personification," three persons—Berek and Ruchel Zielonka and their daughter Julie—were getting on the train in Vilna on their way to Japan. Notwithstanding months of daily visits to the office issuing Soviet visas and late-night interviews, Berek, so urbane and affable a deal maker, with all his resources, was simply getting nowhere. Each time the standard reply was, "'Come back tomorrow.' It was not only frustrating, but it seemed like lunacy in a way to plead to go to Russia when Jews were being sent to forced labor camps in Siberia. And making all these applications gave the Russians dossiers on us. At one point, I called Rochelle and asked her to bring Julie. Julie was attending a nursery school in Vilna. She had learned in the school some Russian slogans about Stalin and communism, all that sort of thing, and she could sing Russian songs, like 'Meadowland.' So we took her to the viceroy's office in Kovno. When he saw Julie, he turned to Rochelle and said, 'Why did you bring her? Do you want to soften my heart?' But maybe we did the right thing, because on the same day we brought Julie in, after four months of applying for the visa day after day, the viceroy called us in and told us we were getting it." The Zielonkas spent three days at the Nova Moskowskaja Hotel, "a new, very modern hotel," in a beautiful suite on the fifth floor. "They commenced to wine and dine us with first-class treatment. But they insisted that we also stay three days in Moscow, and even go to two theaters there—as if we were "tourists" on a holiday. They also required that the very religious Jews who were given visas pay for food on the railroad even though they brought their own kosher food. They said, 'You don't have to eat the food, just pay for it.'" A Russian couple identifying themselves as Jews stalked them through Moscow using every opportunity to provoke them into making compromising statements. "'Do you know who lives across from here?'" Bernard remembers the bearded "professor" trying to entrap him. "We happened to be exactly across from the Kremlin. But we played dumb. The agent provocateur then said, 'Over there lives the biggest murderer of humanity in the world.'" On December 31, the Zielonkas and seventy-seven other Jews departed on the eleven-day trip across Siberia. Rochelle Zell remembers her sigh of relief that she felt when the train left the station as "the best New Year's Eve present I could have had." They endured the "primitive" conditions of the rail trip, frightening incidents in the Soviet Pacific port of Vladivostok, three rough days on a freighter to Tsuruga, where they were greeted by the Kobe reception committee and taken by rail across the island. They had to wait for five months before they could leave for the United States and their new lives. Bernard Zell and his children became major factors in Chicago real estate and philanthropy.

• Victor Erlich, his new wife, Iza, his mother, brother, and sister-in-law were living in hiding since the Soviet incursion of June 15. The brief encounter with the Soviets during the previous fall and his father, Henryk's, arrest and disappearance prompted him not to underestimate Soviet record keeping. "We were under constant threat of arrest," Professor Erlich recalls. Their Bundist friends were able to obtain a few extra visas from Sugihara so the Erlichs did not have to risk standing in line; the Jewish Labor Committee in New York sent money for forty endangered

Bundists. They were most reluctant to leave father and grandfather behind. But "staying in hiding would have been much too dangerous."
NKVD record keeping may not have been all that good, after all. A Soviet
official did try to make a spy of this son of irredeemable Menshevik/
Bundist/bourgeois origins. After making their way across the Soviet
Union and into Japan, they tried to obtain U.S. visas but, for "technical
reasons," could not. With the assistance of the Polish Embassy in Tokyo,
they received visas to Canada and set sail in summer 1941. Victor, beloved
to many generations of Yale students, still speaks of his "profound gratitude" to Sugihara.

• The two Irenes from Lodz again parted ways in September 1940. Irene
Malowist's father, a medical doctor and Zionist, was able to exchange
some medical services for food and hard cash as well as precious British
certificates for Palestine. The family arrived in Japan in October 1940, but
it was clear they would not be able to get the visas enabling them to double back westward to the Holy Land via Hong Kong, Singapore, India,
and Iraq. "The British were afraid of sabotage along the pipelines," the
stranded family was told. To take advantage of the underutilized Polish
quota for visas to the United States was also no easy matter. Irene Malowist remembers how the American diplomats in Tokyo "kept telling
Washington that we must be spies to be let out of the Soviet Union."
Sugihara's ten-day visa was extended to nearly five months until, with the
intervention of Rabbi Stephen Wise, the family received emergency political visas and arrived in San Francisco in March 1941. Now retired in
southern Florida, Irene Rothenberg speaks so movingly of the "not 100
but 110 miracles" that she witnessed. Irene Dynenson's (Dwinson on the
list) family, energetic and clever like that of their friends the Malowists,
were not as fortunate. They received their Sugihara visas at the end of
July, relatively early, weeks before the Malowists. Daily, they went to the
Soviet office where the names of those who received exit visas were
posted. No response. In early June 1941, Irene went to a town a few miles
east of Vilna to visit her uncle's family. Three weeks later when the Nazis
captured Vilna, her family was caught and eventually murdered. Irene escaped into the interior of the Soviet Union, where she spent the war
years, only to be reunited with her childhood friend, Irene Malowist,
nine years later when both were living in the United States. It took her a
good deal of time "to face," Irene Steinman of Nyack, New York, now
recalls, "that the whole family had perished."

• Ludvik Salomon (Lewis Salton) too, individualist and secularist, was at
a dead end in September 1940. The high-risk player, so skilled at manipulating the manipulators, could not get everything to work for him to-

gether at the right moment. Night after night he would explain to his interviewers how heartbroken he was over the thought of leaving the
"worker's paradise" but how much he missed his family in America. He
also dramatically demonstrated to his interviewers his absolute unsuitabil-
ity to spy on behalf of the Soviet Union, another demand often thrown
into the deal. After weeks of waiting in line for a Soviet visa from the
NKVD, he now discovered that the Intourist office was demanding its
payment fully in dollars. The official exchange rate was approximately
five lits to the dollar; on the black market you had to pay thirty. He returned to the NKVD office and mustered his righteous indignation: "I
am a *rabochni narod,* a working man. I went to your Intourist office and
they insisted on dollars. What do you want me to do, go to the black market?" He was sent back to the Intourist office with assurances. "When the
NKVD official called me *"Tovarisch"* (Comrade), I knew I would be on
my way." The officials at the Intourist office now were frightened and
quickly issued his tickets and accommodations on payment of rubles. "For
a young man of twenty-eight, it was very exciting, a lot of adventure."
On his lapsed U.S. visa and with Sugihara's transit visa, he made it across
the Soviet Union and into Japan. As he had done more than a year earlier
in Cracow, in Tokyo he tried to befriend some of the diplomats at the
American Embassy. "But it was taking too long. I received a visit from the
Japanese Police. My Japanese visa had expired. They offered me transportation to Shanghai." A cousin in America had sent him a ticket but he
could not receive it with his expired visa. He made his way to the Imperial Hotel, where he met an old friend from Cracow. By the afternoon he
had a visa to Curaçao with a transit visa to Panama, "not worth the paper
that it was printed on," Salton says. "Diplomats were making money in
Tokyo," he adds. A day before the boat on which he sailed reached
Panama, three men boarded the ship falsely identifying themselves as representatives of HIAS and other Jewish organizations. "Everyone told
them their *tsuris* (troubles). They really were American immigration officers!" Consequently the Jewish passengers were not let off in Panama and
the Japanese ship was forced to drift around the Latin American coast.
Eventually, Mexico took in the Jewish refugees. Salton, with the help of
his cousin with political influence, was able to make it to New York.

• Benjamin Fishoff, disciple of Benjamin Franklin as well as the Kovno
mussarniks, contemplative ethicist, entrepreneur, and communal leader,
still shudders when he tells his story. He and his twelve friends had "missed
the boat" on the Curaçao visa. By the time they decided to leave,
the Dutch consulate was closed. His fellow Yeshiva student Nathan
Gurtwirth, with the Dutch connections, was already on his way east; he

would spend the war years in the Dutch East Indies, a Japanese POW. Fishoff was distraught and confused. But the young *mussarnik* and his friends ultimately demonstrated initiative of a most worldly sort in making use of their Sugihara visas. Not all the rabbis of Vilna advocated the *"shev ve'al taase"* of the late Rabbi Grodzinski, the militant passivity that the rabbi proposed in confronting the risks and uncertainties of escape. Fishoff encountered Rabbi Simon Kalischer, better known as the Amshinover Rebbe, the leader of one of the Hasidic movements in town. That rabbi, similar to the religious Zionist leader Zorach Warhaftig, was urging Jews to obtain whatever visas they could. The rebbe suddenly secured a Japanese transit visa for Fishoff and other stranded Yeshiva students. Fishoff now understands that Sugihara, by the last days in August, was issuing "fictional transit papers without a visa for a final destination" to any Jew who arrived at his door. With the Soviets tightening their grip on everything and with the Japanese Consulate about to close, some of the rabbis and *bukhurs* realized this was the last opportunity to help Jews escape. These religious Jews began to organize still another fiction, concerned, as they were to make the most of all available documents. Though the Yeshiva world was chaste to the extreme, generally advocating separation of the sexes, Fishoff and others were urged to participate in hastily organized "marriages" to enable some stranded young women to benefit from the same visa. But when Fishoff arrived in Kovno, it was decided that the seventeen-year-old was too young-looking to make a convincing-looking groom. Moreover, Fishoff and his fellow students did not have the $180 or so needed to arrange for their Intourist transit through the Soviet Union. Hearing a rumor that in Riga it was still possible to purchase rail tickets to Vladivostok in rubles, they headed to that city. They also hoped they would be able to do some *"schnuring,"* to fundraise for travel money from some of the local magnates. By the time they arrived, however, local Soviet officials had tightened things up in Riga and there were no generous patrons to be found. The Yeshiva students returned to Lithuania, making their way to the border city of Baranowic, where they were able to take a local milk train across what was left of the Soviet border. With rubles, they purchased tickets to Moscow. There they wandered around the railroad station helplessly trying to figure out how to make their way to their next stop—Vladivostok. Fishoff remembers that sojourn as a "wild, irresponsible adventure, the equivalent of sticking one's head into the mouth of a lion. Every minute we were liable to get arrested and be sent to Siberia. How is it that we did not realize this?" He now realizes what his fate would have been had he not been so bold! A Soviet sailor—Jewish, as it turned out—appeared out of nowhere and helped the students purchase their railroad tickets with rubles rather than dollars. Fishoff and his twelve friends had to traverse a third of the world's circumference on hard wooden benches. Many Mirrer Yeshiva students traveling east at that time, such as Moshe Zupnik, Laizer Portnoy, and Leib Mallin, because of their overseas connections afforded better accommodations. But some of their fellow Yeshiva students—with no miraculously appearing sailors or distant patrons—had no seats at all. Mojsze and Sara Grynberg left Kovno on January 7, 1941, at the same time as many of the Yeshiva people, all with their precious Sugihara visas. They remember the "blind passengers." These, as they explain, were vision impaired by nothing other than where they traveled in the train; they traveled in a class of their own: "No tickets, no documents," Mojsze Grynberg recalls with astonishment. "There was a Japanese man in our compartment. I think that he was an ambassador returning to his country. I saw a Yeshiva *bukhur* speak with him." During the course of the next eleven days, Grynburg reports, every time a conductor and border police would pass through the train, the students would climb under the seats. The diplomat's wife would carefully arrange a blanket, spreading it across the seat and down to the floor. The ambassador and his wife would return to their seats, conveniently concealing them. The "blind passengers," too, made it to Vladivostok. That was not the end of troubles for many. Nei, the Japanese consul in that city, an old schoolmate of Sugihara, seemed to be particularly helpful to those bearing Kovno visas. By early spring 1941— perhaps because so many Jews were in Japan with no place to go and the Japanese, in anticipation of war, were eager to be rid of foreigners—officials at Tsuruga actually refused landing to more than seventy bearers of Sugihara's visas, including Ben Fishoff and friends. With what despair they returned to Vladivostok, hoping that a kind official would allow them to return to Lithuania and not imprison them in Siberia. But the refusal of the Soviets to "repatriate" these Jews and the determined efforts of the Amshinover Rebbe, who procured Curaçao visas from a Dutch official in Tokyo, enabled them to return to Tsuruga. Fishoff and his friends and most of the Mirrer Yeshiva students spent the war years in Shanghai in relative safety. Thereafter, some settled in North America, some in Palestine. For Ben Fishoff, as for many Sugihara survivors, expressing gratitude for Sugihara's act is a *mitzva,* itself, an act of ultimate significance.

• Dr. Zorach Warhaftig and his Aliya Committee, by the end of September 1940, had helped approximately 1,200 people obtain documents, by one route or another, to Palestine. Though from day to day the Soviet crackdown was more intense and his activities more dangerous, he continued to contrive more and more schemes—transit through Turkey, Curaçao visas, made-in-Sweden, imported through a Rabbi Shlomo

Wolbe, settlements in Chile or Brazil, Paraguay or Australia. Warhaftig pursued them all while avoiding the pursuit of the Soviet secret police. He had passports, tickets, Soviet transit visas, Sugihara visas, and whatever else it would take to get himself, Naomi, and their small son, Emanuel, to Palestine. But he continued to postpone his own departure, hoping to initiate still another emigration scheme. And then, one Saturday morning as he was about to return home from the synagogue, he noticed his landlady in front of the house gesturing him to move on. He wandered the streets, soon ascertaining that the NKVD was looking for him. Hastily, he completed his own travel arrangements. For eighteen most anxious days, he and his family—guests of another Soviet agency, Intourist—ever-too-slowly made their way to Japan. There he did what he always did best—he organized. He became an international switchboard, coordinating desperate appeals with imaginative if not always implementable rescue plans. In the spring of 1941, he moved with his family to the United States where he spent the next six years, active in Zionist politics. He arrived in Israel in time to participate in its founding parliament and every successive one for nearly four decades and was minister of religion from 1962 to 1974. In his memoirs, written in the early 1980s, he laments opportunities to rescue additional Jews, missed because of a paucity of funds and political support. The British in Tokyo under Ambassador Craigie were wholly uncooperative; the Americans issued a very few visas; the Polish Embassy was more helpful. Excepting some officials, Warhaftig praises the Japanese government. Of its former vice consul in Kovno, Warhaftig speaks warmly but not exuberantly. They met for a second time when Sugihara was invited to Israel in 1969. Sugihara's own modesty in discussing his visa-issuing activities seems to have been too convincing. Warhaftig was impressed by his "moral integrity," by his liberal mindedness, his opposition to the Japan-German connection, and his regret at having had to close his consulate in August 1940.[2] Sugihara—typically Japanese—seems to have emphasized his "loss of face" over any other losses and risks. Warhaftig in recent years more enthusiastically acknowledges the magnitude of Sugihara's act.

• The Ganors, the Brauns, the Minkewiecs, Jewish friends of Sugihara, gracious hosts to so many Polish-Jewish refugees—what happened to them? There are hardly any Lithuanian Jews on Sugihara's list. Not refugees themselves, they took less initiative than others to leave, believing that Lithuania would preserve its neutrality. And after the Soviet annexation, they were forced to become Soviet citizens, unable to obtain Soviet exit and transit visas. Sugihara could be of no help. They suffered the fate of Lithuanian Jewry, of whom over 90 percent were murdered.

• And finally, Moses Beckelman from the Bronx. "Those were the days," he would write, "when relief workers became not only relief workers but also geography experts, travel agents, experts in visas and passports, experts in photographic processes connected with visas, experts in foreign exchange, finance, and currency."[3] He might have laid claims to several other areas of expertise. Yet he found himself more and more unable to respond to the enormous needs all around him. The $25,000 per month that came from New York was hopelessly meager; since the Soviet takeover, that money was frozen by the U.S. government. He was increasingly frustrated that Jews abroad were not doing enough and considered leaving. Yet he stayed, particularly trying to assist the emigration, believing perhaps that as an American, he had "greater latitude." Even after December 31, 1940, when the Soviets closed all foreign operations, Beckelman stayed, helping Jews with Curaçao and Japanese visas to gather their last papers and get out. He was full of praise for the Japanese, yet he never mentioned the name of Japan's own consul, who, in fact, gave Beckelman a visa. Leaving some time around the middle of February 1941, he traversed the route that thousands of Jews with Sugihara visas had already taken and, according to his estimate, eight thousand more still in Lithuania were prepared to take if only American Jews would solve "the problem of unblocking the jam in Japan." He visited Shanghai on his way back to the States. Part of the war years he spent in the U.S. Army with some intelligence involvements. After helping with relief to the DP camps, he worked for the JDC for several years in France and Morocco, dying in 1952.

And so it went. They and we have no way of explaining what transpired. Thousands of "dehumanized" refugees, each facing danger in one way or another, made it across continents to safety in Japan, bearing Sugihara's scrawling. Soviet officials inefficient, perhaps. Japanese officials, inexplicably cooperative. But what accompanied Sugihara's visas and what powers of "personification" did they unleash?

Marvin Tokayer aptly called it the "Fugu Plan." The Jews, similar to the fish—delicious and dangerous—would foster Goto's colonialism, *bunso teki bubi,* military preparedness in civil garb. But Japanese fantasies of a Japanese Birobidzhan, in the fall of 1940 and the spring of 1941, might have saved Jewish lives in a different way.

A U.S. intelligence intercept—documented in a CIA file but now, apparently, lost—reports Japan secretly attempting to "buy" Jewish scientists from Nazi Germany. The Japanese were shocked that the Nazis held to their convictions on "racial purity" with such tenaciousness that they would compromise their worldly interests. Why get rid of such useful scientists when they could advance the Axis effort? It made no sense to the Japanese. Indeed, they would be happy to arrange for their transport to Japan.[4]

For some of Sugihara's colleagues in the Japanese government, Jewish refugees posed at best a mixed blessing. In the past, Tokyo worried that their entrance would antagonize would-be German and Italian allies. Yet if Japan did welcome them, it could demonstrate its singular graciousness, its moral superiority to the West—*and* gain talented, resourceful, entrepreneurial immigrants in the bargain. Such immigrants would also strengthen Japan's economic and demographic stake in Manchukuo. Clearly, there were many factors to consider.

It took one official to have the guts and determination, to balance the pros and cons, and to act. Sugihara initiated that "conspiracy of goodness" for humanitarian reasons, perhaps. But rumors made his action plausible; proposals attributed to the highest level of government, even if mooted by indecisiveness and paralysis, lent to his moral action practical and political legitimacy. Such proposals—precipitating more rumors in the air than facts on the ground—might they have influenced those Japanese officials at railroad junctures and border crossings in late 1940 and early 1941, who had to make the lifesaving decisions about Jewish refugees with Sugihara's visas? Perhaps they thought: "Here come the 'capitalists and technologists,' the 'secret scientists,' secret, so very secret that nobody informed us of their arrival!"

And Sugihara and his family? Sugihara stepped off the train in the Nazi capital, probably on September 5, 1940. He well might have wondered about reactions in the German Foreign Ministry, in the Gestapo, to his visa–issuing activities in Kovno. With whatever apprehensions, he and his family spent pleasant days in Berlin. Years later, he would recall being "pleased" as well as recognizing "dangers" in Berlin. But this was in connection with his Berlin rendezvous with Kuba and Daszkiewicz, his Polish spy friends, his retrieval of the consular car, and his risky smuggling of a flag and photo album of Pilsudski for the Polish underground. There were seemingly no negative reactions—neither Japanese nor German—to his last days in Kovno.

In fact, during those very days, Matsuoka launched mass firings in his diplomatic corps. Shigenori Togo, the Japanese ambassador to the Soviet Union, tells us about the "Matsuoka Purge," of which Togo was a victim. As the foreign minister launched his "tricky business," he seemed to want to consolidate control. Other than his ambassadors in London and Berlin, "the rest of the ambassadors and the majority of the ministers were recalled."[5] The sacked diplomat Togo returned home on the very same train on which Jews with Sugihara's visas escaped the fate of so many in

Sobibor and Siberia. Sugihara, about whose activities even Japanese sea captains were complaining, that "rule-breaker," we are startled to realize, inexplicably survived the purge. He was appointed vice consul to Prague.

Those Berlin days for Sugihara, however, were deceptively calm. While the Nazis seemed to be indifferent to his rescue of Jews, they had been monitoring some of his other activities.[6] On September 11, the eve of Sugihara's departure for Prague, the German Foreign Ministry makes its inquiry to the German Embassy in Kovno. The "Top Secret" report arrives on October 2. As we have seen, it raises some questions about whether Sugihara is "German-friendly." His intense interest in "military questions" suggests that his position as a consul may be "merely a disguise." The report expresses concern over the Japanese citizenship and employment that Sugihara offered to "two former Polish citizens," Kuba and Daszkiewicz, both known to be "English-friendly." The German Embassy in Kovno's advice: "caution" in regard to Sugihara. The Germans probably did not make a fuss about the exposed spy, perhaps because of the delicacy of German-Japanese relations, perhaps, in accordance with the arch-principle of international intrigue: big spies lead to still bigger spies.

Why the Japanese Foreign Ministry sent Sugihara to Prague is not clear. But it does appear that there was internal opposition to this move at an early point. In a cable of October 17, 1940, from the Japanese Embassy in Berlin to the *Gaimusho,* Japanese Ambassador to Berlin Kurusu enthusiastically endorses Königsberg as an ideal site for "collection of intelligence on the Soviets" and "Berlin-Moscow relations." Furthermore, he argues, it is important for the "rare jewel of Tokyo-Berlin relations" that Japan learn more about German internal affairs. But what he really seems to be arguing for is "to close our office in Prague."[7] Here he may have been conveying the request of the German Foreign Ministry. Like the Soviets in Kovno, perhaps the Germans saw foreign consulates in annexed territory interfering with their new claims to sovereignty. But in this regard, perhaps they were not as ruthless as the Soviets. They attempted persuasion rather than decrees. Ribbentrop himself, according to Sugihara's friend and protégé Kasai, visited Prague in early 1941. At a meeting in which he instructed foreign diplomats to leave, Sugihara boldly challenged him.[8] If this did happen, it surely did not ingratiate him with the Germans, who were already advising "caution" about him.

The Sugiharas enjoyed the city of Kafka. It was another place where they could live the "gorgeous life." We do not know what rides into the countryside he made and what other information he could gather there. Sugihara did help organize a Japanese craft exhibition in Prague from October 7 to November 3, attended by 7100 people, "extraordinary for a foreign culture exhibition," as he boasted to his foreign minister.[9] He seems to have retained contact with Kovno—perhaps through his Polish connections—as indicated in a cable of February 17, 1941.[10] By early December, Sugihara is already visiting Königsberg for two weeks. "He is said to open up a Japanese consulate general which is said to take over the function of the former Japanese offices in the Baltic States," according to German records. It was only on March 7, 1941, however, that Sugihara raised questions about Königsberg real estate with Tokyo.[11]

It was precisely in Prague on February 4, 1941, that Sugihara seemed to be called to account for all those visas. In a cable from Matsuoka, Sugihara was ordered to report "how many transit visas you issued to Jewish refugees when you were in Kovno, name, destination, numbers, and date of issue." From the formal style of the cable, it is difficult to tell whether there was any reproach in his minister's request. The next day, Sugihara responded that he had issued 2,132 visas of which 1,500 were to Jews. This is probably the origin of the Sugihara list, though how it was compiled remains a mystery.[12] What may have prompted Matsuoka's interest in visas in Kovno might have been the arrival at that moment of many Jews with Sugihara's visa and the "bottleneck." Foreign embassies in Tokyo were parsimonious in the distribution of end-point visas. Craigie might have been right in his warning about "stranded" Jews!

Whether or not Sugihara felt anxious about the *Gaimusho*'s February 4 inquiry, it did not deter him from issuing still more visas to stranded Jews, John Stoessinger, now distinguished professor of international relations at Trinity University in San Antonio, Texas, remembers. He was then thirteen years old and called Hans; his grandparents were in serious conflict with his stepfather.[13] "'You are an adventurer,' my grandparents shouted to my father. 'This is after all the twentieth century; it can't get any worse.'" His stepfather, "who seemed to understand Hitler, insisted upon leaving Europe immediately." Though the local Chinese ambassador had issued a visa to the Stoessingers for an exorbitant sum, there was no way of getting to Shanghai. But soon, "news had spread like wildfire that a new consul was issuing Japanese transit visas via Kobe to hundreds of desperate Jews. After several days in line, we were ushered into the office of an elegant, kindly looking man who, after patting me on the head, issued us three visas without the slightest difficulty. 'Good luck,' he said to us in German."[14] As young Hans tearfully parted from his beloved grandparents at the Prague railroad station, he was not particularly grateful to Sugihara. Nearly fifty-four years later, during a lecture in Kobe, he suddenly realized who rescued him. Sugihara is not the only Japanese diplomat to whom the professor is now grateful. Stoessinger had the opportunity to express his gratitude to Dr. Ryoichi Manabe. The Japanese diplomat in their compartment on the Trans-Siberian Railroad was so warmhearted. He subsequently helped the Stoessingers greatly when their paths crossed again in Shanghai. The kind and protective Manabe was, in fact, the *Gaimusho*'s German hand who years earlier had translated Hitler's *Mein Kampf* into Japanese.

The German Office of Foreign Affairs in Prague notes that on February 15 the Japanese consulate was closed and on that same day Sugihara was appointed head of the consulate in Königsberg. The consulate itself was open only on March 6. The official notification from the Japanese Embassy in Berlin was not made until April 10.

By May 21, Sugihara's past was catching up with him: "We received information about this man previously from the former German Embassy in Kaunas." By June 5, we hear of trouble! The Oberpräsident (district commissioner) of Königsberg writes a complaint to the Office of Foreign Affairs in Berlin. Sugihara was not one to delay action though the formalities were taking so long. The Oberpräsident was not impressed by Sugihara's breach of formalities in inviting him to consular parties and, when he refused to attend, inviting the Oberpräsident's subordinate. When that official refused because of formalities, Sugihara invited some of his subordinates. This district head summoned Sugihara to "discuss social and diplomatic customs."

Whatever was going on in regard to Sugihara's disregard for local custom and the finer points of diplomacy, it seems that this angered Oberpräsident had other reasons to complain about "Sugihara's professional behavior." Sugihara was asking questions about German intentions in the Ukraine, troop movements, evacuation of children, and the like. The Oberpräsident was taking seriously the warnings of the German Embassy in Kovno to act with "caution in regard to Sugihara." Moreover, it was just at about this time that Sugihara's Polish friend Kuba got into serious trouble in Berlin. Ostensibly, he was involved in some indiscreet liaison with a German woman—inconveniently, the wife of a Gestapo officer! Perhaps his arrest was an act of revenge. But the intelligence agencies that had been keeping track of him may have felt he had outlived his usefulness as bait for "bigger fish." Kuba was tortured, subsequently imprisoned, and murdered, notwithstanding some Japanese efforts to free their national. We do not know how but can well assume that Sugihara was compromised in all this.

By June 7, the Königsberg Oberpräsident is calling for Sugihara's removal. Additional reports about Sugihara's contacts with the American consul in Königsberg as well as his drive through the countryside in mid-June strengthened the Oberpräsident's determination to be rid of him. And all of this was occurring in the tense moments of Germany's greatest and most secret mobilization, as they were about to launch Operation Barbarossa against the USSR and the beginning of the mass murder of Jews.

The Japanese had their own sense of propriety. The question boiled down to whether Sugihara could be dismissed before he was officially appointed by the Emperor! By September 10, it would seem, Sugihara was both hired and fired. Two days later, the Germans report notification that Sugihara is being transferred to Ankara. On October 7, the Oberpräsident complains of a letter that he received from the Japanese consulate stating that "an official who has been recalled from his position should not be stripped of his functions until he has actually left." Sugihara, the Oberpräsident was informed, is not being transferred to Ankara but is merely "planning a vacation in Japan with his family." Whether in fact Sugihara did return to Japan at this time is not known. The war between Germany and the Soviet Union that was already in its fourth month made travel through Siberia impossible. Was there any other route by which Sugihara could have gone to Japan and returned within two months? Neither do we know what Sugihara accomplished during this beleaguered period. But as the records, right in the *Gaimusho,* indicate, he did distribute at least thirty-two visas to Jews.

On December 21, 1941, the United States intercepts the following message: "Cable no. 222 from Bucharest to Tokyo. Sugihara has arrived at his post." Sugihara spent over two years in Bucharest, at least initially enjoying the "gorgeous life." From the few cables that we have of colleagues, it seems that Sugihara was following one of his special areas: he was keeping tabs on White Russians and the responses of different governments to this international community with which Sugihara had had family connections for eleven years in Harbin.

At the end of the war, the Sugiharas were held in relatively benign confinement by the Soviets, first in prison camps along the Black Sea, then farther east in the interior. A report found in the State Archives of the Russian Federation in Moscow provides a rare glimpse into the prison life where Sugihara, one of "seventeen former workers of the Japanese Embassy in Rumania," was held in Camp 380. The diet included one pound of meat and two pounds of fish per month, tomato paste, and two pounds of bread per day. Their release was approved in the summer of 1946. A message from Odessa in November states that "the Ministry of Internal Affairs has no objection to sending them through territories of the Soviet Union to return to their motherland." They left the prison camp and spent several months on a very slow train, arriving in Vladivostok on April 10, 1947. There is some indication that American pressure may have been behind the repatriation. The report concludes with a list of what was confiscated from these Japanese: From Sugihara, we are not surprised to discover, "books on Russia in German and in English; seven notebooks."

Returning to war-shattered Japan, the Sugiharas might not have had as good a diet as they did in Soviet prison camps. Indeed, there are reports that Sugihara makes his first visit back to his hometown of Yaotsu in this period in search of rice. Rules of the General Headquarters of the U.S. Occupational Forces may have resulted in his getting into trouble in this period. As an indication of the social climate of the times, Ryuko Nakamura, Sugihara's sister, recalls her desperate efforts to locate her missing brother. She made a special trip to Tokyo to visit her brother's old friend from the years of the "wetties," Chu'ichi Ohashi, who managed to attain a high position in the first postwar Japanese government. The young Ryuko had spent her adolescence with her brother in Harbin and had been particularly close to the Ohashi family. When she accosted them after the war asking for information about her brother, not only did they deny knowing anything about his whereabouts but they feigned not recognizing Ryuko—nor even ever hearing of her brother. This was perhaps indicative of the way in which he would be received.

The family still tells the story with pain. In the spring of 1947, shortly after his repatriation, Chiune Sugihara was summoned to the Japanese Foreign Ministry in Tokyo. He was ordered at that time to tender his resignation, which he submitted on May 28. It was accepted on June 7, 1947. "Since I would like to resign please give permission to that effect. Signed, Sugihara." How voluntary this resignation was and what prompted it is not clear. The Foreign Ministry still claims that he was given a termination fee of 7,605 yen and a starting pension of 1,613 yen. The ministry further claims that this was a result of retrenchment. Indeed, whatever statistics we have on the Japanese government indicate large-scale forced resignations and particularly strong retrenchment in the diplomatic wing of the Foreign Ministry. An occupied country does not need many diplomats.[15]

The family claims that Sugihara was forced to resign. He was being punished for the "Lithuanian incident." The claims are difficult to assess.

What is clear is that Sugihara himself believed he was being punished. In later years, he even told foreigners that he was listed as a criminal of war by the American forces.[16] There is no evidence for this, notwithstanding his close relations with Hiroshi Oshima and Togo, who were subsequently placed on trial. It also seems clear that an official forced to resign because of insubordination or any other criminal charges would not have been awarded a termination fee and lifelong pension. If his were truly deemed to be criminal behavior, he would have been punished long before. But given Sugihara's second-tier status within the Foreign Ministry—not a graduate of Tokyo University—it is likely that he would be a prime candidate for forced resignation. Even with the democratization introduced by General MacArthur's staff, the *Gaimusho* was not a bureaucracy immediately reorganized to recognize achievement. At the same time, there is no evidence that his visa-granting activities and some of the complications that they subsequently caused were an altogether neutral factor in forcing him to quit. For years, his existence and his act were denied by *Gaimusho* officials; several people who tried to locate Sugihara attest to this. It could be that the Japanese officials who made the decision to fire Sugihara harbored some resentment, even based on Sugihara's rescue of Jews.

The years that followed were not happy years for Sugihara. He moved around trying to support his family at odd jobs. In 1951, Leo Hanin, one of the leaders of the Kobe committee, worked with him in the Ponve Department store, a Jewish-owned store in the Ginza district of Tokyo that catered primarily to American GIs. Hanin remembers Sugihara as dour and depressed, "a difficult man to approach, he felt himself above others but had lost face." Hanin believes that Sugihara lost his pension or at least claimed this to be the case; the Personnel Office of the *Gaimusho* rejects this claim. Sugihara's lifesaving acts on behalf of Jews were known at that time, Hanin further claims, but Sugihara did not want to discuss them. "On one occasion he did explain what he did as the "finger of God."[17] By the second part of the 1950s, Sugihara obtained his first job drawing on his abundant talents. He worked for several years for the NHK Radio Broadcasting Services, translating Russian reports into Japanese. Co-workers in that period remember him as a teacher, as fatherly.[18]

In 1960, following still another reconciliation between Japan and the Soviet Union and the opening of trade, Sugihara was invited to work for a Japanese trade company in Moscow. This was the beginning of a decade and a half of sojourn in the Soviet capital. He was deeply involved in the opening of that trade, working more to help orient Japanese to Soviet conditions than actually as a tradesman. His former colleagues vary in their assessment of his business skills. What they do agree upon is his charm, his impressive linguistic abilities, and his intuitive sense of how Russians think. Even the hardest Soviet officials seemed to respond with a special warmth to Sugihara. This special knack for getting around Soviet bureaucracy was extremely useful to his employers; hearing these exuberant reports from his former bosses about these uncanny abilities with Russians encourages us to imagine more than we can possibly explain about Sugihara's conspiracy of goodness as it was implemented in 1940–41 up and down the tracks from Kovno to Vladivostok and the lives it saved.[19]

During this period, he made but occasional visits to Tokyo to see Yukiko and his three children. But he seemed to keep tabs on things back home and wrote with authority to his children, reminding them to do their homework or to prepare for promising careers with Toshiba or ANA. It was also in this period that he was discovered by several of his survivors who were living in Israel and invited to that country, where he was honored.

By 1975 age and infirmity made it difficult to return to Moscow. But relations with his wife Yukiko seemed to be fairly strained. They settled down to an uneasy life in Kamamura, a bedroom suburb of Tokyo. By 1980 he was being discovered in his own country. Sugihara survivors who visited him at that time wanted to hear about his heroism; he wanted to hear about their children and grandchildren. He died on July 31, 1986.

The small-town road leads to the Sugihara monument on Humanity Hill, past the dam, and on to Joe Iwai's home. Iwai lives in the actual home of Chiune Sugihara's mother, somehow inherited by his side of the family. The Iwai family homestead sprawls in the old style, sliding doors opening on a sitting room, with many small rooms on the other side of paper partitions. The house is surrounded by 330 square meters of land and other hints of Grandma's samurai bearing. The house with its straw mat floors and large chairless sitting room is little changed from the days, a century ago, when Sugihara's mother frolicked in her parents' home. I marvel at the continuity and rootedness that a Japanese man of Sugihara's generation could feel, much as his country endured great changes and he observed global upheavals.

Cousin Joe Iwai tells me of Sugihara's visit to Yaotsu upon his return from Europe after World War II. For reasons that no one quite understood, he now went under the name of Sempo Sugiwara. True, this was but an alternate pronunciation of the equivocal Japanese characters that represent his name. But this was still recognized for what it was—an unexplained name change.

The man who had spent more years of his life in such remote places as Seoul, Harbin, Kaunas, and Moscow certainly impressed family and townspeople with his worldly ways. He arrived in town wearing suit, tie, and jacket rather than more familiar Japanese garb. Rumors circulated as to the exact number of foreign languages in which this son of Yaotsu could comfortably express himself. A grandniece remembers him from her childhood most clearly because he shook hands, European-style and egalitarian, rather than bowing in the prescribed Japanese manner that combines salutation with affirmation of social standing. As struck as Cousin Joe and others were by his suaveness, they were equally impressed and more surprised by the intensity of Chiune/Sempo's cherished childhood memories of summer days in Yaotsu and visits to grandmother's house; their kinsman, who had seen so much of the world, still felt a special warmth for them and experienced their shared town of Yaotsu as home.

No one asked much about what he had done in the interim years. Sugihara seems to have remembered Yaotsu as a nurturing place. The former diplomat, returning to his vanquished country after the war, would go back to his provincial roots in Yaotsu in search of food. In his last years he would come around for occasional visits, circulating among distant relatives and systematically gathering information to compile his family tree. Again, he impressed the locals, this man of the world with so much to remember, so concerned with his connectedness to and memory of the ancestors. They sensed though that he was not sure what the ancestors would think of him and his family, that he had somehow "lost face." He discussed with his cousin buying a small plot of land and returning to the family homestead. But ultimately, he had painful misgivings as to whether his life added to the honor of his ancestors.

I leave Cousin Joe thinking about the classical Yiddish story, *"Bunche Schveig."* In the highest heavens, the most beautiful splendor is being prepared, with the greatest excitement, for a truly righteous person who has just died. Upon his arrival, Bunche the Silent One is asked by God to make his fondest wish for eternity. The heavenly court breaks down in uncontrollable sobbing when Bunche asks for a hot buttered roll. Sugihara the cosmopolitan returns home, if only as a "tragic hero," Japanese-style.

Are There Lessons?

Ordinary People and the Banality
of Goodness, Altruism, and Sacrifice

We all want to help one another. Human beings are like that.
We want to live by each other's happiness, not by each other's
misery. But we have lost the way.

—Charlie Chaplin
   The Great Dictator

O n October 15, 1940, another man, like Sugihara, who took pleasure in the trout fishing of Gifu Prefecture and made of dissembling an art, Charlie Chaplin, premiered in his magnificent film, *The
Great Dictator.* Chaplin plays a Jewish barber, traumatized in the perpetra-
tion of a heroic act as a German soldier in World War I, released from a
mental hospital after years of confinement. He has no understanding of
the changes that have taken place in the New Germany. The Jewish barber resembles the great dictator, also traumatized by that war, not necessarily a hero, but whose Nazi hooligans now are taking over the streets
with which the disoriented man is trying to regain familiarity. The re-
semblance between the two is so great that ultimately Charlie Chaplin is
taken for Hitler himself. The mantle of leadership falls on Chaplin's
shoulders, and he is compelled to address a huge Nazi rally. Charlie Chaplin, ordinary man personified, steps up to the podium and silences the
masses, who are enthusiastically cheering for the man they believe to be
their leader. He gazes for a long moment across those people prepared to

commit unspeakable horrors in his name and has a profound fantasy of *history as it could have been,* of a leader like Hitler at that very last moment, who "cries out for the goodness" rather than arousing the darkest and most demonic forces in the masses, who encourages his nation to "live by each other's happiness" rather than preparing them for the guilt-free murderousness of the Holocaust.

On that October 15 neither Chiune Sugihara, by now settled with his family in Nazi Prague, nor the thousands of Jews in Soviet Lithuania who possessed his visas and were trying to complete arrangements for their departure, much as they may have liked new movies and were enamored of Charlie Chaplin, were in places where this subversive parody against totalitarianism and dictatorship would be screened. But they themselves were living an epic tale of the "contagiousness of goodness," of how compassion rather than destructiveness can be, as social scientists would say, "disinhibited."

We twist our kaleidoscope and configure the biographical and historical data on Sugihara one last time: He was "kind to all people"; his first wife, Klaudia, with such exuberant fondness remembers even sixty years after they were divorced and last saw each other. He was energetic, even ingenious at being "a step ahead" of others; often, he even went "a step too far," his buddy Shimura so obligingly recalls of their experiences at the "wetties." Sugihara was so cosmopolitan, we observe, with his extraordinary talent for languages, his great ease with foreigners, his love of that American "pickpocket" sport, baseball, his capacity for Russian vodka. And yet we find him to be as Japanese as the forty-seven *ronin.* Similar to the loyal disciple and masterless Oishi, Sugihara may have been so skilled at strategizing that he was able to convince others, even himself, that he really had no strategy! He rehearsed for virtuosity in his piano playing, as he did as a mass rescuer. But the single piece/single act man expressed himself in music as he did in reflecting on his motives, in a manner considered by some as "most banal."

The profile of Chiune Sugihara emerges; the portrait of a mass rescuer still eludes us. Let us try to imagine the making of a mass rescue beyond, what was in this situation, a momentary relationship between the rescuer and rescuee. This strong personality—Zorba the Greek-like character in Japanese body—exuded such warmth: Sugihara seems to have catalyzed cooperation, even participation in the rescue act among networks of unwitting and uncoordinated collaborators, including Japanese and Soviet officials who may have remembered him with such fondness from years back, partying in Moscow or Nikolaevsk, in Tokyo or Harbin. These officials were now posted at important decision-making points and geographic locations up and down the escape route. The stamps, the seals, the signatures on Sugihara's visas—even for those Soviet officials who may not have been able to read them—*personified* those Jews who had been stripped of their dignity by Nazi antisemitism and violence. As those Jews passed through the many checkpoints and border crossings—frightening places for anyone, how much more so for refugees—at which they had to make convincing impressions of somehow being legitimate, Sugihara's scraps of paper gave them the courage and conviction to manage such intimidating transactions. The visas provided official protection against border guards and bureaucrats who had life-and-death powers to ignore a questionable or missing document, to overlook one or another regulation. The absurd situation that Sugihara created—thousands of people presenting visas for which, by any strict interpretation of the rules, they could not have qualified—may have evoked a tongue-in-cheek response among these otherwise humorless officials; it may have helped them overcome their own resistance to taking risks. Were they not trained to respond to ambiguous situations by erring on the side of caution even if that meant returning refugees to their tormentors? Sugihara's act may have "disinhibited" their own compassion; it may have aroused among bureaucrats, trained to be unmoved, a deep sense of loathing for that wasting of life that would surely follow their decision to send these people back.[1]

And perhaps with no better explanation, we must conclude that goodness is ultimately as "contagious" as evil. What seems clear is that Sugihara's rescue efforts did not end with a smile or with walking his rescuees to the door, launching them on the road to survival; those efforts may have accompanied them far along the roads away from Kovno. And yet he had little more to say of what he did than "I acted according to my sense of human justice, out of love for mankind."

We are left frustrated, even a bit angry at Sugihara because he tells us so little about himself. We want to connect the portrait of the individual to the profile of the role of rescuer. Not all people who are compassionate or bold or cosmopolitan or well connected become mass rescuers, and certainly not successful ones. We cannot depict Sugihara as a Chaplin-like character, humoring us by tripping over his own feet, stumbling into the role of mass rescuer. His early years demonstrate his propensities for those very actions that turned out to be lifesaving during a few days in the summer of 1940. Yet he did not and could not have done what he did without the special circumstances and opportunities that he understood and pursued, with "vigor and vitality," as his teacher, Goto, would put it. Are there in the life and rescue efforts of Sugihara lessons to be learned? How do we become like Sugihara? How do we foster the growth and education of lots of little Sugiharas? Or in trying to draw such profiles of a rescuer, are we substituting Sugihara's banality with an arrogant banality of our own? Would it not be more edifying to marvel at the mystery of goodness, of mercy, of compassion as it radiates on rare occasion in this world, rather than trying to reduce it to biographical and psychological factors? Would the great Raoul Wallenberg, who while rescuing tens of thousands of Jews wrote home to his mother from Budapest on September 29, 1944, about inviting home for dinner Adolf Eichmann, "quite a nice man," be able to teach us important lessons about his "work?"[2] Would the courageous people of Le Chambon who rescued all the Jews in their village—but years later could say little more than that it was "natural"—guide our efforts in educating future rescuers? The memory of these people and events is an inspiration. But the analysts of great acts of rescue may have to conclude what the analysts of great acts of art have been saying for a long time: The performer is not necessarily the most insightful interpreter.

In recent years there has been much interesting interdisciplinary research on rescue. Notions of altruism, with all their ambiguity, have been attached to the rescuer as the altruistic personality par excellence. Here is not the place to systematically analyze how Sugihara's biography and psyche support notions of the "altruistic personality" and related theories from the growing literature on rescue, such as the marginality of the rescuer or the identification of the rescuer with the victim. Suffice it to say that altruism is usually contrasted with egoism on the one hand and individualism on the other; the two are most obviously not the same.[3] But sacrifice has become an integral aspect of altruism—as claimed by the sociobiologists for ants and the social psychologists for humans. Insofar as rescuers are deemed altruistic, sacrifice and risk-taking become items on their "job description." That heroic rescuers often make sacrifices moves from the descriptive to the normative—rescuers *should* make sacrifices, even that the essence of rescue is sacrifice. But making this connection between sacrifice and rescue may have more to do with some needs that we, the observers, seem to have, rather than with the needs of the rescuer. The call for various types of self-destructiveness is sufficiently alarming to make us skeptical about sacrifice as a motive for human action, even recognizing as we do that sacrifice is often initiated with pure intents and consummated with positive consequences.[4]

There is no reason to assume that the rescuer is prompted by needs for sacrifice or to evaluate the rescue activity by the degree of sacrifice and risk-taking that it required. There are "Righteous" people—as the Israel Holocaust authority, Yad Vashem, tries to identify—whose righteousness is manifest in other human motives. This "love of life" is broadly evoked by many religions as it is emphasized by the French Jewish philosopher Henri Bergson in the 1930s. Even the sociobiologists, who contributed so significantly to the discourse on altruism and sacrifice, now speak of "biophilia." This love of life and revulsion to the wasting of life, it seems to me, is a more reliable motive and prompter for rescue activity. Love of life, rather than degree of sacrifice, provides a basis for honoring heroes and rescuers. Insofar as they are recognized for the love of life that they manifested in their courageous acts, it does not render everything that follows in the lives of these precious individuals who deserve our sustained admiration a letdown and anticlimax.

On occasions that I have mentioned this "love of life" as a lesson that I bring to my life from the life of Sugihara, I have evoked in others disappointment bordering on the hostile! "What, is that all you learn from all of this? Who needs anyone to tell us about 'love of life'? We're doing pretty well, thank you." We should not confuse egotistical hedonism or self-indulgent individualism with the love of life. Sacrifice may at times be a necessary consequence of that love of life, but it is not a necessary condition.

We know how ordinary people, rather than born sadists and demons, can become mass murderers at the desk or in the field. This realization of the human condition is a difficult legacy for us all. And yet whether it can be proven by any evidence of history, by any methodology of the social sciences, it is important for us to maintain the vision of ordinary people, not born heroes or saints, as mass rescuers. We need this vision if for no other reason than to make the refusal to "stand on blood" an achievable standard of behavior and to protect ourselves from despair.

The Sugihara for whom I have been searching is human, all too human and more likable than I might have expected. He is warmer and more vulnerable than the Sugihara sculpted in bronze on the windswept Yaotsu mountaintop. He presents himself neither as hero nor as martyr, unlike the bigger-than-life image projected by those busily at work writing the legend. Sugihara's ordinariness is perhaps what is so extraordinary about this story. In illustrating for us how a common person can perpetrate a most uncommon act, he empowers us all as he challenges us to greater responsiveness and responsibility.

Notes

Prelude

1. In a growing literature on rescuers, a catalogue of the best known may be found in Eric Silver, *The Book of the Just: The Silent Heroes Who Saved Jews from Hitler* (London: Weidenfeld and Nicolson, 1992).
2. Interview with Jan Zwartendyk Jr. June 2 and September 21, 1994, State College, Pa.
3. Keneally claims to use "the textures and devices of a novel to tell a true story." These departures from historical evidence make assessments of motives and transformations particularly speculative. Spielberg's Schindler does not do any more than hint at inner transformations prompting Schindler to action. Some critics, in fact, compliment Spielberg for not indulging in "psychobabble" in regard to motives. But this contributes to a measure of flatness in the portrayal of Schindler and the passivity of the Jews that he rescued.
4. The assumption that identification fosters empathy and helping behavior is strongly held in research on the Holocaust. Some recent social psychological field studies support this link. It makes Sugihara's response all the more significant. See Saul Friedländer's comment "To help the outsider against the insider requires a strong motivation indeed" in "Some Aspects of the Historical Significance of the Holocaust," *Jerusalem Quarterly* 1 (February 1976): 52.
5. Interview, Michael Menkin, January 24, 1996, New York.
6. This is the basic story and standard version as presented in several interviews of them that I have done in 1994 and 1995, consistent with what Mrs. Sugihara writes in her memoirs.
7. There is no evidence from survivors who actually were inside the consulate or from any other source that Sugihara was compiling a list. Months later, when thousands of Jews were arriving in Japan and the fuller magnitude of Sugihara's activities in Kovno became known, he was asked for an accounting as indicated in Foreign Minister Yosuke Matsuoka's cable of February 4, 1941. He responds on February 5 that he issued 1,500 transit visas to Jews out of 2,132 visas given to Lithuanians and Poles. But there were hardly any Lithuanians on the list and a not wholly reliable analysis of names points to considerably more Jews. Another document in the same file indicates that an additional 3,448 visas were issued in Kovno for a total of 5,580. "Reports of Visas Issued to Foreigners by Consulates in Europe," J-2-3-0-J/x2-6, vol. 11. It is impossible to estimate the number of "forged" visas issued in Sugihara's name during and after his stay in Lithuania. For example, most recently, I have received a report from Professor Ryszard Frelek of Warsaw re-

garding some Jesuits in Vilna who were issuing Sugihara visas with seals that he had left behind and did not destroy, long after the Japanese diplomat had departed. The committee of Jewish representatives in Kobe, Japan, that helped Jewish refugees, in a report submitted to the Japanese government, estimated that 1,300 of the approximately 4,000 Jews that passed through Kobe between July 1940 and April 1941 were from Poland. These Polish Jews, if not at least a few of the German Jews, arrived on transit visas issued by Sugihara. Alex Triguboff, one of the members of that committee, in a 1985 interview done by Bill Craig, estimates the number of refugees arriving with Sugihara's visas to be 2,500: It could be that refugees with independent resources who arrived with Sugihara visas were not taken care of by this committee and do not figure in their statistics. Moreover, not all recipients of Sugihara's visas who did exit Lithuania passed through Vladivostok, Tsuruga, and Kobe. Some took the southern route through Korea, often ending up in Shanghai. All told, visas covering 10,000 Jews plus an unspecified number of other refugees is a reasonable estimate. "Miscellaneous Documents Regarding Ethnic Issues: Jewish Affairs," vol. 10, 1940, Diplomatic Record Office, Japanese Foreign Ministry, Tokyo.

8. Interview, October 3, 1994, New York City; Isaac Lewin, *Remember the Days of Old* (New York: Research Institute of Religious Jewry, 1994), 172.

9. Jack Levin and James Fox, *Mass Murder: America's Growing Menace* (New York: Plenum, 1985), 16, 32–33, 58, 66–67, 87; Michael Newton, *Mass Murder: An Annotated Bibliography* (New York: Garland, 1988).

10. Friedländer, "Aspects of the Holocaust," 36.

11. Whether Craigie was using "personification" in its literal sense supported by the *Oxford English Dictionary,* complaining about the emotional response of Sugihara and others who were humanizing, as it were, the plight of the refugees, or whether he was using a consular term to question the authority of refugee certificates to Palestine is not clear. On this point, I have consulted several scholars including Martin Gilbert, A. J. Sherman, and the Honorable Jim Poston. The consensus seems to support the position of Keith Hamilton, the Historian of the Foreign and Commonwealth Office, London, in a personal correspondence of November 20, 1995: "it looks to me like a grammatical error on the Ambassador's part" and that Craigie was concerned with impersonation.

12. From Gustave Le Bon, the nineteenth-century social theorist, observing the "crowd" of the French Revolution from the safety of his garret and bemoaning the decline of Western civilization, through Sigmund Freud, turn-of-the-century Vienna, wondering about what he has learned from the dark side of the soul that explains regression and destructiveness in leaders and group behavior, to generations of empiricists "counting noses," taking aerial photos of mobs to perceive hidden aggressive patterns: conspiracies are views as "contagious"; like germs, they are regressive, and they disinhibit violence.

13. Hannah Arendt, *Eichmann in Jerusalem: A Report on the Banality of Evil* (New York: Viking, 1963), 26.

14. Erik H. Erikson, *Young Man Luther: A Study in Psychoanalysis and History* (New York: Norton, 1958), 58. Erik Erikson says about Luther, "we must view the scant data on Luther's upbringing, sometimes surer of the forces than of the facts." This is all the more so in regard to the study of Chiune Sugihara, whose life was so much less documented and who himself was so much less expressive than Luther. Sugihara did not obligingly leave his biographers with treatises on the door or anywhere else.

15. *Soren Kierkegaard's Journals and Papers,* Howard Hong and Edna Hong, editors and translators (Bloomington: Indiana University Press, 1967), 450.

Chapter 1

1. Richard Beardsley, John Hall, and Robert Ward, *Village Japan* (Chicago: University of Chicago Press, 1959), 219–20, 237–38.

2. Interview with Ryuko Nakamura, Sugihara's sister, July 6, 1994, Nagoya.

3. Interview with Joe Iwai, July 1, 1993, Yaotsu.

4. Junichi Saga, *Memories of Silk and Straw: A Self-Portrait of Small-Town Japan,* trans. George Evans (Tokyo: Kodansha International, 1987), 25–26.

5. Robert Whiting, *The Chrysanthemum and the Bat: The Game Japanese Play* (Tokyo: Permanent, 1977), 3.

6. Inazo Nitobe, *Bushido: The Soul of Japan* (Rutland, Vt.: Charles E. Tuttle, 1993); Kurt Singer, *Mirror, Sword, and Jewel* (Tokyo: Kodansha International, 1973).

7. Carol Gluck, *Japan's Modern Myths: Ideology in the Late Meiji Period* (Princeton: Princeton University Press, 1985), 19, 24, 184.

8. Masao Maruyama, "Patterns of Individuation and the Case of Japan: A Conceptual Scheme," *Changing Japanese Attitudes Toward Modernization,* ed. Marius B. Jansen (Princeton: Princeton University Press, 1965), 511, 521.

9. In 1868, the Meiji Emperor decreed modernizing edicts from the top down, influencing the childhood world of Chiune's parents. See G. B. Samson, *The Western World and Japan* (New York: Knopf, 1950), 310–504.

10. Gluck, *Japan's Modern Myths,* 19, 38, 78.

11. M. K. Dziewanowski and Joseph Pilsudski, *A European Federalist, 1918–1922,* (Stanford: Hoover Institution Press, 1969), 36–37.

12. Jerzy Lerski, "A Polish Chapter of the Russo-Japanese War," *Transactions of the Asiatic Society of Japan,* 3d Series, no. 7 (November 1959): 74.

13. Nurit Govrin, *Devora Baron, The First Half, Early Stories* (Hebrew), ed. Avner Holtzman (Jerusalem: Mosad Bialik, 1988), 143–44, 367–69.

14. Louis Greenberg, *Russian Jewry,* (New Haven: Yale University Press, 1951, 1953), vol. 2, 52–53; John D. Klier and Shlomo Lambroza, ed., *Pogroms: Anti-Jewish Violence in Modern Russian History* (Cambridge: Cambridge University Press, 1992), 278.

15. Mehahem Ponansky, ed., *Maihayai Yosef Trumpeldor* (Tel Aviv: Am Oved); Shulamith Laskov, *Yosef Trumpeldor* (Haifa: Shikmona, 1972), 17–24.

16. Raymond A. Brighton, *They Came to Fish* (Portsmouth, N.H.: Portsmouth 350, 1973), 212.

17. Eugene Trani, *The Treaty of Portsmouth: An Adventure in American Diplomacy* (Lexington: University of Kentucky Press, 1969), 7.

18. Ibid., 8.

19. Ibid., 31.

20. Ibid., 30–32. The phrase "Yellow Peril" was apparently first popularized by German Kaiser Wilhelm.

21. Richard Charques, *The Twilight of Imperial Russia* (London: Oxford University Press, 1958), 87.

22. Alexander Kuprin, *The River of Life and Other Stories,* trans. S. Koteliansky and J.M. Murry (Boston: John W. Luce, 1916), 54. His story, "Captain Ribnikov," is about a Japanese spy whose mastery of Russian culture was so nuanced that his physiognomy did not interfere with his passing for a tsarist military officer back from the war in Manchuria. Here we might have an instructive portrait of Sugihara and his ability to "pass" when he was at his professional prime. At the "Glory of Petrograd," the race track, and other pleasure palaces of the tsar's court, as depicted by Alexander Kuprin, sighs about political discord were expressed self-servingly during these days when Russia was losing everything to Japan and still playing hard to get with Roosevelt.

23. Gary Dean Best, "Financing a Foreign War: Jacob H. Schiff and Japan, 1904–1905," *American Jewish Historical Quarterly* 60, no. 4 (June 1972): 313.

24. Cyrus Adler, *Jacob H. Schiff, His Life and Letters,* Vol. 1 (New York: Doubleday, 1928), 213.

25. A.J. Sherman, "German-Jewish Bankers in World Politics: The Financing of the Russo-Japanese War," *Leo Baeck Yearbook* 28 (London: Secker and Warburg, 1983), 59–73.

26. "Portsmouth's Big Day," *New Hampshire Sentinel,* August 9, 1905, 1.

27. Quoted in Peter Randall, *There Are No Victors: A Local Perspective on the Treaty of Portsmouth* (Portsmouth: Portsmouth Marine Society, 1985), 25.

28. Ibid.

29. Abraham Yarmolinsky, ed. and trans., *The Memoirs of Count Witte* (New York: Howard Fertig, 1967), 163–64; Trani, *The Treaty of Portsmouth,* 134.

30. Trani, *The Treaty of Portsmouth,* 95–157.
31. Alexander Lenson, *The Damned Inheritance* (Tallahassee, Fla.: Diplomatic, 1974), 361–445.
32. Randall, *No Victors Here,* 52–54.
33. Ibid., 221–25.
34. Beardsley, Hall, and Ward, *Village Japan,* 378–79, 384.
35. Gluck, *Japan's Modern Myths,* 30.
36. Ibid., 207.
37. Robert Bellah, *Tokugawa Religion: The Cultural Roots of Modern Japan* (New York: Free Press, 1957), 5.
38. Gluck, *Japan's Modern Myths,* 159.
39. Ibid., 207. Similarities to problems of modernization in Germany, what Jeffrey Herf calls "reactionary modernism," are striking.
40. Ibid., 166.
41. Ibid., 168.
42. Ibid., 169.
43. Ryuko Nakamura, July 6, 1994, Nagoya.
44. We may need additional help from techniques other than those oriented to discovering the "true story." We must imagine, as Hayden White suggests, the "real story," that story "within or behind the events that come to us in the chaotic form of 'historical records.'" In addition to the careful reconstruction of that historical evidence, that "true history," the records that were preserved but for no discernible reason or even by criteria that are tendentious, we must try to get to the "real history" by "fashioning human experience into a form assimilable to structures of meaning that are generally human rather than culture-specific." Narrative, as White suggests, or telling stories about stories "might well be considered a solution to a problem of general human concern, namely, the problem of how to translate *knowing* into *telling.*"
45. Gluck, *Japan's Modern Myths,* 224–25.
46. A.B. Mitford, *Tales of Old Japan,* (Tokyo: Charles E. Tuttle, 1966), 15–41; Takeda Izumo et al., *Chushingura (The Treasury of Loyal Retainers),* trans. Donald Keene (New York: Columbia University Press, 1971).
47. Ruth Benedict, *The Chrysanthemum and the Sword: Patterns of Japanese Culture* (Boston: Houghton Mifflin, 1946), 199.
48. Nitobe, *Bushido,* 25.
49. Gluck, *Japan's Modern Myths,* 221.

Chapter 2

1. *Alumni List of Harbin Gakuin National University* (Tokyo: 1987), 2–9.
2. George Alexander Lensen, *Japanese Recognition of the USSR: Soviet-Japanese Relations, 1921–1930* (Tokyo: Sophia University Press, 1970), 85.
3. Giichi Shimura, a contemporary of Sugihara and friend from the Harbin period who did work with and have a direct relationship with Goto in the early 1920s, equivocated on the point of Sugihara's relationship with the elderly statesman. A check of the Goto letter index, Yenching Library, Harvard University, provides no evidence of an exchange.
4. Cited in Joshua Fogel, *Life Along the South Manchurian Railway: The Memoirs of Ito Takeo* (Armonk, N.Y.: M. E. Sharpe, 1988), 8, 14.
5. Interview July 12, 1994, Tokyo. Inspiring awe through big buildings and the development of the infrastructure was one of Goto's strategies for colonial rule and control that he practiced earlier in his career in Formosa. For a description of this fervor for economic development, particularly in the Manchukuo period, see Louise Young, "Total Empire: Japan and Manchukuo 1931–1945" (Ph.D. diss., Columbia University, 1993).
6. Interview, Japan.
7. Mo Shen, *Japan in Manchuria: An Analytical Study of Treaties and Documents* (Manila: Grace Trading Company, 1960), 14–22, 48–50.
8. Ramon H. Myers, "Japanese Imperialism in Manchuria: The South Manchuria Railway

Company, 1906–1933," in *The Japanese Informal Empire in China, 1895–1937,* Peter Duus et al., ed. (Princeton: Princeton University Press, 1989), 101–4.

9. Ibid., 126; Yukiko Hayase, "The Career of Goto Shimpei: Japan's Statesman of Research, 1857–1929" (Ph.D. diss., Florida State University, 1974), 124.

10. Ibid., 68, 95.

11. Ben-Ami Shillony, *The Jews and Japanese: The Successful Outsiders* (Rutland, Vt.: Charles E. Tuttle, 1991), 213.

12. John W. Powell, "Japan's Germ Warfare: The U.S. Cover-up of a War Crime, *Bulletin of Concerned Asian Scholars,* vol. 12, Oct.-Dec. 1980, pp. 2–17; Robert Gomer et al., "Japan's Biological Weapons: 1930–1945. *Bulletin of Atomic Scientists,* 37, no. 8 (October 1981), 44–52.

13. In recent years and particularly among alumni, it is occasionally referred to as a university. But there is no evidence that the focus of the curriculum was ever broader than to include the Russian language and the geopolitics of the Soviet Union, with a few commerce-oriented courses.

14. "Documents Regarding the Harbin School; the Former Japanese Russian School," 1919-December, 1924, Diplomatic Record Office, Foreign Ministry of Japan, Tokyo, no. 267, July 7, 1921. I 1506b. Records do show that in 1921, the indefatigable Goto, now mayor of Tokyo as well as head of the Japanese Russian Association, is requesting revisions of the *gakuin's* charter. Significantly, his epistles were addressed to the minister of foreign affairs, Yasuya Uchida, which surely indicates something about the support and affiliation; it also suggests that spies more than scholars were trained at this Japanese school in Harbin. With deft politicking, Shimpei Goto later brought the minister of education into the loop, too.

15. Andrew C. Nahm, *Korea Under Japanese Colonial Rule* (Kalamazoo: Western Michigan University, 1973), 17–38.

16. Han-kyo Kim, "The Japanese Colonial Administration in Korea: An Overview," in ibid., 46–47.

17. Interview with Ryuko Nakamura, Sugihara's sister, July 7, 1994, Nagoya.

18. Interview with Sugihara's oldest son, Hiroki Sugihara, July 3, 1993.

19. Correspondence with Professor Chizakao Takao, October 5, 1994.

20. Hiroki Sugihara, August 19, 1994. Sugihara's wife, Yukiko, in her memoirs indicates that he was simply ordered to study Russian. He describes his preparations in an article that he wrote in *Juken E Gakusei* [Taking Examinations for Students] 3, no. 4 (April 1919): 52–61.

21. Peter Berton et al., *The Russian Impact on Japan: Literature and Social Thought* (Los Angeles: University of Southern California Press, 1981), 7.

22. Ibid., 114, 116.

23. Ibid., "The Rules of the Japanese Association School," article 6.

24. Ibid., article 43.

25. Ibid., article 9.

26. Ibid., articles 32 and 35. Takeo Ito, a South Manchurian Railway employee in Peking in 1924, discusses a stipend that he negotiated on behalf of an "indolent villain" who had had the good fortune of attending kindergarten with the head of the General Affairs Department of the SMR. He was given a monthly salary of 300 yen, about which Ito comments, "quite high for the time." Fogel, *Life Along the South Manchurian Railway,* 64–66. Whatever the cost of living differential between Peking and Harbin, this provides some measure of the value of Sugihara's salary.

27. Cited in ibid., 8.

28. Interview with Professor Evsey Domar, Lincoln, Mass., March 9, 1994.

29. Boris Bresler, "Harbin Jewish Community (1898–1958) Politics, Prosperity, Adversity," presented at the Symposium on Jewish Diasporas in China: Comparative and Historical Perspectives, John K. Fairbank Center for East Asian Research, Harvard University, Cambridge, Mass., August 16–18, 1992, 2.

30. Mark Wischnitzer, *Visas to Freedom: The History of HIAS* (Cleveland: World, 1956), 40–49, 62.

31. Ibid., 84–89.

32. John Stephan, *The Russian Fascists: Tragedy and Farce in Exile, 1925–1945* (New York: Harper and Row, 1978), 40.
33. Joshua Fogel, "The Jewish Community of Harbin, 1898–1950," presented at the Symposium on Jewish Diasporas in China: Comparative and Historical Perspectives, John K. Fairbank Center for East Asian Research, Harvard University, Cambridge, Mass., August 16–18, 1992, 2.
34. Peter S. H. Tang, *Russian and Soviet Policy in Manchuria and Outer Mongolia 1911–1931,* (Durham, N.C.: Duke University Press, 1959).
35. Ibid., 55–56, 64.
36. Ibid., 114.
37. Ibid., p. 145.
38. Interview with Yukiko Sugihara, July 5, 1993, Tokyo.
39. According to Professor Takeshi of the National Institute for Defense Studies, Tokyo, the 79th Regiment, part of the 20th Division, was based near Seoul all through the 1920s.
40. Interview July 3 and 9, 1994, Tokyo.
41. I have interviewed some of these former colleagues providing journalists with this information. Their leathery cheeks take on a youthful pink hue in more candid moments, when they remember their own dalliances. Some of these old samurai have little reason to be indignant about Sugihara's relationships with women or sentimental about their own. Jealousy of Sugihara's growing reputation is clearly a factor. But it also may be that Japanese like their heroes tragic; there is nothing that can ruin the reputation of a "tragic hero" more than success!
42. Sanford F. Borins, "Management of the Public Sector in Japan: Are There Lessons to Be Learned?" *Canadian Public Administration* 29, no. 2 (Summer 1986): 175–196. In this regard, old cronies of his who spent their entire professional lives in the military may have had an advantage.
43. *Pearl Harbor as History: Japanese-American Relations, 1931–1941,* Dorothy Borg and Shumpei Okamoto, eds. (New York: Columbia University Press, 1973), 1–23.
44. Stephen and Ethel Longstreet, *Yoshiwara: The Pleasure Quarters of Old Tokyo* (Tokyo: Yenbooks, 1988), 31–69. Without being ponderous and overly academic about what could simply be a good story, to be told without apologia, it must be said that a variety of institutions were to be found in any Japanese red light district. Geisha were artists, highly trained dancers, singers, and musicians who graced the banquets of Japanese gentlemen with their charms and added to the aesthetic pleasure of their experience. They formed what was virtually a guild. Other women provided more varied services. Whether Geisha offered food, drink, or erotic services, "refined and detailed debauchery" varied with the classiness of the institution. Indeed, class is part of the point of the story that Shimura tells.
45. Ibid., 20.
46. This is named for a Japanese island where silk of particularly fine quality is woven.
47. A well-placed Japanese son-in-law may have helped Klaudia's father retain his position, notwithstanding agreements between the Soviet Union and China that the railroad would not employ White Russians. Lensen, *The Damned Inheritance,* 15.
48. Personal correspondence with Michael Apollonov, May 1995. For background on Semenov, his politics, and his patrons, see Stephan, *Russian Fascists,* 32–33.
49. Ibid., 57, 156–59, 183.
50. Cited in Fogel, *Life Along the South Manchurian Railway,* 9.

Chapter 3

1. John J. Stephan, *The Russian Fascists: Tragedy and Farce in Exile, 1925–1945* (New York: Harper and Row, 1978), 69–70.
2. Interview with Tadakazu Kassai, July 6–7, 1994, Gifu City, Japan.
3. Ohata Tokushiro, "The Anti-Comintern Pact, 1935–1939," in *Deterrent Diplomacy: Japan, Germany, and the USSR, 1935–1940,* ed. James Morley (New York: Columbia University Press, 1976), 10–11.

4. Yale Candee Maxon, *Control of Japanese Foreign Policy: A Study of Civil-Military Rivalry, 1930–1945* (Westport, Conn.: Greenwood, 1973). 82–85, 104–5; Richard Storry, *The Double Patriots: A Study of Japanese Nationalism* (Boston: Houghton Mifflin, 1957), 54–95.

5. There appear to be two résumés or work records on file at the Japanese Foreign Ministry. One begins with his birth, has Sugihara's personal seal on the front page, and likely was reviewed by him at the end of his career. The other has his name inscribed in large, roman characters on each page. It is more formally formatted, begins in 1921 with his first appointment, and seems to emphasize his work history, though it has a postscript announcing the birth of his first son written in a different handwriting. The two résumés are largely consistent with each other. The Personnel Office of the Japanese Foreign Ministry indicates that the second is the official departmental record, but there was no explanation of the fact that the entire record covering twenty-five years appeared to be in the same handwriting. Perhaps this record, too, is a summary of departmental records gathered at the time of retirement.

6. Joshua Fogel, *Life Along the South Manchurian Railway,* (Armonk, N.Y.: M. E. Sharpe, 1988), xi.

7. George Alexander Lensen, *The Damned Inheritance: The Soviet Union and the Manchurian Crises, 1924–1935* (Tallahassee, Fla.:, Diplomatic, 1974), 201–11.

8. Alvin Coox, *Nomohan: Japan Against Russia, 1939,* Vol. 1 (Stanford: Stanford University Press, 1985), 1, 44.

9. Stephan, *The Russian Fascists,* 63.

10. Interview, March 9, 1995, Lincoln, Mass.

11. Interview with Ryuko Nakamura, July 5, 1994, Nagoya; July 7, 1994, Yaotsu, Japan.

12. Ben-Ami Shillony, *Revolt in Japan: The Young Officers and the February 26, 1936, Incident* (Princeton: Princeton University Press, 1973), 3–55. In fact, unlike in neighboring China, the number of Japanese actually joining the Communist Party before World War II was never more than one thousand.

13. Amleto Vespa, *Secret Agent of Japan* (Boston: Little, Brown, 1938), 60.

14. Ibid., 57–58.

15. Coox, *Nomohan,* vol. 1, 22–35.

16. Vespa, *Secret Agent,* 58.

17. Ibid., 75–77, 86–87; Stephan, *The Russian Fascists,* 63–64.

18. Chalmers Johnson, *An Instance of Treason: Ozaki Hotsumi and the Sorge Spy Ring* (Stanford: Stanford University Press, 1964), 80–81.

19. Vespa, *Secret Agent,* 26–31.

20. Cited in Mo Shen, *Japan in Manchuria,* 296.

21. Extemporaneous Address Delivered at the Fourteenth Plenary Meeting," in Yosuke Matsuoka, *The Manchurian Question: Japan's Case in The Sino-Japanese Dispute as Presented Before the League of Nations* (Geneva: Japanese Delegation to the League of Nations, 1933), 165–66.

22. Mo Shen, *Japan in Manchuria,* 451–53.

23. Interview with Yoshito Ogino, July 7, 1994.

24. Kurt Singer, *Mirror, Sword, and Jewel* (Tokyo: Kodansha International, 1973), 77.

25. Stephan, *The Russian Fascists,* 65–66.

26. Vespa, *Secret Agent,* 78–79.

27. Stephan, *The Russian Fascists,* 81–90.

28. Vespa, *Secret Agent,* 57–58.

29. Military Intelligence Division, G-2, Intelligence Branch, August 14, 1933, quoted in Lensen, *The Damned Inheritance,* 398.

30. The following quotations of Togo are taken from the unpublished chapters of his memoirs, *The Cause of Japan* (New York: Simon and Schuster, 1956), 222–29, covering the prewar years. I am grateful to his daughter, Ise Togo, and grandson, Shigehiko Togo, for making this material available to me.

31. Ibid., 252–53.

32. Ibid., 327–34.

33. Ibid., 138.

34. Coox, *Nomohan*, I, 79.
35. Mamoru Shigemitsu, *Japan and Her Destiny: My Struggle for Peace* (New York: Dutton, 1958), 94–95.
36. Ben-Ami Shillony, *The Jews and the Japanese: The Successful Outsiders* (Rutland, Vt.: Charles E. Tuttle, 1991), and David Goodman and Miyazawa Masanori, *Jews in the Japanese Mind: The History and Uses of a Cultural Stereotype* (New York: Free Press, 1994).
37. Marvin Tokayer in his book *The Fugu Plan* summarizes plans for Jewish settlements made in the late 1930s. These discussions of what the Soviets were doing in Birobidzhan pre-date those plans by several years.
38. Interview with Hiroo Yasue, August 22, 1994. Yasue and his activities on behalf of Jews continues to be a matter of controversy. See articles of Masanori Tabata in the *Japan Times*, December 16 and 17, 1994.
39. "Miscellaneous Documents Regarding Ethnic Issues: Jewish Problems," vol 7, 1940, Diplomatic Record Office, Tokyo.
40. Louise Young, "Total Empire: Japan and Manchukuo 1931–1945" (Ph.D. diss., Columbia University, 1993).
41. Tokushiro, "Anti-Comintern," 18.
42. Coox, *Nomohan*, I, 77.
43. Michael Montgomery, *Imperialist Japan: The Yen to Dominate* (New York: St. Martin's, 1987), 355, 415–21.
44. Carl Boyd, *The Extraordinary Envoy: General Hiroshi Oshima and Diplomacy in the Third Reich, 1934–1939* (Washington, D.C.: University Press of America, 1980), 18–26.
45. Ibid., 17.
46. Cited in ibid., 123.
47. Ibid., I.
48. Interview with Ise Togo, August 23, 1994, Tokyo.
49. Cited in Shillony, *The Jews and Japanese*, 184. Kotsuji heard Matsuoka make similar statements; David Kranzler, *Japanese, Nazis, and Jews: The Jewish Community of Shanghai 1938–1945.* (New York: Yeshiva University Press, 1976), 333.
50. I thank Ulrich Straus of Silver Spring, Md., for providing this memoir. Personal correspondence, November 30, 1994.
51. Ministry of Foreign Affairs Report, vol. 22 (Tokyo: 1937), 362: 14, 20.
52. *Le Corps diplomatique au Moscou* (Moscow: People's Commissariat of Foreign Affairs, January 1938), 15.
53. George Alexander Lensen, *Japanese Diplomatic and Consular Officials in Russia* (Tokyo: Sophia University Press, 1968), 51, 103, 159.
54. *The Schellenberg Memoirs,* Louis Hagen, ed. and trans. (Worcester, Mass.: André Deutch, 1956), 152–53.
55. Letter from M. Rybikowski to Dr. J. W. M. Chapman, Sussex, England, January 3, 1978. Rybikowski's papers are preserved at the Polish Military Intelligence Archives, Warsaw.
56. Rybikowski's notes on Jakubianiec, 4.
57. Cable no. 6207, March 4, 1938, Paris to Foreign Ministry.
58. David M. Crowe, *The Baltic States and the Great Powers* (Boulder: Westview, 1993), 26.

Chapter 4

1. An American intelligence report from as late as July 26, 1940, taken from a Japanese Foreign Ministry source from February of that year and marked "Reliability: Excellent," indicates that Lithuania is covered by the consul to Latvia, Shojiro Otaka, and makes no mention of Sugihara. Could it be that this is the way the ministry still viewed the arrangement? Report #10,155, July 26, 1940. Military Intelligence Division War Department General Staff Military Attaché Report. Subject: "Japanese Diplomatic Representatives Abroad." From an earlier Foreign Ministry source from the Japanese Embassy in Paris, March 4, 1938, cable no. 6207 proposing an appointment of Sugihara that was not made, it is stated, "Upon your decision of transfer of Mr. Sugihara, you are kindly requested to

arrange that his transfer will never be recorded in the official gazettes, the list of government officials and the like, and that his passport will be issued in the name of XX (false name)." Public records, apparently, did not reflect the true arrangements.

2. "Documents of Appointment to Each Japanese Consulate," folio M2/10 10-92, no. 25574.1, Cable No. 50.

3. Ibid., Cable No. 52, August 9, 1939.

4. Ibid., Cable No. 97.

5. Ibid., Cable No. 108.

6. Emmanuel Ringelblum, the chronicler of the Warsaw Ghetto, sees that support as the exception rather than the rule. See his *Polish-Jewish Relations During the Second World War,* Joseph Kermish et al., eds. (Jerusalem: Yad Vashem, 1974), 8–9, 206–7, 216–17.

7. Rabbi Marvin Tokayer, former chief rabbi of Japan and one of the first Jews to seek out Sugihara in the late 1960s, confirms this. Interview June 19, 1994, Great Neck, N.Y.

8. The actual negotiations seemed to begin in late February, early March of 1939. As the moment approached, Hitler and Ribbentrop deceived Japanese representatives with regard to their plans to invade Poland. This likely increased Japanese distrust of Germany as alluded to in Sugihara's letter.

9. Gerhard Krebs, "Japanische Schlichtungsbemühungen in der deutsch-polnischen Krise 1938/39," *Japanese Studies: Almanac of the German Institute for Japanese Studies of the Philipp Franz von Shebold Foundation* 2 (1990): 207–53.

10. John Strawson, *Hitler as Military Commander* (London: Batsford, 1971), 83–84.

11. Alvin Coox, *Nomonhan: Japan Against Russia, 1939* (Stanford: Stanford University Press, 1985), 2: 893–95.

12. Johanna Meskill, *Hitler and Japan: The Hollow Alliance* (New York: Atherton, 1966), 3–19. Many Japanese were themselves preoccupied with the question of Japanese exclusiveness; with whatever ardor they otherwise supported the pro-Germany faction, they were more than suspicious about Nazi Germany's true feelings toward Japanese. This suspicion was increased, in at least some notable cases, as Japanese encountered the anti-Jewish policies of the Nazis.

13. *Documents on Polish-Soviet Relations, 1939–1945,* General Sikorski Historical Institute (London: Heinemann, 1961), 1: 47–48.

14. Memoirs of Ludwik Hryncewicz, cited in Ewa Palasz-Rutkowska and Andrzej Romer, "Wspolpraca Polsko-Japonska W Czasie II Wojny Swiatowej" [Polish-Japanese Relations in World War II], *Biblioteka "Kultury"* 487 (1994): 9.

15. Coox, *Nomohan,* 2: 869.

16. David Kranzler, *Japanese, Nazis, and Jews: The Jewish Refugee Community of Shanghai, 1939–1945* (New York: Yeshiva University Press, 1976), 330. Interview with Hideaki Kase, August 4 and 15, 1994, Tokyo.

17. Lithuania, December 1939, Ar 33/44, Folder no. 731, Archives of American Joint Distribution Committee, New York.

18. Cable No. 9, from Sugihara to Foreign Minister Nomura, October 18, 1939.

19. Interviews, May 12 and July 5, 1995, Kaunas.

20. There is independent confirmation of his spying preserved in various archives, as indicated below. Why the Germans, aware of these activities at least from the late Kaunas period if not earlier, allowed him to continue has to do with the technical assessments of intelligence services regarding the damage that might result from his efforts versus the promise that he might lead to higher and more pernicious networks of spies. The Germans also might have wanted to avoid reprisals against one of their own diplomat/spies in Japan.

21. From unpublished memoirs of Bernard and Rochelle Zell, edited by Richard Gambino. I thank Professor Gambino and the Zell family for permission to cite this document.

22. Personal correspondence of Irene Malowist, May 15 and 25, 1995; Irene Dwynson, March 14, 1995.

23. This report, in galleys, along with a letter written by Morris Waldman, secretary of the American Jewish Committee on February 17, 1941, indicating that it had been sent to Wallace Murray, chief of division of Near Eastern Affairs, the State Department, is in the

National Archives, declassified only in 1980. David Grodner is apparently the pseudonym of a prominent Polish Jew. It was ultimately published in *Contemporary Jewish Record* (March 1941): 136–47. Had more Jews receiving visas from Sugihara been able to continue to the United States, they would have risked the trip to Japan and been rescued.

24. Interview, July 26, 1995, New York.
25. Interview, August 7, 1995, New Haven, Conn.
26. YIVO Archives, New York.
27. Paul Baerwald cites Beckelman's report of October 17 in his report to the Red Cross on November 14, 1939 (date handwritten). JDC Archives, New York.
28. Jewish Telegraphic Agency, March 10, 1938.
29. Memorandum of October 24, 1939, HIAS Archives, YIVO, New York.
30. Ibid.
31. Owen J. C. Norem, *Timeless Lithuania,* 2d ed. (Cleveland: League for the Liberation of Lithuania. 1967), 272–78.
32. No. 4,368 (Diplomatic) Jewish Emigration from the Klaipeda (Memel) Territory and Lituania Major, National Archives.
33. David Wyman, *Paper Walls: America and the Refugee Crisis 1938–1941* (Amherst: University of Massachusetts Press, 1968), 67–68, 174, 184–205.
34. No. 150 (Consular) "Registration of Aliens at Kaunas, Lithuania," National Archives, Washington, D.C.
35. No. 731, JDC Archives, New York.
36. No. 730, JDC Archives, New York.
37. October 31, 1939, ibid.
38. Ibid.
39. Ibid., November 3, 1939.
40. Interview, June 28, 1994, Herzelia, Israel. Some of the following quotes are taken from an early draft of his beautiful memoirs that he was kind enough to share with me. *Light One Candle: A Survivor's Story of Holocaust Demons and Japanese Heroes* (New York: Kodansha International, 1995).
41. My appreciation to Jaak Treiman, the Estonian honorary consul in Los Angeles, who provided this biographical information on Jaan Lattik in a personal correspondence of August 15, 1995.
42. Interview, November 24 and December 23, 1994, Los Angeles. Dr. Jack Brauns kindly provided a copy of the privately published memoirs of his father.

Chapter 5

1. Usui Katsumi, "The Role of the Foreign Ministry," in *Pearl Harbor as History,* ed. Dorothy Borg and Shimpei Okamoto (New York: Columbia University Press, 1973), 127–48.
2. Togo, unpublished memoirs, 216.
3. The following files are the primary repository for documents regarding Sugihara and the issuance of visas: "Miscellaneous Documents Regarding Ethnic Issues: Jewish Affairs," I 460 1–2 vol. 9, Jan.–May, 1940; Report on the Issuance of Passports and Visas for Foreigners by Overseas Japanese Diplomatic Establishments in Foreign Countries in Europe, Jan. 1940, J 230 J/x2–6, vol. 2; J 230 J/x 1–3, Diplomatic Record Office, Tokyo.
4. Cable No. 383/1, January 10, 1940.
5. Cable No. 182, no date.
6. "Miscellaneous Documents Regarding Ethnic Issues: Jewish Problems," vol. 7, 1938, Diplomatic Record Office, Japanese Foreign Ministry, Tokyo, Cable No. 1162. A conference of five ministers, allegedly taking place on December 6, 1938, endorsed policies protective of the Jews. This meeting is often cited in the publicistic literature of the time and later historical works. There is no evidence that this meeting actually took place and that specific ministers attended. I thank Mr. Masaaki Shiraishi, the archivist of the Diplomatic Record Office, in his correspondence of June 16, 1995, for clarifying this point.
7. Cable No. 124, January 16, 1939.

8. Little is known about Garson. David Kranzler, *Japanese, Nazis, and Jews* (New York: Yeshiva University Press, 1976), 244, even suggests this might be a pseudonym for an American Jew, perhaps with JDC connections. In several cables at the end of December 1939 and at a meeting of the Jewish communities of Manchukuo, settlement proposals were discussed. These continued through the summer of 1940. In the several rounds of correspondences with Rabbi Stephen Wise, the American Jewish leader was cautious in regard to the intentions of the Japanese and his perceptions of U.S. State Department policy. Given the lives that were at stake, some might say that the rabbi was being overly cautious and not making the most of his influence. These initiatives have been examined by Dicker, Kranzler, Tokayer, Shillony, and Ross, among others, but there are still many unanswered questions. Insofar as these initiatives were *in the air*, they likely affected the manner in which Jews with visas from Sugihara were received in Manchukuo and Japan.

9. Cable of December 23, 1939.

10. Quoted in James Ross, *Escape to Shanghai: A Jewish Community in China* (New York: Free Press, 1994), 56–58.

11. On that same day, a British Passport Control officer in Berlin, Captain F. Foley, raised objection to Jewish immigration to Shanghai, allowed by the Nazis, as he believed, "as their shipping companies are paid for the freight . . . it might be considered humane on our part not to interfere officially to prevent the Jews from choosing their own graveyards. They would rather die as freemen in Shanghai than as slaves in Dachau." Quoted in A. J. Sherman, *Island Refuge: Britain and Refugees from the Third Reich 1933–1939* (Essex: Frank Cass, 1973), 210.

12. Elhanan Joseph Hertzman, *The Miracle of Rescue of the Mir Yeshiva* (Jerusalem: n.p., 1976), 31, 44.

13. Zorach Warhaftig, *Refugee and Survivor* (Jerusalem: Yad Vashem, 1988), 63.

14. Ibid., 64–65.

15. Ibid., 86.

16. I am grateful to his daughter, Ruth Beckelman, of Paris for providing a copy of his unpaginated diary covering October 1939–March 1940. If he kept a diary beyond that period, it is missing.

17. February 16, 1940.

18. Moses Beckelman's diary.

19. Kasai, Sugihara's younger colleague in Harbin and fellow Gifuite who was at the time in the Manchukuo Embassy in Berlin, remembers Sugihara obtaining documents for Poles that apparently involved his embassy. It is likely that Sugihara procured Manchurian documents for these Poles as well; he could have provided them with more plausible biographies, similar to those of the White Russians that he knew so well in Harbin, than to claim that they had lived in Japan.

20. That danger was underscored by the Gestapo's subsequent arrest, torture, and execution of one of Sugihara's "Polish friends," Captain "Kuba" Jakubianiec, in June 1941. While Kuba ultimately compromised his position through a libidinous entanglement with some Gestapo agent's wife in Berlin, his threat to the interests of state were such that the Nazis were willing to risk a rift with their Japanese allies by refusing to recognize the diplomatic immunity and Manchurian citizenship that Sugihara had provided.

21. Johanna M. Meskill, *Hitler and Japan: The Hollow Alliance* (New York: Atherton, 1966), 89–90.

22. I have located two specific reports from the Kaunas period in the German military archives, the Militärarchiv of the Bundesarchiv, Freiburg, Germany. One is sent from Kaunas on November 15, 1939, by the office of the German military and airforce attaché reporting on some diplomatic scuttlebutt in which Sugihara seems to be involved. The second was written by the German Legation in the same city on October 2, 1940, reporting on Sugihara's military interests and his Polish companions. That warnings about Sugihara did not include any mention of his most public activity of issuing visas to Jews is rather strange, to put it mildly, and calls for some explanation. Politisches Archiv des Auswärtigen Amts, Abteil Kovonau, 2, 108 Japan/Sugihara, band R 119860.

23. Ibid.

24. C. R-1019, s. 1, f.17, 161. Lithuanian Central Archives, Vilnius, Lithuania.
25. Warhaftig, *Refugee,* 119–21.
26. Political Archives of the Foreign Office.
27. Daszkiewicz, unpublished memoirs, 15. Rybikowski collection at Polish Military Intelligence Archives, Warsaw.

Interlude

1. Unpublished memoirs of Jan Daszkiewicz, 23. Rybikowski Collection at Polish Military Intelligence Archives, Warsaw.
2. The original typescript has handwritten in its margin "Sugihara reports 3,500." The copy of these memoirs currently in the Polish Military Intelligence Archives in Warsaw was originally in Michal Rybikowski's possession, and it is likely he added this note.
3. A letter from Col. Carlisle, War Office, Whitehall, to Mr. Mackenzie, June 11, 1941, at the Public Record Office, Kew, Foreign Office files, C62424/248/55, F0371 26730, challenges the impression Daszkiewicz conveys that it had to do with Jews' lack of patriotism and loyalty. "I spoke this morning to M.I.5 and to Col. Tokasz who is the Polish Liaison Office with M.I.5. According to their statements, there are under a hundred volunteers in Tokyo of whom only eight to ten are to be considered genuine as the rest are Jews. Col. Tokasz was anxious to prevent these Jews being sent to Canada where he thought their appearance in so large a majority in the recruiting camps just formed on the American frontier would make an unfavorable impression. I understood him to say that the Canadian Government would not give visas to these Jews . . . On the other hand they are anxious to despatch the Jews in order to make more Japanese transit visas available for genuine Polish volunteers."
4. Col. Rybikowski's memoirs are in the Polish Military Intelligence Archives, Warsaw.
5. Onodera's widow claims that Sugihara and the general met after the war and casually shared such "war stories." I thank her for this information and the Onodera-Rybikowski correspondences that she shared with me.
6. I thank his son, Dr. Jan Zwartendyk Jr., for providing documents from his father's archives.
7. Yukiko Sugihara, *Rokussenin no Inochi No Biza* [Visas to a New Life for 6,000 People], unpublished English translation (Tokyo: 1990), Chapter 1, Part 2: 1–6. I thank Hiroki Sugihara for providing this translation.
8. July 5, 1993, Tokyo.
9. Yukiko Sugihara, *Visas for Life,* trans. Hiroki Sugihara, ed. Lani Silver and Eric Saul (San Francisco: prepublication copy, 1995). These memoirs have been published in two Japanese editions, in French, and now in English. It is my impression that revisions have been made beyond basic "fact checking" and not necessarily in consultation with Mrs. Sugihara.
10. At the beginning of Yukiko Sugihara's memoirs, she brings several quotations that she identifies as "from the notes of Chiune Sugihara." In an interview she indicated that at some point in his last years he began to write these notes about his life but did not get far. There he indicates, "I will never forget that it was the end of July in 1940" as the date of "unusual noises." *Visas to a New Life for 6,000 People,* 1st ed. (Japanese), 1. Mrs. Sugihara specifies July 27, 1949 [1940]. This is, indeed, the first day on which Sugihara issued more than a few visas, in accordance with his list, but by no means when he began issuing visas.
11. "Reports of Visas Issued to Foreigners by Consulates in Europe," J-2-3-0-J/x2-6, vol. 11. The surveys in this file go as far back as October 1939 and include some records of December 1942. There seems to have been an order issued by the Foreign Ministry at the end of 1939, earlier and independent of any reaction to Sugihara's visa-issuing activities, demanding quarterly reports from individual consulates on the number of visas issued.
12. Bill Craig, *Pacific Stars and Stripes,* June 23 and 30, 1985, Part I, 12. Bill Craig was kind enough to share the tape of this interview as well as his notes and other documents that he found at the time of writing this article.

13. I have discussed this with those closest to Warhaftig in this period, including Issy Graudenz and Josef Orgler, but have not received any more specific information. Sugihara in later years did recall a 1940 meeting with Warhaftig, but he may have been conflating this with visits of other Jewish representatives.

Chapter 6

1. John Toland, *The Rising Sun: The Decline and Fall of the Japanese Empire, 1936–1945* (Toronto: Bantam Books, 1988), 68–99.
2. Interview with Mel Goldstein, New York, September 12, 1995.
3. David M. Crowe, *The Baltic States and the Great Powers: Foreign Relations, 1938–1940* (Boulder: Westview, 1993), 156–58.
4. Interview with Julie Baskes, Boston, November 11, 1995.
5. Interview with Lucille Camhi, New York, October 26, 1995.
6. Interview with Lewis Salton, New York, November 7, 1994.
7. Interview with Mojsze and Sara Grynberg, Boston, October 26, 1994.
8. Zorach Warhaftig, *Refugee and Survivor* (Jerusalem: Yad Vashem, 1988), 92–95.
9. Ibid. Representatives of the foreign Jewish organizations seemed to be less convinced that the Zionist organizations were well coordinated in regard to organizing emigration and less confident that Warhaftig and colleagues would be able to continue operations in any manner under Soviet occupation. Israel Bernstein, the Hebrew Immigrant Aid Society (HIAS and HICEM) representative in Riga writes to his organization's offices in Lisbon and New York in regard to Latvia and Lithuania on July 4, 1940, "The continuation of the Palestine Amt offices is uncertain." One week later, he writes to the same correspondents: "the Pal Amyt in Kaunas, the most popular in the Baltic States, has discontinued its activities. The emigration to Palestine hampered and handicapped by the war has now been dealt a staggering blow." HIAS-HICEM I, section xii Baltic States, 2a, 5, 7. These archives are preserved at the YIVO Institute for Jewish Research, New York.
10. Several leaders, in Lithuania and abroad, negotiated with the Soviets to allow Jewish transit. These include the chief rabbi of Palestine, Rabbi Herzog, who, earlier that year was encouraged by his discussions with the Soviet ambassador to Great Britain. Some historians explain the unusual response of the Soviets as an expression of their concern about absorbing so many Polish Jews into the new Sovietized Lithuania. But the Soviets had no such problems elsewhere, resorting when needed to violence. In Beckelman's cables, letters, reports, and diary, from the earliest hints of his contacts and negotiations with the Soviets for permission for Jews to leave or traverse the Soviet Union, the primary issue was money. In a cable of April 1, 1940, to HICEM, Lisbon, Beckelman writes: "ESTIMATED COSTS PER PERSON ISTANBUL ONE HUNDRED TOKIO TWO HUNDRED DOLLARS STOP IMPERATIVE WE HAVE YOUR DECISION SOONEST STOP." By July 1, HIAS seemed to establish the policy that their local representatives "cannot contribute more than two hundred dollars per person." Emigrants were to encourage relatives abroad to provide money for their emigration as well as to sell their personal goods. Intourist generally charged $180–$200 for railroad tickets and Moscow accommodations, though some survivors remember paying more, presumably for a higher class of service when, as was often the case, standard accommodations were already booked. As Intourist became better institutionalized, as we shall see, it was made more difficult for refugees to pay in rubles or in other local currencies. Strained communications between field offices and headquarters continued to take place over sums of money available both for refugee assistance and emigration. Beckelman, in a HICEM-Lisbon communication as late as December 27, 1940, was quoted as saying that the Soviet authorities were willing to continue activities with Intourist as intermediary as long as Jewish organizations can participate with "fonds substantiels" (substantial funds). To his shock and chagrin, those funds were not always available. Dina Porat, "Conditions and Reasons for the Granting of Soviet Transit Visas to Refugees from Poland," *Shvut* 6 (1979): 66, estimates that Jewish organizations provided $300,000 to the Soviets as partial funding for the transit in this period.

11. A polish naval officer, O. Koreyewo, in his report in December 1940 on arriving in Tokyo writes how a Mr. Panoff and other Soviet officials pressured him into promising to spy in the future in exchange for a visa. Other survivors acknowledge similar experiences, reluctantly speaking of them, even a half-century later, with fear!

12. Some entrepreneurial Jews such as Bernard Zell and even the JDC developed "transfer" schemes to enable Jews with surplus cash to deposit their money with Jewish organizations in Lithuania helping to fund operations. They were promised reimbursement in dollars on arrival in the United States. Josef Szimkin, in a 1985 interview with Bill Craig, claimed that a substantial part of the funding came from this source rather than from abroad.

13. Frank Iklé, *German-Japanese Relations: 1936–1940* (New York: Bookman, 1956), 156–63.

14. Toland, *The Rising Sun,* 68–99.

15. Togo, in his unpublished memoirs, pp. 219–34, wryly describes the spread of this motto as part of the shift taking place that summer in favor of the pro-Nazi faction.

16. Norman Graebner, "Hoover, Roosevelt, and the Japanese," in *Pearl Harbor as History: Japanese-American Relations, 1931–1941,* ed. Dorothy Borg and Shumpei Okamoto (New York: Columbia University Press, 1973), 25–52.

17. Ibid., 43.

18. Ibid., 45.

19. U.S. Department of State, *Papers Relating to the Foreign Relations of the United States: Japan, 1931–1941.* Proclamation no. 2413 (Washington, D.C.: 1943).

20. Toland, *The Rising Sun,* 53.

21. Kakegawa Tomiko, "The Press and Public Opinion in Japan, 1931–1941," 546–47; Ito Takashi, "The Role of Right Wing Organizations in Japan," 505–9, in Borg and Okamoto, ed., *Pearl Harbor as History.*

22. These documents are preserved at the Diplomatic Record Office of the Japanese Foreign Ministry in a file entitled "Miscellaneous Cases in Racial Problems—Jewish Affairs." I, 460 1–2, vol. 10, June-December 1940.

23. Ibid., 142.

24. This may have been but one of several proposals discussing the settlement of Jewish refugees in the Far East. Kranzier, Tokayer, and Eruse Cramer, "The Berglas Plan for Jewish Settlement in China," *Leo Baeck Institute News* 62 (Winter 1995): 1.

25. Cable No. 87.

26. Cable No. 97.

27. Cable No. 123

28. Toland, *The Rising Sun,* 69–76.

29. Interview, Amsterdam, June 29, 1994; personal correspondences, April 26 and September 25, 1994.

30. Samuel Schreig, "The Angel of Curaçao," *B'nai B'rith Messenger,* Los Angeles, January 24, 1963.

31. Letter from Jan Zwartendyk. Rotterdam, to Benjamin Grey, Los Angeles, August 21, 1963.

32. Ibid. Zwartendyk uses a similar phrase in a letter to H. Shapiro, Baltimore, January 22, 1967. There he emphasizes that he had not consulted Sugihara nor the Soviet authorities "beforehand."

33. Interviews, June 2 and September 21, 1994, State College, Pa.

34. Letter from Nathan Gutwirth to Rabbi Marvin Tokayer, September 24, 1974.

35. *Zutfense Krant,* Zutfen, Holland, December 24, 1963.

36. Dr. Warhaftig notes that he met the governor of Curaçao after the war and asked him whether he indeed would have admitted Jews possessing the "Curaçao visa." He led Warhaftig to believe that there would have been angry shipping companies!

37. Daszkiewicz specifically mentions that Preston did not support the Curaçao scheme.

38. This cable is in a file marked J,2,3,0 j/x i-iii, "Report on the Issuance of Passports and Visas for Foreigners by Overseas Japanese Diplomatic Establishments in Foreign Countries in Europe," January 1940-, no. 22785, no. 50 local.

39. Isaac Lewin claims that his wife, Pesi, was the first to receive a Curaçao visa. She, her brother, and her husband indeed appear at an early point on Sugihara's list. Gutwirth claims that he had a prior relationship with Zwartendijk. He, too, claims to have written the Dutch ambassador in Riga but does not state the exact date.

40. These letters are proof texts for memoirists as well as some recent scholars that Sugihara asked permission from the *Gaimusho* to issue visas, straightforwardly, and was denied.

41. Warhaftig, commenting years later on the complaints in the Jewish agency against Rabbi Herzog for acting out of turn in negotiating with the Soviets for Jewish transit, saw this as further evidence of the poor grasp that Jewish organizations had on this unusual rescue opportunity.

42. Sugihara in interviews late in his life and Yukiko Sugihara in interviews and memoirs tell about a meeting with five Jews, including Warhaftig, in which these leaders explained what the situation of Jews in Europe was and why they needed visas. Warhaftig does not write about this meeting and in interviews presents the vaguest details of personal discussions at the time. It is my impression that Sugihara needed no such explanation. Insofar as he did have a longer meeting with any applicants, it may have been with representatives of the Mirrer Yeshiva, probably at a somewhat later date.

43. G-2 Military Intelligence Documents Regional Files for the Country of Lithuania, file No. 2020, National Archives, Washington, D.C.

44. Foreign Service Archives, National Archives, Washington, D.C.

45. HIAS Archives, xii–5, YIVO, New York.

46. Ibid. The archives preserve only an unsigned carbon copy.

47. Interview with Rabbi Moshe Portnoy, New York, the son of the late Rabbi Eliezer Portnoy, September 7, 1995.

48. Cables of July 30 and 31 to JDC, New York, JDC Archives, Folio No. 731.

49. Foreign Minister Arita, for example, cables his ministers for more information on Jews and Freemasons. One senses the degree to which Japanese officials are influenced by the policies of other countries having more experience with Jews, but also the extent to which they want to form their own judgment.

50. Interview with Rabbi Moshe Zupnik, New York, August 16, 1995.

51. Cable Nos. 67/26809.

52. Foreign Service Archives, National Archives, Washington, D.C. Rybikowski in this period also mentioned visas for six hundred.

53. In his letter to the Polish underground he says, "During a period of 10 months [days], I regularly had to send a telegraph to the ministry in Tokyo for advice regarding these visa for Polish refugees." The Hebrew translation uses "advice," whereas the Russian, probably the original, uses a word implying "permission."

54. Interview with Moshe Zupnik, New York, August 16, 1995.

55. Interview with Michael Menkin, New York, January 24, 1996.

56. Bill Craig, "A Beacon of Humanity in a Malevolent World," *Pacific Stars and Stripes,* June 23, 1985, Part I, 13–14.

57. Cable No. 27,465. This cable refers to cable No. 22, "How to handle the refugees."

58. Crossed out in the written draft of the cable are the words "we have done what you have suggested." Perhaps this refers to Sugihara's suggestion in Cable No. 67 on August 1 or 2 that refugees whose paperwork is not completed should not be allowed entry. In an interview on July 4, 1994, in Tokyo, Hisanobu Mochizuki, a spokesman of the Japanese Foreign Ministry, indicated to me that this cable was the official reprimand of Sugihara for his visa-granting activities. The attention that Sugihara has received in recent years has left Japanese officials in something of a quandary. At times, they deny his alleged dismissal from the Foreign Ministry in response to his visa-issuing activities while at the same time trying to justify it. It is not clear why this should be seen as a reprimand.

59. Unpublished interview of Brian Oxley.

60. Ivan Morris presents a fascinating analysis of this social type: *The Nobility of Failure: Tragic Heroes in the History of Japan* (New York: Noonday, 1975).

61. Cable No. 1169, 69, National Security Agency (NSA).

Conclusion

1. "Reports on the Issuance of Passports and Visas to Foreigners by Consulates in Europe," J-2-3-0 J/x 2-6, Diplomatic Record Office (DRO), Japanese Foreign Ministry, Tokyo. This is a compilation from individual reports, some of which actually provide statistics on Jews in the column "nationality," others providing names, including "Israel" and "Sara," made mandatory by the Nazis. Temporary consulates in other cities such as Hamburg might have issued additional visas.
2. Zorach Warhaftig, *Refugee and Survivor* (Jerusalem: Yad Vashem, 1988), 110.
3. Moses W. Beckelman, "Polish Refugees Eastward Bound," *Jewish Social Service Quarterly* 18, no. 1 (September 1941): 50–54.
4. Interview with Irving Petlin, New York and Paris, October 1994. He was a U.S. soldier, 1957–59, posted at the Army Record Center in St. Louis. He claims that Soviet and Japanese officials made privy to this plan whose record he saw might have thought that the refugees bearing Sugihara's visas were those who had been authorized under this program. A search for this file has been unsuccessful. A major section of the St. Louis facility was devastated by fire in the 1960s, and other parts of the collection seem to have been scattered to regimental archives now housed at several university libraries across the United States.
5. Shigenori Togo, unpublished memoirs, 219, 224.
6. Bundesarchiv, Militärarchiv, Freiburg, Germany. Sugihara's coded identification seems to be II 108. Material in this collection covers Sugihara's activities in Konigsberg, described below. A twelve-page memorandum entitled "Japanische Spionage im Reich," sent on August 7, 1941 to Ribbentrop from the security police (signed, as it appears, by Reinhardt Heydrich) indicates Nazi awareness of Sugihara's connections with Polish spies and with Onodera and Rybikowski in Stockholm, and the possibility of the leakage of valuable information to British intelligence.
7. Cable No. 1346, Japanese intercepts, National Security Agency (NSA), National Archives, Washington, D.C.
8. Yukiko Sugihara records this incident, likely hearing it from the same source, Kasai. Checking Ribbentrop's travel schedule for this period at the Archives of the German Foreign Ministry, I was told that there is no indication that Ribbentrop was in Prague in this period.
9. "Exhibitions on Japan Held Abroad," E-2-8-0-7-1, No. 127 (DRO).
10. Cable No. 016, NSA.
11. Cable No. 002, NSA.
12. "Reports on the Issuance," J-2-3-0 J/x 1-3, DRO. Moshe Zupnik who, we remember, spent two weeks in the Kovno consulate, has some memory of visa applicants filling out an application and a list being maintained. But there is no corroboration for this. The list itself is almost entirely in the same handwriting.
13. Personal correspondence and interview, December 20, 1994, San Antonio, Texas, and unpublished memoir, "Good Men in Dark Times," November 1994.
14. In Cable No. 24 sent by Sugihara on May 18 from Königsberg, he acknowledged that he had issued thirty-six visas in Prague out of which thirty-two were to Jews. *Gaimusho* records indicate thirty-eight—close enough to be a validity check.
15. Interview with K. Umemoto, deputy director, Personnel Division, Japanese Foreign Ministry, July 3, 1994, Tokyo.
16. Interview and personal correspondence with Gerhard Dambmann, January 4, 1995, Mainz-Drais, Germany. A German TV correspondent in Japan during the 1970s, Dr. Dambmann met Sugihara and was so impressed that he dedicated his book to him.
17. Interview, May 29, 1994, Los Angeles. Another postwar report is provided by Konuma, husband of Setsuko, Yukiko Sugihara's sister who was with them for the approximately eight years that they were in Europe. Setsuko met her husband in Bucharest. She died shortly after their return to Japan. He recently spoke about his late brother-in-law, Chiune Sugihara, in most negative terms, saying that in the period in which he knew him, Sugihara was very much disliked by people in the *Gaimusho*. He also claims that Sugihara

had large foreign bank accounts with money that must have come from Jewish bribes. There is no credible and independent evidence to corroborate any of this. Interviewed by T. Shino, March 12, 1996, Morioka.

18. Interview with Okamoto, former boss at Mihon H.S. Kyokai (NHK), July 9, 1994, Tokyo.

19. Interviews with Noby Yoshimura and Kikuya Jimma, July 1, 1994, Tokyo.

Postlude

1. We have already noted the impression of Dr. Isaac Lewin, who had a Sugihara visa, that the Japanese officials at border points were not particularly careful in examining documents. Hamaji Uewo, an administrator of Japan Travel Bureau in Manchuria during World War II, corroborates this, even claiming that some 30 percent of the Jews who passed through had no visas at all. "They had to pay 30 yen in order to get in." He was not sure whether he was there when refugees with Sugihara's visas were passing through. Interview on July 10, 1994, Tokyo. In a subsequent interview appearing in an article "Making of a Myth: Sugihara's Story Debunked" by Masanori Tabata in the *Japan Times,* December 17, 1994, Uewo spoke with greater certainty about being in Manchouli on the Soviet-Manchurian border in the summer of 1940. He reported to his boss that many of the refugees did not qualify for admission. "To my surprise, my boss said it's OK. I didn't know at that time but now I suspect my boss knew something much more than what I was officially briefed on."

2. Perhaps this was "disinformation" to confuse Nazi censors and observers. There is no reason to believe that Wallenberg harbored any general fondness for the Nazis, notwithstanding the involvements of his family business with Nazis like Eichmann in Vienna. But anti-Jewish sentiments have not impeded some from courageous acts of rescue, as noted in the fine work of Pearl and Samuel Oliner, Nechama Tec, Eva Fogelman, and other researchers.

3. Kristen Renwick Monroe, "Fat Lady in a Corset: Altruism and Social Theory," *American Journal of Political Science* 38, no. 4 (1994): 861–893. See Emile Durkheim's definition of altruism in his classical study, *Suicide.*

4. The work of Kenneth Burke and René Girard, in particular, warns us of these dangers. Sacrifice, particularly self-sacrifice, raises complex issues. In the history of Judaism, a fascinating multigenerational Talmudic discourse develops out of the flagrant position taken by the second-century Rabbi Yose. A contemporary of abortive rebellions that resulted in much sacrificial behavior, he seems to argue against sacrifice, even in what appears to be a discretionary activity, like laundering, and even if the lives of others may be at stake. This discourse on Rabbi Yose's laundry can be traced from its early source in *Tosefta, Baba Metsia,* 11, as it is argued through the generations.

Bibliography

Adler, Cyrus, *Jacob H. Schiff, His Life and Letters.* vol. 1. Garden City, N.Y.: Doubleday, 1928.

"Alumni List of Harbin Gakuin National University." Tokyo: 1987.

Arad, Yitzhak. "Concentration of Refugees in Vilna." *Yad Vashem Studies* 9 (1973): 201–14.

Barak (Brick), Zvi. "Plitei Polin be-Lita bashanim 1939–1941" [Polish refugees in Lithuania in 1939–1941]. In *Sefer Yahadut Lita.* Edited by Chasmon: 353–70.

Bauer, Yehuda. *American Jewry and the Holocaust: The American Jewish Joint Distribution Committee, 1939–1945.* Jerusalem: Institute of Contemporary Jewry, Hebrew University, 1981.

Bauer, Yehuda. "Rescue Operations through Vilna." *Yad Vashem Studies* 9 (1973): 215–23.

Beardsley, Richard, John Hall, and Robert Ward. *Village Japan.* Chicago: University of Chicago Press, 1959.

Beckelman, Moses W. "Polish Refugees Eastward Bound." *Jewish Social Service Quarterly* 18 (September 1941): 50–55.

Bellah, Robert. *Tokugawa Religion: The Cultural Roots of Modern Japan.* New York: Free Press, 1957.

Benedict, Ruth. *The Chrysanthemum and the Sword: Patterns of Japanese Culture.* Boston: Houghton Mifflin, 1946.

Berton, Peter et al. *The Russian Impact on Japan: Literature and Social Thought.* Los Angeles: University of Southern California Press, 1981.

Best, Gary Dean. "Financing a Foreign War: Jacob H. Schiff and Japan, 1904–1905." *American Jewish Historical Quarterly* 61, no. 4 (1972): 313.

Borg, Dorothy, and Shimpei Okamoto, eds. *Pearl Harbor as History: Japanese-American Relations.* New York: Columbia University Press, 1973.

Borins, Sanford F. "Management of the Public Sector in Japan: Are There Lessons to Be Learned?" *Canadian Public Administration* 29, no. 2 (1986): 175–96.

Boyd, Carl. *The Extraordinary Envoy: General Hiroshi Oshima and Diplomacy in the Third Reich, 1934–1939.* Washington, D.C.: University Press of America, 1980.

Bresler, Boris. "Harbin Jewish Community (1898–1958): Politics, Prosperity, Adversity." Paper presented at the Symposium on Jewish Diasporas in China: Comparative and Historical Perspectives, John K. Fairbank Center for East Asian Research, Harvard University, Cambridge, Mass., August 16–18, 1992.

Brighton, Raymond A. *They Came to Fish.* Portsmouth, N.H.: Portsmouth 350, 1973.

Chapman, J.W.M. "The Polish Connection: Japan, Poland and the Axis Alliance." *Proceedings of the British Association for Japanese Studies.* vol. 2. (n.p.) 1977.

Charques, Richard. *The Twilight of Imperial Russia.* London: Oxford University Press, 1958.

Coox, Alvin. *Nomohan: Japan Against Russia, 1939.* 2 vols. Stanford: Stanford University Press, 1985.

Cramer, Ernst. "The Berglas Plan for Jewish Settlement in China." *Leo Baeck Institute News,* no. 62 (1995).

Crowe, David M. *The Baltic States and the Great Powers: Foreign Relations, 1938–1940.* Boulder: Westview, 1993.

Dicker, Herman. *Wanderers and Settlers in the Far East: A Century of Jewish Life in China and Japan.* New York: Twayne, 1962.

Diplomatic Record Office. "Documents Regarding the Harbin School, the Former Japanese Russian School." Foreign Ministry of Japan, Tokyo, January 1919–December 1924. Mimeographed.

Diplomatic Record Office. "Miscellaneous Documents Regarding Jewish Affairs." Foreign Ministry of Japan, Tokyo, January, 1940.

Diplomatic Record Office. "Reports of Visas Issued to Foreigners by Consulates in Europe, 1939–1941."

Diplomatic Record Office, ed. *Dictionary of the History of Japanese Policy.* Tokyo: Yamakawa, 1992.

Dower, John. *War Without Mercy: Race and Power in the Pacific War.* New York: Pantheon, 1986.

Dziewanowski, M. K. and Joseph Pilsudski. *A European Federalist, 1918–1922.* Stanford: Hoover Institution Press, 1969.

Eggar, Steven A. *Serial Murder.* New York: Praeger, 1990.

Erikson, Erik H. *Young Man Luther: A Study in Psychoanalysis and History.* New York: Norton, 1958.

Fogel, Joshua. *Life Along the South Manchurian Railway: The Memoirs of Ito Takeo.* Armonk, N.Y.: M. E. Sharpe, 1988.

Fogel, Joshua. "The Jewish Community of Harbin, 1898–1950." Speech or paper presented at the Symposium on Jewish Diasporas in China: Comparative and Historical Perspectives, John K. Fairbank Center for East Asian Research, Harvard University, Cambridge, Mass., August 16–18, 1992.

Fogelman, Eva. *Conscience & Courage: Rescuers of Jews During the Holocaust.* New York: Doubleday/Anchor, 1994.

Foreign Ministry of Japan, "Gaimusho Kiko Hensen Zu" [History of Foreign Ministry's Reorganization, 1868–1971]. Tokyo: 1971.

Friedländer, Saul. "Some Aspects of the Historical Significance of the Holocaust." *Jerusalem Quarterly 1* (Fall, 1976): 36–59.

Friszke, Andrzej. "Dialog Polsko-Zydowski W Wilnie [Polish Jewish Dialogue in Vilna, 1939–40]." *Wiez* 4 (1987): 88–90.

Gilbert, Martin. *The Second World War.* New York: Holt, 1989.

Gluck, Carol. *Japan's Modern Myths: Ideology in the Late Meiji Period.* Princeton: Princeton University Press, 1985.

Gomer, Robert et al. "Japan's Biological Weapons: 1930–1945." *Bulletin of Atomic Scientists* 37, no. 8 (1981): 44–52.

Goodman, David, and Miyazawa Masanori. *Jews in the Japanese Mind: The History and Uses of a Cultural Stereotype.* New York: Free Press, 1994.

Govrin, Nurit. *Dvora Baron, The First Half, Early Stories.* Edited by Avner Holtzman. Jerusalem: Mosad Bialik, 1988.

Graebner, Norman. "Hoover, Roosevelt and the Japanese." In *Pearl Harbor as History: Japanese-American Relations,* edited by Dorothy Borg and Shimpei Okamoto, 25–52. New York: Columbia University Press, 1973.

Greenberg, Louis. *Russian Jewry.* 2 vols. New Haven: Yale University Press, 1951, 1953.

Grodner, David. "In Soviet Poland and Lithuania." *Contemporary Jewish Record* (March 1941): 136–47.

Hagen, Louis. ed. and trans. *The Schellenberg Memoirs.* Worcester, Mass., André Deutch, 1956.

Hallie, Philip P. *Lest Innocent Blood Be Shed: The Story of the Village of Le Chambon and How Goodness Happened There.* New York: Harper & Row, 1979.

Herf, Jeffrey. *Reactionary Modernity: Technology, Culture, and Politics in Weimar Third Reich.* Cambridge: Cambridge University Press, 1986.

Hertzman, Elhanan J. *Nes Hahazla Shel Yeshivat Mir* [The Miracle of Rescue of the Mir Yeshiva]. Jerusalem: n.p., 1976.

Hirschman, Albert O. *Shifting Involvements: Private Interest and Public Action.* Princeton: Princeton University Press, 1982.

Hitchins, Keith. *Rumania 1866–1947.* Oxford: Clarendon, 1994.

Hong, Howard V., and Edna H. Hong, eds. *Sören Kierkegaard's Journals and Papers.* 1, A–E. Bloomington: Indiana University Press, 1967.

Hunt, Morton. *The Compassionate Beast: What Science Is Discovering About the Humane Side of Humankind.* New York: Morrow, 1990.

Hyase, Yukiko. "The Career of Goto Shimpei: Japan's Statesman of Research, 1857–1929." Ph.D. diss., Florida State University, 1974.

Iklé, Frank. *German-Japanese Relations: 1936–1940.* New York: Bookman, 1956.

Izumo, Takeda, Miyoshi Shoraku, and Namiki Senryu. *Chushingura (The Treasury of Loyal Retainers).* Translated by Donald Keene. New York: Columbia University Press, 1971.

The Japan Biographical Encyclopedia and Who's Who, 2d ed. Japan: Rengo, 1961.

Johnson, Chalmers. *An Instance of Treason: Ozaki Hotsumi and the Sorge Spy Ring.* Stanford: Stanford University Press, 1964.

Kahan, R. Shoshano. *In Faier Un Falamen.* [In Fire and Flame] Buenos Aires: Central Organization of Polish Jews in Argentina, 1949.

Katsumi, Usui. "The Role of the Foreign Ministry." In *Pearl Harbor as History: Japanese-American Relations,* edited by Dorothy Borg and Shimpei Okamoto. New York: Columbia University Press, 1973.

Klier, John D., and Shlomo Lambroza, eds. *Pogroms: Anti-Jewish Violence in Modern Russian History.* Cambridge: Cambridge University Press, 1992.

Korbel, Josef. *Twentieth-Century Czechoslovakia.* New York: Columbia University Press, 1977.

Kranzler, David. *Japanese, Nazis, and Jews: The Jewish Refugee Community of Shanghai, 1938–1945.* New York: Yeshiva University Press, 1976.

Krebs, Gerhard. "Japanische Schlichtungsbemuhungen in der Deutsch–Polnischen Krise 1938/39." *Japanese Studies: Almanac of the German Institute for Japanese Studies of the Philipp Franz von Shebold Foundation* 2 (1990): 207–53.

Kuprin, Alexander. *The River of Life and Other Stories.* Translated by S. Koteliansky and J. M. Murry. Boston: John W. Luce, 1916.

Laskov, Shulamith. *Yosef Trumpeldor.* Haifa: Shikmona, 1972.

Le Corps diplomatique au Moscou (Moscow: People's Commissariat of Foreign Affairs, January 1938).

Lensen, George A. *Japanese Diplomatic and Consular Officials in Russia: A Handbook of Japanese Representatives in Russia from 1874 to 1968. Compiled on the Basis of Japanese and Russian Sources with a Historical Introduction.* Tokyo: Sophia University Press, 1968.

Lensen, George A. *Japanese Recognition of the USSR: Soviet-Japanese Relations, 1921–1930.* Tokyo: Sophia University Press, 1970.

Lensen, George A. *The Damned Inheritance: The Soviet Union and the Manchurian Crises, 1924–1935.* Tallahassee, Fla.: Diplomatic Press, 1974.

Lerski, Jerzy. "A Polish Chapter of the Russo-Japanese War." *Transactions of the Asiatic Society of Japan* 7, 3d Series (1959): 74.

Levenson, Joseph R. *Confucian China and Its Modern Fate: A Trilogy.* Berkeley: University of California Press, 1965.

Levin, Jack, and James Alan Fox. *Mass Murder: America's Growing Menace.* New York: Plenum, 1985.

Lewandowski, Jozef. *Swedish Contribution to the Polish Resistance Movement During World War Two (1939–1942).* Uppsala, Sweden: Acta Universitas Upsaliensis, 1979.

Lewin, Isaac. *Remember the Days of Old: Historical Essays.* New York: Research Institute of Religious Jewry, 1994.

Leyton, Elliot. *Compulsive Killers: The Story of Modern Multiple Murder.* New York: New York University Press, Washington Mews Books, 1986.

Longstreet, Stephen, and Ethel Longstreet. *Yoshiwara: The Pleasure Quarters of Old Tokyo.* Tokyo: Yenbooks, 1988.

Macaulay, J., and L. Berkowitz. *Altruism and Helping Behavior.* New York: Academic, 1970.

Mandelbaum, David. *Yeshivat Hakhmei Lublin.* 2 vol. Jerusalem: Center for the Encouragement of Cultural Projects and Torah Research in Israel, 1994.

Maruyama, Masao. "Patterns of Individuation and the Case of Japan: A Conceptual Scheme." In *changing Japanese Attitudes Toward Modernization,* edited by Marius B. Jansen. Princeton: Princeton University Press, 1965.

Matsuoka, Yosuke. "Extemporaneous Address Delivered at the Fourteenth Plenary Meeting." In *The Manchurian Question: Japan's Case in the Sino-Japanese Dispute as Presented Before the League of Nations.* Geneva: Japanese Delegation to the League of Nations, 1933.

Maxon, Yale C. *Control of Japanese Foreign Policy: A Study of Civil-Military Rivalry, 1930–1945.* Westport, Conn.: Greenwood, 1973.

Meerhof, Ron. "Consul Sugihara and the Jews: A Perspective on International Relations. Germany, Japan, Lithuania, and the Soviet Union on the Eve of World War II." Ph.D. diss., Master's thesis. Rijksuniversiteit Leiden, 1992.

Meskill, Johanna M. *Hitler and Japan: The Hollow Alliance.* New York: Atherton, 1966.

Ministry of Foreign Affairs Report. vol. 22, no. 362. Tokyo: Foreign Ministry of Japan, 1937.

Mitford, A. B. *Tales of Old Japan.* Tokyo: Charles E. Tuttle, 1966.

Monroe, Kristen Renwick. "Fat Lady in a Corset: Altruism and Social Theory." *American Journal of Political Science* 38, no. 4 (1994): 861–93.

Montgomery, Michael. *Imperialist Japan: The Yen to Dominate.* New York: St. Martin's, 1987.

Myers, Ramon H. "Japanese Imperialism in Manchuria: The South Manchurian Railway Company, 1906–1933." In *The Japanese Informal Empire in China, 1895–1937,* edited by Peter Duus et al. Princeton: Princeton University Press, 1989.

Nahm, Andrew C., ed. *Korea Under Japanese Colonial Rule: Studies of the Policy and Techniques of Japanese Colonialism.* Kalamazoo: Center for Korean Studies, Western Michigan University, 1973.

Newton, Michael. *Mass Murder: An Annotated Bibliography.* New York: Garland, 1988.

Nimmo, William F. *Behind a Curtain of Silence: Japanese in Soviet Custody, 1945–1956.* Westport, Conn.: Greenwood, 1988.

Nitobe, Inazo. *Bushido: The Soul of Japan.* Rutland, Vt.: Charles E. Tuttle, 1993.

Oliner, Pearl M., and Samuel P. Oliner. *The Altruistic Personality: Rescuers of Jews in Nazi Europe.* New York: Free Press, 1988.

Oliner, Pearl M., and Samuel P. Oliner, Lawrence Baron, Lawrence A. Blum, Dennis L. Krebs, and M. Zuzanna Smolenska, eds. *Embracing the Other.* New York: New York University Press, 1992.

Oren, Baruch. "Mi'Vilna Derech Yapan ed haolam hachofshi" [From Vilna via Japan to the free world]. *Yalkut Moreshet.* no. 11 (1969): 470–71.

Palasz-Rutkowska, Ewa, and Andrzej T. Romer. "Wspolprac Polsko-Jaonska W Czasie II Wojny Swiatowej" [Polish-Japanese Relations in World War II], *Biblioteka "Kultury"* 487 (1994): 3–43.

Peck, L. "Unzer Arbet Far Retung Un Pletim-Hilf" In *Unzer Kamf.* New York: Poale Zion Zeire Zion, 1941.

Porat, Dina. "Nessibot Vesibot Lematan Visot Ma'avar Sovyetiyot Liflitei Polin" [Conditions and reasons for the granting of Soviet transit visas to refugees from Poland]. *Shvut* 7 (1979): 54–67.

Powell, John W. "Japan's Germ Warfare: The U.S. Cover-up of a War Crime." *Bulletin of Concerned Asian Scholars* 12 (1980): 2–17.

Randall, Peter E. *There Are No Victors Here: A Local Perspective on the Treaty of Portsmouth.* Portsmouth: Portsmouth Marine Society, 1985.

Ringelblum. *Polish-Jewish Relations During the Second World War.* Edited by Joseph Kermish et al. Jerusalem: Yad Vashem, 1974.

Ross, James. *Escape to Shanghai: A Jewish Community in China.* New York: Free Press, 1994.

Rushton, J. Philippe, and Richard M. Sorrentino, ed. *Altruism and Helping Behavior: Social Personality and Developmental Perspectives.* Hillsdale, N.J.: Lawrence Erlbaum, 1981.

Saga, Junichi. *Memories of Silk and Straw: A Self-Portrait of Small-Town Japan.* Translated by George Evans. Tokyo: Kodansha International, 1987.

Scholes, Percy A. *The Oxford Companion to Music.* London: Oxford University Press, 1938.

Schreig, Samuel. "The Angel of Curaçao." *B'nai B'rith Messenger,* January 24, 1963.

Shen, Mo. *Japan in Manchuria: An Analytical Study of Treaties and Documents.* Manila: Grace Trading Company, 1960.

Sherman, A. J. "German-Jewish Bankers in World Politics: The Financing of the Russo-Japanese War." In *Leo Baeck Yearbook* 28. London: Secker and Warburg, 1983.

Sherman, A. J. *Island Refuge: Britain and Refugees from the Third Reich 1933–1939.* Essex, England: Frank Cass, 1973.

Shigemitsu, Mamoru. *Japan and Her Destiny: My Struggle for Peace.* New York: Dutton, 1958.

Shillony, Ben-Ami. *Revolt in Japan: The Young Officers and the February 26, 1936 Incident.* Princeton: Princeton University Press, 1973.

Shillony, Ben-Ami. *Politics and Culture in Wartime Japan.* Oxford: Clarendon, 1981.

Shillony, Ben-Ami. *The Jews and Japanese: The Successful Outsiders.* Rutland, Vt.: Charles E. Tuttle, 1991.

Shogan, Robert. *Hard Bargain: How FDR Twisted Churchill's Arm, Evaded the Law, and Changed the Role of the American Presidency.* New York: Scribner, 1995.

Silver, Eric. *The Book of the Just: The Silent Heroes Who Saved Jews from Hitler.* London: Weidenfeld and Nicolson, 1992.

Singer, Kurt. *Mirror, Sword, and Jewel.* Tokyo: Kodansha International, 1973.

Sophie, Dubnov-Erlich. *The Life and Work of S.M. Dubnov.* Bloomington, Ind.: Indiana University Press, 1991.

Stephan, John J. *The Russian Fascists: Tragedy and Farce in Exile, 1925–1945.* New York: Harper and Row, 1978.

Storry, Richard. *The Double Patriots: A Study of Japanese Nationalism.* Boston: Houghton Mifflin, 1957.

Strawson, John. *Hitler as Military Commander.* London: Batsford, 1971.

Sugihara, Yukiko. *Rokusen Nin No Inochi No Viza* [Visas for Life for 6000 People]. Orien, Japan: Asahi, 1990.

Tabata, Masanori. "Mystery Behind the Myth." *Japan Times Weekly* (December 17, 1994): 6–7.

Tang, Peter S. H. *Russian and Soviet Policy in Manchuria and Outer Mongolia 1911–1931.* Durham, N.C.: Duke University Press, 1959.

Tec, Nechama. *When Light Pierced the Darkness: Christian Rescue of Jews in Nazi-Occupied Poland.* New York: Oxford University Press, 1986.

Thorne, Christopher. *Allies of a Kind: The United States, Britain and the War Against Japan, 1941–1945.* New York: Oxford University Press, 1978.

Togo, Shigenori. *The Cause of Japan.* Translated and edited by Togo Fumihiko and Ben Bruce Blakeney. New York: Simon and Schuster, 1956.

Tokayer, Marvin, and Swartz, Mary. *The Fugu Plan: The Untold Story of the Japanese and the Jews During WWII.* New York: Paddington, 1979.

Tokushiro, Ohata. "The Anti-Comintern Pact, 1935–1939." In *Deterrent Diplomacy: Japan, Germany, and the USSR, 1935–1940,* edited by James Morley. New York: Columbia University Press, 1976.

Toland, John. *The Rising Sun: The Decline and Fall of the Japanese Empire, 1936–1945.* Toronto: Bantam Books, 1988.

Tory, Avraham. *Surviving of the Holocaust: The Kovno Ghetto Diary.* Edited by Martin Gilbert. Cambridge: Harvard University Press, 1990.

Trani, Eugene P. *The Treaty of Portsmouth: An Adventure in American Diplomacy.* Lexington: University of Kentucky Press, 1969.

U.S. Department of State. *Papers Relating to the Foreign Relations of the United States: Japan, 1931–1941.* Proclamation no. 2413. Washington, D.C.: 1943.

Vespa, Amleto. *Secret Agent of Japan.* Boston: Little, Brown, 1938.

Vizulis, Izidors. *The Molotov-Ribbentrop Pact of 1939: The Baltic Case.* New York: Praeger, 1988.

Wallenberg, Raoul. *Letters and Dispatches, 1924–1994.* New York: Arcade 1995.

Warhaftig, Zorach. *Palit Vesarid* [Refugee and Survivor]. Jerusalem: Yad Vashem, 1984.

Warhaftig, Zorach. *Refugee and Survivor.* Jerusalem: Yad Vashem, 1988.

Whiting, Robert. *The Chrysanthemum and the Bat: The Game Japanese Play.* Tokyo: Permanent, 1977.

Wischnitzer, Mark. *Visas for Freedom: The History of HIAS.* Cleveland: World, 1956.

Wyman, David. *Paper Walls: America and the Refugee Crisis 1938–1941.* Amherst: University of Massachusetts Press, 1968.

Yarmolinski, Abraham, editor and translator. *The Memoirs of Count Witte.* New York: Howard Fertig, 1967.

Young, Louise. "Total Empire: Japan and Manchukuo 1931–1945." Ph.D. diss., Columbia University, 1993.

Zuroff, Efraim. "Rescue via the Far East: The Attempt to Save Polish Rabbis." *Simon Wiesenthal Center Annual* 1 (1984): 153–83.

Acknowledgments

This investigation into the mystery of goodness has surrounded me, to an uncanny degree, with good people. Lack of space prevents me from saying as much as I would like about each of those who have conspired with me, offering insight, encouragement, unanticipated kindnesses, and companionship along the way. They include Noboyasu Abe, Dina Abramowicz, Petras Anusas, Mira and Albert Appel, Michael Apollonov, Masayoshi Arai, David and Madie Arnow, Joan and Robert Arnow, Toyomi Asano, Hans Baerwald, Chaim Bargman, Donna Bascom, Julie and Roger Baskes, Yehuda Bauer, Ruth Beckelman, John and Charlotte Bemis, Gordon Berger, Dennis and Janice Berkowitz, Elizabeth Berman, Joanna Binkowski, Laurel Brake, Jack Braun, Arie Bucheister, Sara Bush, Susanne Carter, J. Chapman, Max and Ida Cohen, Robert Cohen, Bill Craig, Gerhard Dambmann, Bill Doyle, Susan Erony, Sidra Ezrahi, Yaron Ezrahi, Morris and Lynne Faiman, I. E. and Billie Farber, Marcos, Stephanie, and Leslie Fastlicht, Helen and Eli Feller, Joshua Fogel, D. F. Freed, Randy Freed, Ronald Freed, Saul Friedlander, Etsuka Fujii, Nobuo Fujiwara, Satako Fujiwara, Richard Gambino, Martin Gilbert, Sumner Glimcher, Denise Gluck, David Gordis, Felice Gordis, Alvin and Sally Greenberg, Andrzej Guryn, Milt Gustafson, Nathan Gutwirth, Moshe Halbertal, Tova Halbertal, Frederick Harris, Roberta Herche, Kazuko Hirano, Yumiko Hirobe, Barry Hoffman, Mel Howard, Hiroshi and Terukio Ichikawa, Moshe Idel, T. Ikami, Martin Indyk, Nathan and Myrtle Isaacson, Stanley and Joyce Kalendar, Nat Kameny, Nancy Kaufman, Maria Keipert, Erazim Kohak, Nobyuki Koide, Akira and Yuriko Kondo, Takeshi Kondo, Regina Kopilevich, Roman Korab-Zebryk, Makoto Kosaka, Stawomiv Kowalski, David Kranzler, Irene Kveraga, Dan Kyram,

Irving and Evelyn Lamm, Steve Lavine, Hugh Lawson-Tancred, Aryeh Lebeau, James Lebeau, Andzej Lechowski, Estelle, Saul and Meri Manski, Naoki Maruyama, Tim McDaniel, Ron Meerhof, Bernard and Emily Mehlman, Ronit Meroz, Meredith Meyers, Catherine Minkiewicz, Gretchen and Henry Mittwer, Toshio Mochizuki, Yukuto Motomatsu, Ichiro Nakata, Mayumi Nakatsuka, Setsuko Naoe, Takeo Nishioka, Eric Nooter, John O'Brien, Sarah Ogilvie, Yukio Okamoto, Yuriko Onodera, Josef and Bernard Orgler, Hiroko Oyama, Mordecai Paldiel, Tadeusz Panecki, Helen Petter, A. Piliponis, Andrew Plaks, David and Muriel Pokross, Jim Poston, Dolly and Irving Rabb, Gila Raumas-Rauch, Ruth Rauch, Tova Reich, Walter Reich, Edith and Mel Roebuck, Natasha Rohlina, Aaron Roland, Dan and Joanna Rose, Emily Rose, Lana Rosenfeld, Henry Rosovsky, Edmund de Rothschild, Sophia Rybikowska, Eric Saul, Henry Schwab, Vera Schwarcz, Nobuhiro and Rea Sera, Ari Sherman, Kanako Shiga, Ben-Ami Shillony, Susumu Shimazono, Barry Shrage, Frank Shulman, Lani Silver, Melissa Silverman, Abraham Sirkin, Susannah Sirkin, Alex Spear, Arnold and Ruth Stein, Adin Steinsaltz, Janet Sternburg, Esther Stohl, Ulrich Straus, Zbigniew Swiecicki, Jan Swyngedouw, Sam and Bertha Szmurlowicz, Andrew Tagliabue, Yuji Takechi, Hara Takeshi, Larry Taub, John Taylor, Anghel and Emmanuel Tchividjian, Shigehiko Togo, Marvin Tokayer, Sidney Topol, Avraham Tory, Jaak Treiman, Teruo Uemura, Ezra Vogel, Glenn Wallach, Robert Wargo, Irving Warner, Marek Web, Anita Weiner, Charlotte White, Russell Whitmont, Helen Whitney, Elie Wiesel, Rowena Winik, Rachel Wizner, Jason Wolfe, Robert Wolfe, Junka Yamada, Kaoru Yamamoto, Akio and Hideo Yoshida, John Zamparelli, Rochelle Zell, Sam Zell, Lidia Zimmermann.

I have gained much insight into Sugihara and his times from questionnaires and extensive interviews. Many members of his immediate and extended family, friends, and survivors have been enormously helpful in providing information. Only some could be mentioned in detail in this book. All contributed to my understanding. Among those rescued by Sugihara who were so generous with their time, Masha Leon, Sam Manski, and Leo Melamed deserve particular thanks.

For several periods during this research, I was the guest of Logos Theological Seminary in Kyoto and its affiliate churches throughout Japan, as well as Tokyo University. I shall always remember the warm hospitality and inspiring collegiality I found there. Limits on space prevent me from mentioning the names of many who, over the course of these years, patiently and competently translated language and other elements of culture, in Japan and China in particular, enabling me to find meaning and familiarity beneath threatening surfaces of strangeness.

I thank, for their diligence and patience, librarians and archivists at the following institutions who helped me trace a complicated paper trail: the National Archives and Library of Congress in Washington, D.C., YIVO, HIAS, and the American Joint Distribution Committee archives in New York; the Widener, Mugar, and Hebrew College libraries in Boston; the Portsmouth Atheneum and Strawberry Banke in Portsmouth, New Hampshire; the Hoover Institution in Palo Alto, California; the British Library, the Foreign Office Archives at Kew, the Polish Underground Movement Study Trust, and the Sikorski Institute in London. The military archives in Freiburg and the German Foreign ministry in Bonn; the Polish Military Intelligence Archives in Warsaw; the Lithuanian Central Archive, Vilnius; the Russian State Archives in Moscow; Yad Vashem, the Hebrew University and National Library, and the Joint Distribution Committee archives in Jerusalem; Harbin Technical University Library in Harbin, Diplomatic Records Office, Tokyo University Library, and the National Institute for Defense Studies in Tokyo.

Rysard Frelek helped me make Polish connections, and Vulf and Natasha Slobodkin added pleasure to my Moscow visits as they oriented me to the realities of archival research in their country. Their beloved children, Anya and Igor, so eagerly would arrange for the shipment of archival material. May the memory of two beautiful but tragically abridged lives be a source of inspiration.

I thank Sandra Dijkstra, my literary agent, for her assistance and good advice and her most competent staff, and the same appreciation to Junzo Sawa and William Miller at the English Agency in Tokyo. At Simon & Schuster/Free Press, I thank Adam Bellow, my devoted editor, and David Bernstein, Edith Lewis, Bob Niegowki, Jessica Osorio, Miriam Rosen, Tom Stvan, Abigail Strubel, and Gene Taft. Edward Cone copyedited with skill and concern. Friends and colleagues have discussed this work with me, carefully reading and commenting in detail on earlier drafts of this book. I thank them for significant editorial and substantive contributions. They include Larry Harmon, Jennifer McPeak, Dan Pake, John Rauch, Henry Rosovsky, Lauri Slawsby, Eugene Weiner, Katherine Whittemore, and Naoko Takeda Yarin.

Among my many friends in Japan, I happily remember prominent representatives of that goodness who have been so encouraging. Masaru Ohtsuki wisely advised me at every step of this search, Teruhisa Shino provided much information from his abundant knowledge of Sugihara, and Kiyoshi Suwa spared no trouble to ensure my ability to do this research and to understand its complexities. Closer to home, Helena and David Kazhdan shared with me Japanese films and words of Torah, always inspiring.

Lauri Slawsby, my friend and colleague, coordinator now of several such projects, brought keen insight and good judgment to every phase of this research and writing. Her diplomacy, competence, and loyalty are much appreciated. Alan and Alex Slawsby offered their own help and encouragement.

This search involved voyages in which my family escorted me along inner and outer paths. That they were so eager to join me has been truly a blessing. The accompaniment is found on every page. With Shulamith, Hephzibah Nehamah, Tiferet Ahavah, and Haninah Zephaniah Peretz, I have been engaged in the most formidable theoretical discussions of the "love of life." But their influence on me has been no less great in the very profound and deliberate manner in which each of them practices that love.

Index